The beginning of ideology

THE BEGINNING OF IDEOLOGY

Consciousness and Society in the French Reformation

DONALD R. KELLEY

CAMBRIDGE UNIVERSITY PRESS

Cambridge

London   New York   New Rochelle
Melbourne   Sydney

Published by the Press Syndicate of the University of Cambridge
The Pitt Building, Trumpington Street, Cambridge CB2 1RP
32 East 57th Street, New York, NY 10022, USA
296 Beaconsfield Parade, Middle Park, Melbourne 3206, Australia

First published 1981
First paperback edition 1983

Printed in Great Britain at the
University Press, Cambridge

British Library Cataloguing in Publication Data

Kelley, Donald Reed
The beginning of ideology.
1. France – Civilization – 1328–1600
2. France – History – 16th century
I. Title
944'.028   DC33.3   80-41237

ISBN 0 521 23504 9 hard covers
ISBN 0 521 27483 4 paperback

Contents

Contents

Preface

This book represents an experiment in history – intellectual history, I suppose it must be termed, or perhaps social history of ideas, except that this phrase has been pre-empted for rather different approaches to the interpretation of the past. It also represents the results of over twenty years of digging into and reflecting upon the literary remains of sixteenth-century Europe. It builds in some ways on two related products of these investigations, one a history of historical thought and scholarship and the other a biography of one of the more active and controversial protagonists of that age.[1] But while it goes over some of the same ground, it departs both from the narrative and chronological form of the latter and from the analytical (and as historians of science would say, 'internalist') approach of the former. The present strategy I think of as synthetic; and since a number of its tactics may seem questionable as well as unfashionable, I may begin by acknowledging and if possible justifying my choices.

My original aim was to try to recapture certain aspects of sixteenth-century experience, thought and behavior which, falling between the history of ideas on the one hand and the history of society and institutions on the other, might yield a more comprehensive and coherent picture of that time than is normally attempted. In keeping with this, and in opposition to current intellectual fashions which value quantitative and objective science and social reality above subjective experience, I have chosen to begin with and to place primary emphasis (though I hope not uncritically) on subjective testimony. 'Subjectivity is truth', Kierkegaàrd has taught; and while the subjectivity in question here must at best be taken at second hand, it should not for that reason be dismissed as inferior to more inert kinds of evidence. Not that I believe that history is moved by minds alone (or stomachs or fists or tools, for that matter); but I do believe that current preoccupations with material factors and subverbal behavior have obscured the force and relevance of individual emotion, thought and dis-

---

[1] Donald R. Kelley, *Foundations of Modern Historical Scholarship* (New York, 1970) and *François Hotman: A Revolutionary's Ordeal* (Princeton, 1973).

course in the complex process of history. In any case my strategy has been to move from consciousness to society rather than the reverse.

There is epistemological as well as methodological justification for this view. Owen Barfield has made an important point about natural science which seems even more pertinent to the study of human culture. 'Physical science has for a long time stressed the enormous difference between what it investigates as the actual structure of the universe, including the earth, and the phenomena or appearances which are presented to normal human consciousness. In tune with this, most philosophy – at all events since Kant – has heavily emphasized the participation of man's own mind in the creation, or evocation, of these phenomena.'[2] Too many historians, it seems to me, are still operating in a pre-Kantian world in search of an 'actual structure' discernible apart from human consciousness, their own as well as that of their subjects; to avoid such methodological hubris I have tried to eliminate surreptitious (and pseudo-) objectivity. My explorations into past consciousness and society are indeed the reconstructions of a late-twentieth-century North American interested in social and cultural sciences as well as history. Obviously I cannot see the hearts, minds and behavior of sixteenth-century humanity without distortion, cannot ask significant questions without disturbing the field of inquiry and reorganizing the data.

In the course of the following series of analyses there will be occasion not only to venture into a variety of sub-fields of history (history of religion, education, law, printing and so forth) but also to touch upon more alien areas (such as the psychology and sociology of a similar range of behavior) and often to encounter various controversial problems, including conflicts between the sexes and generations, religious and political conversion, exile and martyrdom, the significance of oral, scribal and print culture, the conceptual value of rhetoric and jurisprudence, the use of literary criticism in intellectual history, the phenomenon of propaganda and its forms, the nature of political parties, and of course the problems of ideology itself, which involve the sociology and anthropology of knowledge. It is tempting to inject various extra-historical and inter-disciplinary concepts on these occasions, but for the most part I have tried to avoid gratuitous (and perhaps meretricious) applications of theories derived from other contexts. For the reconstruction of sixteenth-century mentalities and ideology, it seems to me, Freudian psychoanalysis or Marxian class analysis is no more (and perhaps is less) suitable than Lutheran or Thomist theology. Quite to

---

[2] *Saving the Appearances* (London, n.d.), 12.

the contrary, I prefer to assume that an exposure to sixteenth-century experience and modes of thought may itself have something to offer to other disciplines, whose evidence and perspectives seldom extend back so far. There is no reason to suppose that religious motivations or political convictions conform to modern conventions, or that psychic or social – oedipal, say, or class – behavior preserves a constant pattern. These are questions to be asked, not categories to be applied.

On such grounds I do not aspire, for example, to apply what currently passes for 'psychohistory' to the profound and shattering experiences of sixteenth-century observers and actors (although the work of Erik Erikson, so grounded in such experience, is not without relevance). It is obvious that sixteenth-century materials are rich in subjects for psychohistorical analysis in a general sense – testimonies of generational conflict, conversion, martyrdom, confessional and personal quarrels, autobiographical revelations and even formal theology – but it is difficult enough to find patterns in such evidence without imposing some apparatus of prejudgment. And as I choose not to rely on Victorian theories of psychology (except inadvertently), so I choose not to place my trust in Victorian views of social structure and process (except again to the extent that a subliminal kind of Marxism is unavoidable); and I might say the same thing about any Christian perspective. If I had a preferred model, it would be that of cultural anthropology: the past is also a foreign country, and we need to approach it as a kind of alien and perhaps unsettling field work, not expecting satisfaction or confirmation from the results. Although I entertain high hopes about the possibilities of exploring sixteenth-century consciousness and the social formations which they reflect, I do not pretend to account for the upheavals of the sixteenth century in a demonstrative fashion. In general my purpose is not to seek causes but rather to reveal patterns, not to reduce but to reconstruct experience, not to 'explain' but to interpret.

In this hermeneutical effort I have hoped that reliance on imaginative reconstruction of a wide variety of testimony from several points of view might reveal ties and continuities with our own age which a more positivistic, literal-minded and intra-disciplinary approach would overlook or reject. This presents a difficulty, for these days we are not used to feeling kinship with any century before the seventeenth. Was not that period the 'age of genius', when the world began to be transformed jointly by an irreversible 'revolution' in natural science and a profound 'general crisis' in European society? Well, perhaps; but I do not want to regard the question as closed. The scientific revolution has deeper roots than earlier historians suspected; it produced some misshapen progeny which mar the success story usually passed off as the history of science; and in general the legacy of rationalism, naturalism and scientism has been neither so beneficial nor so enlightening as some apologists have argued. As for the seventeenth-century 'crisis', this controversial thesis is predicated on a particular conception of demographic transformation, class conflict and 'modernization' (our equivalent of the 'Whig fallacy' or the idea of Progress?) that seems altogether too indiscriminate, materialistic and unilinear to accommodate an appreciation of historical experience in general and our various predicaments in particular. What this amounts to, I suppose, is another plea – every generation seems to need one – for an historical approach that is relevant without being anachronistic, meaningful without being myopic, illuminating without being apologetic.

A larger difficulty: in pursuit of these objectives – reaching for some of the human meaning of sixteenth-century experience and relating it to our contemporary human condition – I have relied on a conceptual device which many historians avoid or at least conceal (often from themselves). This device is what may be termed a historical generalization; and the form it takes is not a statically defined category but rather a reconstructed, or at least historically inferred, temporal continuum. Certain ideas, institutions, types of behavior, although they may vary widely, or wildly, in time, nevertheless establish traditions or processes which demand coherent historical definition and analysis. Such abstractions as 'art', 'science', 'representation' and 'property' have changed radically in content over the centuries; and yet these terms, nominally anachronistic, have a necessary function in giving conceptual coherence to the process of history. Previously, I have advanced similar arguments for two more concretely definable continua – one that scholarly cast of mind which came to be called 'historicism', and the other an early illustration of 'revolutionary' thought and action. The 'historicism' of Budé can hardly be identified with that of Mommsen, still less the 'revolutionary' attitude of Hotman with Marx; and yet both cases, it seems to me, suggest historical connections and retrospectively justify the positing of a 'historical generalization'.[3] Such is also the rationale for the conceptual perspective of this book, namely, the notion of 'ideology', which seems to me a promising way of tracing some of the most fundamental ties be-

[3] Analogous perhaps to the 'concrete universals' discussed by Paul Ricoeur, *The Symbolism of Evil*, trans. E. Buchanan (Boston, 1969), and Peter Munz, *The Shapes of Time* (Middletown, Conn., 1977), 321, and traceable to Hegel.

tween our world and that of pre-scientific and pre-industrial Europe.

What I understand historically by 'ideology' will appear in the course of the book. Let me conclude these preliminary remarks by suggesting the reason for subsuming my investigations under this outlandish (and to many historians, no doubt, distracting) category. Why, in particular, the *beginning* of ideology? What is at issue is not *the* beginning of ideology in a specific historical sense, of course, but rather the 'beginning of ideology' as a general feature of historical experience, as a problem of the human condition. Some years ago there was much talk about the obverse of this epiphenomenon, that is, the 'end of ideology'; and despite compounded confusions – centering less on the emotive term itself than on the question, *'whose* ideology?'* – the problem is of continuing importance.[4] The phenomenon, or non-phenomenon, of the exhaustion of ideals, the collapse of collective determination and the onset of disillusionment is central to an understanding of history, which has seen many ideologies rise and fall – and indeed rise again after the societies which spawned them were long gone. Presupposed by this problem, however, is another and even more fundamental question arising at the other end of the ideological process, which is the *generation* of values and ideals and of the activity attendant upon these. This book, focussing upon one of the seminal periods of European history, takes as its point of departure precisely the posing of this problem, 'the beginning of ideology'.

Aspirations and pretensions aside, I have tried to pose some rather obvious questions about part of what used to be regarded as 'modern history'. Given the nature and scope of the subject, it would be a largely irrelevant affection to refer to the sort of manuscript sources which garnished my two related books; on the other hand it is necessary to apply to a considerably wider range of printed materials, which are very far from being exhausted for this period. Media limitations have unfortunately prevented consideration of visual and iconographic sources; ignorance has made it unfeasible to explore such more remote expressions of 'ideology' as the play element, various aspects of material culture and less accessible patterns of behavior which historians, unlike anthropologists, can seldom hope to observe. As for my point of view, while I do not want to read the twentieth century back into the sixteenth, at the same time I cannot pretend *not* to write from the perspective – and with some concern for the predicaments – of this age; and to some extent I do see this as a case study of a larger and more general

---

[4] *The End of Ideology Debate*, ed. Chaim I. Waxman (New York, 1968).

phenomenon that is psychological, sociological and perhaps anthropological. Because my presentation (if not my approach) is deliberately systematic, chronology may be violated; but Clio herself, I hope, will retain some of her charm as well as utility, if not her virtue. Such at least are my good intentions: only God and the Reader – in this secular age perhaps only the Reader – can judge what road they have taken me down.

Research for this book has been carried out, over the past decade and more, in many libraries on two continents. The writing was made possible by extended sojourns at Harvard and at the Institute for Advanced Study; and in this connection I am indebted especially to the late Myron Gilmore, Giles Constable, Felix Gilbert and John Elliott, as well as the John Simon Guggenheim Foundation and the University of Rochester. Personal obligations are beyond counting, and I will not test friendships by associating my intellectual creditors in this rash undertaking. More generally, however, and in keeping with the topical approach of this work, I may single out my mother's side of my family for their efforts (largely in vain) to instill a fundamentalist faith (chapter III), certain friends and colleagues at Rochester for intensifying my appreciation of the educational and political dialectic (chapters IV, VI and VII), members of Clifford Geertz and Albert Hirschman's seminar at the Institute for Advanced Study (especially Quentin Skinner) for encouraging me to think more broadly about this subject than a historian's training might allow (chapters I and VIII), and above all Bonnie and John Reed Kelley, for helping me on the most fundamental level of socialization (chapter II). This book is for them, in recompense.

D.R.K.

Abbreviations

In general the sources for this book are of three kinds: conceptual aids (especially in the first and last chapters), secondary literature (most important for chapters II–VI) and primary sources (limited in general to printed material and most conspicuous in chapters V–VIII). It is impossible to do justice to any one type: the first I have had to suppress forcibly, except at a few crucial points; the second I have been able to suggest only selectively, since each chapter involves at least one discipline with its own apparatus and historiography; and the third I have had to present even more arbitrarily because the ocean of early modern printed material (here, for the most part, French, Latin and English) has been neither classified nor even charted. Here is a list of the common abbreviations used in the notes:

AC   *Archives curieuses de l'histoire de France*, ed. L. Cimber and F. Danjou. Paris, 1834: 15 vols
Allen   P. S. Allen (ed.), *Opus Epistolarum Des. Erasmi Rotero-dami*. Oxford, 1906–58: 12 vols
Argentré   Carolus du Plessis d'Argentré, *Collectio judiciorum de erroribus*. Paris, 1724
Ars.   Bibliothèque de l'Arsenal (followed by shelf-mark)
Aspects   *Aspects de la propagande religieuse*, ed. E. Droz. Geneva, 1957
BHR   *Bibliothèque d'Humanisme et Renaissance*
BM   British Museum (British Library) (followed by shelf-mark)
BN   Bibliothèque Nationale (followed by shelf-mark)
Bordier   Henri Bordier (ed.), *Le Chansonnier huguenot du XVIe siècle*. Paris, 1870
BRN   *Bibliotheca Reformatoria Neerlandica*. The Hague
BSHPF   *Bulletin de la Société de l'Histoire du Protestantisme Française*
Bulaeus   C. E. Bulaeus, *Historia Universitatis Parisiensis*. Paris, 1673: 6 vols
CHF   *Catalogue de l'histoire de France*, I (Bibliothèque Nationale). Paris, 1855

CO	*Ioannis Calvini Opera quae supersunt omnia*, ed. Baum, Cunitz, Reuss. Braunschweig, 1872–9: 59 vols
Crespin	Jean Crespin and Simon Goulart, *Histoire des martyrs*, ed. D. Benoit. Toulouse, 1885–9: 3 vols
Crevier	J.-B.-L. Crevier, *Histoire de l'Université de Paris*. Paris, 1761: 6 vols
De Thou	J. A. de Thou, *Histoire universelle*. The Hague, 1740: 11 vols
Fournier	Marcel Fournier (ed.), *Les Statutes et privilèges des universités françaises*, IV: *Strasbourg*. Paris, 1894
Haag	Eugène and Emile Haag (eds.), *La France Protestante*. Paris, 1848–58: 10 vols; 2nd edn, 1877–8: 6 vols
Hauser	Henri Hauser, *Sources de l'histoire de France, XVIe siècle*. Paris, 1906–15: 4 vols
HE	*Histoire ecclésiastique des églises réformées au royaume de France*, ed. Baum and Cunitz. Paris, 1883: 3 vols
Herminjard	A. L. Herminjard (ed.), *Correspondance des Reformateurs dans le pays de langue française*. Geneva, 1866–97: 9 vols
Isambert	F. Isambert, A. Jourdan, A. Decusy (eds.), *Recueil général des anciennes lois françaises*. Paris, 1821–33: 29 vols
Isnard	A. Isnard (ed.), *Catalogue général des livres imprimés de la Bibliothèque Nationale, Actes Royaux*, I. Paris, 1910
L'Estoile	Pierre de l'Estoile, *Journal pour le régne de Henri III*, ed. L. Lefèvre. Paris, 1943
LN	R. O. Lindsay and J. Neu, *French Political Pamphlets 1547–1648*. Madison, 1969 (followed by pamphlet number)
MC	*Memoires de Condé*. London, 1740: 6 vols
ME	*Memoires de l'Estat de France sous Charles neufiesme*, ed. S. Goulart. 'Meidelbourg' (Geneva), 1578: 6 vols
Pithou	Nicolas Pithou, *Le Protestantisme en Champagne*, ed. C. Recordon. Paris, 1863
Raemond	Florimond de Raemond, *L'Histoire de la Naissance, Progrez et decadence de l'heresie de ce siecle*. Rouen, 1648
STC	A. W. Pollard and G. R. Redgrave, *A Short-Title Catalogue of Books Printed in England, Scotland & Ireland. . . .* London, 1926
Sleidan	Johann Sleidan, *De Statu Religionis et Reipublicae Carlo quinto Caesari Commentarii*, ed. J. G. Boemius. Osnabrück, 1968 (repr.)

Abbreviations

Table Talk	Martin Luther, *Table Talk,* ed. and trans. T. Tappert, in *Works,* vol. LIV. Philadelphia, 1967
Tractatus	*Tractatus universi juris.* Venice, 1584: 15 vols

Prologue:
The problem of ideology and
the process of history

In the fall of 1789 Vice-President John Adams found himself, like so many of his successors, with time on his hands; and spurred by the news of recent turmoil in France, he turned to one of his favorite topics, the phenomenon of Revolution. In order to examine the subject systematically he chose what we should call a historical 'model' from his own knowledge of the European past. Not altogether surprisingly, the model he decided upon was very close to the subject of this book, namely, the tumultuous social, political and intellectual background of the wars of religion. His views were derived from the seventeenth-century history by Davila, which along with De Thou's *History* furnished so much of the substance of the historical education of Englishmen and Americans. In the spring of 1790 Adams published, first as a series of articles and then as a book, his *Discourses on Davila*, in the hope of shedding light on the meaning of the feudal and popular upheavals which were threatening the French monarchy.[1] About the Protestant opposition, the Huguenot party, Adams had mixed feelings. On the one hand he commended their principle of 'liberty of conscience', but on the other he deplored the partisanship which had divided and then wasted Europe. In the long run he believed that this civil conflict had prepared the ground first for absolute government and eventually for the ruination of French society. His fear – and his message – was that France was beginning this process all over again.

Almost a quarter of a century later Adams thought he saw the fulfillment of his prediction. In 1813, still following the news from France closely, he came across a speech by Napoleon in the Tuileries just after the ignominious retreat from Moscow.[2] The target of the Emperor's rhetoric was what he called 'idéologie'. This term had been coined in the late eighteenth century by Destutt de Tracy to distinguish a philosophical approach to human society from formerly prevailing theological attitudes, but characteristically Napoleon gave a pejorative twist to the term. For him 'ideology' was 'an obscure

---

[1] *Discourses on Davila* (Boston, 1805), published originally in the *Gazette of the United States* 'by an American citizen'.
[2] See Zoltán Haraszti, *John Adams and the Prophets of Progress* (Cambridge, Mass., 1952), 166–7.

metaphysics' that proposed an abstract and unhistorical approach to government – and that lay at the roots of his own mounting difficulties. Who but the purveyors of ideology, he asked the assembled court and citizenry, 'proclaimed the principle of insurrection as a duty . . ., flattered the people by proclaiming for them a sovereignty . . . [and] destroyed the sanctity and the respect for the law?' Indeed, he might have added, the ground he stood on had more than once been splattered with the blood of men and women who had fought over ideology in one form or another, as Davila's historiographical successors had and still have reason to note.

Adams was so pleased with this testimony to his foresight that he made his own note in the flyleaf of his copy of the *Discourses on Davila* written a generation before, and in the course of his remarks introduced the term 'ideology' into American English. 'The political and literary world are much indebted for the invention of the new word IDEOLOGY', he wrote. 'Our English words Ideocy or Ideotism express not the force or meaning of it.' A profound science it is, he continued, deeper than the divers in the *Dunciad*. 'It was taught in the school of folly, but alass Franklin, Turgot, Rochefoucauld and Condorcet, under Tom Paine, were the great masters of that academy.' And now, a revolution later, Adams saw his prophecy realized. Playfully he interpreted Napoleon's speech as a 'comment' on his book, and in his own counter-comment he summed up the lesson of his *Discourses*. 'Napoleon!', he exclaimed, 'this book is a prophecy of your empire before your name was heard.' *Mutato nomine, de te fabula narrabitur*, Adams aphorized: the names are different but the music is the same. If they could agree on nothing else, these two old revolutionaries, the ex-President and the soon-to-be ex-Emperor, were united in their opinion that 'ideology' – in that minimal sense of a doctrinaire program intended to move the world through words and arguments, through the mobilization of consciences – was the major disturbing (if not propelling) force in modern history.

Adams also wrote to his old friend Thomas Jefferson about the problem.[3] Speaking of Lafayette, he lamented the 'Grossness of his ignorance of Gover[n]ment and History' and grouped him with Turgot and the rest as displaying 'this gross Ideology of them all'. Three years later he was no longer concerned about Napoleon, but the 'Idiologians' (in his uncertain spelling) still troubled him. Jeffer-

---

[3] *Adams–Jefferson Letters*, ed. L. Capon (Chapel Hill, 1959), II, 355, 471, 500 (to Jefferson, 13 July 1813, 3 May and 16 Dec. 1816), and 505 (from Jefferson, 11 July 1817); and see now E. Kennedy, *A Philosophe of the Age of Revolution: Destutt de Tracy and the Origins of 'Ideology'* (Philadelphia, 1978).

son, who knew Destutt de Tracy and who indeed had been in on the secret of the book's authorship, told Adams about the treatise on ideology. '3 Vols. of Ideology!', marvelled Adams. 'Pray explain to me this neological Title! When Bonaparte used it, I was delig[h]ted with it, upon the Common Principle of delight in every Thing we cannot understand. Does it mean Idiotism? The Science of Non compos Menticism? The Science of Lunacy? The Theory of Delirium? Or does it mean the Science of Self love? Amour propre? of the Elements of Vanity?' Adams was being facetious, but his presidential successor set him straight by explaining, 'Tracy comprehends under the word "Ideology" all the subjects which the French term *Morale*, as the correlative to *Physique*.' So Jefferson tried to give a balanced and philosophical interpretation of the notion of ideology as the study of consciousness, distinguished from that of the natural and material world, in a way that would seem to offend neither historians nor contemporary sociologists. Whatever one might think of ideologists or of Tracy's coinage, the concept itself could be understood as referring to a legitimate object of study.

The theoretical interchange between these two revered figures, who were no mean ideologists in their own right, serves to introduce the general subject of this book, which is the rise of ideology, its impact, transmission and transformation, in the context of one of its most seminal periods. For some (like Napoleon) 'ideology' is a red flag; for others (like Adams) it is a barbarism; and to still others (like Jefferson) it suggests a general concept that may be put to philosophical and historical use. I incline to the latter opinion and, in keeping with modern sociological usage, take 'ideology' as a conceptual convenience, a way of relating the study of society, whether in terms of institutional or class structure or set of cultural forms, to particular human thought and testimony – which after all is the historian's last court of appeal as well as his first professional concern. Like Adams (though I appreciate his literary sarcasm) I feel that English does not possess another word of appropriate force and comprehensiveness; like Jefferson (though I realize he was merely reporting the ideas of Tracy) I assume that the term need not be taken invidiously, that it serves at least to distinguish human consciousness (*Morale*) from the material side of existence (*Physique*); and I believe that only a foolish literalism would prevent its employment to give meaning to one dimension of the historical process.

As a term, 'ideology' is less than two centuries old, but as a concept it can be traced much further back. In a pejorative sense it is associated with the particular scholarly 'deceits' (*borie*) distinguished by Vico, and before that with the famous 'idols' of Bacon. Less directly it recalls the critical views of human knowledge reflected in skeptical thought, for instance in the attack by Henry Cornelius Agrippa of Nettesheim on 'the vanity of learning' in the whole range of human and natural sciences.[4] In a more specifically political sense it suggests a connection with the old distinction between declared policy and actual strategy (the *arcana imperii* of classical devising) – between the politics of the palace, according to Machiavelli, and that of the public square.[5] But the view of ideology I want to make use of here goes beyond concepts of 'false consciousness' and of public positions as contrasted with private convictions. Rather it involves a distinctive and more or less coherent conglomerate of assumptions, attitudes, sentiments, values, ideals and goals accepted and perhaps acted upon by a more or less organized group of persons. It is both more and less than a philosophy: more because it includes the emotional, the subconscious and the irrational and must be linked to particular social patterns; less because it stops short of a rational and self-enclosed system of thought. At the same time it is more explicit and systematic than 'mentality' or, to use the terminology of Edward Shils, 'outlook', which characterizes a stable and pluralistic society.[6] More comprehensive in scope and more urgent in appeal, ideologies demand 'consensus' and some sort of collective embodiment, referred to by Shils as the 'ideological primary group'. Moreover, an ideology speaks for a 'transcendent entity', that is, an ideal going beyond material interest, involving alienation from society as a whole and perhaps the creation of a counter-culture, not to say counter-society and (as sixteenth-century observers would conclude) a counter-state.

In general 'ideology' is centered upon that pivotal and almost inaccessible juncture between society and consciousness – the historical equivalent, one might suggest, of that crucial pineal gland which, Descartes speculated, linked mind and body. What is the nature of this bond between consciousness and society? The precise relationship no doubt involves a meta-historical question, but the futility of trying to explain one in terms of the other should be evident to most historians (as it has been to most sociologists) by now. Such an approach involves either the most vulgar sort of Marxism or the most naive idealism, doctrines which may comfort but which seldom enlighten. It is not the historian's business to

---

[4] Cf. p. 178 below, n. 7.
[5] Karl Mannheim, *Ideology and Utopia*, trans. L. Wirth and E. Shils (New York, 1952), 56.
[6] *The Intellectuals and the Powers* (Chicago, 1972), 23 ff.; cf. C. Geertz, *The Interpretation of Cultures* (New York, 1973), 193–233.

choose between Hegel and Marx – or between More and Machiavelli – to discover the secret springs of the historical process by *a
priori* assumptions; this is the secular equivalent of finding the
workings of Providence in history. Rather (so I assume) it is to
investigate both of these transitory human creations – the processes
both of thought and of society – and to suggest some of the interac-
tions between them. Taking into account the inside as well as the
outside of the human condition, the concept of ideology opens the
possibility of suggesting some of the general meaning of a particular
field of experience – the meaning not simply in a philosophical sense
but also the sort of significance which evolves retrospectively in later
ages, whether causally (historically?) or by imputation and interpretation (hermeneutically or mythically?).[7]

In any case, the problem of ideology, though unfortunately
monopolized by sociologists and philosophers, seems to me to be in
a most fundamental sense historical. It may be possible to study this
problem in the static terms of particular established social groups,
but such a focus will surely miss the significance of ideology as a
force which can challenge, disturb and perhaps transform the status
quo. Indeed it might be argued that established ideologies themselves remain largely inarticulate until facing such challenges. At no
time does the phenomenon of consciousness, especially social and
political consciousness, become more accessible to the historian than
in the confrontation of ideology and counter-ideology. This seems in
accord with the experiences both of Napoleon and of Adams – and
certainly of the model chosen by Adams to illustrate that most
intensely ideological of phenomena: revolution.

If 'ideology' is a conceptual device that needs justification, the
'process of history' refers to a real puzzle of which we are all pieces,
a labyrinth from which none of us can emerge in this life. It is a
continuum of experience that can hardly be grasped from the inside
and in any general way must be expressed through metaphor. One
of the best known of these metaphors is history as a seamless web. It
is indeed plausible, this image of Maitland's, recalling as it does the
last attire of Christ as well as the complacent Victorian gradualism
which assumed that the historical fabric was woven by men of
reason, learning and especially of law. Yet there is good reason to
question the simile even if intended casually, because it suggests a
simplicity, a regularity and a homogeneity altogether foreign to our
experiences and so to our perceptions of history. It is not merely that

---

[7] Emilio Betti, *Teoria generale della interpretazione* (Milan, 1955).

the search for 'revolutions', 'crises', and turning-points where history did in fact turn has become fashionable among historians and social scientists, or that we have come to appreciate more fully the dark forces of the unconscious. It is also that recent lines of questioning and means of suggesting answers have made us more aware, more sensitive to the rents, patches and even seams of the human past – of the discontinuities, upheavals, cross-currents and reversals of the process of history. Whatever we may think of the integrity of Christ's cloak, the myth of history as a regularly bestowed inheritance hardly seems appropriate to an understanding of the human predicament in any age. Certainly, it was not accepted by either Napoleon or Adams, except as a political and social ideal.

Such a warning seems particularly necessary for the sixteenth century, that least placid and most parlous of times (which may indeed account for Maitland's admission that he 'liked most centuries better'). Men of that age would have appreciated the sentiment. For some who had come of age by 1500 it was a time of bitter disappointment, and indeed political observers like Machiavelli and Guicciardini illustrate in many ways that intellectual syndrome called the 'end of ideology'. For others, it is true, the fashion was to speak of a time of renewal and peace, an 'age of gold'. Erasmus, Budé, Lefèvre d'Etaples, Vives, More and even Luther spoke in such optimistic accents. But such hopes had soured before the century was a quarter past. 'No one will undo this universal tragedy except God', remarked Erasmus to Melanchthon about the Lutheran schism.[8] And the younger generation of humanists was even more intensely aware of the disastrous turn which the celebrated 'novelty' of their age had taken. When Budé's leading disciple came to list the central achievements of the modern world, he did not omit to mention the already famous triad of printing, the marine compass, and gunpowder; but then he went on to point out a few less productive 'marvels', including the new form of venereal disease.[9] Syphilis was not the worst plague, however. 'In addition', continued Louis Le Roy, 'sects have sprung up in all countries, which have greatly disturbed the public peace and chilled the mutual charity of human beings . . . Everywhere states have been afflicted, disturbed or ruined; everywhere religions have been troubled by heresies. Everything is pell-mell and in confusion; nothing is as it should be.' The world was not only being renewed, in short; it was also, according to the old topos, 'turned upside down'. Sons turned

[8] Allen, IX, no. 2343 (7 July 1530).
[9] Louis le Roy, *De la vicissitude ou varieté des choses en l'univers* (Paris, 1575), fol. 249.

against their fathers, subjects against their rulers, the faithful against their church. Neither the web of history nor the robe of Christ would ever be the same.

How had this come about? In general terms the answer is, and was, obvious. The source of this turmoil was that primal scream of the modern world we call the Reformation. Whether regarded as the culmination of a long tradition of religious and social disaffection, as a renewed but now inwardly turned crusade, or as an incipient struggle for autonomy and liberty, the Reformation was a traumatic human experience, or complex of experiences, whose effects went beyond religious allegiance and persisted long after specific doctrinal conflicts had ceased to be relevant. From the earliest stages, in fact, the multivalent character of the Reformation was apparent to any eyes that would see. For within a generation the ostensibly religious upheaval precipitated by Luther involved not only the formal break-up of Christendom but a whole range of secular disturbances: economic ferment in all classes, the transformation of institutions on all levels from the family to the state, a series of national uprisings, the most radical questioning of conventional values and goals, and the first and in some ways most unsettling world war in modern times. What we have, in sum, is many ingredients of a modern 'revolution'; and the temptation to apply this unwieldy abstraction to the sixteenth century often becomes irresistible. If I do not make systematic use of this fashionable model in any systematic way, it is because 'model' suggests mechanical toy as well as conceptual device, and because further reflection and investigation may indeed reveal it as immature, if not childish. But whatever the appropriate label, the transfiguration of European society in the age of the Reformation ought to be understood not merely as a changing design upon a historical fabric but as a violent, multi-dimensional, and perhaps multi-directional process which needs examining from several angles, through a variety of sources, and by a number of methods.

How does one go about grasping the process of violent social change? How, that is, while at the same time being reasonably comprehensive yet not unreasonably impressionistic, being penetrating yet not overly myopic? Not, from the point of view at least of the historian, by relying on some reductionist key, whether economic, political, intellectual or psychological: such a procedure, no matter how sophisticated or persuasively argued, can act only as an impediment to novel lines of research, set up barriers between disciplines, discount certain kinds of evidence and in general tend to dehumanize history. Nor should one restrict oneself to the superficies of human behavior, whether on the level of public affairs, of commercial activity or of conscious discourse: such an attitude too often excludes the unconscious, mythical, instinctive and in general non-functional aspects of human behavior. Nor finally, it seems to me, should one attend exclusively either to the specificity of individual action or to the anonymity of collective behavior: such a choice between biography and statistics tends to eliminate the middle ground of human participation in and reaction to society, ground which is properly that of the historian, inaccessible as it may seem methodologically.

The dilemma, though posed in historical terms, is the old problem of universals – or the newer one of statistical conformity to law – and if it is ultimately insoluble, the historian is bound sometimes to make the attempt. To clarify the dilemma we may consider two methodological extremes. A locus classicus of sociological method is Durkheim's *Suicide*; and however dated, the discussion illustrates the virtues and limitations of the attempt to explain in collective terms what after all is a very personal affair.[10] The result is indeed to explain 'voluntary death', that is, to link it with social 'causes' in a way that makes classification and even prediction possible. What it does not do, cannot do, is to relate this analysis with particular human motivations or extend causal analysis to particular cases. From the heights of sociological generalization, psychological motivation represents at most a kind of Brownian movement that in no significant way affects larger currents and patterns. The suicide of a statesman or an author does not count for more than one of a psychopath or mortally ill person. The trouble with this view is that the problems of the *quality* of consciousness do not arise, and so the problem of 'ideology' cannot be confronted in a meaningful way. Not only are we humanly, perhaps, curious about the 'why' of individual choices, and about the patterns of these whys, but for some purposes of cultural understanding we need to make qualitative distinctions between cases in terms of public impact and historical significance. As there are charismatic individuals, for example, there may be exemplary or symbolic cases that transcend their classification – transcend, sometimes, their historical context and assume mythical proportions. And some acts – consider religious conversion or that special kind of suicide that receives recognition as martyrdom – have ideological repercussions beyond statis-

[10] E. Durkheim, *Suicide: A Study in Sociology*, trans. G. Simpson (London, 1952); cf. his *Sociology and Religion*, trans. D. Pocock (New York, 1974) and J. Douglas, *The Social Meaning of Suicide* (Princeton, 1967).

tical assessment; and no methodological totems or taboos should be allowed to obstruct investigation of them.

At the other extreme from such quantitative analysis we have what Bernard de Voto somewhere called 'history by synechdoche'. His assumption was not only that some sort of methodological individualism was necessary to capture the experience (say) of the mountain men but also that in order to appreciate any sort of historical experience, even the most humdrum, we need a human encounter; we need to stand, vicariously, in the moccasins of another. Whether a single case is representative, exceptional or unique may be debated; but the effort of understanding brings a depth of insight that collective examination must forego. For only synecdochically can we appreciate the emotions, values and thoughts of humanity – and so reconstruct the ideological substance of the past. One area in which such a discriminating method is essential is intellectual history, not only because this field is elitist (in a vulgar sense) but also because it must assume for its own purposes that ideological factors are more enduring than the social and political structures of which they were a part – in other words, that they have an afterlife in consciousness – not only in books but in memory, myth and folklore. Following the posthumous life of ideology (as of ideas) also depends upon an approach that is critical and selective, if not invidious and arbitrary – why not call it 'qualitative history'?

Is it possible to combine these approaches – combine, that is, macro- with micro-history? To see the texture as well as the structure, some of the trees as well as the forest? Perhaps not; one can hardly imagine Durkheim and De Voto joining forces in such an enterprise. Yet some such illicit union seems to be necessary to acquire any sort of general understanding of the process of history. In accordance with this hybrid approach I propose to move from the examination of particular personalities, experiences, events and institutions toward more general historical patterns, and so to reach for some of the human meanings of the historical process in the sixteenth century. The direction is from history as synechdoche, then, to history as structure. As an analogy one might consider the 'historical semantics' of Leo Spitzer, which proceeds by moving back and forth between 'word details' and the conceptual locus to which they refer in order to transcribe a 'historical circle' of meaning, analogous to the 'hermeneutical circle' described by Gadamer and others.[11] Some such figurative reconstruction will appear, I hope, in

---

[11] Leo Spitzer, *Linguistics and Literary History* (Princeton, 1948), 33; and cf. H. Gadamer, *Truth and Method*, trans. G. Barden and J. Cumming (New York, 1975), 167.

the course of the following explorations of the historical process in Reformation Europe.

To conclude these preliminary assumptions and admissions, let me confess that, despite the apparently systematic form of presentation, literary models may in many ways offer the best hope for the primary aim of this book, which is to reconstruct the subjective side of the Reformation, the experiences and consciousness of its actors and observers, and the intellectual expressions thereof. I mean this in the sense not only that techniques of literary criticism, language analysis, tracing of genres and *topoi* are essential for any historical enterprise relying primarily on written discourse, but also that the *form* of presentation may derive something from this source. The Reformation was indeed a historical drama – a collective 'agony', with ideology identifying the various protagonists and antagonists, formulating their speaking parts, shaping their actions and to some extent determining their fates. It was also a sort of epic – the story of heroic (though perhaps misguided) effort, grandiose designs and finally (for posterity) mythical achievement. It is appropriate and perhaps necessary that an effort of 'qualitative history' should have recourse to such pre-historical forms as well as to more systematic kinds of analysis. Let us begin then *in medias res* with a dramatic and at the same time paradigmatic episode in the ideological *Agon* of the Reformation.

1 · Context:
The egg that Luther hatched

Erasmus innuit, Lutherus irruit, Erasmus parit ova,
Lutherus excludit pullos, Erasmus dubitat, Lutherus
asseverat.

Florimond de Raemond

Utinam Lutherus taceret.

Melanchthon

1 · Context:
The egg that Luther hatched

APOLOGUE: THE AFFAIR OF THE PLACARDS
(1534)

Two or three hours after midnight on Saturday, 17 October 1534, a number of religious enthusiasts, adherents of the 'so-called reformed religion', went out, some of them armed, into the streets of Paris and other French cities upon a dangerous mission. On walls and other prominent places they posted broadsheets which had been printed in Neuchâtel and recently smuggled into France.[1] These placards, measuring less than 14 by 10 inches and printed in a modest but clear *bastarda*, had been composed by Antoine Marcourt, pastor and propagandist of Neuchâtel, and published by the transient printer Pierre de Vingle. The next morning, on their way to church, the citizens of Paris, Orleans, Blois, Rouen, Tours, and Amboise could read the French text, which was headlined

THE TRUE ARTICLES AGAINST THE HORRIBLE, GROSS, AND INSUPPORTABLE ABUSE OF THE POPISH MASS, invented directly contrary to the holy supper of Jesus Christ.

The preacher, who was a 'sacramentarian' rather than a Lutheran (though the distinction was too fine for most orthodox folk), continued:

I invoke heaven and earth as witnesses to the truth against this pompous and arrogant popish mass, by which (if God does not prevent it) the whole world will be ruined, cast down, lost and desolated.

He concluded by setting down four articles repudiating the idolatrous error of transubstantiation and affirming the spiritual character of Christian faith and worship. The papists are like 'ravaging wolves', he concluded. 'They kill, burn, destroy and murder all who oppose them. The truth escapes them, but this same truth will seek out and soon destroy them. Fiat. Fiat. Amen.'

---

[1] The most detailed account is now Gabrielle Berthoud, *Antoine Marcourt* (Geneva, 1973); the placard itself is reproduced in *Aspects*. Cf. Herminjard, III, 225.

Shocking sentiments these, directed as they were against the primary rite and mystery of Christendom, the ultimate symbol of orthodoxy and legitimacy. More than heretical, they were treasonable; certainly King Francis I thought so, when on Sunday morning he found his personal copy attached to his bedchamber door in the château of Amboise. The previous year he had allowed a papal bull to be translated and published calling for 'the extirpation of the Lutheran heresy and other sects swarming over the country'; now he began to campaign in earnest. Two days after the affront to his royal person he set in motion the machinery of repression – the Gallican church, the Sorbonne, and the Parlement of Paris – appealing to his subjects' national pride and sense of religious unity. He assigned to the theologian Jerome de Hangest the job of replying in print to these 'offspring of the devil' and to the lieutenant-general of Paris, Jean Morin, that of tracking down the 'imitators of the Lutherans'. In his 'perpetual and irrevocable edict' of January he added that informers would be rewarded with a quarter of the confiscated property of any convicted members or accomplices of the seditious sect.[2] The 'ravaging wolves', it must have seemed to evangelical sympathizers, had struck again.

The royal crusade did not succeed, but it was not for lack of trying. Rumor had it that up to 400 persons were imprisoned. In fact at least a dozen men had been arrested and convicted by the end of the year. Nine of them were burned at the stake after other conventional indignities, one was banished (after a flogging), and two escaped punishment, according to a contemporary witness, 'because they accused many others'. Altogether, for the year following the affair of the placards, over 120 victims have been identified, although there were surely others, including some 'thrown into the Seine', according to ancient custom. In general the group constituted a fair cross-section of French urban society. The majority was middle-class: shopkeepers and merchants, including possibly one Italian (Louis de Medici by name), and only three nobles, all of whom escape into exile. A considerable number were intellectuals of a sort: ten churchmen (priests and friars), ten printers and booksellers, one lawyer (who was dispossessed and banished), and three formally associated with the university (though there were surely others concealed by the vagaries of the record). More than half of those convicted managed to escape into exile, including two authors of considerable renown, Clement Marot and Mathurin

---

[2] *Ordonnance du Roy François contre les imitateurs de la secte Lutherienne et recelateurs d'iceaux*, 1 Feb. 1535 (BN F.35149); Isambert, xii, no. 211 and (16 July) no. 216. Cf. P. Feret, *La Faculté de theologie de Paris*, ii (Paris, 1900), 28.

Cordier, but all were condemned *in absentia*. Basing himself on a hated popish formula (the canonist *de motu proprio*), the king ordered in July that the property of these should be confiscated without trial.

What was the offense of these demonstrators? One woman was condemned allegedly because she ate meat on Fridays and Sundays and a man for donating money to a Lutheran group; but for the most part they were partners in the same crime, and this crime was literary. It was, specifically, possession or distribution of suspect books or pamphlets. The conclusion of the same ordinance of July made official intransigence unmistakable: 'It is forbidden to all . . . to read, dogmatize, translate, compose, or print, publicly or privately, any doctrine contrary to the Christian faith.'

One of those who had fled into exile in the wake of this affair was a young French scholar already at work on a book which would give classic form to many of these same condemned doctrines. Jean Calvin had gone to Basel to publish his *Institutes of Christian Religion*, and in the late summer of 1535 he addressed his preface to Francis I in defense of the martyrs of that year. What he did not scruple to call 'our cause', though indeed contrary to the degenerate custom of recent times, was neither novel nor seditious nor the source of public disorder; and he warned the king not to heed the maligners of true religion. Even if spreading the gospel did involve conflict, he added, this was no more than the apostles themselves had suffered; and like the apostles the new evangelists were ready to face such dangers and even death. Although couched in respectful language and denying any imputation of disobedience, Calvin's plea ended with a challenge as unmistakable as the king's own thundering declarations. 'The strong hand of the Lord . . . ', he concluded, 'will surely appear in due season, coming forth armed to deliver the poor from their affliction and also to punish their despisers, who now exult with such great assurance.'[3]

The affair of the placards broke upon the French scene just seventeen years after Luther had publicly displayed his own placard, the Ninety-Five Theses, thirteen years after his doctrines had been condemned in France, and perhaps a year after the conversion of Calvin. In the act itself there was little novelty: placards had been distributed earlier, men (especially authors and printers) had faced martyrdom and exile, and governments had adopted a policy of repression before. But this particular affair was pivotal for a variety of reasons. It marked a turning-point in the fortunes of French

---

[3] *Institutes*, preface.

Protestantism, which from this time became a largely underground movement; it displayed the irreversible polarization of French society in painfully obvious terms and intensified it by provoking more extreme statements on both sides, ranging from Calvin's *Institutes* to Guillaume Budé's *Transition from Hellenism to Christianity*, which defended the royal policy of persecution; and it destroyed prospects for an accord between France and the Lutheran princes of Germany, which was being negotiated with the help of Philip Melanchthon.[4] Clearly religious affairs were having a shaping and even determining effect upon social and political history.

Still more significant, perhaps, was its symbolic and in a sense mythical value. For the affair of the placards constituted a veritable microcosm of the Reformation, illustrating as it does all of the primary factors of ideological change in the sixteenth century. It was, first and most obviously, a display of an unexpectedly well-organized opposition movement with a coherent and indeed fanatic doctrinal base. The only concession to propriety was the omission of the names of Luther or other heterodox figures; but the intemperance of the language – 'horrible et execrable blaspheme', 'Paovres idolatres', 'telles pestes faulz antichristz', etc. – was uncompromising. So the lines were drawn, the enemy was identified and, especially with the attack on 'ce gros mot Transsubstantiation', doctrinal bridges were burned. The confrontation was familiar: an idealistic and even fanatical minority demanding a return to a purely spiritual commitment and confronting a responsible but materialistic and authoritarian establishment with other values and priorities. What was emerging into public view was not only a 'sect' but potentially a party that would not accommodate itself to the world as it was being run.[5]

No less shocking than the radicalism of these sacramentarians was the extent to which the contagion of protest had spread, both vertically and horizontally, into European society. Bad enough that the new doctrines had been broadcast in every part of the Holy Roman Empire, including even the Netherlands, which was Charles V's own domain; but that the realm of the 'Most Christian King' should be infected from top to bottom and throughout was intolerable. By 1535 almost fifty towns had been perceptibly touched by heresy, and the great period of expansion was just beginning. What is more, the missionary zeal of French Protestants had reached the

[4] Guillaume Budé, *De Transitu Hellenismi ad Christianismum* (Paris, 1535); French trans. M. Lebel (Paris, 1973), English trans. D. F. Penham (unpublished Ph.D. thesis, Columbia University, 1954).
[5] See below, pp. 118–28.

pitch of facing not only outlaw status at home but also martyrdom and – which was worse in terms of social stability, the integrity of property and the continuity of succession – exile. What resulted was a growing community of refugees fleeing to Strasbourg, Basel, Zurich, and especially to Geneva, which was soon to become the principal haven and nerve-center of international Protestantism. 'The blood of martyrs is the seed of the church' became a motto of the reformers, but the actions of exiles was in the long run more effective in the propagation of their faith.[6]

In the vanguard of this new church were the intellectuals, and their influence far outweighed their numbers. At first Francis I had tended to attribute 'Lutheran' errors to 'people of low status and lower understanding', but by 1535 he must have known better, if only because of the condemnation of scholars like Lefèvre d'Etaples and Louis Berquin, who had been executed some six years earlier. He was surely aware of the threat posed in particular to the University of Paris, that 'eldest daughter of the church', which had been among the first to come out against Luther; for in 1533 statutes were passed against the 'impudent books of the heretics'. After the affair of the placards, in which the university community had been so deeply implicated, the ideological menace seemed much more immediate; and in the spring of 1535 the king issued a personal warning to the faculties to see to it that their charges were properly 'indoctrinated', as he put it.[7] But it was increasingly difficult to regulate the influx of new ideas, especially in the German nation and in the embryonic 'college of three languages', that seed of the Collège de France which Francis had planted just five years before. Always an arena of disputation and turmoil, the university had become a center of a kind of counter-culture which promoted a conflict not only of faculties but also of generations and of ideological factions – and which challenged not only pedagogical but also paternal and political authority. From the universities of Paris, Orleans, Bourges, and elsewhere came many of the Protestant leaders of the next generation, new-style intellectuals who wanted to make academic learning the agency of a profounder transformation.

What the escapade of the placards demonstrated most conspicuously was that printing had come of age as a vehicle of propaganda as well as a source of public enlightenment. It offered an irresistible platform for men like Marcourt, who demanded that the placards 'be published and displayed in every public place' – men, that is, who were driven to bear public witness to their beliefs and to broadcast

[6] See below, p. 277, n. 51.   [7] Bulaeus, VI, 252–3. See below, pp. 143–58.

them to the world. As a means of testifying to and propagating the faith, of course, the printing press had been used effectively since the first years of the Lutheran scandal, which spread almost immediately, especially through translations, to the rest of Europe. The ideological explosion of the 1520s had been accompanied by an enormous increase not only in the quantity of books but also of the means and rapidity of distribution. The international character of publishing is well illustrated by these placards – composed by a Swiss pastor, published by a French printer, posted simultaneously in five cities and sent or reported to persons outside France (to Melanchthon, for example) as well as inside. Of course the threat posed by printing to religious orthodoxy and social order had been recognized from the first. As early as 1523 'Lutheran' literature was publicly burned in France, and official censorship was instituted in the form of a royal ordinance, the first of a long and repetitive line, devoted to the extermination of the heretical 'vermin' set loose in Germany. This campaign of censorship reached its highest point in the wake of the affair of the placards, when Francis I, still in the throes of his anti-sacramentarian tantrum, tried to abolish printing altogether.[8] This ludicrous order was never enforced (and indeed the text was not preserved), but it does suggest the depth of official apprehension about the force of publicity.

It may be said in general that official attitudes toward Protestants constituted a sort of counter-fanaticism, and their declarations a counter-propaganda. In edict after edict, appearing increasingly in printed form as well as being 'published at the sound of trumpets' on street corners, the accursed sect was denounced and its 'extirpation' and 'extermination' announced to be royal policy. In mid-January the king staged a great spectacle in Paris, a counter-demonstration celebrating national unity and orthodoxy.[9] It began with a mass in Nôtre-Dame, included an elaborate procession of the Gallican clergy, and ended with the public execution of six heretics. The purpose, significantly, was the repudiation not merely of heresy but of lese-majesty – of treason. Two weeks later this position was made even clearer when Francis I declared to the Protestant princes of Germany (whom he was already courting because of rivalry with Charles V) that his displeasure was directed not against Lutheranism as such but against the seditious behavior of those who, behind their theological 'paradoxes', were subverting French society.[10] Even more than his treaty with the Turks of this same year, this act of the

---

[8] See below, p. 238, n. 58.
[9] G. Corrozet, *Les Antiquitez de Paris* (Paris, 1586), fol. 157, and see below, pp. 193–203.
[10] Herminjard, III, 249.

French king signified what Garrett Mattingly called 'the breaking-up of Christendom' and in general the replacement of the religious question by politics.

As in the case of Luther himself, in short, the fundamental issue was not merely doctrinal disagreement but obedience to established authority. The main target of the sacramentalists was the central ceremony of the Christian faith, but it is essential to understand that the eucharist had an ideological as well as a Christological significance. Protestants of a sacramentarian persuasion put their faith in a transcendent God, and so they regarded the Catholic doctrine of transubstantiation not only as idolatrous but as materialistic to the point of obscenity, implying physical consumption of the Divine Being. 'Their god is the belly', wrote Calvin of his enemies, and a pamphleteer of the religious wars attacked more explicitly those 'Antromorphites, who made God carnal'.[11] This sort of 'Communion' was a metaphor for defiling not only the divinity but also the entire ecclesiastical establishment which claimed legitimacy on that basis. Corresponding to the idea of an 'immanent God', in other words, is that idea that the visible church, its institutions and its traditions, are divinely sanctioned – that human organization embodies divine authority.[12] And as they abhorred the notion that the Lord's Supper was a blood sacrifice, so Protestants rejected the notion that the priesthood was a sacred office. This abhorrence and rejection was expressed not only in vituperative and sometimes scatological language but also in physical violence, iconoclasm representing an uncontrollable abomination for debased religion.

To this extent official fears about the inseparability of heresy and sedition were not without foundation. The threat of Lutheran 'liberty' and sacramentarian anarchy was made manifest in the year of the placards. To reject immanence, and thereby traditional authority, on grounds of private conscience was merely heretical; but to proclaim these views publicly was treasonable. What was most ominous about the affair of the placards was the prospect of social revolution. It did not take modern anthropological insights into the social function of religious symbols, especially one so sensitive as the eucharist, to reveal this to contemporaries.

---

[11] *Discours politique*, in *ME*, III, fol. 15ᵛ.
[12] See Guy Swanson, *Religion and Regime* (Ann Arbor, 1967), and among various reactions to it, those of H. G. Koenigsberger and Natalie Davis in *Journal of Interdisciplinary History*, I (1970–1), 380ff. See also below, p. 36, n. 35.

Context: the egg that Luther hatched

THE IDEA OF REFORM

'In the beginning was the word': here is a text dear to the hearts of theologians and essential to their method of inquiry. For historians, however, the opposite must be assumed: the 'word' – generalizations, conclusions and even precise definitions – must come at the very end, and historically speaking the end never quite comes (so far, at least). The Reformation presents such a dilemma. Contemporaries knew what it signified: the realization, or alternatively the subversion, of the true church. With hindsight, however, we cannot be so sure. All historians can say is that 'the Reformation' refers to a set of religious, social and finally political phenomena which came to dominate individual consciences and eventually public opinion as a whole during the sixteenth century.[13] What we are confronted with, in fact, is not a perceivable phenomenon in an ordinary sense but rather a historical epiphenomenon that acquired meaning only retrospectively. In the interpretation which has been developed by observers and historians over four centuries and more, the Reformation is a 'sacred history' which gave its participants values, standards of judgment and transcendent goals. It was a new creation, or a re-creation, whose moving spirits were not ordinary individuals, even the least of them, but heroes and shapers of history. So the official historian of Lutheranism, Johann Sleidan, while not neglecting the drums and the trumpets, told his story of the times as an epic struggle between the forces of darkness and the children of the light. So counter-historians like Florimond de Raemond, seeking an appropriate literary form, turned to tragic drama – 'Histoire Tragique de ce Schisme Luthero-Calvinique', Raemond called his book, written in part to counteract that of Sleidan, 'the Livy of the Lutherans'.[14] Raemond was no less convinced than Sleidan that the coming of Luther was supernatural; but for him it was demonic rather than miraculous, having been foretold by astrological signs and the outcries of the people, who were no less infallible prognosticators. Fortunately, he added, fate determined at that very moment that Cortés should be carrying the banner of Christ against the Aztec 'idolaters', though of course this hardly made up for the Lutheran mischief.

To friends and foes alike, in short, the Reformation represents a

---

[13] A fundamental work is G. Ladner, *The Idea of Reform* (Cambridge, Mass., 1959), with his 'Die mittelalterliche Reform-Idee und ihr Verhältnis zur Idee der Renaissance', *Mitteilungen des Instituts für österreichische Geschichtsforschung*, LX (1952), 31–59; but for our period there is nothing of this sort, nor anything comparable to W. Ferguson, *The Renaissance in Historical Thought* (Boston, 1948), except the controversial work of Konrad Burdach, including the essay *Reformation, Renaissance, Humanismus* (Berlin, 1926), and of course an unmanageable quantity of discussion of individual 'reformers'.

[14] Sleidan; Raemond, 4–5, 26.

sort of myth, in just the sense that Mircea Eliade uses the term, a myth which transcended human experience and the historical process. Almost from the beginning it appeared as a fulcrum of modern history, a cataclysm which turned the world upside-down and dominated western society for generations. To later interpreters it was the enacting of a spiritual 'agony' so profound that neither what came before nor what came after possessed the same creative (or catastrophic) force as the set of events fired by the symbolic act of Martin Luther. To many modern historians, too, the Reformation has posed intimidating problems that go beyond the explanatory powers of any single discipline. In the work of Weber and Troeltsch, for instance, it has posed an intimidating *Problematik* which has inspired and confused generations of scholars; such are the forms that myths take, it seems, in this secular age.[15]

If the Reformation may be construed as a myth in this positive sense, it was of course not an original construction. It was rather a recapitulation of an earlier 'sacred mystery', which was the rise of Christianity itself. The 'imitation of Christ' was literally the defining theme of the religious movements of the sixteenth century. Conceptually, the link was in the time-honored and multi-faceted idea of reform, which had a number of ancient roots but which received characteristic formulation in Christian antiquity. Cosmological notions of renewal, especially those of a cyclical nature, vitalistic notions of revival, often associated with the idea of the 'Renaissance', and utopian notions of a new age all went into the making of the sixteenth-century idea of reform; but the most direct antecedent again was Biblical. Specifically, the source was the notion of personal regeneration, or conversion, the spiritual experience of being 'born again', which involved a fundamental change of attitude from evil to good accompanied by feelings of guilt, revulsion and repentance. Underlying this was the desire to suppress or wipe away an evil past, an attitude symbolized by the sacrament of baptism. 'Water purifies and regenerates because it nullifies the past', remarked Eliade, 'and restores – even if only for a moment – the integrity of the dawn of things.'[16] So with the cleansing by water in Protestant confessions. Baptism nullifies by death, that is, immersing, according to Luther; and it restores by resurrection, that is, emerging. In a way, it was a replica both of the pervasive myth of the Reformation,

---

[15] The historical misconceptions of Weber and even more the sociological misconceptions of most of his critics have deprived the literature of much of its usefulness for historians and sociologists alike; but the 'Weber thesis' is still an unrivalled attempt to interpret Protestant ideology in its formative period.

[16] Mircea Eliade, *Myth and Reality*, trans. W. Trask (New York, 1963), 2.

a return to the lost innocence of the 'primitive church' and of the conscious experience of conversion.

'Reform', in the sense of this Pauline and Augustinian 'change of mind', was extended also to social and institutional transformations; and indeed during the middle ages much of the substance of historical change was expressed, or justified, in terms of reformation and restoration, of improvement by return to the supposed good old days. Let us do away with papal bureaucracy, pleaded religious reformers, and return to the days of apostolic simplicity; let us decrease litigation and venality of justice, pleaded French legal reformers, and return to the days when St Louis decided cases under the great oak of Vincennes. 'Reform' of religious orders, of universities, of guilds, of the army, of the laws, of the Empire, of the church as a whole – these programs recurred through western history from the patristic period down to modern times. There was nothing novel about the sixteenth-century idea of reform, then, except perhaps for its inflation, which led enthusiasts like Erasmus to proposals for reforming the whole world. Nor would such oecumenical schemes and retrospective utopian dreams be discouraged even by the worst horrors of religious war.

In 1512 John Colet, friend and in some ways mentor to Erasmus, gave a famous sermon to Convocation in which, scolding King Henry VIII as well as the assembled prelates of England, he sounded the basic theme of reformation. 'Be ye not conformed to the world', he quoted – 'to this age' (*a ce siècle*), as his colleague Lefèvre d'Etaples had it – 'but be ye reformed in the newness of your minds . . .'[17] This same text, Romans 12:2, he had quoted fifteen years earlier in lectures delivered at Oxford; but now, addressing the monarch as well as the Anglican church, he extended his message more especially to the human evils within Christendom. 'Reformation' demanded not merely individual repentance but also the restoration of the ancient laws and customs of the church against all kinds of worldliness, bureaucratic corruption and the resulting sin of simony; and it was to apply to laity as well as to clergy. It was much the same spirit that informed Erasmus's 'philosophy of Christ' and inspired, or at least reinforced, Luther, who at this very time was likewise irretrievably involved in Pauline theology.

These years witnessed a growing if dissonant chorus of pleas for the reformation of European society from top to bottom, and to an older generation of historians this commotion seemed sufficient explanation for the greater Reformation inaugurated five years later.

[17] Translated in F. Seebohm, *The Oxford Reformers* (London, 1869), 230ff., and cf. Lefèvre's translation of the New Testament.

'Reform in head and members', as the phrase went: reform through the papacy, as ventured in the Lateran Council, meeting also at just this time (1512–17); reform by particular prelates, such as Cardinal Ximénez and Bishop Guillaume Briçonnet; reform in particular orders, such as the Dominicans in Germany and the Franciscans, the spiritual branch of which was at last recognized in 1517, a victory of the 'reformed' over the 'deformed'; and reform in various academic circles by Christian humanists of varying degrees of devotion.[18] There was also much talk of 'reform' in particular 'national churches', especially the Gallican, clinging to the 'liberties' achieved a century earlier during another period of 'reform', that is, the period of Conciliarism, a doctrine officially discredited but still supported north of the Alps; in the ecclesiastical establishments, secular and regular, of territorial and urban governments, especially in Germany, Switzerland and the Netherlands; and in various popular movements, such as the Modern Devotion and various religious sodalities, and more radically in peasant and urban groups. 'Reform', finally, was sought by the descendants of medieval heresies, including the Waldensians, Hussites, Lollards and less easily identified dissenters such as the proto-sacramentarians of Germany and the Netherlands. Hardly anybody, it seems, was satisfied with the 'form' of the world as it appeared in the sixteenth century.

But most of this chorus was just that – cries of outrage and murmurs of discontent, but in the end only noise. Reformation had little relation to social reality or ideological change but referred mainly to the rhetoric of a number of conflicting groups seeking the betterment of their own positions and elimination of abuses and inequities as they appeared on their particular horizons. National interests, secular and ecclesiastical authorities, urban and agrarian groups, university faculties – each had its complaints and remedies; but the conflicts and contradictions of each were even more conspicuous and prevented reform from finding either a particular focus or a single direction. What sense could be made from such ideological pandemonium?

Perhaps the easiest answer was given by political realists like Machiavelli and Guicciardini, who tended to discount such ideals as either dreams or pretexts, and in both cases politically useless or detrimental. Religious movements seemed hardly to penetrate their consciousness or historical writing and were certainly not given a place in the realm of public affairs along with war and diplomacy. At the opposite extreme were optimists like Erasmus, Lefèvre

[18] H. Jedin, *A History of the Council of Trent*, trans. E. Graf, 1 (London, 1957); J. Moorman, *A History of the Franciscan Order* (Oxford, 1968), 581.

d'Etaples and perhaps Thomas More, who professed to believe that the world could indeed be shaped by ideas and that they could, in Lefèvre's words, 'aspire to see our age restored to the likeness of the primitive church'.[19] In the middle (if a middle position can be distinguished at all) were traditionalists like Claude de Seyssel, for whom established religion was one of the bulwarks of society and state and for whom reform meant Gallican independence and suppression of heresy. Three modes of perception, then, and three types of social consciousness: the Machiavellian, the Utopian and the traditionalist. Each of them, in its own way, elitist, rationalistic and a bit shallow – and none of them prepared to cope with or even account for the phenomenon of Luther and the form of the world that emerged in the wake of his career.

In this maze of attitudes, this blur of differing viewpoints, Luther came to represent a clear and sharply focussed vision of the world, of this one as well as the other; in a riot of 'outlooks', to use Shils's terms, Luther offered a definite ideological choice. He made a leap into the radical theology of St Paul and in some ways beyond; and among contemporaries of almost all persuasions his fundamentalism produced a shock, whether of revulsion or of recognition. For his overall idea of reform was absolute, total, uncompromising. He wanted to wipe away not only the filth of human traditions but also the false glitter of humanist hopes, rejecting the degeneracy of the one and the hubris of the other. So he turned first to himself, then to his Book and to the transcendent God he discovered, or rediscovered, there. Where 'there' was has often been debated – whether in the text of Paul's epistle to the Romans or in his own conscience – but in any case Luther found a way to justify both his God and himself. Then, having passed through the phase of personal reform, he turned to his public work, which was the Reformation of religion in more general terms, to give public reality to a private ideal. So at least the story goes in the form that it has been handed down from those crucial years.

The key to Luther's idea of reform lay in the Christian doctrine of penance, which had long been the subject not only of ecclesiastical abuse (as Luther interpreted it) but also of scholarly criticism; and Luther's reformulation was indebted to both of these traditions. On the one hand he was revolted by the canonist theory and practice of *poenitentia*, which was materialistic and utilitarian, having become the basis of a major source of papal revenue, a practice illustrated most flagrantly by the contemporary sale of indulgences. On the other hand he drew upon the humanist critique of the Biblical basis

---

[19] Preface to commentaries on the four evangelists (1522), in Herminjard, I, 93.

for this, especially that of Lorenzo Valla and Erasmus, which argued on grammatical as well as theological grounds that the meaning of the text 'Repent ye!' was not external but spiritual – that is, not to do penance but to feel penitent. In logical if not in emotional terms the line from this, the first of Luther's Ninety-five Theses, to his rejection of the entire canonist tradition, was continuous and straight. In public terms the road was marked by a series of 'disputations', an academic institution which would later become a primary vehicle of formal 'reformation'.[20] Intellectually, the terminal point came in 1520, when Luther dramatized his complete rejection of ecclesiastical tradition and the 'power of the keys' by publicly burning the corpus of canon law. Like water, fire also purifies; and in this second act of academic defiance Luther symbolically wiped away the past in order to begin anew, although the final burning of his bridges did not come for another few months, when he took his famous and potentially martyrly stand at the Diet of Worms on the dual grounds of Conscience and God's Word. Not that, at this point, he distinguished much between the two.

In this way Luther fashioned his own myth; and the myth was ratified officially when ecclesiastical and secular authorities branded him excommunicate and outlaw – not so much for his unorthodoxy as for his defiance; for disobedience was his unforgivable error. By that time his idea of reform was largely formulated. In three famous works of 1520 (four, if one includes his justification for burning the books of canon law) Luther explained the principles of intellectual and social as well as religious reformation. In the tract on 'Christian Liberty' he discussed what might be regarded as the religious psychology of Lutheranism, the state of inner confidence and freedom from 'human traditions' which accompanied reformation. In the work on the 'Babylonian Captivity of the Church' he introduced a prominent metaphor of polemical anti-Romanism and gave his judgment on penance and the other sacraments. In his vernacular 'Address to the Christian Nobility of the German Nation', finally, Luther presented systematically his griefs against his 'Romanist' enemies and set down a comprehensive program of reform, which included not only religion but also society, learning and education, especially in the universities, where among other things civil law was to be restricted, Aristotle largely eliminated and canon law banished. In this way, out of Luther's struggles with his conscience and with his enemies (and with the support of a

[20] Cf. G. Olsen, 'The idea of the Ecclesia Primitiva in the writings of the twelfth-century canonists', *Traditio*, xxv (1969), 61–86. The term 'primitive eglise' appears also in the Concordat of 1516 (Isambert, xii, 36).

growing number of friends and disciples), there emerged first an academic scandal, then a religious 'sect' and finally a full-fledged ideological movement.

One other element deserves notice. Lutheran ideology involved not only a program of reform and a vision of the future but also a new perspective on the past, which was even more important in social and political terms.[21] According to this perspective, which reinforced and in some ways broadened that of Renaissance humanism, the Christian past exhibited three principal phases, corresponding to three mythical constructs that had long been part of the mentality of religious reformers. The first was the myth of the primitive church in which the 'pure word of God' had been established and which, perhaps, had been preserved in the hearts of a few saintly persons. The second was that of progressive degeneration through 'human traditions' and idolatry resulting from the secularization of the church. Finally came the restoration of pristine Christianity by purging of worldly institutions and reviving of spiritual values. Formation, deformation, reformation: this was the original dialectic of modern history, and it runs through all levels of experience encountered in this book.

THE SEVEN HEADS OF MARTIN LUTHER

The symbol, the cynosure and the starting point of the Reformation as an historical experience was Martin Luther, and some appreciation of his impact is essential for any understanding of the sixteenth-century climate of opinion. Even in recent times his presence is imposing – whether fulfilling the Hegelian role of 'world-historical figure', Weber's Charismatic Leader, Erikson's archetypal Troubled Youth, or a monstrous creation of modern publicity, an original personality cult. In his own century Luther's public image ranged from the demonic to the divine, from the heroic to the villainous, from the infantile to the paternal. In a contemporary cartoon gracing an early, hostile biography he was presented as a seven-headed monster.[22] Characteristic of Reformation religious caricature, this conceit will also serve to suggest the various uncommon faces which Luther presented to contemporaries and to posterity, and to anticipate, on the biographical level, the principal themes of later chapters.

---

[21] Essential is John Headley, *Luther's View of Church History* (New Haven, Conn., 1963).

[22] Cochlaeus, *Septiceps Lutherus* (Paris, 1564), with the epithets 'confusius, impius, spernis, ethnicus, haereticus, indoctus, duplex anima'.

The seven heads of Martin Luther

First there is Luther the Angry Young Man: confused, mal-adjusted, floundering in an 'identity crisis', resolving it and willfully trying to project his solution on the rest of mankind. Then Luther the Teacher: explaining the meaning of the Bible and human existence to souls in his cure, disciples, visiting supplicants, the German nation and the world at large. There is Luther the Pastor: similarly broadcasting concern for his own and for his followers' souls to a wider audience and apostolically trying to disseminate his message to as much of Christendom as could hear his voice. Supplementing these roles, Luther the Author: unleashing a flood of propaganda and in the process transforming the art of printing from a source of enlightenment into a means of inflaming society. Luther the National Hero: leading his followers out of a Roman bondage to a 'liberty' that was German as well as Christian. Luther the Authoritarian Father-figure: attracting the filial obedience and emulation of a younger generation and offering them answers to big questions and a way to a new and more fulfilling life. And finally Luther the Rebel: questioning and rejecting ecclesiastical authority and inspiring, however inadvertently, a movement which brought civil war to Germany, schism to Christendom and a model of revolution to posterity.

Why, to look at Luther's first aspect, was he so angry? In recent years Luther's psyche has been the target of much investigation and speculation, not only because it was situated in the eye of one of the great storms of western history but also because it seems to afford access to a certain kind of religious and political pathology which has sometimes complicated the historical process.[23] In many ways Luther seemed to typify, or perhaps to magnify, tensions and conflicts of late-medieval Christianity in his search for that peace of mind which represents the psychological basis of the doctrine of salvation. He was, perhaps, fighting death, and the fear of death, in the cultural symbols of his own time. In succession he sought answers in ecclesiastical institutions, in monastic life, in an academic career, in traditional theology and finally, and most characteristically, in scriptures. Death was in the world; life in the Book. The failure of all but the last of these solutions was marked by a series of 'crises' which almost shattered him but which in the end drove him down that fateful road to Worms.

Martin Luther was an intractable man; he must have been a willful child. Though prejudiced, Raemond was not necessarily wrong when he reported that 'Margaret his mother had more than one

[23] On Erik Erikson's celebrated *Young Man Luther*, see Roger A. Johnson (ed.), *Psychology and Religion* (Philadelphia, 1977).

occasion to believe that she had given birth to a flaming torch.'[24] His father had even more cause to complain when Martin, after his famous oath in the thunderstorm in 1505, chose a dismal monastic life over a lucrative legal career, though not without a certain sense of guilt, to which he later testified. More doubtful is the story about Luther's 'fit in the choir', told by the same biographer who gave him seven heads, and the accompanying suggestion that Luther feared demonic possession, inferred from the cryptic 'It is not me' (*Ego non sum*) produced by the Biblical text about the possessed child brought to Christ. In any case these became part of the Lutheran legend. More certain and more immediately relevant is his 'tower experience', his conversion coming probably during his intensive study of St Paul for his lectures of 1515, which marked the founding both of his inner conviction and of his future program. In general, however seriously one decides to take the Eriksonian analysis, one cannot doubt that Luther passed indeed through a crisis of identity and indulged in increasingly bold acts of defiance until his decision to give public notice of his beliefs in 1517. Luther was a resistant child; he became a rebellious man.

This was the darker or at least more instinctual side of Luther's nature – the compulsiveness emphasized by his enemies, admitted by Luther himself but played down by his followers, who preferred to see his more rational and pedagogical face. As an intellectual Luther seems in many ways modern: a scholar fully abreast of humanist learning, a literary artist who played a major role in creating German prose style, and a popular author who exploited the new medium of print. Yet in general Luther was the product of a fairly standard scholastic education. He saw the world, and tried to change it, within the framework of late-medieval learning.[25] His doctor's degree, obtained at the University of Wittenberg at the age of twenty-eight, was not only a source of personal and professional pride but also a prime justification for his mission to instruct humanity in its duties and purpose. To Luther the doctor's thesis certified what was at least the second-highest human calling – discovering the truth, achieving 'mastery' over its dissemination, and defending it to the world. The central, revolutionary act of his career, his posting of the Theses in 1517, was itself a quintessentially academic gesture, and the challenge to debate them illustrated the highest goal of scholastic education, which was the ability to dispute (successfully).

In many ways Luther drew strength from his academic base. It was in

---

[24] Raemond, 26, following Cochlaeus.
[25] See E. H. Harbison, *The Christian Scholar in the Age of the Reformation* (New York, 1956), and more specifically on the University of Wittenberg, E. Schwiebert, *Luther and his Times* (St Louis, 1950).

the course of his teaching duties, especially his lectures on Paul's epistle to the Romans, that he made his major intellectual break-through. In his responsibilities as adviser to candidates in theology he came to appreciate the power of pedagogy to win over the next generation and so not only to undermine an old tradition but also to create, or to maintain, a new one.[26] Such discipleship appeared almost immediately in Wittenberg, increased during his early de-bates, and spread to Erfurt and other parts of the German and European university community. Through the formation and 'refor-mation' of academic institutions by such scholars as Johann Sturm and Philip Melanchthon, the Protestant educational system became a leading carrier and disseminator of the Lutheran message as well as creator of future leadership. The Reformation began as an academic affair, and in many ways the academy continued to be a major vehicle of ideological and social change.

A related aspect of Luther's charismatic function, his third face, was his work as confessor, counsellor and especially preacher. In some ways this pastoral function was even more fundamental to the maintenance of his church, involving as it did a profounder appeal to a much wider range of persons and classes; and in fact Luther distinguished clearly between the Latinate intellectualism of his lectures, commentaries and disputations and the simple messages and vernacular exhortations of his popular preaching. It was the cure of souls, his parishioners' as well as his own, that had impelled him in the first place to resist the materialism embodied in the sale of indulgences. From this defensive position he moved to an attack on the foundations and superstructure of the church,[27] arguing that the justification for the ecclesiastical hierarchy, that is, the power of the keys given by Christ to St Peter, had actually been assigned thereby to all ministers of the Word. Indeed this commis-sion, together with his doctoral degree, constituted his credentials as director of consciences of all men. The evangelizing process, whether through sermons, letters of spiritual counsel or talk over the dinner table, whether through exhortation, dialogue or exam-ple, constituted the ideological life-principle of a Christian com-munity – nourishing its leadership, its fellowship and its follower-ship. For Luther the true church was defined in terms of a doctrinal or spiritual and not an institutional or human tradition, in terms of the vitality of the Word and not the authority of the government; and in keeping with this spiritualizing process, propagation re-

[26] F. Painter, *Luther on Education* (Philadelphia, 1889).
[27] G. Rupp, *The Righteousness of God* (London, 1963), among many analyses.

placed ordination – Preacher replaced Priest – as the center of the religious community.

Called to be pastor and trained to be pedagogue, Luther was able to expand both functions through the new and rapidly growing medium of print; and so he found another public role, that of author.[28] He had a spectacular model in Erasmus but far surpassed him in the intensity of his message and, because of his mastery of the vernacular, in popularity. In the decade following the appearance of his Theses, in fact, he became the most published writer in modern history. Luther affected to scorn his books, ostensibly fearing that they would obtrude themselves between Christians and their scriptures, as patristic and scholastic commentaries had done; and he explicitly asserted the superior efficacy of the spoken word. Yet there is no doubt that Luther took his authorship seriously. He took the trouble to project into print many of his oral creations – lectures, polemics, debates, confessions, hymns and especially his interpretations of the Bible. The editions and copies of these works reached unheard-of quantities during the 1520s, setting off a veritable firestorm of propaganda through the European reading public – and of course provoking counterattacks from established authority. In this way, too, Lutheranism was a religion of the book. One measure of the impact of print culture almost as direct as the number of publications was the variety of attempts to control or to suppress distasteful literature; and it must be acknowledged that Luther himself was not opposed on principle to this practice. In any case contemporaries seemed to perceive in these developments a double revolution – the upsurge of German heresy and the coming of age of the (likewise German) art of printing – with Luther riding the crest of both.

If it was the invention of printing that gave Luther best access to the public arena, it was his relation to secular power that assured his ecclesiastical leadership. In his address to the German princes in 1520 Luther not only laid out his reform program but also consciously assumed the posture of the religious leader of the German-speaking people. What resulted was a new ideological base for the principalities (including his own Saxony) and cities that had long been struggling for political and ecclesiastical independence. In the mid 1520s this constitutional movement merged with Lutheran reform to create a party which took formal shape at the Diet of Speier in 1529, and the next year this party adopted the Lutheran Confession of

[28] M. Gravier, *Luther et l'opinion publique* (Paris, 1942); A. G. Dickens, *The German Nation and Martin Luther* (London, 1973); J. Benzing, *Lutherbibliographie* (Baden Baden, 1966).

Augsburg as its religious program. At the same time Luther and his followers labored to give structure and sustenance to their ecclesiastical organization; and in this effort they turned to the old German institution of the territorial church (*Landeskirche*) under princely protection. It was in this novel situation – the Reformation publicized and politicized – that the authoritarian and illiberal aspects of Luther began to make their appearance. It is difficult to argue that Luther was a man of vision in political and social matters. He hated foreigners and Jews and scorned the German peasant as drunken, swinish and rebellious; and his political philosophy hardly went beyond the famous Pauline formula of divine right, though privately he suggested that politics was Satan's (or the lawyers') business. On the one hand he celebrated the Germanic virtues and 'liberties' which since Tacitus had become part of a national mythology; on the other hand he accepted without question the powers that be – or were – including the territorial church, which in a more up-to-date and Erastian form became the basis for the Augsburg peace settlement after his death: *Cujus regio, ejus religio*, the German equivalent of the national church. Liberty and order – internal liberty, that is, and external order: it was a paradoxical solution which not only suited Luther's conscience but also informed German political consciousness for centuries.[29]

As head of a family Luther was hardly less authoritarian than as national leader. In general, Luther's 'political thought' probably should not be taken very seriously; the truth is that his understanding of public affairs was basically a projection of his understanding of private life (just as his view of 'reformation' was a projection of the Pauline idea of spiritual renewal); and despite pontifications about political and cosmological matters, his intellectual horizons hardly extended beyond the family. For this institution Luther had the highest regard, and despite his own youthful behavior, he took it as a model system of authority. After his marriage to Katherine von Bora in 1525 he presided over a large and changing household, which included, in addition to four children, a variety of friends and visitors, who all formed a discussion circle around Father Martin. Here he could vent his feelings, tell his jokes, ranging from the mild to the most obscene, and discuss his likes and especially his dislikes, most prominently lawyers, usurers and fornicators. But most of his pronouncements were about domestic concerns – the joys of marriage, problems of sex, the difficulties of matchmaking and the duties

[29] L. Krieger, *The German Idea of Freedom* (Chicago, 1957), traces the later career of this attitude.

of wives and children. A troublesome son himself, Luther became a supportive and providing father not only for his own kin but also for countless members of the younger generation and for various factions of squabbling progeny, moderates and ultra-Lutherans fighting for the doctrinal inheritance after his death. Even for Protestants of deviant confessional positions Luther appeared as the ideological patriarch as well as paradigm of the Reformation.

The most striking of Martin Luther's personae, to friends and foes alike, and especially to the later sixteenth century, was surely that of Rebel. The longer the perspective, the easier it is to interpret his career as an ascending series of rejections – beginning with paternal authority and going on to canonist tradition, papal supremacy, the old sacramental system and finally the Emperor himself. To critics this pattern seemed diabolical, a repetition of the Devil's own 'I will not serve' (*Non serviam*). To friends and followers it was liberating and purifying; and if some of them went further than Luther would have wished, he himself had gone further than he had expected – as far, in fact, as his conscience had required of him. The key to Luther's subversive stance, though he did not understand it at first, was his fundamentalism, whether expressed in his conception of scriptures, the Primitive church, God's grace or his own conscience. It may be, it has been argued, that his fundamentalism has a psychological as well as a doctrinal base; in any case it produced a series of large and potentially explosive equations that set, for example, the Word over the Law, Conscience over Tradition, and Liberty over Authority. In principle, then, Lutheran ideology seemed to have no necessary social base. It appealed not to community interest but to meta-historical standards, whether a utopia of the past, an inner light or a transcendent God; and as with the Bible itself this rationale was open to a wide variety of interpretations. As Luther himself showed in his discussion of Bible translation, 'interpretation' was a very flexible and debatable matter indeed.[30] That it could be avoided Luther truly believed, but the process of history, those 'human traditions' he so much deplored, insured that it would take place.

About the question of rebellion in a human sense, about armed resistance, Luther seemed to leave the door open even more deliberately. It is true that in general he forbade this on the basis of the famous Pauline text and that in particular he denounced the seditious behavior of the German peasants in 1524 and other

[30] See Luther's prefaces to his translation of Acts and Romans; also S. Berger, *La Bible au XVIe siècle* (Paris, 1879), and W. Schwarz, *Principles and Practice of Bible Criticism* (Cambridge, 1955).

uprisings later; but in the course of the civil war between the 'Protestant' princes and the Emperor he was more ambiguous. In this case, in fact, he deferred to the lawyers whom he otherwise so much scorned. 'We have placed this proposition before the jurists', he wrote in 1531: 'If they find (as some think they do) the imperial law teaches resistance as a matter of self-defense in such a case, we cannot check the course of temporal justice.'[31] 'Our office', he explained, the office, that is, of a pastor, 'cannot so recommend; but jurists may find human grounds for resistance' – and indeed it was the jurists eventually who took over this question from the theologians later in the century and who thus further 'politicized' the Reformation. A few years later he suggested more directly, 'If one may resist the pope one may also resist all the emperors and dukes who contrive to defend the pope . . .' In general the radical structure and implications of Lutheran doctrine continued to provide the emotional and intellectual foundations for ideas of resistance and, in effect, rebellion. In number of ways Lutheran 'reform' represents, however remotely, a prototype for the modern idea of revolution.

Here then are seven aspects of Martin Luther which preserved his ideological presence long after his death in 1546. The Angry Young Man may have been forgotten for the most part, but many other angry young men appeared to trouble the European scene, consciously or unconsciously recapitulating Luther's defiant early career. The Father may have been lost; but that role, too, was exemplary; and it merged with that other incarnation, the National Hero, to form a vast and growing legend exploited or attacked by many generations and varieties of ideologists. The Teacher and the Preacher were remembered and replaced by others who aspired to Luther's model and achievement; and the Author continued to be prolific and to find even greater popularity as his works were translated and disseminated, taught and disputed, celebrated and denounced in many other places and contexts. Finally, Luther the Rebel grew in stature, inspiring some and appalling others, but continuing to provoke interpretations and controversies, some of the most intense within his own following. In general this seven-headed monster that was the public and the posthumous Martin Luther haunted the conscience of Europe through the entire century and beyond, representing not only a primal generator of ideology but

---

[31] Letter to Spengler, 18 Mar. 1531, and disputation of 8–9 May 1539 in Lowell H. Zuch (ed.), *Christianity and Revolution* (Philadelphia, 1974), 134. See also H. Scheible (ed.), *Das Widerstandsrecht als Problem der deutschen Protestanten 1523–1546* (Gütersloh, 1969), and Q. Skinner, *The Foundations of Modern Political Thought* (Cambridge, 1978), I, 199ff.

also in a sense a model and microcosm of the Reformation experience.

DIMENSIONS OF REFORMATION

Luther gave the 'Reformation' substance in people's thoughts, but what about its worldly form? What, to put it as simply as possible, were its size, shape and duration in terms of European consciousness? What were the perceived human, geographical and temporal dimensions of the Reformation? For some persons, of course, 'reformation' was still a private matter that proceeded soul by soul and was an ineffable spiritual process. For others it was Luther's message, advertised and available to all from its first appearance. For still others it was a goal never entirely reached but the object of a war that would go on until the final judgment – a 'continuous reformation', to paraphrase another charismatic leader. In worldly terms, however, there was remarkable agreement by friends and foes about the quantitative aspects of the question. Hostile observers like Florimond de Raemond as well as apologetic historians like Johann Sleidan and Jean Crespin agreed on the plot of the story. For purposes of context it will be useful to review the background of this story – to map the general terrain of the Reformation before beginning particular soundings.[32]

Politically the history of sixteenth-century Europe, at least from the beginning of the Italian wars in 1494 down to the treaty of Cateau-Cambrésis in 1559, was dominated by the problem of Italy, or rather of who was to control Italy; and no amount of spiritual turmoil could disguise the realities of power politics. After the emergence of Luther the second phase of this struggle, the Habsburg–Valois wars, broke out and furnished, intermittently, the background action for the first generation of the Reformation. Although united in their opposition to the new religious opinions, the Emperor Charles V and his French adversaries Francis I and (from 1547) Henry II carried on their political duel until the very eve of the civil wars in France, when different international configurations began to appear. This conflict, especially when Henry II began to align himself with the Protestant princes who were defying the Emperor's authority, generated its own considerable controversy, although it could not

---

[32] Since Sleidan set the standard and laid the foundations in 1556, surveys and special studies of Reformation history have multiplied incalculably, and must go largely unnoticed here except as they bear on particular points.

indefinitely be kept separate from religious questions. Sleidan tried to make just this separation in his great survey of European history from 1517 to 1555, but he admitted that such an effort was like sundering body and soul. The truth is that for the power elite of the sixteenth century it was still politics as usual even during the most ideologically agitated times, to the extent at least that they were able to control affairs.

This was the age too of the consolidation of national monarchy, especially in France, Spain and England; and although Germany and Italy seemed to be exceptions to this trend, state-building did take place on another level, that of the principalities and the cities. The classic example of the marshalling of national 'force' and institutional controls was France, for which Claude de Seyssel's *Grand Monarchy* of 1515 was an equally classic description.[33] This process of consolidation can be traced on a number of levels, most notably in the theory and practice of absolute government, reflected particularly in legislative efforts; in the elaboration of governmental machinery, especially the organization of counsel, the expansion of judicial and fiscal offices and the institutions of new diplomacy; in the establishment of the national church (fixed by the Concordat of 1516); and in the search, ultimately as vain as it was voracious, for new sources of revenue. But above all, the ever-present aim was organization for war, defensive if not offensive, for honor if not for profit. Seyssel's book is usually read for its description of the political and social structure of the French monarchy; but it should not be overlooked that the argument was finally concerned – as was most of Seyssel's own political career – with the 'augmentation' of the state, its relations with neighbors and especially with the machiavellian problem of 'how to conquer states and maintain them'.

Yet these same consolidating processes had centrifugal and destructive effects. The ever-present fact or threat of war intensified international hatreds as well as national sentiment and tended to preserve the political power as well as the social position of the nobility, as in a different way did the proliferation of administrative offices and the abuse of 'venality', the transformation of office into transferable property. In general, as we have come to appreciate, there was an actual revival of feudalism in the course of this century. The third estate, too, whose social mobility was celebrated by Seyssel, became increasingly unmanageable; and cities not only in Italy, Germany and the Netherlands but also in France began to display attitudes of political independence. La Rochelle, for exam-

---

[33] See below, p. 188 at n. 26.

ple, was 'rebelling' against royal taxes long before it was involved in religious protest.[34] Economic dislocation also affected the lower classes and made them susceptible to even less clearly focussed discontent. Meanwhile, the problem of the church persisted; for if the Gallican settlement in 1516 resolved the relationship with the papacy, it did not remedy old questions of pluralism, neglect and corruption. In this social and institutional turmoil it became even more difficult to separate secular questions from those of religion, especially from a 'so-called reformed religion' that claimed to provide universal remedies for the ills of society as well as of souls.

As for the religious sphere itself, contemporaries of Luther were aware not only that reform movements were already in progress in parts of Europe but also that there had been various traditions of 'pre-reform', including the conciliar movement of the previous century and, for Luther's admirers, a spiritual heritage of anti-Romanism consisting of such 'proto-martyrs' as Wycliffe and Hus. Nevertheless, for all parties the magical and mythical birthdate of the Reformation was All Saints' Eve of 1517, and as has been said, the Lutheran program was virtually completed within three years of this. By 1525 the radical phase of Lutheranism was over. In Germany evangelical reform, converging with and then being submerged in the constitutional conflict between Charles V and a number of 'protesting' princes and cities, was politicized, first in the League of Schmalkald in 1531 and then, more radically, in the resistance to the imperial 'Interim' pacification in 1548. At the same time the Lutheran Confession of Augsburg, in the first of its formulations by Melanchthon in 1530, joined with the constitutional protest to form an ideological program that would be a central factor in German history from this time on. In the Peace of Augsburg in 1555 Lutheranism was finally legalized; it was also localized, confined in effect to Germany and to Scandinavia, and became largely peripheral to the career of international Protestantism.

Throughout much of Europe the 1520s were a period of furious activity and expansion of evangelical reform. The main centers were the cities of Switzerland and the Rhineland, starting in Zurich, where Zwingli began evangelizing in 1519. By 1524 Zurich was politically as well as confessionally 'reformed' and soon would be followed by Strasbourg, Bern, Basel, Constance (and consequently by smaller towns and the countryside) and a decade later by Geneva, Lausanne and others.[35] In general the process of 'reforma-

---

[34] See below, p. 286.

[35] Besides the classic study by Hans Baron, 'Religion and politics in the German imperial cities during the reformation', *English Historical Review*, LII (1937), 405–27, see B. Moeller, *Imperial Cities and the Reformation*, trans. H. Midelfort and M. Edwards (Philadelphia, 1972); S. Ozment, *The Reformation in the Cities* (New Haven,

tion' followed a regular pattern, of course with local differences: first a stage of preaching by one or more charismatic figures; then a period of agitation and disputation, private and public, which may be regarded as the stage of 'socialization'; and finally the stage of legalizing, institutionalizing the new religious forms. Although reforming edicts can be dated precisely, the whole process, even when permanently successful, could take a generation; and so Geneva, for example, officially 'reformed' in 1534, was not settled under Calvin's control for another twenty years.

Outside Germany and some of the free cities the progress of evangelical religion was carried out under difficult conditions of mounting resistance and official oppression. In Catholic areas like Italy and Spain there were a few small groups, but for the most part they were covert operations. In the Emperor's Burgundian territories the reformed religion made greater advances, especially in the north, and from the 1520s imperial legislation attempted continuously to root it out. After mid-century Calvinism exhibited a tendency similar to that of Lutheranism in that it began to join with feudal and commercial interests into nascent political opposition. In England Protestantism was a marginal issue under Henry VIII, being located mostly in university circles. The evangelical movement was more successful under the young Edward VI, who for a time was one of the hopes of international Protestantism; but on the accession of his sister Mary in 1553 persecutions like those in the Empire and France were set in motion. The exiles of this Marian period put English Protestantism into direct contact with the continental movement.[36] After the accession of Elizabeth many at least unofficial connections were maintained with French and Swiss reformers and of course more directly with Scotland, which was 'reformed' by Knox after his return from exile. The international, though amorphous, character of Protestantism in the mid sixteenth century is well reflected in Sleidan's more or less official Lutheran history, written in Strasbourg (which had French and English as well as German communities and visitors from all parts of Europe) and attempting to cover every corner of the 'Christian Republic' of Europe.

For the religious question as for so many others, however, France was the center of attention and of political maneuvering and finally the principal battleground for the wars of the later sixteenth century. Like his rival the Emperor, King Francis I tried to stem the 'Lutheran' tide through legislation and the agencies of the faculty of theology of

Conn., 1975); O. Olsen, 'Theology of revolution: Magdeburg, 1550–1551', *Sixteenth Century Journal*, III, 56–79; R. Benert, 'German resistance theory and the German Constitution', *Il Pensiero Politico*, VI (1973), 17–36; and most recently T. Brady, *Ruling Class, Regime and Reformation at Strasbourg 1520–1555* (Leiden, 1978).

[36] C. Garrett, *The Marian Exiles* (Cambridge, 1938), but a new study is needed.

the University of Paris, the 'Sorbonne', and the sovereign court of the Parlement of Paris. From the 1530s and more especially under the reign of Henry II (1547–59) attempts were made to 'exterminate' heresy. As in the Empire these efforts were futile, and again by mid-century Calvinism had established a network of congregations throughout France, again with more or less direct connections with Geneva, Strasbourg, Basel and other centers of the 'so-called reformed religion' (*Religion prétendue reformée* or '*R.P.R.*'). The first national synod of the reformed churches of France met secretly in the spring of 1559, just a few months before the death of Henry II threw France into political chaos and created the conditions for the civil wars which to most contemporaries seemed inevitable.

The high tide of evangelical reform, the second quarter of the sixteenth century, was also a period of fragmentation for international Protestantism. Divergences appeared not only between Lutherans and the Swiss but also between the Swiss, Zwinglians or sacramentarians, and other confessions (not to speak of the anabaptist or 'catabaptist' radicals who were abominated by all groups). The major break was with the Lutherans, who had become conservative on many issues, most disturbingly on the eucharist, with the ambiguous doctrine of consubstantiation, which implied something uncomfortably close to the horrible notion of 'real presence' and all the degeneracy this implied. Public breaks were usually expressed in terms of the sacraments, but arguments about the mass or predestination concealed other equally fundamental divergences on social, political or national grounds. Even within Lutheranism a rift appeared between the 'ultras' and the moderate 'Philippists', that is, the group of Melanchthon which maintained good relations with English and French confessions. In this riot of confessional differences Calvinism emerged in the third quarter of the century as the most successful and cohesive of all sects, having restored friendly relations with the Zwinglians if not with the Lutherans. By then the 'Calvinist International' was a world-wide community with missionary colonies all over Europe, especially in France and the Netherlands, and soon it would expand also into Scotland, England, Germany (Rhine Palatinate), eastern Europe (Poland and Hungary) and even into the New World.[37] By this time, too, that is, after mid-century, this international threat was opposed by an increasingly organized Catholic opposition, whose own program was being

---

[37] R. Kingdon, *Geneva and the Coming of the Wars of Religion in France* (Geneva, 1956); H. de Vries de Heekelingen, *Genève pepinière du calvinisme hollandais* (Freiburg, 1918); Ch. Martin, *Les Protestants anglais refugiés à Genève au temps de Calvin* (Geneva, 1915).

fashioned, or refashioned, at the intermittent Council of Trent (1545–63). The publication of the Tridentine canons and decrees prepared the ground ideologically for the wars that began in the 1560s and continued for the rest of the century and beyond.

These international wars continued the old Habsburg–Valois conflict but added an ideological element which, in unprecedented ways, made them 'total' in a modern sense. In France the civil conflict of Catholics and 'Huguenots' became increasingly entangled with the war of liberation between the Dutch and the Spain of Philip II. On the one hand the Protestants were supported to varying degrees by the Swiss, German Lutherans and Elizabethan English; on the other hand the Catholics seemed to be moving toward some kind of Tridentine, ultramontane league under the leadership of Spain and the papacy; and this polarization, appearing in particularly stark form after the massacres of St Bartholomew in 1572, challenged the peace and stability of Europe for more than a generation. It was in this context that evangelical religion and militant Catholicism were politicized and, consequently, that there arose the most massive upsurge of public controversy in modern times: a 'beginning of ideology'.

The social dimension is much less accessible than the political. In many respects the Reformation was a popular phenomenon, and even Raemond cited the old maxim, 'the voice of the people is the voice of God', in connection with the wave of religious sentiment preceding and accompanying the Lutheran movement.[38] Nevertheless, the social strength of the Reformation lay in the urban, literate and articulate middle classes. The cities along the Rhine axis from Amsterdam to Basel were vital for its expansion and preservation, though it by no means follows that Protestantism was a class phenomenon or in any meaningful way 'bourgeois' ideology. From the beginning, to be sure, artisans and lower-class and 'illiterate' persons were often involved, as authorities often had occasion to lament; and they figured prominently, if often anonymously, in the martyr rolls which formed much of the substance of Protestant historiography. No doubt they also figured prominently in the mass gatherings at outdoor sermons, in iconoclastic outbreaks and in the larger-scale conflicts of the civil wars themselves. Even more essential to the political (and military) strength of international Protestantism was the landed aristocracy, to some extent the office-holding nobility but more especially the high nobility, which combined its

[38] Raemond, 13, '. . . voix populaire comme une Heraut et Trompette, par cry commun et consentement universal . . . pre-anounce et pronounce son jugement sur les choses non advenuës plus certain que quand il parle des presents . . .'.

own feudal arrangements with the congregational organization of religious groupings taking their lead from Geneva and other centers of reform. But the large social base of the reformation movement – certainly from the point of view of public visibility and ideological force – continued to be the urban classes, including defecting secular and especially regular clergy, members of the professions, especially the law, university scholars and other members of the intelligentsia (and its literate following) on which the international character of Protestantism was based.

The Reformation in Europe can also be measured in generational terms, although this can only be suggested by rather superficial characterization of the leading figures, as they were judged by public opinion. The period of the Reformation at the center of the present discussion covers roughly three generations between the emergence of Luther and other early 'magisterial' reformers around 1520, especially Melanchthon, Zwingli, Bucer, and perhaps Farel and Lambert, down to the bloodily 'political' final stages of fighting. Taking two decades as a rough generational unit, the second generation, represented by Calvin and Viret and perhaps Bullinger and Sturm, became prominent around 1540. This was followed by the disciples and successors of Calvin, including Beza, Hotman, Crespin and Knox, who began to assume leading roles and radical postures in the early 1560s; and their major ideological efforts appeared in the wake of the massacres of St Bartholomew. The 1580s saw the rise of a new mood of 'politique' realism and resignation and new leadership, that of Henry of Navarre.[39] His success and (as Beza would see it) defection from the evangelical ranks marked, in a sense, the 'end of ideology', at least for the Reformation drama set in motion by Luther.

In general the cycle of ideology to be traced here covers the period from the public appearance in the 1520s of 'Lutheranism' – though in fact reformed doctrine was as often 'sacramentarian', whether specifically Zwinglian or in some other version – down to the 1580s, when ideological conflict had become in effect institutionalized and internationalized; that is, when the social ideals and the political program of the 'Huguenots' had been formulated in the face of an apparent anti-Protestant crusade led by the papacy and Philip II. It is impossible to understand this tumultuous period, however, without attending to the penumbral areas of earlier and later generations. A proper perspective, in other words, should include the background of the reformation movements and, over as much as a

[39] See below, pp. 185–93 and 203–11.

century, their various social and institutional vehicles. Not only must we see 'the Reformation in medieval perspective', in fact, but we should recognize many elements of medieval society persisting and even becoming stronger in Reformation society. Similarly it is necessary to consider at least peripherally some later survivals and repercussions of sixteenth-century phenomena; and indeed the whole strategy of interpreting politico-religious movements in the Reformation as forms of 'ideology' involves some assumption about the continuity of these patterns into more recent times – in areas of education, propaganda, professional behavior and partisan conflict as well as religion and politics. For good or ill, and perhaps largely for ill, the political, social, intellectual and psychological legacy of the Reformation has continued to shape the modern world and, at least indirectly, our own human predicament.

THE HUMAN CONDITION AND THE BEGINNING OF IDEOLOGY

The conceptual problem of 'reform' has been posed, the human starting-point has been examined, and the historical situation has been outlined; it remains to suggest the method that will be followed and the kinds of questions asked. The major source for an examination of sixteenth-century ideology is the vast body of pamphlet literature scattered in many European and American collections, a kind of material that is forbidding and very difficult to control but which is unrivalled in quantity and variety.[40] The hypothesis is that this pamphlet literature, official as well as unlicensed and subversive, represents the tip of an ideological iceberg; and my intention is to use it, in conjunction with other information and hypotheses, to reveal some of the basic human and institutional patterns and sources of ideological behavior and expression. The aim is to gain some understanding of human experience, private as well as public, unconscious as well as conscious, in the sixteenth-century context. Because of the nature of the sources and the questions, the drift of the discussion is from ideas and attitudes to social structure and process – from intellectual to social history, rather than the reverse. Since the aim is to analyze human experience in its own terms, that is, in terms of ideas, beliefs, sentiments and symbols, the explora-

---

[40] And about which one student (Beaupré, *Pamphlets pour et contre les Guises* (n.p. 1865)) said, 'sous peine d'ennui mortel, il faut se garder de lire au delà du premier feuillet'.

tion will be carried out not in a casual and chronological way but will be organized round particular social forms, institutional frameworks of experience and potentially of ideological expression. In simpler terms the context is a somewhat schematized formulation of what Montaigne – building on Cicero but greatly enriching (and 'modernizing') his notion – called the 'human condition'.

Awareness of the complexities of the human condition were certainly not lacking in the sixteenth century, although they were often couched in a kind of religious and pre-scientific language that does not always impress, perhaps even reach, modern observers. That age may have had to get along with little history and less science in a modern sense; but in its own terms it was not without penetrating psychological acumen and a profound sense of change. Luther himself, though lamentably obtuse (as it may seem to us) in political and social matters, was a man of marvelous insight into the human condition as well as passionately involved in transforming it. About one of the most fundamental patterns, the human life-cycle, he had this to say: 'Young fellows are tempted by girls, men who are thirty years old are tempted by gold, when they are forty years old they are tempted by honor and glory, and those who are sixty years old say to themselves, what a pious man I have become.'[41] These phases of private existence – lust, careerism, ambition, complacency – are as important for ideological movements as the more artificial structures of public careers, though they are seldom accessible to the historian. The natural rhythms of life – growth, conflict, loves, hates, adaptations, achievements, failures – are omnipresent; but it is clear that in a period of crisis and fundamental divisions youthful energies and idealism can be channelled into doctrinal and political causes and transformed, perhaps, into a dogmatic and intransigent adulthood. In succeeding chapters attempts will be made to trace the sources and patterns of ideology through a number of phases that correspond roughly to phases of life and maturing – in a sense, to an ascending scale of consciousness – culminating, logically if not always historically, in ideology in its most intense form.

The first level of investigation is that of individual psychology; and since there is no humanity in isolation, this means that the starting point for the study of ideology is normally the family.[42] In this

---

[41] Luther, *Table Talk*, ed. and trans. Theodore G. Tappert in *Luther's Works*, LIV (Philadelphia, 1967), 158.

[42] For intellectual history modern statistical studies of religious psychology are scarcely relevant, nor do they concern themselves on the whole with periods before the nineteenth century. Still fundamental is William James's *Varieties of Religious Experience*, on which see J. Dittes in *Beyond the Classics*, ed. C. Glock and P. Hammond (New York, 1973), 291–354; also G. Allport, *The Individual and his Religion*

context we must look for the first stirrings of consciousness, the settling of belief and the foundations of ideological commitment. Here we see a microcosm of society in which the most fundamental conflicts make their appearance, especially those between male and female and between generations, and in which the most fundamental choices are made, especially between conformity and non-conformity. Here are presented basic standards and ideals to be accepted or reacted against, and the first confrontations with authority and perhaps injustice. Here, in short, is where the process of identification takes place, and from this base ventures are made into other social situations. There are reasons to think that family relationships and attitudes are recapitulated in other institutional arrangements; and although there is little direct evidence for the sixteenth century, public expressions and ideological style seem to bear this out in many ways. Not only are father-, mother- and brotherhood projected into the world beyond kinship, but the conflicts in that wider arena are frequently expressed if not felt in familial terms. For modern European history the question arises as to whether the family possesses an inherent ideological force that is always available to give impetus to ideological movements.

On this level, too, religious experience begins, not only habits of devotion and conceptions of the divine but also the ideological commitment demanded by organized religion. At its most intense this commitment suggests, for the Reformation or indeed any other large-scale social upheaval involving fundamental transvaluations, feelings of aberration on the one hand, the religious vision or the conversion experience on the other. In general it is clear that sixteenth-century religious experience offers a rich field for psycho-historical investigation, especially with regard to the extremes of sainthood, martyrdom, a variety of fanaticisms and other dysfunctional behavior. This does not entail any particular psychological doctrine (as in recent attempts to interpret conversion in terms of Jung, or theology in terms of Piaget);[43] but it is apparent that religious psychology involves questions that transcend conventional social and intellectual history and (what is distressing to some historians) that cannot be answered through a merely literal reading of evidence. In order to find some of the general patterns it may be useful to view religion in a number of ways which are not necessarily

(New York, 1950); W. H. Clark, *The Psychology of Religion* (New York, 1953), on Rudolph Otto's 'idea of the holy'; J. M. Moore, *Theories of Religious Experience* (New York, 1938); and on methodology more generally, M. Eliade and J. Kitagawa (eds.), *The History of Religions* (Chicago, 1959).

[43] J.-M. Pohier, *Psychologie et théologie* (Paris, 1967), and D. Cox, *Jung and St Paul* (London, 1959).

logically compatible – as a reflection of collective social forces (with Durkheim); more generally (with Geertz) as a 'cultural system' to be defined in relation to, though not necessarily as a direct projection of, its host society; or even (with Otto) as a systematic attempt to cope with the 'wholly other', which (whether accessible or not) constitutes a social as well as a psychological frontier for historians.[44]

Religious psychology and religious sociology suggest many questions essential to the understanding of consciousness – and of course subconsciousness – in history. What, to take some obvious examples, accounts for the extraordinary appeal, charismatic even at second hand, of men like Luther, Calvin or Beza? What accounts, that is to say, for the ideological force of their convictions? What drives men to elevate matters of private 'conscience' to the level of public creed? How can we make sense of the transfer of individual allegiance to an unpopular 'cause', and beyond that the willingness and desire to suffer in consequence exile and even martyrdom? How, more generally, assess the replacement of family and patria by an alien community, of blood ties by ideological enthusiasm? How account for the extension of verbal behavior – praying, sermonizing, singing – into physical action, including iconoclasm, criminal violence and larger-scale militancy? Although there has been extensive empirical and statistical investigation of such problems for recent times and even for the nineteenth and eighteenth centuries, very little has been attempted for earlier periods of history. Yet these earlier ages, especially the sixteenth century, though they will not respond to questionnaires or therapeutic interrogation, will yield much relevant material and perhaps significant insights into the changing human condition.

Paralleling and in some ways reinforcing religious experience are the equally disturbing revelations and behaviour patterns offered by the academy, especially that cockpit of adolescent transformation, the university. Educational psychology brings us into contact with that level of intellectual history I call trivial – not pejoratively but after the subjects of the *trivium*, grammar, rhetoric and dialectic.[45] Here recent work in the history of education is most helpful; but again this is a subject that is not entirely accessible through purely

---

[44] More than the psychology of religion, the sociology of religion has looked to historical evidence, especially in the classic works of Weber and Troeltsch, on which again see Glock and Hammonds, *Beyond the Classics* (contributions by B. Nelson and T. Parsons), 71–130, 156–80; also J. Wach, *Sociology of Religion* (Chicago, 1944), W. Stark, *A Sociology of Religion* (London, 1966), S. Feuchtwang, 'Investigating religion', in *Marxist Analysis and Social Anthropology.* ed. M. Bloch (New York, 1975), 61–82, and C. Geertz, *The Interpretation of Cultures* (New York, 1973), 87–125.

[45] Fundamental, though chronologically remote, is H. Marrou, *A History of Education in Antiquity*, trans. G. Lamb (London, 1956).

literal analysis, especially because the habits and attitudes acquired in school are not all products of deliberate indoctrination. The lessons learned were not always the lessons taught, and students often profited more from one another than from their masters. The impact of particular personalities may be obvious, but what about the overall cultural shock produced by exposure to foreign groups and foreign ideas, especially in the larger universities? The importance of the arts of persuasion and disputation for the propagation of ideas is also clear enough; but what about the indirect effects of classroom techniques of questioning tradition and challenging 'authority' when projected into the realm of private and then public institutions? Such intangibles must be taken into account when one considers how the universities became the breeding-ground for a sort of counter-culture (as many of them did), havens for unorthodoxy and in effect an underground ideology whose base was as international as the European university network itself. No wonder the universities, as headquarters for an increasing (and increasingly restless) lay intelligentsia, became primary generators as well as carriers of ideology – and doctrinal battlegrounds that contributed to as well as anticipated the real bloodshed of the later sixteenth century.

Spanning the academic and the public spheres were the learned occupations, and one in particular was seminal for ideological movements. The profession of law, rivalling that of theology and medicine, lay at the end of the educational process both as a vocational choice and, at least for the favored few, as the gateway to a public career.[46] Although they had their own ties with the *trivium* and often remained within the academy, lawyers had their own distinctive way of seeing the world and of trying to impose their views on others. Through their work as hired advocates and professional ideologists they changed the substance as well as the style of partisan debate and tended to politicize as well as to secularize confessional conflict. Given the conditions of that age, it may well be asked if they did not contribute more to divisiveness than to the rule of law. Their public image and to some extent their social function were contradictory. On the one hand, with their impressive arsenal of learning and argumentation, they were in demand by all parties; on the other hand, projecting their habits of sophistry and chicanery into the realm of political discussion, they became, even

---

[46] The sociology of professions seems another field without much of a historical dimension; fundamental again is Weber (the sections on law in *Economy and Society* (New York, 1968)); also J. Dawson, *The Oracles of the Law* (Ann Arbor, Michigan, 1968), and W. Bouwsma, 'Lawyers in early modern culture', *American Historical Review*, LXXVIII (1973), 303–27.

more than normally, the objects of fear and ridicule. From either point of view they represented the most powerful and visible segment of the lay intelligentsia and arguably the most effective agency of ideology. In general the role of the lawyers raises questions about the significance of professional groups in public life and more particularly of the use and abuse of ideas of law, which was so fundamental to sixteenth-century conceptualization and argumentation.

Like humanists and theologians, lawyers had always been vocal enough, but in the sixteenth-century they became positively vociferous. Though due in part to the intensified demands of partisanship, this was the result most directly of a new force that was regarded as revolutionary even before the emergence of Luther.[47] The 'German art' of printing became a dangerous weapon as well as a source of enlightenment and entertainment, and in the process it became also the basis for a large commercial establishment. Aside from the quantitative production – a veritable journalistic explosion – the subliminal impact of the printed page, psychological and social, is again hard to assess; and it has provoked a number of questions which have attracted and divided scholars in recent years. In the wake of printing there also appeared a new class of experts – authors, printers, distributors and attendant technicians – who found not only a means of subsistence but also a 'calling' in a Protestant sense. Among the results of their labors were a new profession, a sturdy base for the expanding European 'republic of letters', and the pursuits of journalism, organized scholarship, propaganda and to some extent public opinion as we have come to know them. Through the medium of print, too, matters of conscience were transformed into political issues by the act – not new but mightily exalted – of 'publication'; and from this arose some of the less admirable features of intellectual modernization, including preventive censorship, generalized thought-control, and the persecution of intellectuals as well as some hapless readers. These, too, are the fruits of ideology and at least potential characteristics of the human condition in the modern age.

By a number of paths, then – through religious experience, the process of education, professional life and printed communication – we leave the private sphere and enter upon the wider world of publicity and the 'public' in general. We enter the world of what have been called 'greedy institutions', of religious, professional and

[47] Central to this discussion, in terms of questions if not necessarily of answers, are the works of Marshall McLuhan and Walter Ong, and Elizabeth Eisenstein, *The Printing Press as an Agent of Change* (Cambridge, 1978).

political collectives. Each of these aspects of the socializing process, as they may be regarded, created its own tensions, agitations, awareness and forms of expression; but with public life and its political context we must face questions of consciousness and action in a more general sense. For the sixteenth century this means looking not only at classes, at 'orders', but also at other corporate groups and interests that make up the complex fabric of late-medieval society (as well as structures of government, of course), even though sources and strategies prevent consideration of social context in any but the most peripheral (and superstructural) terms.[48] In general the nobility, despite the increasing difficulty of defining that station, maintained its dominant position; and indeed it can be argued that Protestantism did not become a political force until it won over a significant part of the feudal classes – the union of Lutheranism and the 'protesting' German princes furnishing the precedent and the model for both France and the Netherlands, where Huguenots joined respectively with 'Malcontents' and 'Beggars' to resist 'foreign' oppression. This convergence of religion with social and political interest, the classical expression of the generation of an ideological movement, represented the final stage of the polarization of society. This process cut across, if it did not transcend, class interest and class consciousness; and it resulted in that clearest, if not crassest, manifestation of ideology, the party. Whether there is a genetic or only a generic relation to modern political 'parties' may be debated, but there are obvious carry-overs, especially in patterns of organization and propaganda.

So we come finally to the epiphenomenal subject of these partial analyses, which is the emergence of a potentially global ideology, rising out of the matrix of social conflict and torrents of propaganda.[49] The relations between this ideology and lower levels of consciousness and institutional affiliation are unmistakable. although it requires something in the nature of an archeological investigation to uncover them. In a passion-rent, war-torn society the family continued to be a source of discontent as well as of strength; and lamentations about the destructive effects of doctrinal disagreement on this institution (as well as continuing celebrations of its excellence) provided rich themes of propaganda for all parties. The

---

[48] L. Coser, *Greedy Institutions* (New York, 1974); cf. R. Mousnier, *Social Hierarchies*, trans. P. Evans (New York, 1973), and more specifically his *Les Institutions de la France sous la monarchie absolue*, I (Paris, 1974).

[49] The conceptual context here is of course the sociology of knowledge stemming especially from the work of Karl Mannheim; see also Georges Gurvitch, *The Social Framework of Knowledge*, trans. M. and K. Thompson (Oxford, 1971).

university and the legal profession were even more agitated and agitating than in Luther's time; and indeed they became major battlegrounds in their own right, while the medium of print, with its inherent intellectual imperialism, intensified and exploited controversies on all levels. Capping all turmoil was the fusion of feudal and religious organization on an international as well as a local level, and out of this arose what Shils has called the 'ideological primary group' – a group which we may identify roughly with the leadership of the Protestant revolutionary party.[50]

The wider community affiliated with this party, held together at least temporarily by common goals and above all by a common enemy, constituted a public manifestation of private disaffections; but at certain times and in certain situations it could also exhibit the attributes of that more intense collectivity, the crowd (following the old distinction of Robert Park between *Masse* and *Publikum*).[51] Congregations of Huguenots and less single-minded 'malcontents' possessed – in some ways internationally as well as locally – the features attributed by Gustave Le Bon to the crowd: heightened emotions, increased credulity or susceptibility, especially exaggerated and one-sided opinions and intolerance, yet also a capacity for personal disinterestedness and unselfishness. Although difficult to describe concretely, such collective psychology certainly conditioned perceptions and knowledge and produced the sort of 'generalized beliefs' that led not only to particular confrontations and outbreaks but to more general ideological expressions.

There is of course no question of examining the ideological outburst of the later sixteenth century with any attempt at bibliographical completeness or even historical comprehensiveness, nor will it be appropriate even to survey the contents of pamphlet material in any systematic fashion. The aim will be rather to return to certain fundamental questions about the human condition already posed in earlier contexts: problems of authority and of individual liberty and their limits, of resistance and its justifications, and more generally of the nature of society and government. Ideology will be assessed in terms not only of its various psychological, religious, social and political elements but also of the philosophical dimension reached, or at least aspired to, in certain fundamental works forged in the heat of the controversies succeeding the massacres of St Bartholomew. In particular the works of Beza, Barnaud and Hotman and, on the Catholic side, Bodin, represent not only the culmination of an

[50] See above, p. 4, n. 6.
[51] *The Crowd and the Public*, trans. C. Elsner (Chicago, 1972), discussing the views of Gustav Le Bon; cf. N. Smelzer, *Theory of Collective Behavior* (New York, 1962).

ideological movement but a seminal phase in political thought; and on this if on no other level, sixteenth-century ideology survived to impress more than one posterity. With these works, appearing over half a century after the outburst of religious protest, the cycle of ideology seems complete; and with a consideration of the final phase, the 'end of ideology', this interpretation will end. However simplified and idealized, this summary outline provides at least a suitable framework for the particular analyses in the following chapters.

It is probably needless to say, but certainly important to recall, that this Huguenot ideology presupposed a Catholic counter-position – in the sense not only of an established 'outlook' which was, selectively if not wholly, rejected, but more specifically of the mobilized doctrinal program that was formulated, or reformulated, in the course of mounting controversy. Tridentine Catholicism, too – the statement of theological, institutional and cultural values laboriously hammered out in meetings held intermittently over eighteen years at the Council of Trent – also constituted an ideology. Although it was fashioned out of traditional materials, it may be regarded as a 'counter-ideology', since its formulation was provoked by the deviations of Luther and others and indeed its design, like that of much informal Catholic propaganda, was in general a point-by-point refutation or contradiction of evangelical doctrine. Nevertheless, the ultramontane program of Tridentine Catholicism had its own dynamic; and the force and intensity of Huguenot ideology cannot be understood apart from its rival and obverse. Present strategy precludes doing justice to this subject, but then 'doing justice' is a lawyer's concept: the historian's business is probing and understanding even if it means doing violence to his subject.

So much for background, aspirations, intentions, methods and theoretical considerations; now we move from the general to the particular. The inquiry begins with the nature of the religious experience, then proceeds to social repercussions and to more collective forms of ideological behavior.

11 · Family:
Religious experience and
ideological commitment

Ego non intelligo iura, sed ego sum ius iurium in re
conscientiarum.

Luther

La saincte liberté de noz consciences . . .

Prince de Condé

11 · Family:
Religious experience and
ideological commitment

APOLOGUE: THEODORE BEZA SEES THE LIGHT
(1548)

One day in the early fall of 1548 Theodore Beza, not yet thirty years old, already drawn toward the 'so-called reformed religion' and unhappy about the emptiness of his existence, was precipitated into a desperate decision. The impetus, as Beza later recalled, was provided by God himself.[1]

He approached me through a sickness so severe that I despaired of my life. Seeing His terrible judgment before me, I could not think what to do with my wretched life. Finally, after endless suffering of body and soul, God showed pity upon His miserable lost servant and consoled me so that I could not doubt His mercy. With a thousand tears I renounced my former self, implored His forgiveness, renewed my oath to serve His true church, and in sum gave myself wholly over to Him. So the vision of death threatening my soul awakened in me the desire for a true and everlasting life. So sickness was for me the beginning of true health.

Within a few days, even before recovering from his illness, Beza left the 'Egypt' that France had become.

I burst asunder every chain, collected my efforts, forsook at once my native land, my kinsmen, my friends, that I might follow after Christ, and, accompanied by my wife, betook myself to Geneva in voluntary exile.

In that promised land his new life began.

Though Beza's choice was spontaneous, in a deeper sense it was the product of many years of struggle. His own interpretation was set down at a later time in a letter to his revered mentor, Melchior Wolmar. Beza had been born in the Burgundian town of Vézelay, about mid-way between Paris and Lyon, in the year (1519) when Luther's complaints were first being attended to in France. He 'thanked God' for his noble birth, and although this claim was

---

[1] *Correspondance*, III, 45 (no. 156 to Wolmar, 12 Mar. 1560), trans. in H. Baird, *Theodore Beza* (New York, 1899), 355–67; cf. P. Geisendorf, *Théodore de Bèze* (Geneva, 1949), 1–31.

exaggerated, the very precariousness of his social status may have intensified his class allegiance. His upbringing was irregular and unsettling. Before the age of three he was taken to Paris by a paternal uncle. His mother, who had opposed the move 'as though foreseeing disaster', died soon after. His father barely figured in his memory. Beza grew up in the tumultuous university quarter of the city; and his earliest recollections were mostly dismal, focussing upon a chronic skin disease and an impulse, apparently encouraged by his uncle, to self-destruction.

A fortunate turn came at the age of nine, when Beza was taken by another uncle, also an advocate by profession, from Paris to Orleans and sent to take lessons from the Greek scholar and jurist Wolmar, a 'Lutheran' sympathizer. This step Beza celebrated 'not otherwise than as a second birthday', and Wolmar himself Beza honored in no less than paternal terms. First at Orleans and then at Bourges Beza was introduced to the delights and the discipline of the 'new learning', which to him implied religious enlightenment as well as classical studies. Unfortunately, Beza's father cut this short by calling him back to Orleans for a proper legal education. But Beza had been spoiled for conventional scholastic learning, especially for the 'Bartolo–Baldizing' field of law; and in the classic fashion of Petrarch he turned away from this barbarous subject (though he did receive his license in 1539) for the pleasures of poetry, and came back to Paris to pursue a literary career. He 'took philology as a wife', as he told a friend in 1542, and he published his youthful verses just a few months before making his momentous religious decision.

Yet neither literary fame nor material success was enough to satisfy Beza's deeper needs. He was profoundly alienated, as we might say, yet at the same time trapped – caught in a web of family and professional connections, tempted by the pleasures of Parisian society, compromised by the revenues of several unsolicited benefices and generally depressed by the prospect of an easy worldly existence. What he really wanted was to follow Wolmar into Germany and to resume his pursuit of true learning, and he began to seek ways to change his life. His first act of resistance was his secret marriage which he hoped later to celebrate publicly within the true church. These were the crucial years, the mid 1540s, when Luther was living out his life as head of his own church and when Calvin was in the process of establishing another. For Beza it was a time of struggle, intense self-doubt, and remorse, until at last it ended with his conversion experience; it was a time, in short, of ideological regeneration.

Beza's predicament, attitudes and especially later career made him the very prototype of a second-generation reformer, though in some ways he was cast in an older mold. In general terms his conversion followed the trajectory set by Luther some third of a century earlier: disillusionment with established religion, remorseful search for a new system of values, attachment to the scholarly standards of humanism, a long crisis of personal doubt, revulsion from paternal and institutional authority, and finally a sudden life-choice leading to conviction and a new form of existence. The process was literally one of reformation in the Pauline sense of inner transformation. For Luther this may have been a solitary experience, but for his spiritual descendants of a later generation it signified what might be called an 'ideological epiphany' and entailed allegiance to a new social community as well as a confessional elect.

The conscious point of departure for Beza, as for most evangelical reformers, was the 'new learning' of the Renaissance, with its emphasis on pure doctrine, original sources and the consequent attitudes of fundamentalism and hostility to scholasticism. His principal contact with the first generation of Protestants was Wolmar, who not only introduced him to Latin, Greek, and the elements of jurisprudence, but who also prodded his conscience (as he had prodded Calvin's) in matters of religion.[2] During the 1520s Wolmar had taught at Paris, where he had found the religious climate too oppressive; at Orleans, where he had first met Beza; and at Bourges, where Andrea Alciato was in the process of establishing the new humanist school of jurisprudence. Finally, he returned to Germany to take the chair of law at the University of Tübingen. Wolmar took a special interest in Beza and even tried to arrange to take him back to Germany. In any case it seems clear that Wolmar held a higher place in Beza's affections than any blood relative, particularly his father, whom (he later told Wolmar) 'the calumnies of certain persons had alienated from me'. It may be suspected that this alienation of affection was at least as significant, and certainly chronologically prior to, the intellectual impact of classical learning. Critics like Raemond thought so, too, and charged Beza not only with hypocrisy but with 'cruel parricide'.[3] To what extent the replacement of paternal by pedagogical authority was ideologically formative may be debatable, but it certainly prepared the way for Beza's more-than-filial relationship with another of Wolmar's pupils, Jean Calvin.

No less crucial in Beza's experiences were the negative impulses, especially the worldly snares set to distract and to corrupt him.

[2] D. J. de Groot, 'Melchior Volmar', *BSHPF*, LXXXIII (1934), 416–39.
[3] Raemond, 1045.

Despite pride in his birthright, Beza obviously regarded the attendant pleasures and rewards as more of a burden than a legacy. The net of relationships, commitments, and emoluments into which he was born only heightened his awareness of the materialism of French society, especially the mercenary character of the Gallican church and the legal profession. Every prospect seemed designed to entrap him: the string of benefices falling to him either directly or through his brother and uncle; the legal career which he found distasteful and hypocritical; and even his seductive mistress 'philology', at least in the hedonistic form she took in his early poems (of which he later repented). The security promised by this patronage and growing fame did not give Beza peace of mind; on the contrary it agitated his conscience and alienated him further. For Beza and others of his generation, identifying the enemy and renouncing it were necessary preliminaries to the conversion experience.

Beset by these forces and awed by the magnitude of his choice, Beza came to see his early life as a great cosmic drama – a struggle between the forces of good and evil for the possession of his soul. Ordinary people, including his idealized mother, his intimidating father, and Wolmar himself, appeared essentially as agents of these forces, either helping him toward or obstructing him from his final goal. 'I found an infinite number of snares laid for me on every side by Satan', he remarked of his early years. Ultimately it was the Devil, working especially through his father and uncle, who threatened his life and his very soul through illness, suicide, and worldly corruption. Only through the grace of that transcendent 'Best of Fathers' was Beza able to cling to his oath based on 'an entire repudiation of the papal religion'. It was God, in short, working through Wolmar and especially through Calvin, Who preserved him from these threats, Who led him to 'good letters', Who rescued him from vanity and idleness, and Who finally propelled him forcibly into his new life. So Beza was saved for his destiny, which was, to be Calvin's spiritual heir and eventually to take over leadership of God's chosen people.

If conversion in such a context may be taken as an ideological epiphany, then the subsequent adaptation may well be considered a sort of ideological commitment. In Geneva Beza came out of hiding, began calling things by their right names, and – rejecting the hypocritical 'nicodemitism' condemned by Calvin – bore public witness to his faith. For Beza rebuilding his life in his thirtieth year was a process of total re-identification: the restructuring of old patterns of behavior, the transvaluation of old values, the setting of new goals. Most important was the substitution of confessional roles for familial ones – of blood ties by ideological ones – so that Calvin psychologically as well as honorifically 'became Beza's 'father' and his fellow exiles his brothers and sisters. At the same time, Beza's commitment to philology was transformed from self-indulgent versifying to a more useful evangelism. He did not entirely lose his sense of humor, as can be seen from his satirical attacks on popery and Sorbonism, but theology had come to replace literature in his affections. The question of a career remained. At one point Beza apparently considered going into the printing business with his friend Jean Crespin, the future Calvinist martyrologist; but Calvin had other plans for his young convert. So Beza spent the next decade teaching Greek to young Protestants at the Academy of Lausanne and pursuing his theological studies. From then on, spreading the Word, in one way or another, would be Beza's true vocation.

In Beza's traumatic experience of October 1548 we can see all the essential ingredients of Protestant psychology, and especially the notions of Conscience, Conversion, and Confession. This ideological triad implies a whole range of positive values: idealism, self-sacrifice, personal conviction, and selfless action toward a common cause. But of course these ideas also had negative connotations. Beza had to reject not only family but also patria, and of course he was repaid in kind. In Paris he was burned in effigy, and among orthodox folk his 'black legend' approached those of Calvin and even Luther. In his efforts to find an individual standard of judgment, to reject traditional authority and to support an alien and eventually antagonistic community, Beza had performed a comprehensive and irremediable act of rebellion. He had made a commitment which was to transform confessional loyalty into a dynamic, militant and ultimately treasonable Cause.

AGENBITE OF INWIT

What distinguished Beza's lifetime from most ages before and since was the primacy of the inner life, or rather the collective behavior attendant on this condition of heightened consciousness. Private conviction, fashioned in the crucible of family life, replaced public norms as the ultimate standard of action: the 'internal forum', to put it in sixteenth-century terms, replaced the 'external forum'. So 'conscience' became a moving force in history, and at least for a time material self-interest became subordinate – to the confusion of men of authority and to many later historians.[4] In this radicalizing and often irrational shift Luther was again a central figure, but he was by no means alone in his audacity. In schools, churches, monasteries and market-places all over Europe young men and women were turning away from the faith of their fathers to seek their own paths to salvation, or fulfillment, reinforced perhaps by his example, though not necessarily persuaded by his particular doctrinal solution. In this unmistakable though not always immediately perceptible phenomenon we can sense the individual aspect, the psychological dimension of 'reform'; and it was given social expression in a bewildering variety of unorthodoxies, dissents and separatisms which emerged or re-emerged, subdivided and expanded in patterns forming a veritable kaleidoscope of ideological ferment.

How can we make sense of these patterns? The neatest way was suggested by Luther himself, who distributed them along a spectrum from left to right (from popery to anabaptism, reversing the modern convention) and measured the degree of dissent from his presumed central position by the extent to which the orthodox system of seven sacraments was modified or discarded. It will not be possible even to begin to penetrate early modern consciousness without acknowledging the life-enhancing, or intimidating, force of the doctrines of the eucharist, baptism, penance, marriage, ordination, confirmation and extreme unction. Of these Luther kept only the first three (penance with crucial reservations), Calvin the first two, while Zwingli cast doubt on the eucharist, and the anabaptists threw out infant baptism as well. The permutations and combinations were almost endless. According to one ex-Protestant, 'I have seen seven sects of sacramentarians, all different and each defend-

---

[4] On the idea of conscience the literature is extensive but technical and not on the whole relevant to the history of consciousness or ideology. Among the most useful works are H. Appel, *Die Lehre der Scholastiker von der Synteresis* (Rostok, 1891); A. Cancrini, *Syneidesis* (Rome, 1970); J. Lecler, *Toleration and the Reformation*, trans. T. Westow (New York, 1960); C. A. Pierce, *Conscience and the New Testament* (Chicago, 1955); and J. Stelzenberger, *Syneidesis, Conscientia, Gewissen* (Paderborn, 1963).

ing its opinion in the most dogmatic fashion.'[5] The one position common to all, whatever other disagreements they had, was the appeal from authority to conscience, from a conventional and consensual to an unconventional and personal reading of scriptures. In this shift above all we can see the opening up of the Pandora's box of ideology. It was the unleashing of ego, in other words, that freed the unending swarms of eponymous '-isms', anti-'isms', '-olatries', '-phobias', and '-manias' which, in conjunction with more familiar human needs and drives, transformed the face if not the soul of modern society. To orthodox critics, at least, the appeal to conscience seemed hardly less 'libertine' than the motto of Rabelais's Abbey of Thélème: 'Do what you will.'

By Luther's time the idea of Conscience had had a long and, despite its anti-social potential, largely honorable history. Its emergence is a major episode in the story of human consciousness in general, and like other guiding concepts of western thought it had a dual pedigree. One was Greek, and most notably the Platonic directive to self-knowledge; the other the Judaeo-Christian preoccupation with guilt and the impending judgment of a wrathful God. These attitudes converged in the grand tradition of Christian humanism, extending from Paul, Jerome and Augustine down to Erasmus, Luther and Calvin. It may seem parochial to insist upon the Christian nexus; for the ancient Greeks had entertained notions of secrecy and guilt that went beyond simple self-awareness to a moral self-criticism (*syneidesis*), and Judaic views required the use of this same term in the Septuagint. Nevertheless, it was that archetypal 'divided self' (in William James's term), that tortured Jew and cocksure Christian convert Saul/Paul, who first gave expression to the specifically Christian idea of conscience, associating it with faith, atonement and the wrath of God, thus characteristically 'internalizing' the concept.[6] The discussion and rationalization of 'conscience' was continued by a distinguished line of medieval theologians, who considered as well such related puzzles as that of the 'erroneous conscience' and whether the seat of conscience was the will or the intellect. It was Abelard who had set 'conscience' at the center of moral theology by equating sin with violation of conscience (*Quod peccatum non est nisi contra conscientiam*).[7] The problem was taken up afresh and less systematically by humanists, including Marsilio Ficino and Erasmus, who turned back to the Platonic (and Pauline)

[5] *Responce pour le chevalier de Villegaignon* (Paris, 1561; BN Lb33. 19), 12.

[6] K. Stendhal, 'The Apostle Paul and the introspective conscience of the west', *Ecumenical Dialogue at Harvard*, ed. S. Miller and G. Wright (Cambridge, Mass., 1964), 236–56; cf. C. Trinkaus, *In Our Likeness and Image* (Chicago, 1970), I, 633.

[7] Abelard, *Ethics*, ed. D. Luscombe (Oxford, 1971), 54.

tendency toward internalization, and who thus seemed to speak more directly to the individual. Such laicization (and in a sense Biblicization) of conscience was taken up in various ways by the magisterial reformers, whose concern as well was to bestir self-consciousness in others – for example, by discussion of 'how to confess' and in general how to be awakened and transformed by religious experience.

Though Christianized and Reformed, Conscience never lost its psychological duality. Egoism and altruism, self-advertisement and self-doubt, autobiography and confession: these have been the roots of individuality, the well-springs of dissent and the seed-beds of ideology. Self-consciousness permitted one to question tradition; remorse of conscience – that 'agenbite of inwit' of Anglo-Saxon formulation – impelled one to reject it. Such was the Pauline dialectic, criticizing the literal and deadening Judaic law and replacing or rather reforming it by the life-giving spiritual message of Christ, which was given to 'free' consciences. Such was the ideological pattern recapitulated by Luther, too, although characteristically he pushed the idea to a further extreme. As this 'man of abnormal introspection', as he has been called, radicalized Paul's doctrine of faith – faith alone! was, despite his Biblical literalism, his persistent interpretation – so he radicalized the Pauline view of conscience.[8] 'Liberty of conscience' was Luther's innovation; and notwithstanding some equivocation, the effect was to substitute private judgment for custom, tradition and especially 'law', which connoted the sinful legalism not only of the Old Testament but also of the Roman Ecclesia. In Luther's obstinate declaration at the Diet of Worms, that 'it is neither safe nor right to act against conscience', the basic issue was not heresy but disobedience (that is, to the order of silence). His stand was a locus classicus of subversion, and in the course of the next two generations it made 'liberty of conscience' a burning issue – a scandal to some, a slogan to others.

There was something paradoxical in this, especially for one who was shortly to become not only a champion of secular authority but also a vociferous critic of the idea of 'free will'. Aside from the implied Pelagian error in this notion, what about the factor of human weakness? 'What of the occasion when conscience strikes the mind, and presently it turns away from God and dreads Him as a cruel murderer?', asked Luther's colleague Melanchthon.[9] Yet without conscience, he immediately added, men were truly slaves. For

[8] G. Rupp, *The Righteousness of God* (London, 1963). 150ff., 117; and see now M. G. Baylor, *Action and Person: Conscience in Late Scholasticism and the Young Luther* (Leiden, 1977), arguing for Luther's modernity and activism.
[9] *Loci Communes*, 'sin', in *Melanchthon and Bucer*, ed. W. Pauck (Philadelphia, 1969), 42.

Calvin, too, conscience was not only an 'undoubted sign of the immortal spirit' but also a source of fear, despair and outright rebelliousness that played into the hands of Satan – or perhaps of 'libertines' like Rabelais, whose Abbey of Thélème allowed its members to spend their lives 'not in laws and statutes but according to their own free will and pleasure'. Then of course there was the problem of the conscience 'not thine own', as Calvin quoted from St Paul, 'but of the other'.[10] Most problematical of all, however, was the relationship between social convention and individual judgment: on the one hand the bondage of 'human traditions', especially the Roman constitutions, and on the other hand man's conscience, which 'watches and observes all his secrets so that nothing may remain in darkness', and which finally governed thought, if not action. Luther acknowledged the dilemma. 'I don't understand law', he reportedly claimed, 'but I am an authority in matters of conscience.'[11] So was Calvin, and he also set himself up as a court of appeal. What neither seemed to understand, or would acknowledge, was that by disparaging human laws they were setting up conscience itself as law. In the long run the effect was not only to confuse but also to politicize 'liberty of conscience'.

It may well be a misreading of the thought of Luther and Calvin to assign them retrospectively to a tradition of political libertarianism, as certain philosophical idealists and liberal historians have done. Ever since Peter Abelard 'intention' has been essential to the assessment of guilt, and certainly neither Luther nor Calvin had intentional political defiance on their consciences. Yet as all teachers and authors have cause to realize, the message sent is not always, and perhaps is never, the message received. One major thesis of Luther was 'the freedom of the Christian man', and though he meant freedom under law, the Christian had always to ask, whose law? Not, certainly, the law of the church; and indeed it was on the basis of substituting 'conscience' for canon law that lawyers like Charles Dumoulin (as well as theologians) opposed the old-fashioned canonist restriction on usury. Why should other areas of secular concern not be judged in the 'internal forum'? Such seemed also to be the message of Calvin, who opened the door further to subversion. To him 'Christian freedom' meant 'that the consciences of believers . . . should rise above and advance beyond the law, forgetting all law righteousness'. Different circumstances – and different consciences! – could make this a call not only to nonconformity but also to rebellion. And so it happened as a result of the extraordinary resonance between the conscience, and ego, of Luther, and those of so many disaffected contemporaries. Whatever

[10] Calvin, *Institutes*, III, xx, on I Corin. 10:29.   [11] Luther, *Table Talk*, 131.

psycho-social reality underlies this metaphor of 'resonance', it acted quite directly to raise – or to lower – Luther's attitudes from the level of ideals to that of ideology. It was a process more easily begun than controlled or suppressed.

So it was that, in the later sixteenth century, the problem of conscience was transformed from a theological dilemma into a burning political and social issue, and then the duality was not so much a divided soul as a divided allegiance. The official view, political as well as ecclesiastical, recognized individual conscience to be a root cause of disorder, and the reaction was a mounting wave of legislation designed to enforce religious uniformity. It was pressed not only by the Catholic monarchs of France, Spain and the Empire but also by Lutheran and Calvinist governments; and the 'forced' or 'terrified consciences' became the center of a debate about the nature and limits of religious toleration. One of the main targets, though a declared champion of 'liberty of conscience', was Calvin himself; and according to one of his most insistent critics, religious zealotry, wherever and however directed, was the bane of his age. 'The principal and efficient cause of the malady [of France], of this tormenting sedition and war', wrote Sebastien Castellio in the very first year of civil conflict, 'is the forcing of consciences' (*forcement des consciences*).[12]

By this time liberty or 'repose' of conscience had become a major plank in the Huguenot political and ecclesiastical platform. In the so-called conspiracy of Amboise in the spring of 1560, which was in effect the premature curtain-raiser for the civil wars which broke out two years later, 'those of the religion' petitioned the king to allow them to follow 'the purity of the Gospel and the repose of their consciences'; and indeed the royal edict which attempted to settle the disturbance peaceably seemed to hold out just this promise. This edict, even more than that of January 1562 and the long series of 'pacification edicts' over the rest of the century, constituted the best hope, slim as it was, of satisfying the consciences of the 'so-called reformed religion'. Yet these hopes, at least until the Edict of Nantes, were not realized; and running contrapuntally with the legislative declarations of good intentions were the counter-legislative complaints of the Huguenots. From the very beginning the party line established its religious legitimacy on two points. One was the gospel; the other, proclaimed by the Prince of Condé in the summer of 1562 as he marshalled forces and arguments in Orleans, was 'the holy liberty of our consciences' (*la saincte liberté de noz consciences*).[13] This theme clashed painfully with the

[12] Calvin, *Institutes*, III, xix.
[13] *Conseil a la France desolée* (n.p., 1562), 6; cf. Michel de l'Hôpital, *Oeuvres complètes* (Paris, 1824), I, 471, and on Baudouin, pp. 85–7 and 161–3 below.

old premise of Gallican unity and uniformity – 'one king, one faith, one law' – and the resulting cacophony dominated public opinion for a generation and more.

From at least one point of view, then, violated conscience lay at the roots of much of the disorder of the age, and much of the propaganda of the civil wars was cast in these terms. The truth was that conscience was no longer a private matter. To those who protested on its behalf it had become an article of faith and the basis for a program of action. To judicial authority like the Parlement of Paris – though its members, too, acted 'according to their con-sciences'[14] – it was a blight on the tree of the commonwealth, and hence a proper object of political surveillance. But then, as later, the inner life would not be shaped by external force, and hardly even restrained by institutional means, at least until time, disillusionment and ideological exhaustion could set conscience at rest.

THE ROAD TO DAMASCUS

Awakened, conscience is a personal discomfort; activated toward a goal, it can be a disruptive force in society. What William James called 'the hot place in a man's consciousness', the center of intellectual energy and potentially of religious enthusiasm, was ignited with unusual ease in the sixteenth century and, joined in a mass, led inevitably to larger ideological conflagrations. This phe-nomenon, which from an individual point of view constitutes the conversion experience, also had a long career in western culture, and again there was a twofold heritage.[15] One corresponded to philosophic conversion, as manifested for instance in the dazzling vision appearing at the end of Plato's cave. The other was the emotional, often guilt-ridden seizure, as experienced for instance by Paul on his way to Damascus, also accompanied by blinding light.

[14] *MC*, III, 396; cf. I, 63, 102, 109, 334, 388, 654, 899, etc.; Pithou, 130, 139; P. Belloy, *Conference des Edicts de Pacification* (Paris, 1600), and below, pp. 255–60. On Montaigne's 'De la liberté de conscience', K. Cameron in *Renaissance Quarterly*, XXVI (1973), 285–94. Cf. Calvin, *Institutes*, III, xvii, 1.

[15] In general, B. Citron, *New Birth, A Study of the Evangelical Doctrine of Conversion in the Protestant Fathers* (Edinburgh, 1951); W. L. Jones, *A Psychological Study of Conversion* (London, 1937); P. Aubin, *Le Problème de la 'conversion'* (Paris, 1963); J. R. Neal, 'Conscience and the Reformation Period' (unpublished Ph.D. thesis, Harvard University, 1972). But on the *experience* of conversion there is little of historical value beyond A. D. Nock's classic *Conversion* (Oxford, 1933) and nothing compar-able for medieval and early modern times, despite many shelves of autobiographi-cal and apologetic discussion and, more recently, sociological and statistical studies. One special work of interest is F. W. B. Bullock, *Evangelical Conversion in Great Britain 1516–1695* (St Leonards on Sea, 1966).

Change of mind – change of heart; turnabout of attitude – transformation of character; act of will – reaction of conscience: such were the principal forms of conversion experience, or at least the conventional ways of perceiving and expressing them.

The word 'conversion' has been rich in signification. It has encompassed various sorts of fundamental change, ranging from the solitary decision to enter monastic life (becoming a *conversus*) to political revolution (as in Jean Bodin's adaptation of the Polybian cycle of constitutions, *anacyclosis*).[16] In individual terms it was associated with Greek ideas of repentance (*metanoia*) and the turning from evil to good (*epistrophe*), and as such it was related to the idea of conscience. In the sixteenth century the process of conversion was central to all varieties of reformed faith, for it (and not the mass or any external observance) signified the most direct encounter between humanity and divinity. It was associated closely with the sacrament of penance as reformulated by Luther and others. 'Repent and turn yourselves from all transgressions' was one of the Old Testament texts used by Calvin to illustrate the process, and of course such 'turning' was identified with conversion in a modern sense: 'Convert me, O Lord, and I will be converted.'[17] Although Protestant theology generally denied that this act was truly voluntary, it was in many cases intellectualized – inspired by reading, hearing or debating a particular passage of scripture – and usually it was accompanied by revulsion from an environment perceived as corrupt and identified as a source of malignancy.

Not only did conversion represent the pivotal point in the experience of many persons in this age, it suggested also a basic explanation for the turn which history as a whole seemed to be taking. Most generally, in other words, the conversion experience was connected to the idea of reform itself in its several senses of restoration, renovation, regeneration and resurrection – a vision of lost innocence recaptured. The basic text was the Pauline exhortation not to conform but to be 'transformed in the newness of your minds' (*reformamini in novitate sensus*), which Colet and others took as the initial step in the reconstitution of church and society in general.[18] Like 'conscience', then, 'conversion' reflected directly and dynamically the psychological aspect of the Reformation and, elaborated in countless works of theology, history and popular literature, became one of the most powerfully transforming myths of modern times.

Although the idea seems simple, the experience is hard to

---

[16] H. Workman, *The Evolution of the Monastic Ideal* (London, 1913), 4. Bodin, *Method for the Easy Comprehension of History*, trans B. Reynolds (New York, 1945), 158.
[17] *Institutes*, II, v, 8–9; III, iii, among others.   [18] See above, p. 22.

describe and harder to classify. All too few conversions have been recorded even by major figures, and no systematic studies have been made for earlier ages. To sixteenth-century reformers the example of ancient Christianity was important, but the parallel was not really very close: the road from Athens to Jerusalem was longer but more clearly marked than that from Rome to Wittenberg – or to Geneva. The classic point of departure for the latter journey would seem to be the sudden conversion (*conversio subita*), most dramatically illustrated by the case of St Paul and recapitulated in modern times by Luther, at least as he reconstructed his experience in retrospect.[19] The crucial point of his life, whenever it came, was the epiphany induced by his penetration, after long struggle, of the phrase in Romans 1:17, 'The just shall live by faith.' The scholarly discussion of this passage had a significant history going back to Lorenzo Valla, who some seventy years before had corrected the translation by changing it from present to future tense; but – thus Protestantism built upon as well as departed from Renaissance humanism – Luther's interpretation went beyond grammar to a transcendent principle.[20] His conviction was that faith alone, and so inferentially his conscience alone, furnished ultimate justification. This sudden insight, the Lutheran counterpart to Paul's fall from his horse, established not only a key doctrine of reformed religion but also a modern archetype of conversion experience. The only comparable magisterial conversion was that of Zwingli; and his personal crisis, coming in the wake of a near-fatal illness, also set a precedent for the next generation, followed notably by Beza and Hotman.

The symbol and often catalyst of conversion in the sixteenth century was the book,[21] and most recollections of the sacred and pivotal time of revelation revolve around a reading experience like Luther's storied *Turmerlebnis*. As the world appeared as a book to some philosophers, so the book could be a metaphor for the world, a gateway to cosmic or microcosmic discovery. 'Take, read', Augustine had repeated (*tolle lege, tolle lege*); and his advice might serve as the motto of the great tradition of Christian humanism, of the Biblical version of that Greek cultural ideal (*paideia*) which was itself, as Werner Jaeger observed, a kind of conversion.[22] It was from the same passage of the *Confessions* that Petrarch, during his famous climb up Mount Ventoux, was vouchsafed sudden insight and

---

[19] G. Swarts, *Salut par foi et conversion brusque* (Paris, 1931).
[20] See above, p. 32, at n. 30.
[21] See E. R. Curtius, *European Literature and the Latin Middle Ages*, trans. W. Trask (New York, 1953), chapter 16, 'Book as Symbol'.
[22] Jaeger, *Paideia*, trans. G. Highet (Oxford, 1939–44), II, 295.

self-revelation; and such bookish enlightenment was even more crucial to evangelical reformers. 'I seem to belong to a new creation', remarked Guillaume Farel after his conversion.[23] 'I understood the meaning of the scriptures; the light was lit in my soul.' A generation later a similar experience was recalled by the great evangelist Guy de Brès, though his attitude was not quite so pioneering. 'I took the road', he wrote of his struggles to understand the Word, 'which had been taken by the prophets, the apostles and indeed the son of God, our Lord Jesus Christ, and so many thousands of martyrs . . .'[24] Such bookish experiences may have been reserved largely for the literate and the reflective, but certainly the pattern of conversion was representative of a broader range of social types. The executioner converted at the last moment by his victim is only one of many stories about such experiences, or at least a convention presumed to be widespread.

Throughout the sixteenth century sudden conversion ostensibly continued to be a common occurrence; and certainly it fulfilled the requirements of doctrinal purity, which assumed a single moment of grace, a threshold of enlightenment and perhaps a flash of literary insight. Yet history as well as psychology suggests that reality was more complicated. For many persons the road to Damascus, even if they did not follow it to the end, was neither straight nor narrow. Sometimes it resembles rather the winding path taken by Petrarch in the ascent of his symbolic mountain, especially in contrast to the path chosen by his brother, who as a monk was literally a 'convert'. For others it was a continuous struggle toward the light; and it is perhaps not surprising that such reliers on scholarly effort, including Erasmus and Melanchthon, inclined toward an exaggerated view of free will and that error of 'synergism' which has man co-operating with God in the process of grace. Religious vacillation and the recurrence of doubt further undermine the interpretation of conversion as an instantaneous experience, though particular theories of salvation might well require it. In human terms, then, one does not have to fall off a horse to achieve grace.

For these and other reasons it seems useful to try to understand patterns of conversion in terms of the human condition rather than as a soteriological ideal, as a process involving some sort of mental and moral *preparatio evangelium*. As modern religious psychology

---

[23] *Guillaume Farel . . .*, par un groupe d'historiens, professeurs et pasteurs de Suisse, de France et d'Italie (Neuchâtel, 1930), 105; J.-D. Burger, 'La conversion de Farel', *BSHPF*, CXI (1965), 199–212; and H. Meylan, 'Les étapes de la conversion de Farel', *L'Humanisme français au début de la Renaissance* (Paris, 1973), 253–9.

[24] E. Braekman, *Guy de Brès* (Brussels, 1960), 38.

suggests and sixteenth-century experience bears out, conversion begins not with the pursuit of righteousness but with the struggle against sin: before knowing God men had to see the Devil, and this required some passing involvement in the world. The pursuit of righteousness was itself a journey marked by several stages.[25] So it had been with Luther, beginning with his entrance into monastic life. So it was also, contemporaneously, with Zwingli, who moved from Biblical study to ego assertion – the 'pure invocation of God' without intermediaries – to his final rejection of the mass. And so it would be with Guy de Brès, who recorded a long intellectual journey, completed only after extended reflection and psychic turmoil. In a human sense, then, the best model may be not that of Paul but that of Augustine, whose transformation was bound up with memories of a devout mother, a deeply classical education and long struggles against sinful and pagan inclinations. In general this Augustinian paradigm, though it contained Pauline as well as Platonic elements, was not an emotional seizure but an intellectual pilgrimage.

The conversion process was also in some ways congruent with mental history, that is, with the complicated business of growing up and in particular with what William James called the 'growth crisis'. One threshold is the discovery of a 'calling', whether choosing the profession of a 'religious' (as did Luther) or making an intellectual commitment (as did Melanchthon), and starting on a line of thought leading to criticism of established ideas and institutions. This stage may be complicated by family as well as by scholastic and professional pressures. Another stage involves struggle and discontent, arising characteristically from a sense of sin, guilt and purposelessness, and coming to a conviction about the nature and source of evil; and this is often capped by the classic 'sudden conversion', when things fall into place, a remedy is discovered (if only in personal terms), and a decision is taken to enter upon a new course of life. Finally, if the decision is firm, comes the time to make some public profession of faith, for only in a social context can this process of re-identification be completed. Questioning traditional values, transvaluation of these values and the publication of them to a wider world: such, at least in psychological terms, were the stages of 'the beginning of ideology' in modern times.

Supplementing the stories of ostensibly 'magisterial' converts was the more common incidence of what might be called 'discipular

---

[25] Emile G. Leonard, *A History of Protestantism*, trans. J. Reid and R. Bethell (2 vols, London, 1965–7), I, 294.

conversion', a secondary phenomenon resulting in part from charismatic force and necessarily less well documented. Such, to one degree or another, was the relationship of Farel to Lefèvre d'Etaples and Bucer to Luther (both in 1519), and countless others to all of these. Perhaps most dramatic was the case of François Lambert, that free spirit who, like Erasmus and Luther, became disgusted with monastic life (after almost a quarter century of it) and fled to the purer atmosphere of Switzerland and Germany. Although a champion of the gospel for a number of years, Lambert did not make his breakthrough to evangelical understanding until he came to Zurich in 1522 in order to deliver a sermon to an audience that included Zwingli himself. When Lambert dropped a favorable remark about the Virgin Mary, Zwingli could not restrain himself. 'Brother, you are wrong!', he interrupted.[26] In an ensuing debate Lambert was brought around to Zwingli's way of thinking; and a few months after that he made a pilgrimage to Wittenberg, where, with Luther's encouragement, he publicly 'threw off his cowl' and mounted an assault upon the Catholic church.

In the next generation acts of conversion became more stereotyped and even socialized; for while the first generation of Protestants (roughly those born before 1500) had blazed their own trail, their heirs and epigones – their converts – had a somewhat easier time of it and models to imitate, if not maps to follow. Four years after his own crisis Beza effected the conversion of Louis de Masures, just returning from Rome; and this young man recalled the encounter in glowing but not uncharacteristic terms.[27]

> On the shores of Geneva's lake,
>   And never shall I forget the day,
> Returning from the conclave of Rome,
>   I stopped and I heard you say:
> Receive and cling to the truth,
>   And never lose the certain way.

By then conversion implied not only an expression of conscience but also an initiation into a religious community.

For this very reason the process of conversion could not be fulfilled simply by attaining an inner state of conviction; it had to

[26] R. Winters, *Francis Lambert of Avignon* (Philadelphia, 1938), 30.
[27] Meylan, 'La conversion de Bèze', *Genava*, n.s. VII (1959), 104:
> O comme de bon coeur et de fidèle voix
> Sur le bord sablonneaux de beau lac Genevois
> Un jour, dont à jamais il me souviendre, comme
> Passant je retournois du conclave de Romme,
> Tu m'enhortas de suivre et fermement tenir
> La verité certaine, et que pour l'avenir
> Laissant l'oblique et faux, au droit sentier j'allasse
> Hors du chemin d'erreur, ou le monde se lasse.

become manifest as well by some public sign. This was the position taken with peculiar adamance by Calvin, especially in his assaults on those 'Nicodemites' afflicted with timidity or hypocrisy.[28] For him, no one could participate in the abomination of the Roman mass, or say 'Hail Mary', even to avoid persecution, and remain a member of the elect. This requirement became even more essential in the face of scandalous defections, including (Raemond remarked with relish) Calvin's first convert, Louis du Tillet. Other instances were those of the Sieur de Villegagnon, who turned his polemical talents against his former co-religionists, the Seigneur du Rosier, who had two conversions (to 'Huguenotterie' and back to Catholicism) within a year, and François Baudouin, who was accused of changing faith seven times – not to mention the case of Henry of Navarre, who turned back to Catholicism twice, once in 1572 to save his life and again in 1594 to save his crown.[29] No doubt some of these stories of religious 'vacillation' were, to say the least, exaggerated, as were those of deathbed conversions, or recantations, about which Erasmus warned (thinking in particular of the case of Louis Berquin). What is significant is the priority given to the profession of faith as the key to social identity and sometimes to survival.

How did one demonstrate membership in a particular religious community? Liturgical propriety was not always enough. For some it meant taking up some sort of evangelizing work, broadcasting the Word in oral or written fashion. The culmination of Luther's 'conversion' process was the publication of his Ninety-Five Theses, and of Zwingli's, his New Year's sermon in the pulpit of Grossmünster in 1519; and the pattern was carried over into many discipular conversions. Often the decision to go public was more crucial than the original act of religious choice, involving as it did entering the ministry – the reformed counterpart of ordination. For others it required flight from an inhospitable environment. Peter Martyr, for example, after his conversion on Christmas Day 1542, could no longer bear to preach or to hear the old doctines – 'unless I would either have darkened the truth, or have professed things which are plainly false' – and fled into exile.[30] So did many young men, especially in France and the Empire, and by mid-century religious emigration became a major social phenomenon. Here, too, we can see the transition from religious experience to ideological commitment.

[28] See C. Ginzberg, *Il Nicodemismo* (Turin, 1970), and E. Droz, *Chemins de l'hérésie* (Geneva, 1970–6).

[29] R. Kingdon, 'Problems of religious choice for sixteenth century Frenchmen', *Journal of Religious History*, IV (1966), 105–12; cf. A. Guerin, *Epistola ad Franc. Balduinum apostatum* (n.p., 1564).

[30] P. McNair, *Peter Martyr in Italy* (Oxford, 1967), 263.

Although the phenomenon of conversion forms part of the very substance of history, it is difficult to discover and to assess in social terms; and since evidence is anecdotal and even legendary in character, it is hardly accessible in any direct way to statistical methods or to prosopography. Yet the consequences are unmistakable, and so is the obvious snowballing effect of the conversion process. Among the converts of Farel after his own experience was Pierre Viret, who was an even more remarkable missionary preacher. It was said that the entire faculty of medicine of the University of Montpellier was converted by him, and so apparently were some villages.[31] Stories were told, and grew with the telling. We hear of people being converted at outdoor sermons, in secret services, in their travels and at executions. Defections from the old religion could be detected within the secular and regular clergy, in the professions of law and medicine, in schools and guilds, in the nobility and even in houses of royal blood. Whole families went over to the reformed religion and often into exile, such as the Budés of Paris and the Colladons of Bourges. The Parlement of Paris was crawling with heresy, or so it was popularly and officially supposed. The loss of souls was denounced by orthodox critics and legislation on the one hand and applauded by advocates of reform on the other, and published works as well as oral discourse resounded with problems of inner turmoil.

Behind this uproar lay a whole world of human experience, a transmutation of thought, feeling and value, whose significance went beyond the immediate issues of conscious debate. Old notions of social order were damaged beyond repair. European society was certainly not renewed according to the expectations of the reformers, but it was shaken up and set on a path that brought change in an even more striking fashion, confirming their sense of evil if not their hope of restoration. What their ideal of conversion helped to bring about was indeed a transformation – but in the sense (to use a popular phrase of sixteenth-century journalism) of a 'world turned upside-down'.

THE PRIMAL DIALECTIC

The roots of religious experience and social consciousness are mostly sub-historical (if not psychohistorical) and inaccessible even to contemporary observation, located as they are in the context of the family and having a largely unconscious and pre-conceptual charac-

---

[31] J. Barnaud, *Pierre Viret* (Saint-Aman, 1911), and R. Linder, *The Political Ideas of Pierre Viret* (Geneva, 1964); cf. Louis Raynal, *Histoire du Berry* (Bourges, 1844), III, 347.

ter.[32] A child takes for granted the little world of the domestic circle and has small means of criticizing it directly, even in later life. In the family are set basic patterns of self and the other, love and hate, work and play, co-operation and competition, obedience and defiance. It was a truism that

> A good child does always his mother and father obey.
> A bad one, even when beaten, rebels and goes astray.[33]

It was in what Renaissance pedagogues called 'first infancy', up to the age of five or so, that the child's 'nature' was formed. However conceived, this nature corresponded in many ways to the first stage of social consciousness, the stage of domestic ideology, as it might be called; and however inaccessible, this seminal phase may be appreciated at least indirectly in terms of family relationships and especially of the perceived parental roles.

In the sixteenth century the family appeared to be a little cosmos of blood ties and instinctual relations which was incorrigibly and indeed prehistorically conservative. Lines of descent were set by custom, rationalized by lawyers and celebrated by genealogists. In particular 'grades of cognation and agnation' fixed pedigree and inheritance, determined the complex web of kinship and defined the domestic horizons of individuals, at least until marriage widened or confounded them. The young François Hotman, while in the throes of religious doubt, devoted his first major work to this subject and laid out the structure of kinship according to the conventional civilian pattern of laterally and vertically expanding lines.[34] Conceptions of the family were more conspicuously and more controversially displayed in contemporary discussions of dynastic theory and succession, and indeed almost forty years later Hotman contributed substantially to this related subject in his defense of the succession of Henry of Navarre to the French throne. In terms both of social and political theory, then, the family was fundamental – more so, indeed, than intellectual historians have acknowledged. In general the family was a human web, defined by blood and marriage, reaching into past and future as well as out into society, maintained ultimately by considerations of succession and heritable wealth, and possessing still largely unappreciated significance for the study of ideology.

---

[32] In the crush of recent work on family history there is little that concerns intellectual history; of older works the most relevant are G. Le Pointe, *La Famille dans l'ancien droit* (Paris, n. d.), P. de Félice, *Les Protestants d'autrefois* (Paris, 1897), and C. Ribbe, *Les Familles et la société avant la Révolution* (Tours, 1879), I.

[33] J. Le Coultre, *Mathurin Cordier* (Neuchâtel, 1926), from quatrains on 'Le bon enfant'.

[34] *De Gradibus cognationis et affinitatis libri duo* (Paris, 1547) and *De Jure successionis regiae in regno Francorum leges aliquot* (n.p., 1588).

The traditional image of the family was a tree; and it was as a tree that the extended family, that 'society intended for domestic welfare and profit', was elaborately pictured by another contemporary social theorist. For Guillaume de La Perrière this tree grew on feudal as well as sacramental soil and required the most careful cultivation, for its life-principle was 'Fidelity' – meaning fidelity to one's self and kin (*proches*) as well as to office, sovereign and God.[35] The human foundation was marriage, and this La Perrière also likened to a tree, supporting life through the rights and obligations of husband and wife. The resemblance between these domestic institutions and the great 'tree' of the republic itself was not accidental, for the family, like the institution of marriage, was indeed regarded as a political entity (a *civitas* or *res publica*). As Jean Bodin wrote, the family was 'the true seminary and beginning of every Commonweale and also a principal member thereof'.[36] Social stability, therefore, required that governments protect the family from internal dissension, external attack and material diminution; and sixteenth-century legislation reflected this official solicitude.

In this domestic republic children were essentially without legal rights. Father and mother were 'visible gods', since they were creators of their offspring; and disobeying them was the worst of crimes, leading directly to heresy, atheism and sedition. The lives, educations and inheritances of children were at the parents' disposal. There was no appeal from the fifth commandment, and according to the old proverb quoted by Luther, 'The Devil brings up all whom fathers and mothers can't.'[37] Over such children the only control was the magistrate, the only punishment prison or the gibbet. Since the central problem was generational stability, blood tradition as it were, one of the most sensitive issues was the control of succession, which is to say marital choice. In this connection the sort of secret marriage indulged in by Beza and Hotman was clearly a threat to social order, and it became a special target of royal displeasure. In 1556 Henry II issued the first of a series of edicts 'concerning marriages clandestinely and irreverently contracted by children of a family'.[38] The next year this principle was elaborately endorsed by the jurist Jean de Coras, who condemned the practice as 'not only against the law of God and nature but against all human law and reason'. Honoring parental wishes, according to Coras, was one of the traits distinguishing humans from animals. Assertions of youthful ego, whether through carnal or religious passion, could not be tolerated in any institutional context.

[35] *Le Miroir politique* (Paris, 1567; 1st edn, 1555), 25ff.
[36] Bodin, *Les six livres de la Republique* (Paris, 1576), I, 2; Bucer, *De Regno Christi*, in Pauck (ed.), *Melanchthon and Bucer*, II, 15. [37] *Table Talk*, 68.
[38] *Edict du roy sur les marriages clandestines* (Paris, 1556 [1557]; BN F. 46814.5 and Harvard); also in Isambert, XIII, nos. 1309–10.

In the establishment of 'domestic ideology' the primal influence was maternal. This began with nursing, and one contemporary author expressed 'horror' at any female who refused 'perhaps the only good thing she can do in her life'.[39] After this, during the 'second infancy', the mother was literally the 'conscience' of the child and introduced him to his catechism and the Bible before passing him on, at the age of six or so, to the schoolmaster. A classic example of maternal influence was Augustine, whose conversion was in a sense a return to the teachings of his pious mother. And many reformers – Luther, Beza and Hotman among them – held their mothers in fond recollection, in more or less invidious contrast to their fathers. Of course such influence was almost by definition domestic rather than social, moral rather than political. The teachings of mothers concerned personal relations rather than larger questions of public behavior and ideals. In the popular mind women were associated neither with inner torment nor with social turmoil and certainly not with the moving forces of history, except indirectly, or if by mischance power fell into their hands.

Such attitudes were reinforced by a stereotype deeply embedded in western intellectual tradition, as reflected in the Homeric formula cited by Aristotle, that 'Silence is a woman's first glory.'[40] Speech, rationality and hence political activity, the inference was, belonged to men; and in the sixteenth century this continued to be a common-place view. Counterbalancing the celebration of the 'dignity and excellence of man', a theme popularized by Pico, was that of the dignity of woman; but when noted at all, this obverse theme was normally elaborated in terms of beauty, domestic efficiency and a retiring disposition (*excellentia ex taciturnitate et silentio* was the phrase of the jurist Barthélemy de Chasseneux, who raised the contrast to an almost metaphysical level in his encyclopedic *Catalogue of the Glories of the World* of 1529).[41] In such euphemistic phrases he denied women authority, learning and civilized discourse, which in practical terms meant office, university advancement and political opinions.

In France these assumptions were part of the very substance of law and custom. It was generally assumed that only men could preserve the 'honor', which is to say the material integrity, of the family. André Tiraqueau, for example, who sat in judgment on many

---

[39] Félice, *Les Protestants d'autrefois*, IV, 6; cf. P. Ariès, *Centuries of Childhood*, trans. R. Baldick (New York, 1962); revised French edn, *L'Enfant et la vie familiale sous l'ancien régime* (Paris, 1973).
[40] *Politics*, I, 13.
[41] *Catalogus gloriae mundi* (Lyon, 1529), 17ᵛ; cf. Pierre Boaistuau, *Bref discours de l'excellence et dignité de l'homme* (Paris, 1559), 12.

an accused heretic, published a massive treatise on the principles of male supremacy and succession; and his authoritative work typified official attitudes toward social and political order.[42] This view received further confirmation from that incorrigibly popular legend, the 'Salic law', which excluded women from royal succession. 'Women do not succeed to a fief', explained the feudist Jean Pyrrhus d'Angelberme, 'much less to a kingdom.'[43] During the last stages of the civil wars, when Henry of Navarre had become a claimant to the crown, this customary rule was elevated to the level of 'fundamental law'. In its support one partisan cited the 'five reasons' of the fourteenth-century jurist Baldus for the superiority of men: invidiously expressed, they centered on women's indecisiveness and inability to keep a secret. For such reasons not only political 'virtue' but also royal 'majesty', or sovereignty, were masculine monopolies; and so even anti-feminism was politicized in this divisive age.[44]

With these judgments, permeating the subconscious as well as the consciousness of Europe, Protestants had no particular quarrel. A woman was the mere 'shadow of a man', according to one evangelical poet engaged in the pastime of celebrating the dignity of man.[45] There were some dissenting views, including those of Calvin's friend and classmate François Connan, who opened the door to the feudal rights of women; but the majority opinion was in keeping with orthodoxy. Evangelical heroines there were, but among those who might be regarded as professional ideologists – university scholars, theologians and pamphleteers – women figured hardly at all. Women did teach in schools, it is true, but mainly as an extension of their domestic function; and the notion of a woman preacher was as unthinkable as a woman priest, even though Protestants were not bound by the same theological inhibitions against the feminine gender. One woman's proclamation that she was a female 'Christ' was denounced as a 'horrible thing' by Protestants as much for its sexual impropriety as for its theological presumption.[46] In the political sphere religious protest seemed to intensify this prejudice, at least partly as a result of the widely condemned incompetence and villainy (according to Protestant charges) of such figures as Catherine de Médicis, Margaret of Parma and Mary Tudor. In these cases female incompetence was compounded by female malice, but

42 *Commentarii de nobilitate et iure primigeniorum* (Lyon, 1566), 431.
43 *De Lege Salica*, in E. Forcadel, *De Feudis* (Hanover, 1603), 100: 'dignior est masculus quam femina in rebus publicis.'
44 Pierre du Belloy, *Examen du discours . . . sur la loy Salique* (Paris, 1587), 57ff.
45 Barthélemy d'Aneau, *Picta poesis* (Lyon, 1552), 79. Cf. Connan, *Commentariorum Juris Civilis libri X* (Paris, 1553), I, 8.
46 P. Feret, *La Faculté de théologie de Paris*, I (Paris, 1900), 145.

this was a magnification rather than a contradiction of the stereotype, and it was not without precedent. The Biblical model was Jezebel, while in the secular sphere French scholars could point to Queen Brunhild for a vicious and bloodthirsty example. Sensational cases, no doubt, but civil war did bring ordinary anti-feminism to such extremes.

One striking (and ideologically telling) mark of the low esteem in which women were held in certain quarters was the dethroning and vilifying of the Virgin Mary. 'Anti-Marian' blasphemy, a common complaint to the Inquisition in the later middle ages, became even more popular during the sixteenth century.[47] Among the first pro-Lutheran publications in France was a parody of the Sorbonne's characterization of Luther, in which it was sarcastically proposed that Mary was superior to God the Father (an interesting thesis not yet investigated, it would seem, by historians of sexual attitudes); and another satirical work, employing the traditional figure of 'Mother Fool' (*Meresotte*), mocked a book of hours of the Virgin. Probably the most conspicuous sign of heterodoxy in contemporary religious services, aside from dropping the mass, was omitting the 'Ave Maria'. So Farel, for example, signalled his passage from Gallican to evangelical faith; and a host of martyrs gained their credentials by refusing to cry, 'Jesus Maria!'[48] In line with the general progression from vituperation to violence, defacing pictures of the Virgin, or cutting off the nose of her statues, became a popular form of iconoclasm. In general, feminine epithets (next to scatology) were among the commonest forms of abuse. The equation of simony with prostitution made Rome a 'whore' to Luther and the Sorbonne the 'Pope's whoring chamber', while 'Our Holy Mother Whore the Roman Church' was a choice phrase thrown out by Beza in his satirical attack on Pierre Lizet, president of the 'burning chamber' of the Parlement of Paris and arch-persecutor of the French evangelicals.[49]

On the level of popular opinion at least the matter may perhaps be summed up by saying that in the private world women represented the positive virtues of adornment, service and moral strength; in the public world they posed at best a threat to order and at worst a deformation of nature. In most ways, then, the key to sixteenth-century social, religious and political structure – and change – was

---

[47] P. Fredericq (ed.), *Corpus documentorum Inquisitionis haereticae pravatis Neerlandica*, I (Ghent, 1899), *passim*, and see M. Warner, *Alone of all her Sex* (New York, 1976), 285 ff.

[48] Crespin, I, 516, 590; Bulaeus, VI, 180; Anthoine Fromment, *Les Actes et gestes merveilleux de la cité de Genève*, ed. G. Revilliod (Geneva, 1857), 11.

[49] *Le Passavant*, trans. I. Liseaux (Paris, 1875), 84; cf. Luther, cited by W. F. Bense, 'Noel Beda and the Humanist Reformation at Paris' (unpublished Ph.D. thesis, Harvard University, 1967), 316.

the principle of male domination. Europe was still a warrior culture, as Erasmus lamented; and the whole debate over authority and liberty, obedience and resistance, was tied to perceptions and assumptions about lordship and (to use La Perrière's emotive term) 'virility'. Again, religious conflict seemed only to reinforce this tendency. (Essays written 'in praise of beards' celebrated masculinity, but the beard itself seemed to become a symbol of defiance and so was banned not only in the university but also in the Parlement of Paris.)[50] In general, the thrust of the Reformation, and especially the 'magisterial Reformation', was intensely masculine in leadership as well as rhetoric and imagery. God, Pope, priest, king, magistrate, preacher: all of these were men; and so were the rebels who attacked their character and position. All likewise lacked a coequal female partner. In the Reformation, then, sons fought with fathers – symbolically and in reality – and brothers with brothers; and what they fought over, the much abused mystical body of Christendom, was regarded as female, though no longer 'Holy Mother Church'. Lutheranism in particular was a masculine affair; and from it came, according to a great historian of the last century, 'an explosion of anti-feminist and anti-liberal sentiments – war to the knife'.[51]

Within the family masculine supremacy was beyond debating. As Bodin recalled, fathers had the power of life and death. Although the old Roman and Germanic constructions of paternal power (the *patria potestas* and the *mundium*) had been modified in recent times, the father was still, after the divine and royal model, in every sense 'lord', controlling the actions and fates of all members of his household. It was on such grounds, for example, that both clandestine marriage and violation of the father–son relationship were denounced.[52] Bad enough to disappoint paternal ambitions by taking monastic vows, as Luther did; worse to enter the service of a foreign power. Fathers fought, and sued, to protect their offspring from the clutches of the Calvinists on the one hand and the Jesuits on the other. Raemond lamented the Protestant desacramentalizing of marriage which permitted young people to mate without parental consent.[53] On the other side the classic case was that of René

---

50 Among various contributions to the praise-of-beards genre are Pierre Boaistuau, *Bref discours de l'excellence et dignité de l'homme* (Paris, 1559), 12ff., and A. Hotman, *De Barba* (Lyon, 1586).

51 R. Maulde de la Clavière, *The Women of the Renaissance*, trans. G. Ely (London, 1900), 467.

52 Jean de Coras, 'Petit discours sur les marriages contractés par les Enfans sans l'avis, conseil et volunté des Peres', following a new printing (Paris, 1572) of the edict of 1557 (see p. 72 above, n. 38).

53 Raemond, 1032.

Ayrault, who had joined or been taken into the Society of Jesus against the wishes of his father. Pierre Ayrault, who happened to be Lieutenant-criminel of Angers as well as a prominent legal scholar and professed royalist, responded with a scathing criticism of the Society in the form of a pamphlet on 'la puissance paternelle', which was at once an historical sketch and a celebration of the subject. 'This paternal power often has more focus and credit than that of the whole government . . .', he argued, 'more than the magistrate, however organized and armed.'[54]

In a sense, then, the prime source of authority (and so of tyranny) in the sixteenth century, especially in terms of early experience and the immediate substance of life, was not prince or pope but rather father – the original 'papa'. In western history the subordinate and even servile position of children has been a constant condition of life, a central factor in the conflict of generations which at least since Aristotle (or since Homer) has been recognized as an agitating if not a driving force in history. Fathers have always stood for reality and usually for the status quo against the irregular and irresponsible behavior of children; and given the support of laws and institutions, they have usually been successful in preserving at least the semblance of tradition. At certain points in history, however, the struggles of fathers against sons has become intense and widespread, and motives and opportunities for nonconformity have become irresistible. The sixteenth century was a time not only when this happened on a grand scale but also when a rationale and justification for such defiance was formulated. Fatherhood continued to be taken as the ultimate source of authority and meaning; and the Huguenot author of the *Political Discourse* (1574) gave equal ranking to 'these two powers, paternal and civil'.[55] Ultimately, however, Protestants had to subordinate both of them to 'Our Father' in heaven, for to Him, as St Thomas also taught, first allegiance was due (*non est parentis sed ipsius Dei*).[56] Calvin, too, insisted on the fifth commandment to honor the one who shared with divinity the titles of 'father' and 'lord', but he immediately added 'that we are bidden to honor our parents only in the lord'. The unfortunate fact was that earthly fathers were associated with materialism, careerism and the conservatism of

---

[54] 'De la Puissance paternelle', in *Opuscules* (Paris, 1598), 234, and Pasquier, *Les Lettres* (Paris, 1619), xi, 9. Cf. Gaines Post, 'Patriapotestas, regia potestas, and rex imperator', *Explorations in Economic History*, vii (1969), 185–204.

[55] *ME*, iii, fol. 153.

[56] Aquinas's commentary on Peter Lombard's *Sentences*, cited by J. Brissaud, *History of French Private Law*, trans. R. Howell (Boston, 1912), 180.

secular society; and these were precisely the attitudes that stood in need of reform.

In general, paternal power offered the first challenge to as well as model for self-identification, the first obstacle to – if it was not the determinant of – religious awakening. At whatever age and speed it might take place, religious conversion normally erupts in the psychological context of the family, reacting against or reinforced by its values, habits, totems and taboos; and unorthodoxy was an unmistakable challenge to paternal authority. So Luther had taken the initial step, his 'conversion' to monasticism, against the express wishes of his father, who had intended for his son the more lucrative career of a lawyer; and his disobedience troubled him for many years. So it happened with Beza and with his younger friend Hotman, whose father was a royal official attached to the court of the same 'burning chamber' presided over by Lizet and a man who, as Hotman later put it, ended his life 'oppressing a thousand martyrs'.[57] In 1548 Hotman fled Paris without a word and, carefully avoiding the agents sent by his father in pursuit, joined his co-religionists in Geneva. So it must have happened to many young men during the rising tide of emigration in the middle years of the century.

Here we can see one of the first tears in the social fabric arising from religious consciousness – and perhaps some of the first stirrings of the search for a new ideological base. For Luther, as Erik Erikson has argued, the rebellion against his father was the very center of his self-justification; and it formed part of a logical sequence of rejections of authority that ended only when he found a fatherly God whose rule he could accept, and when he could set himself at the head of his own household and religious community. This pattern, which would be repeated many times in the course of Protestant expansion, represents a full and natural cycle of life experience; but in the peculiarly self-generating and mutually reinforcing social movements of the sixteenth century it contributed to an uncontrollable and, in a sense, unnatural process of social change.

Again, direct evidence is scanty, but the massive defection of sons and daughters was surely one of the fundamental elements of historical change in this period. How many left home, or schools, or monasteries, and at what ages, can never be known with accuracy; nor can the overall pattern of religious change. But the increase of discontent and dissension that involved a basic break with blood ties was extraordinary; it began in the 1520s and continued over the next

[57] Letter to Melanchthon, 24 May 1556, in D. R. Kelley, *François Hotman: A Revolutionary's Ordeal* (Princeton, 1973), 47.

two generations. A prominent example was the great printing dynasty, the Estiennes, which developed a Genevan as well as a Parisian branch when Robert fled from censorship problems in 1549. Another was the family of Estienne's most famous author and indeed (with Erasmus) the greatest scholar of his age. Guillaume Budé, who had applauded the policy of persecuting the 'sacramentarians' after the affair of the placards, died in 1540 and so was perhaps spared the knowledge that similar heresy had infected his own household. In 1547 his wife, urged by Calvin himself to flee the 'Babylon' which France had become, emigrated with four of her sons to the new Jerusalem that Geneva had become. In the 1550s there was a growing traffic of such disillusioned or defiant souls making their ways to Geneva, Strasbourg, Basel and other independent havens. In the three years from 1549 to 1552 Geneva received over 300 new 'inhabitants', including scholars, lawyers and especially printers (at least 13); and among those officially registered were Laurent de Normandie, Jean Budé, Conrad Badius, Guillaume de Trie (brother-in-law of Budé, informer on Servetus, and later a casualty of the Conspiracy of Amboise), Robert Estienne, Claude Baduel, Jean Crespin and perhaps, the next year, Jean Bodin ('de sainct Amand, diocese de Bourges'). It was to stem this tide that in 1551 Henry II issued the notorious Edict of Chateaubriand, but the effort was useless except as an expression of official propaganda.[58]

These are only a few examples of the familial and social dislocation of the sixteenth century, and of the mentality of alienation and defiance underlying the struggles of that age. Among the by-products of this estrangement arose who knows what tensions, resentments and feelings of guilt? Of one of Viret's converts an orthodox chronicler reported that it had been accomplished 'to the great regret of his father and brothers' and that he 'resembled the cuckoo which devours the mother that nourishes it'.[59] Yet a younger generation of defectors had recourse to a different value-system. A song was sung about an orthodox mother who had informed on her daughter and repented her action only when the girl faced execution.[60]

> Said the mother, 'My child, go straight to mass.'
> 'The mass', she replied, 'is only abuse.

---

[58] See below, p. 200, n. 57. And cf. *Livre des habitants de Genève*, I, ed. P. Geisendorf (Geneva, 1957), 1–24; later, the figures increase, and in the crucial year 1559, for example, over 1600 incoming French *habitants* are listed.

[59] H. Vuilleumier, *Histoire de l'église réformée du pays de Vaud* (Lausanne, 1927), 61.

[60] B. Vaurigaud, *Essai sur l'histoire des églises réformées de Bretagne* (Paris, 1870), I, 6–7.

Bring my books with my holy vows.
I had rather burn, my ashes scattered,
Than go to mass and break my oath.'

Such martyrly self-righteousness further intensified the gulf between generations.

Behind these attitudes, of course, there were more material, social and economic problems. In France there is a huge record of family divisions, disinheritances and confiscations reflecting a fundamental social disruption a generation before the civil wars. Undeniably there had always been uprooted individuals, homeless vagrants, 'free preachers' and other potential social and religious incendiaries; but never before had there been such a coherent movement involving a presumably stable bourgeois, noble, office- and land-holding society; and this phenomenon made an indelible impact on the soul as well as the face of Europe. Beza paid for his decision by losing his patrimony and enduring the disgrace of being burned in effigy. Hotman also, as Calvin acknowledged, 'abandoned the hope of a fine inheritance in order to fight for Christ';[61] and so it was with many others over the next half-century in the face of repeated legislation ordering the confiscation of the property of heretics, normally reserving a portion of it to any successful informer. Families like the Budés and Hotmans were set against one another. While François Hotman and his son Jean were serving Protestant interests abroad, for example, his brothers and cousins in Paris were actively supporting the Catholic League. One brother was responsible for the defection of Hotman's fourth son Daniel, who was naturally himself disinherited (and later became a member of the Oratory). And there are other examples of this sort of tragic cycle, which agitated social and religious ferment with another more fundamental rhythm based upon blood.

FROM COGNATION TO CONFESSION

If emergent religious and social consciousness could have a shattering impact on particular families, in other ways it reinforced kinship patterns and raised them to a higher or at least more public plane. The result was a shift of emphasis from the relationships of what jurists called cognation to the ideological ties of a common religious confession – a kind of sublimation of blood into belief. This rather intangible process seems to give further support to the thesis referred to earlier, that the distinguishing feature of Protestantism,

[61] Kelley, *Hotman*, 46.

especially the sacramentarian and Calvinist varieties, was its attachment to the principle of 'transcendence', an attitude which purported to restore the idea of the holy – and the community based thereon – to a metahistorical and immaterial level.[62] It was in pursuit of this ideal, consciously or unconsciously, that evangelical reformers devoted themselves to repudiating manifestations of the contrary principle of 'immanence', that is, to purifying the church and in particular the sacramental system linking humanity and divinity. 'Transcendence' provided the rationale of Luther's first act of theological subversion, which was his attack on the Romanist notion of penance as a prescribed act rather than a state of mind and conscience; it provided the rationale, too, of the more general assault on the 'abomination of the mass' as a carnal indulgence rather than a spiritual experience or memorial; and so it underlay both of these symbolic acts repudiating manifestations of 'immanence' – the posting of Luther's theses of 1517 and of the placards of 1534. This shift from immanence to transcendence was recapitulated on the level of individual psychology, in a sense, by the transfer of allegiance from family to flock.

Concomitantly and analogously with this shift, the family itself came to be supplanted by a sort of spiritualized domestic community, which, though constituted on other than blood lines, nevertheless preserved some of the psychology and morality of kin relationships. In this process, commonly accompanying the conversion experience, the most essential step was the transcending of fatherhood – the replacing of one's natural progenitor, as far as life-values and goals were concerned, by a more fulfilling source of authority and purpose. The general pattern, again illustrated by Luther, was the adoption of an elder mentor or confessor whose function was to enlighten and to point the way to salvation, and finally the discovery of the nature of ultimate Fatherhood in the first person of the Trinity. Here, in transcendent form, we can see the reconciliation of paternity and filiality so often denied to humanity. In like manner brotherhood was redefined on confessional rather than cognative grounds. So in a sense was marriage, which Protestant doctrine not only 'desacramentalized' and freed from such superstitions as the notion of 'spiritual cognation' but also in some ways extricated from family control through ministerial influence and at least inadvertently through the device of 'clandestine marriage'. The tendency was to replace kinship with ideology as the basis of the closest and most enduring community.

In various ways the transition from family to flock is apparent in

62 Besides Guy Swanson, *Religion and Regime* (Ann Arbor, 1967), see J. Fisher, *Christian Initiation in the Reformation Period* (London, 1970), and J. McNeill, *A History of the Cure of Souls* (New York, 1951).

theology and in what Joachim Wach called 'the integrating power of worship'. In the church service domestic imagery came to replace Hellenic or Latinate affectation; and so, for instance, arose the 'Lord's supper' (*Nachtmal, Cene,* as distinguished from the hated, hierocratic mass).[63] This communal experience was a spiritual feeding which, like baptism, did honor to divine paternity and also signified the filial relationship of worshippers. Primordially, the eucharist had been a blood sacrifice; but under the spiritualizing influence of Pauline theology the carnal aspects of this sacrament were modified and even, for extreme sacramentalists like Zwingli, eliminated altogether. In more than one sense, then, the bloodthirsty god was domesticated, and indeed sublimated. In any case the meaning of the eucharist, according to Calvin, was that 'God has received us, once for all into his family, to hold us not as servants but as sons.'[64] So God provided not only nourishment but also – the much debated point where Zwingli departed from Luther and Calvin – in some sense his 'presence', as any good father must do, though Calvin was careful to reject the 'blasphemy' that transformed a private experience into a public spectacle and made it a priestly monopoly instead of a fraternal sharing.

The replacement of cognation by confession can also be seen in the interpretation which Calvin placed on the only other sacrament accepted without qualification. Baptism established the essential bond of the extended confessional family which Calvin's church came to resemble, and indeed it was the spiritual counterpart of birth itself. According to Calvin, baptism was 'the sign of initiation by which we are received into the society of the church, in order that, engulfed in Christ, we may be reckoned among God's children'.[65] Thereby, he instructed in his catechism, 'we have a testimony that we, otherwise strangers and aliens, were received into the family of God, so that we are reckoned among his household'. In a sense baptism represented a sort of social compact, a sign of membership in an Elect which encompassed group consciousness in the widest temporal and geographical sense, a covenant in which children also participated. This is why, despite logical and scriptural difficulties, baptism had to be defended against radical advocates of adult baptism, the anabaptists or catabaptists as Calvin called them, who appeared to deny the mystical body of Christ and the reality of Christian brotherhood as well as the legitimacy of secular government. The Elect was not a doctrinal club but a spiritual family.

In conscious terms the nascent ideology of this spiritual family was

---

[63] Bucer, *De Regno Christi,* II, 15; in Pauck (ed.), *Melanchthon and Bucer.*
[64] *Institutes,* III, vii.   [65] *Ibid.* Cf. J. Wach, *Sociology of Religion* (Chicago, 1944), 39.

expressed in a most direct and elementary fashion in that traditional medieval genre, the catechism, again as reformed by Luther and others. To the conventional 'Apostles' ' Creed, the Lord's Prayer and (from the thirteenth century) the Ten Commandments, Luther added chapters on baptism, the Lord's Supper and confession: and the results finally were his big and little catechisms of 1529. According to Bucer, the first purpose of the catechism was to protect children from Satan. Calvin's famous Genevan catechism of 1545, advertised as an intellectual counterpart of baptism and a cornerstone of religious unity, was in form a dialogue between a child and a minister and consisted of a litany of doctrinal points, reflecting complete accord between generations.[66] It followed exactly the fourfold arrangement of the *Institutes*, and indeed of the Apostles' Creed repeated at the outset of the discussion; that is, Father, Son, Holy Spirit and church. The principle of paternalism again seems dominant. 'What is the end of human life?', the minister first asks. 'That men should know God by Whom they are created', the child responds. We are set on earth to know our Father and to be faithful to him, and we call Him 'Father' because He stands in that relationship to Christ, hence to all mankind. Thence the questioning proceeds to topics of theology, law, prayer, the sacraments and the government of the church: everything a Christian needs to know, from cradle to grave.

The emphasis on family spirit and fellowship can be seen in the reformed church of Strasbourg after the liturgical reforms introduced by Martin Bucer at just the time that this independent city was becoming a haven for French evangelicals.[67] Matthias Zell had been preaching the gospel and defending Luther since 1521, but it was not for another three years that the 'German mass' was initiated by his assistant, Diobald Schwarz. Shortly thereafter Bucer took over the task of giving coherence to the Argentine flocks and making them into a true community in Christ (*gemein Christ*). Invocation of saints and the Virgin was discarded, and so was the display of images. Confession, the 'Confiteor', was no longer mumbled by a priest but pronounced audibly by the entire congregation; and like Luther, Bucer encouraged the singing of hymns. There were other signs of domestic informality: use of the vernacular, lay participation in

[66] J. Courvoisier, 'Les Catéchismes de Genève et de Strasbourg', *BSHPF*, LXXXIV (1935), 105–21. Cf. *Le Sommaire de Guillaume Farel*, ed. J. Baum (Geneva, 1867; 1st edn, 1525), summarized in S. Ozment, *The Reformation in the Cities* (New Haven, Conn., 1975), 69–70.
[67] G. van de Poll, *Martin Bucer's Liturgical Ideas* (Assen, 1954), and F. Wendel, *L'Eglise de Strasbourg* (Paris, 1942).

partaking of bread and wine, discarding of clerical robes, and especially rejection of clerical celibacy. In pursuit of the ideal of the priesthood of all believers, emphasis was not on ritual and propriety but on brotherhood and morale, for example through silent prayer. Congregations were also asked to pray for the civil authorities and to attend special meetings in times of political crisis, especially during the Schmalkaldic wars. Community feeling was essential to worship, for as Bucer asked, 'He who does not love his brother . . . how can he praise God?'[68]

Such communal spirit was even more conspicuous in the Calvinist church in exile, which, in Geneva and elsewhere, was in many ways modelled on that of Strasbourg. In 1553 a certain Antoine Cathelan, writing under the sarcastic pseudonym 'Passevent' (borrowed perhaps from that taken by Beza a little earlier for similar libellous purposes), visited the Calvinist colony of Lausanne; and two years later he published his impressions which, despite the disparaging tone, offer valuable insights.[69] The simplicity of the ceremonial, bordering on rudeness, seemed to Cathelan designed to mock God. The people, he noted, 'all called each other brothers and sisters'. Their church was like a classroom, with bare benches and without ornament. Their preachers, poor as friars, affected lay attire like advocates and gave direct instruction, omitting the 'Ave Maria' but regularly leading the singing of psalms. Three or four times a year they held their commemorative 'supper', to which children of eight or ten came. Neither marriage nor baptism called for external pomp. A single 'Je vous baptise' sufficed for a large number of children, and of course names were taken from the Bible rather than the saints' calendar. Perhaps the most remarkable expression of communal feelings was the extreme and carefully cultivated prejudice against all forms of popery, real and imagined. The mass continued to be the ultimate symbol of corruption: brothers and sisters 'went to sermon'; going to mass was slang for visiting the public privy. Anyone who had 'testified for the brothers and the church', as the saying went, perhaps by suffering imprisonment, was welcomed, wrote Cathelan; all others were regarded as papists, idolaters, spies and enemies of the faith. We should not even eat with the openly wicked, Calvin advised his adherents. Such were the demands made upon, such the attitudes generated by, that 'greedy institution', the religious community.

The familial character of this community is illustrated perhaps

---

[68] *De Regno Christi*, I, 2. 9.
[69] *Passevent Parisien Respondant à Pasquin Romain* (Paris, 1875; 1st edn, 1556), 3, *passim*.

most clearly in the paternal role assumed by the pastor, or *antistes*. For evangelical religion did not discard but rather reshaped and secularized the conventional cure of souls (*cura animarum*). 'This human ministry . . .', according to Calvin, 'is the chief sinew by which believers are held together in one body.'[70] In fulfilment of this, Luther and Calvin became not only charismatic leaders but also surrogate consciences and providers for their flocks, in many ways playing father to their extended confessional households. Calvin in particular fed and housed visitors, gave them refuge, counseled them, recommended them for positions, sometimes found wives for them and often continued such solicitude for years. In return, of course, these informally beneficed disciples served Calvin as sources of information and, directly or indirectly, as missionaries, publicity agents and even ambassadors. The flood of propaganda later in the sixteenth century was much indebted to the quasi-familial, confessional network centering on Calvin's paternalistic activities of an earlier period.

Many young men found a father-substitute in Calvin after his permanent installation in Geneva in 1541. Among the earliest and most prominent were Beza and those archetypal sibling rivals, François Baudouin and François Hotman. The relationship between these two competitive protégés of Calvin offers a striking illustration of squabbling over paternal approval and confessional inheritance.[71] In 1545 Baudouin, in flight from his native Arras and in the company of Jean Crespin, came to Geneva, where he swore filial as well as doctrinal fidelity to Calvin; and for a year he served Calvin – 'mi Pater', he addressed him – as secretary before finding a more permanent position as professor of law at the University of Bourges. After fleeing paternal tyranny in Paris in 1547, Hotman followed very much in Baudouin's footsteps, likewise serving Calvin as amanuensis and even more insistently declaring his filial sentiments. 'I have loved no one more', he told Calvin, 'not even my father.' Calvin may have had a hand in Hotman's choice of a wife; he was certain he was responsible for placing him in his first professional position, which was teaching in the Protestant academy of Lausanne. So it happened also to Beza, who in fact accompanied Hotman to Lausanne to begin his own career, under the supervision of Calvin's friend and colleague Pierre Viret, as a teacher and above all as a Calvinist agent.

Of all Calvin's confessional brood, Beza clearly emerged as the

---

[70] *Institutes*, IV, iii; cf. J. Benoit, *Calvin directeur d'âmes* (Strasbourg, 1947).
[71] Kelley, *Hotman*, 47ff.

favorite son and finally successor to the Genevan patrimony. Hotman came in for a certain share, ideologically speaking; but since his chosen career was law instead of theology, he moved further away from the Calvinist family circle and made different use of the confessional legacy. On the other hand Baudouin, following the same path, fell into disfavor and was not only formally disinherited but was also the victim of endless attacks by his former brethren, especially Hotman and Beza.[72] The feud between Baudouin and Hotman was in part personal (charges of plagiarism) and in part professional (Baudouin lost his chair of law at Strasbourg to Hotman in 1556 as a result of Calvinist intrigues), but Calvin had more serious charges. While Hotman was teaching Latin to children in Lausanne and making himself useful by evangelizing or taking over Beza's classes to free him for more important missions, Baudouin was selfishly pursuing a scholarly career at the University of Bourges. His confessional defection was displayed not only in 'nicodemitism', since he attended mass while still pretending to be a Calvinist, but also in his efforts to define a moderate religious and political program independent of Calvin. Worst of all, however, was Baudouin's personal betrayal of Calvin, amounting to a sort of confessional parricide committed against the man whom he had once called 'father'. He was truly a black sheep in Calvin's flock.

The ideological conflict which grew out of this domestic quarrel became a major public issue during the religious wars, but the original quasi-familial pattern was in some respects preserved. Baudouin became weary of the intolerance and tribal attitude – the 'Calvinolatry' – of his former comrades. In the style rather of Erasmus and Melanchthon he favored a more oecumenical, hence vaguer, conception of Christianity; and he continued to promote his 'irenic' program even in the 1560s as violence mounted and civil war loomed. Of course it was hopeless – even Melanchthon became a casualty of the irresistible descent into partisanship – and Baudouin ended by returning to Gallican orthodoxy. For their part, the Calvinists continued to rage against the apostate black sheep, and they did this, characteristically, with the most personal kind of vilification. Baudouin was accused of being a 'hermaphrodite', for example, not only because of his presumably unmasculine indecisiveness and anemic faith but because of his unmarried state. The tone of this controversy was reminiscent of nothing so much as that between Luther and Baudouin's countryman Erasmus, except that tempers and ideological stakes were raised to a higher and more

[72] Kelley, *Foundations*, chapter v.

dangerous level. Baudouin remained an anachronism, a throw-back to the old 'spiritual and interior reformation', as he was still writing during the religious wars, 'which is otherwise called Regeneration'.[73] He was a 'mediator' in a period when there could be no mediation, an idealist in a world of ideologues.

After the massacres of St Bartholomew of 1572 and after Baudouin's death the next year these controversies were still going on, and with a still sharper political edge, as Hotman engaged in a polemical duel with Baudouin's disciple Papire Masson over another and more complicated phase of the ideological debate – and in a literary sense accentuated his arguments by dancing on the grave of his one-time friend and confessional brother. By that time both cognation and confession had been superseded by another ideological community which civil war made into one of the most greedy of all 'greedy institutions' – the Party, which of course had its own claims upon conscience and its own familial overtones.

The connections between familial and religious groups, between kinship and congregation, are many and often explicit. Yet the attempt wholly to replace the first by the second is ultimately inhuman and destructive. In the course of time the mutual reinforcement of the two is a conspicuous feature of a flourishing ideological movement; for it is the function of religion traditionally to build upon and, in a spiritual and universalizing way, to extend positive family patterns. It is time now to examine this socializing function and turn more specifically from family to flock.

---

[73] *Advis de François Balduin jurisconsulte, sur le faict de la Reformation de l'eglise* (n.p., n.d.; BN D. 12839). There is at last a modern critical biography: Michael Erbe, *François Bauduin (1520–1573)* (Gütersloh, 1978).

III · Flock:
Cultivating the faith

Semen ecclesiae sanguis christianorum.

Tertullian (Jean Crespin)

L'Evangile soit semence de rebellion.

Anon. (1577)

III · Flock:
Cultivating the faith

APOLOGUE: THE AFFAIR OF THE RUE ST JACQUES (1557)

On Thursday evening, 4 September 1557, a group of some 400 Parisians gathered in a house in the university quarter, on the street of booksellers near the Sorbonne, to hold religious services. The Bible was read in French, a minister offered prayer, and communion was given to those who felt worthy of it. Then there were more prayers for the king, his realm, and for the church, and the meeting closed with the singing of psalms. Though illegal, it was a conventional-sounding ceremony, like many others during these years of war and economic stagnation. But the context was not normal. Paris was on edge because of the news of the Spanish victory at St Quentin less than a month before and the subsequent breach of the frontier, which in fact may have helped to inspire this gathering of Protestants. And, less than six weeks before, the king had published the notorious Edict of Compiègne, reaffirming the policy of persecution. In this atmosphere of growing unrest, official intransigence and long-festering prejudice, the assembly on the rue St Jacques precipitated a confrontation more ominous than the affair of the placards twenty-three years earlier.[1]

As so often before the volatile character of the university provided the spark. Some priests associated with the College of Plessy across the street, who had for some time been on the lookout for such trouble-makers, gathered to block the entrance to the house, attracting a growing crowd of sympathizers. They started bonfires in the street, collected a supply of rocks, and set up a cry against the 'robbers and conspirators' within. Learning that they were merely 'Lutherans' only infuriated the mob further. Those trapped inside feared that a massacre was in the making, and they renewed their prayers, this time for their own safety. Some, with the help of a few gentlemen who had brought their swords, decided to make a run for it; and many were successful, though a number were wounded and

---

[1] Jehan de Fosse, *Journal d'un curé ligueur de Paris*, ed. E. de Barthélemy (Paris, 1866), 31ff.; *HE*, I, 139ff.; Crespin, I, 543ff.; La Vacquerie, *Catholique remonstrance . . .* (Paris, 1560), 37; cf. L. Romier, *Les Origines politiques des guerres de religion*, I (Paris, 1913), 254, listing the names.

one was stoned to death. The remainder, mostly women and children, waited for the city police to arrive, hoping for protection if not sympathy. When they arrived, the *procureur royal* Martine made an investigation on the spot and, being told of the clandestine ceremony, arrested the hundred or more 'Lutherans' and had them dragged immediately off to prison, some of them suffering further indignities *en route*. The culprits were put together in crowded quarters, where they continued their prayers and psalm-singing.

Legal proceedings began in an atmosphere of extreme prejudice – not that there was any doubt of guilt. Rumor had it that the Protestants had been engaged in a sexual orgy and in eating small children; but the official charge, as usual, was that they were taking part in 'illicit assemblies', heresy, and therefore sedition. The king gave prosecution of this group first priority, and before the month was out seven of them had been executed. Two of them were students, two lawyers, one a physician, another a young lady named Philippe de Luns. About her Beza told an atrocity story to match any Sorbonist concoction: her tongue was cut out and her genitals burnt with a torch before her final execution. The rest, aside from a few who recanted, stayed in jail. If the Cardinal of Lorraine had had his way, it was said, these too would have been done away with. Henry II would not go so far, but neither would he listen to the pleas of the Protestant cantons of Switzerland and the Rhine Palatinate, which had been solicited by Calvin, Beza, and others. Some of the prisoners eventually escaped; others, especially the younger students, were sent off to various monasteries in the hope of reconverting them.

In the end nothing was resolved. A small pamphlet war emerged in the wake of the affair. Orthodox critics accused the culprits of rebellion and atheism and of trying to burn the Sorbonne's books. As usual apologists were put on the defensive and, instead of justifying themselves, had to deny these extreme charges. Calvin himself was much moved and declared that soon 'the whole kingdom will be in flames'.[2]

In the generation between the first reverberations of the Lutheran word in France and the still nominally 'Lutheran' gatherings in the 1550s there had been a fundamental transformation in the pattern of religious behavior. Out of transient and sporadic dissidence the 'so-called reformed religion' had created a coherent movement and an almost corporate organization. Preaching and the pastoral func-

---

[2] Letter to prisoners in Paris, Sept. 1557, *CO*, XVI (no. 2716).

tion, ritual and routine had drawn congeries of stray believers into self-conscious and structured congregations; charisma (in Weberian terms) had been replaced by comradeship. In this process confessional agreement had come in many ways to cut across both age and class lines. The group that dared to hold services in the very shadow of the Sorbonne was not made up of 'people of low condition', as Francis I had characterized those involved in the affair of the placards, but men, women, and children 'of every rank', including sword-bearing gentlemen and university graduates.[3] One of them was François Budé, son of the man who was France's greatest classical scholar and a devoted servant of the crown – and who would surely have been shocked at his son's impropriety and religious inclination. Spiritual communion and group identification were overshadowing class, generational and educational differences, at least in this period of expansion and euphoria.

The flock still needed its pastor, of course, and needed the discipline of instruction from above. Sermons continued to be essential in giving direction and focus to belief. Yet for the most part they were designed to reassure the converted, not to cavil with the doubtful. The vital principle of the congregation was mutual reinforcement. The essential activities of the service were communal, not a priestly sacrament, an elitist mystery vouchsafed to a passive laity, but a shared experience; and as such they seemed quite contrary to the habits of hierarchy sanctioned by the ecclesiastical establishment. Common reading of scriptures in the vernacular, which was in itself suspect; singing psalms in the prohibited translations of Marot and Beza, which was more so; offering up prayers, no doubt for the propagation of the faith as well as preservation of the realm; reciting a confession of faith, as a sign of allegiance; and joining in communion in a most reprehensible style – these were all effective but unorthodox means of promoting a collective spirit. Each congregation so assembled was a society with its own rules and ideals, living in a world apart – and as such a clear and present danger to its host culture.

The public nature of this danger was becoming more evident every day. Just two years before the affair of the rue St Jacques, the first reformed church of Paris had been formed, and in the wake of the commotion Nicolas de Gallars arrived from Geneva to direct its fortunes. It was in these months, too, that the French church began to acquire support from the higher nobility, notably from the King of

---

[3] [A. de Chandieu], *Histoire des persecutions et martyrs de l'eglise de Paris depuis l'an 1557* (Lyon, 1563), xxxix.

Navarre, the Prince of Condé, and Coligny's brother François d'Andelot, who had first seen the light in a Spanish prison after his capture during the battle of St Quentin. The high morale of Parisian Protestants was demonstrated even more vocally during the spring of 1558, when one section of the university grounds (the Pré-aux-clercs) became the scene of regular gathering at which psalms, in the proscribed translations of Marot and Beza, were sung by growing numbers of people, perhaps up to 10,000. And just a year later the first national synod of the French reformed religion was held in Paris.

What was in the process of creation, in short, was not merely a sect but a new church, with all of the mystical, communal and political connotations possessed by this emotive term in the sixteenth century. Both sides acknowledged it. The prisoners taken in the rue St Jacques claimed to represent 'la vraye eglise', while an official critic, the theologian and Celtophile historian Robert Ceneau, felt it necessary to dispute the point.[4] The symbol of this 'false church' was a loaded gun which pointed the way to hell, he wrote, while the sign of the true, the Gallican church was a bell whose sweet sounds opened the gates of heaven. Neither simile seems entirely appropriate; but despite the passive demeanor of those arrested, there was certainly an aggressive potential in the system of beliefs of the reformed religion. Perhaps the first source of this was their own intransigence, or counter-intransigence, which was based upon a fear of hypocrisy and an obsessive need to bear witness. Even more crucial was the absolute rejection of Romanism, the church of antichrist, and all its material trappings and entrapments. It would not be long before such revulsion took the classic form of image-smashing – which leaders such as Beza would justify. Such physical reactions to Catholic assumptions of an 'immanent' church did indeed push heresy to the point of sedition.

Perhaps the most ominous aspect of the religious upheavals of this time was the international repercussions – and more specifically the Genevan reactions. Gaspar Carmel brought the news of the affair of the rue St Jacques to Calvin, who responded by sending several of his agents to ask the Protestant cantons of Switzerland and the soon-to-be-Calvinized Rhine Palatinate to intercede with Henry II. Among these agents were Beza, Farel, and Jean Budé, brother of the imprisoned François; and though their mission was not a conspicuous success, it does show the extent of international sympathy and publicity. Not only Calvin but also the Company of Pastors of

---

[4] *Response catholique contre les heretiques de ce temps* (Paris, 1562).

Geneva sent letters of consolation to those in prison. Once again, too, Calvin appealed to the king in the form of a brief confession of faith on behalf on the 'society of the faithful' and the 'true church'. The last of these articles (and Calvin directed his copyists to see that it was so placed) declared that 'we are bound to obey their laws and statutes, pay tribute, taxes, and other imposts' as long as religion is preserved; but his expectation of royal mercy was obviously not high, and he counseled his Parisian brethren to prepare themselves for the ultimate and most irrevocable form of ideological commitment – martyrdom.

Flock: cultivating the faith

As the horizons of kinship were expanded by conscience to encompass a community based upon a common faith – as family was supplanted by flock – so values, goals, relationships and means of communication were modified; and a new world of consciousness was created. Concurrently, as this consciousness became a social force – as 'confession' became a social rather than merely a private concern – so religious ideas were transformed into a form of ideology. The emphasis was shifted from the old auricular confession to the more public *exomologesis*. 'Confession is demonstrating publicly that you consent in no way to idolatry', declared one Huguenot pamphleteer on the eve of the wars of religion, 'and communicating to others the same doctrine that you embrace.'[5] In some ways the form of one's credo, or credimus, became as important as social status; and this doctrinal *carte d'identité* affected the very quality of the historical process in the sixteenth century. Never were religious changes – conversions, reversions and deviations – so common; and never were signs of religious affiliation – baptism, profession or recantation of faith and church attendance – so much insisted upon. In general the sublimated family that was the confessional group became a polemical and proselytizing cause (*Calvinista causa*, in the words of one critic) and a primary, indeed a revolutionary, source of historical change.

The social basis of this embryonic ideology was most immediately the 'congregation', the term used by Erasmus to designate the church of primitive Christianity, connoting a community of souls united in belief rather than the structured and hierocratic *ecclesia* of canon law. This spiritualized redefinition was urged by Protestants not only as the preferred translation of the Biblical term but also as an ecclesiological and social ideal. Not the Romanist hierarchy but the Augustinian 'congregation of the faithful' (*congregatio fidelium*) or even 'communion of saints' (*communio sanctorum*) was the model of reformation; and so in place of the princely terminology of papal doctrine the dominant image became that of shepherd and flock. Pastoral theology, the art of the care and feeding of sheep, assumed a new importance.[6] The key to this new social unit, the reformed congregation, was collective self-consciousness, and to this the reduced and 'disenchanted' system of sacraments was accommodated. As penance became 'evangelical' instead of 'legal', according to Luther's distinction, so the eucharist became (in the view of Protestant critics) a collective experience rather than a superstitious

[5] *Traité du devoir des princes* (n.p., 1561; BN Ld 176.16), 3.
[6] J. McNeill, *A History of the Cure of Souls* (New York, 1951).

ritual. Baptism, too, appears as a reflection of social consciousness, being defined variously as 'a good conscience before men', as 'true penance' and, in Calvin's words, as 'the mark by which we publicly confess that we wish to be reckoned God's people . . ., by which we openly defend our faith'.[7]

The forms of self-expression of the evangelical cult ranged from the most elevated theological concepts to the most invidious name-calling, from the most structured discourse to the most spontaneous violence; and the generation of ideology ought to be understood through the whole range of such demonstrations of commitment. The life principle of the 'Calvinist cause' in particular was the need to express, to communicate, to penetrate the consciences of others; and its goals included denunciation of the popish enemy as well as evangelical self-advertisement and aggrandizement. The impulse to bear public witness was further reinforced by the need to avoid that most deplorable error, Nicodemitism. All of these incentives and inhibitions, these totems and taboos, left their mark on the more deliberate propaganda and official reactions which constituted the public face of ideology – and which, in surviving written form, represent the foundation of this study.

Not that we must be bound entirely to the printed page, for in fact some sources illustrate ideological behavior that was not exclusively bookish. There is, for example, no more direct expression of the inner harmony and solidarity of a religious community than its music and, as both Luther and Calvin believed, no better way to praise God. The congregational singing of psalms and hymns, in contrast to the priestly chant, spread rapidly and widely. From the early 1520s Lutheran hymns could be heard in Antwerp as well as Strasbourg and other German cities; and from Strasbourg, through melodies as well as lyrics, musical influence penetrated to French-speaking areas. The 'siren song' of the psalms (as one Catholic critic referred to them), especially in the translation of Clement Marot and Beza, represented the most influential of all verbal propaganda aside from the New Testament.[8] In 1531 those of Marot were banned from the university and later, with those of Beza, were subjected to more severe censorship. To Protestants psalm-singing was the most direct communication of all, and on the eve of the religious wars the practice was recommended to the Queen Mother, Catherine de Médicis herself, as the door to evan-

---

[7] *Institutes*, IV, XV.

[8] P. Beuzart, *Les Hérésies pendant le moyen âge et la Réforme* (Paris, 1912), 221; P. de Félice, *Les Protestants d'autrefois* (Paris, 1897), I, 53; E. Baie, *Le Siècle des Gueux*, II (Brussels, 1932), 242; Crevier, V, 258.

gelical understanding. Some were prophetic and perhaps self-fulfilling:

> I am afflicted and ready to die
> From my youth up.[9]

Of course psalms could inflame as well as mourn or enlighten, as exemplified by the notorious 'hymn to violence' of Beza:

> And He shall bring down upon them their own iniquity;
> And shall cut them down in their own wickedness;
> Yea, the Lord our God shall cut them off.

This particular implicit attack upon the Catholic party eventually brought Beza into court to defend himself before the Genevan authorities.

Popular enthusiasm for evangelical religion burst forth in other more scandalous musical forms. As early as 1525 the Parlement of Paris heard complaints about disrespectful *chansons*, but there was no way to stop the chorus of musical defiance. So it was, too, in the Netherlands, where the 'Beggars' Song Book' (*Guezenliedboek*) was the counterpart to the Huguenot *Chansonnier*. Songs about the mass, songs about the Ten Commandments, songs mourning martyrs like Anne du Bourg, songs 'demonstrating the many errors and falsities' in established religion – all these reflected and reinforced the evangelical movement and its growing alienation from orthodox society. Vulgar and sometimes offensive songs chronicled and celebrated many of the major figures and episodes of the new doctrines, often in satirical or scurrilous fashion. One early lyric alluded to the preaching of Michel d'Arande, friend of Lefèvre d'Etaples and member of the circle of Meaux reformers before his return to orthodoxy.

> Don't preach the gospel, Master Michel;
> The danger's too great of landing in jail.

Another attended to the conversion of the 'poor ignorant papists'.[10]

---

[9] Psalms, 94; 23; cf. 88.
[10] Bordier, xv, 97:

> Paovres papistes retournez vous
>   A Jesus qui est mort pour nous.
> Paovres papistes debonnaire
> Qui desirez a Jesus plaire
> Vostre ignorance a trop duré
> Trop avez d'erreurs enduré
> Paovres papistes . . . etc.

From confession to cause

Your ignorance is too deep,
Too long have you lived in error.
Poor Papists return
To Jesus, who died for us.

During the civil wars popular music came to parallel and sometimes to repeat the propaganda of the Huguenot party. It came also to reflect the sensational stories of the times, including assassinations and massacres, and may represent more immediately the climate of opinion and feeling than less spontaneous expressions of hope and fear. Musical behavior is closer not only to emotion but perhaps also to action.

Even before the outbreak of war, music and militancy became increasingly frequent companions. In the 1530s the psalm-singing crowds were common in the Pré-aux-clercs in the Latin quarter of Paris, and sometimes there was violence, as during the May Day celebrations of students. In Rouen people sang songs to ridicule the monks, and both there and in Toulouse the Parlements reported that the singing led to rioting.[11] In Montauban a priest who had taught people to sing psalms was imprisoned, and a crowd of his admirers attacked the jail. From the late 1550s such incidents became more common and widespread. In Paris great lords joined the students in singing in the Pré-aux-clercs. Crowds regularly thronged the streets of Antwerp, singing their way to the sermons of Guy de Brès or Pierre Dathenus, generating excitement even before being stirred by the spoken word. In 1560 in Valenciennes the psalms of Marot and other 'impious songs' were sung and seemed to constitute such a threat to public order that they were banned the next day. In that same year, too, a leading anti-Protestant pamphleteer offered a 'counter-poison' to the false psalms of 'Marot Lutheriste'.[12] Psalm-singing reached a crescendo in the pre-war years. It figured in the affair of the rue St Jacques in 1557; again the next year, a few blocks west, in the turmoil in the Pré-aux-clercs; in 1560 accompanying the conspiracy of Amboise; and then in the 'massacre of Vassy', which most observers took as the opening incident of the religious wars. During these wars the singing of psalms continued to be a heated issue, and at most the practice was legally permitted in private homes. Clearly it had become a public menace.

Of course the martial spirit echoing in Protestant music took more concrete form in these agitated times – sometimes to the detriment of the other fine arts. Of the sacramentarians Raemond complained

---

[11] A. Floquet, *Histoire du Parlement de Normandie* (Rouen, 1840), II, 310; J. B. Dubédat, *Histoire du Parlement de Toulouse* (Paris, 1885), I, 342.
[12] Artus Desiré, *Le Contrepoison des cinquante deux Chansons de Clement Marot* (Paris, 1560), Aiiii.

that the 'principal object of their revolt' was the 'images which they wrongly term "idols"'.[13] Through such hatred of 'idolatry' and 'superstition' the cult of purified religion was easily transformed, by the temperaments of some enthusiasts, into a cult of violence. Iconoclasm, the most direct physical assault on the principle of 'immanence', was a time-honored practice, and sixteenth-century authorities were no strangers to the problem. In 1503 one misguided soul had thrown the host on the ground and stamped on it in the Sainte Chapelle, practically in the presence of the Parlement of Paris; and to one eighteenth-century historian he was a by no means unusual 'precursor of the promoters of Luther and Calvin'.[14] From the 1520s such behavior became chronic and, in reformed territories, even condonable. In Strasbourg pictures and statues were removed from churches as a matter of policy, but elsewhere this sort of religious enthusiasm was indulged in more spontaneously. During the summer of 1528 Parisian vandals mutilated a statue of the Virgin, striking out at the belief in miracles as well as idolatry. In the bishopric of Bern such gestures were carried out by the young converts of Guillaume Farel, his so-called 'infants terribles', including Christophe Hollande, who was finally imprisoned for defacing the altars of his native village of Orbe.[15]

In response to such demonstrations came official retaliation, first with the revival of older legislation against blasphemy and in defense 'of the glorious Virgin Mary', according to an ordinance of 1487, 'and of all the saints in paradise'.[16] Other displays of official and popular displeasure were even more newsworthy. Following the king's own example in the wake of the placards, ceremonies of expiation were held after an iconoclastic outbreak in 1537, another in Nîmes, and two more were ordered by the Parlement of Bordeaux in the 1550s.[17] No social phenomenon better illustrates the polarization of French public opinion than such demonstrations and counter-demonstrations. Not surprisingly, the incidence of iconoclasm and violence under religious provocation or pretext continued to rise, though it is difficult to distinguish this from commoner sorts of crime; and indeed legislators did not make any serious attempt to do so, believing that words, gestures and blows defiantly intended were all within their competence.

---

[13] Raemond, 896. And see N. Davis, *Society and Culture in Early Modern France* (Stanford, 1975), 152 ff.

[14] Crevier, v, 42.

[15] H. Vuilleumier, *Histoire de l'Eglise reformée de pays de Vaud* (Lausanne, 1927), 61ff.

[16] Isambert, xi, no. 59.

[17] Léon Ménard, *Histoire . . . de la Ville de Nîmes*, iv (Nîmes, 1874), 176; Dubédat, *Parlement de Toulouse*, i, 432; C. Boscheron des Portes, *Histoire du Parlement de Bordeaux* (Bordeaux, 1877), i, 146; and cf. P. Imbart de la Tour, *Les Origines de la Réforme*, iii (Melun, 1944), 167.

Communal religious experience centered of course on the service; for here most public projections of religious sentiment, written as well as oral, originated. Some of the more domestic and, as it were, internal varieties have been discussed already, and some of the more politically significant manifestations will be considered later. But to illustrate the process of congregational self-definition, of what might be called a declaration of identity, we must turn to another characteristic and enduring institution of evangelical reform which involved emotion and spectacle as well as reason and discourse. In the sixteenth century the theological disputation, although it was among the most traditional of medieval practices, assumed a new and often sensational importance, being deplored by orthodox observers and celebrated by many Protestants as perhaps the most effective way of persuading and convincing large groups of people.[18] Such debates represented milestones on Luther's road to Worms, and they were likewise vehicles of advertisement and proselytism for Zwingli and other Swiss reformers. At Leipzig in 1519, Zurich in 1523, Basel in 1525 and Baden in 1524, German evangelism found well-publicized forums and an international audience; and this lesson was not lost on French reformers.

Among the most fertile fields for cultivating the new doctrines by confrontation was the bishopric of Bern, where the reformed party achieved a majority in the city council in 1527 and capped their victory with a public disputation the following January.[19] At this disputation there was a French contingent, coming in response to an invitation, and a French version of the theses to be debated prepared by Farel. Ostensibly the purpose was religious unity and rejection of the abominable notion 'that everyone may believe and defend whatever pleases him without regard to the simple knowledge of God's truth'. 'Tumultuous' and 'seditious' behavior was forbidden on pain of death, and so were libels, injuries, provocations and mockeries. Yet everyone realized that the assembly was hardly designed to bring conciliation. The Bishop of Lausanne found an excuse for not attending and the 'Sorbonists' from Paris were soundly defeated by Farel (so observers said, anyway, although the records have been lost, and one must rely on Bullinger, hardly an unbiased witness). The result in general was to advertise the Biblical basis of religion and of course to attack such abuses as the mass, image-worship and clerical celibacy.

More significant for the Francophone world was the Disputation of Lausanne, sponsored by the conquering Bernese eight years later

---

[18] Bucer, *De Regno Christi*, I, 2; Calvin, *Institutes*, IV, i.   [19] Herminjard, II, 55ff.

despite the objections of the Emperor Charles V.[20] This spectacle was also staged by and for Protestants, with the few orthodox participants on the defensive. The ten theses proposed by Viret, the pastor of Lausanne, were opened to debate by Farel, speaking for the 'brothers in Christ'. Among the other evangelical champions were Calvin, Pierre Caroli and Marcourt, author of the placards of recent notoriety; and they carried on their offensive over the whole range of theological and pastoral issues, starting with the mass and images. They were in no mood to compromise. They were happy to hear the Dominican Jean Michod acknowledge the legitimacy of vernacular preaching 'in order to indoctrinate the people'; but they were unwilling to accept the further argument that 'images were the books of the poor people who were not able to read the scriptures'. 'Free speech' and safe conduct was guaranteed for all parties, but it was clear that no amount of argument would change the Word as conceived by Calvin and his colleagues.

The disputatious character of Calvinism became increasingly apparent in the 1540s and 1550s, and the staging of debates became common on all fronts – usually with divisive effects. For moderates like Melanchthon and Bucer disputations and colloquies may have promised ways of compromise and co-operation, at least among Protestant confessional groups; but for militant Calvinists they were ways of defining doctrine, gaining converts and chastising the papists. Among friends they were propaganda platforms, among enemies ideological battlefields. Even the Bernese overlords of Lausanne came to deplore the Calvinist taste for theological jousting; and they clashed with the French faculty of the Academy, including Viret, Beza and Hotman, over the ban on the conventional monthly theological disputations, which were giving too much prominence to the rival Calvinist confession. This conflict with the German Zwinglians eventually resulted in the flight of the French Calvinists, including Hotman, Beza and Viret himself, and a further narrowing of the Genevan ideological base.

Perhaps the most revealing of all sixteenth-century colloquies – the colloquy to end all colloquies for many French Protestants as well as Catholics – was that held at Poissy in 1561 in a last-ditch effort to reconcile Huguenots with orthodoxy, before sticks and stones succeeded the increasingly vicious name-calling to which people were becoming accustomed.[21] To this dramatic confrontation came both

[20] Vuilleumier, *Histoire*, 142ff., and *La Dispute de Lausanne*, ed. R. Deluz (Lausanne, 1936).
[21] See now D. Nugent, *Ecumenism in the Age of the Reformation* (Cambridge, Mass., 1974), and in general D. Ziegler (ed.), *Great Debates of the Reformation* (New York, 1969).

Catherine de Medicis and the Cardinal of Lorraine, who was already regarded as the nemesis of French Protestantism because of his sponsorship of persecutions in his own territories of Lorraine as well as in France. The leader of the evangelical delegation was Theodore Beza, who had explicit instructions from Calvin to concede no point of doctrine; and indeed he behaved as if he were on an evangelizing mission, unabashedly reaffirming the Calvinist confession of faith in the presence of the Queen Mother and the head of the Gallican church. The Colloquy of Poissy was a spectacular but not unexpected failure. What emerged from the addresses and debates was quite the opposite of the ostensible purpose of reconciliation. Rather it fixed the lines of division for a generation and more and set the stage for religious war, which followed the assembly by less than six months.

In all this ideological uproar arising from religious sentiment the most effective agent of transmission remained popular preaching. To this other forms of expression – psalm-singing and iconoclasm, public dialogue and disputation – were subordinate. The sermon elaborated and dramatized other forms of religious expression, including the catechism (which in Calvinist practice furnished material for a year of Sunday preaching) and confession; it gave emotional focus to the congregation and public thrust to its enthusiasm; it gave impetus to other kinds of demonstration, both musical and militant; and in general it represented a prime mover of public opinion. In the context of oral culture, certainly, no other kind of discourse better illustrates the transition from private conviction to public cause, from a profession of faith to concerted propaganda and even a platform of action. In the Reformation as in earliest Christian times the ideological priority was clear –'And the gospel must first be published among all nations'[22] – and so the sermon now becomes the center of our attention.

FIDES EX AUDITU

In the generation of ideology on any level a spokesman must take the lead. In religious associations the charismatic element takes the form of a prophetic agent who, as Max Weber put it, 'by virtue of his mission proclaims a religious doctrine or divine commandment'.

[22] Mark 13: 10.

This was the task of a renewer as well as a founder, and as Luther himself was not too humble to observe, 'I have something of the prophet in me.'[23] In accordance with this role he not only defined doctrine, directed consciences and established goals, but also imposed upon others his vision both of past and of future. Above all – and again like the 'divine orator' Paul – Luther managed in almost unprecedented fashion to catch and to hold the ear of his generation, including even (or perhaps especially) his severest critics. The primacy of hearing over seeing in the sixteenth century has often been pointed out, and this held in particular for cultivating the faith. 'Hearing the word of God is itself faith', Luther declared (*Auditum verbi Dei, id est fidem*).[24] Even in this age of print, then, oral modes of discourse continued to be essential; and indeed it is impossible to understand the explosion of religious enthusiasm in the sixteenth century without appreciating the force of the spoken word, especially in the collective experience of the sermon.

'Preaching is the most effective agent for the conversion of mankind', wrote one early-sixteenth-century authority on the matter, Ulrich Sargant; 'by its means especially sinners are brought to repentance.'[25] Luther followed this advice as well as Sargant's specific prescription for sermon-making. In the course of his career he delivered over 2300 of them, after 1514 mostly in the vernacular.[26] Though impressive, this total was easily surpassed not only by reformers like Calvin and Bullinger but also by some of Luther's predecessors. For despite laments about religious decline, the fifteenth century had in fact experienced a general increase in missionary preaching. This is deducible from the great quantity of extant manuscripts, numbering in the hundreds for such German territories as Westphalia and Strasbourg, as well as some 10,000 printed sermons from the incunabular period; and these must represent a small fraction even of those written down. The popularity of certain published collections was remarkable: the 'Disciple' sermons went through forty-one editions (perhaps 40,000 copies) before 1500, and the 'Sleep well' sermons (named for the peace of mind rather than the tedium they promised) through twenty-four editions. Another measure was the number and variety of such ancillary works as

[23] *Table Talk*, 384. Cf. Weber, *Sociology of Religion*, trans. E. Fischoff, in *Economy and Society*, II (New York, 1968), 399ff.

[24] Commentary on Hebrews cited by R. Mandrou, *Introduction à la France moderne* (Paris, 1961), 70; cf. J.-M. Pohier, *Psychologie et théologie* (Paris, 1967), 146.

[25] Cited by Johannes Janssen, *History of the German People*, I, trans. M. Mitchell and A. Christie (London, 1896), 36.

[26] E. Kiessling, *The Early Sermons of Luther and their Relation to the Pre-Reformation Sermon* (Grand Rapids, Michigan, 1935).

Fides ex auditu

Biblical cyclopedias and *plenaria* designed to provide reference and illustrative material and especially of the treatises on the 'art of preaching' (*ars praedicandi*, analogous to the *artes poeticae, rhetoricae,* and *historicae*), which set down the nature and purpose of sermons.[27]

Although the emergence of new issues affected the contents of sermons, in many ways the forms of pulpit oratory deviated little from medieval tradition. In the later sixteenth century Panigarole, an Italian preacher extraordinarily popular in France, provided a scholastic summary of the 'art of preaching and making a good sermon' for all occasions and purposes.[28] He distinguished four types, only one of which, the didactic, was in any way neutral. Of the others, the first was the demonstrative, intended to distribute praise and blame according to Christian standards; the second was the judicial sermon, designed to accuse or to defend particular persons or causes; and the last was the deliberative type, for persuasion or dissuasion. All these types were grounded in rhetorical convention and thus adaptable to all kinds of polemical and political as well as religious purposes. Under the pressures of religious conflict and fragmentation the full ideological potential of the sermon form, by word both of mouth and of print, was realized in the sixteenth century.

'Cry aloud, spare not, lift up thy voice like a trumpet, and shew my people their transgression': this was the text (Isaiah 58:1) which pulpit orators had practiced as well as preached for centuries.[29] Originally *kerygma* had been the proclamation of a lordly decree to the barbarian, and so it remained in its Biblical form that 'the gospel must first be published among all nations'. For centuries 'imitation of the apostles' had been the motto of monks, friars, and lay preachers; and Protestant pastors may well be seen as riding the crest of a very long wave. The most powerful impulse had come from the great preaching orders, the Dominicans and the Franciscans; and despite their sad decline they had not entirely forgotten their vocation. More recent and perhaps more interesting were their various rivals, including the Albigensians and Waldensians, lay movements like the Modern Devotion, and the 'free preachers' and sermonizing vagrants (*vagabundi*), who added to the noise if not to the piety of the pre-Lutheran age. A similar type were the so-called

---

[27] T. Charland, *Artes Praedicandi* (Paris, 1936).
[28] F. Panigarole, *L'Art de prescher et bien faire un sermon*, trans. G. Chappuis (Paris, 1604).
[29] Michel Ménot, in R. Petry (ed.), *No Uncertain Sound* (Philadelphia, 1958), 30; T. Parker, *The Oracles of God* (London, 1947), 14; E. Douglass, *Justification in Late Medieval Preaching, A Study of John Geiler of Kaisersberg* (Leiden, 1966); cf. M. Vicaire, *L'Imitation des apôtres* (Paris, 1935).

'beards' (*barbes*) of the valleys of the Vaud, itinerant preachers who were still giving trouble to the ecclesiastical authorities on the eve of the Reformation.[30] Claude de Seyssel, Bishop of Turin in his last years (he died in 1519), was much impressed by the purity of their lives even as he deplored the theological errors leading them to a liaison with Protestants of Bern and southern Germany. Like the Lollards of England, the religious communities of the Vaud merged with, and to a large extent were submerged by, the powerful ideological currents of the magisterial Reformation.

One significant novelty from the fourteenth century was the endowment of civic preaching posts. These had proliferated remarkably in the years before Luther's agitations.[31] In 1455 the Council of Geneva, with the assistance of the Franciscans, had established public sermons, although subsequent uproars made the city fathers wonder about the wisdom of their act. In Strasbourg there were a dozen such posts before 1530 and a total of fifty-nine preachers, most with university training. Like the apostles, of course, some preachers, famous 'apostolic preachers' subsidized by the church as well as nameless 'vagabonds', travelled about the countryside in order to bring salvation by word of mouth. But urban missions were by far the more important. 'The Lord says that preachers are to betake themselves to great cities rather than to small towns and villages', was the advice offered in one famous fifteenth-century sermon on Isaiah, 'because more sins are committed there.'[32] The man who made this remark, Michel Ménot, was one of a number of great predicators of the late fifteenth century – Savonarola, Olivier Maillard, John Colet and Johann Geiler of Kaisersberg were others – who might have been as well known as many of the magisterial reformers of the next century, except for political circumstances and the vagaries of fame before printed publicity. In terms of oral culture it might be argued that the high water mark of the preaching tradition was reached in the generation before Luther.

We have been taught – by humanists, Protestant reformers, and historians who accept their criticism at face value – that monkery was inhuman, obscurantist, and reactionary. 'The monk', wrote Rabelais, 'doth neither preach nor teach, as do the Evangelical doctors and

---

[30] A. Méray, *La Vie au temps des libres prêcheurs* (Paris, 1978); *Guillaume Farel . . .*, par un groupe d'historiens, professeurs et pasteurs de Suisse, de France et d'Italie (Neuchâtel, 1930), 286; A. Monastier, *A History of the Vaudois Church*, English trans. (London, 1848), 47.

[31] E. Lengweiler, *Die vorreformatorische Prädikaturen der deutschen Schweiz* (Frieburg, 1955), 18; H. Naef, *Les Origines de la Réforme à Genève* (Geneva, 1968), I, 166; S. Ozment, *The Reformation in the Cities* (New Haven, Conn., 1975), 39ff.

[32] Petry, *No Uncertain Sound*, 30.

school-masters.'[33] And yet, judging from individual performance if not institutional achievement, the regular clergy was in fact a major source of enlightenment and reform. Classical scholars like Lorenzo Valla and Erasmus, who had nothing but contempt for the 'profession of the religious', could hardly be expected to take this view. Valla told a story about a certain Franciscan friar who explained that the 'Apostles' Creed' was so named because each of the original twelve had contributed one clause, and to him this epitomized mendicant ignorance. But such literary snobbery did not impress popular preachers. 'Lorenzo Valla and other classicists criticize theologians for their vulgar language', remarked Geiler, 'but that is beside the point.'[34] What did count was their effectiveness, and this was remarkable. In 1478 a French Franciscan had stirred up a great uproar over his criticism of all levels of society; and when King Louis XI forbade further preaching, people reacted violently, some women, it was said, throwing rocks at officials who came to silence him. More famous was the Franciscan Maillard, who raised his voice in 1494, and again in 1496 and 1508, against a wide range of vices; and despite the rudeness of his speech, including an annoying habit of clearing his throat, he had an impact not only in his own age but two generations later when his criticisms were revived by the Huguenot publicist Henri Estienne.[35] Best known of all was the 'trumpet of Strasbourg', Johann Geiler, who preached reform from 1492 to 1511, echoing Savonarola and anticipating John Colet's famous sermon to Convocation in 1512. 'O holy bishops', Geiler exclaimed, 'wake up and reform your church according to the Holy Gospel, the Apostles and the teachings of the true church.'[36]

For such men the sermon was not merely instruction and consolation, it was a call to battle, and their mission was Biblical - 'for preachers today', declared Michel Ménot, 'succeed in the office of apostles, which is to preach the word of God'. Consequently they never hesitated to break the rules and forms of the *ars praedicandi* and indeed of all polite discourse. Although they used Latin notes, they spoke in the vernacular, in a rambling manner and often at

[33] *Gargantua*, Chapter 40.
[34] Ch. Schmidt, *Histoire littéraire de l'Alsace* (Paris, 1879), 335ff.
[35] Estienne, *Apologie pour Hérodote*, ed. P. Ristelhuber (Paris, 1879), I, 75, citing passages from Ménot as well as Maillard. In general A. Samouillan, *Olivier Maillard, sa prédication et son temps* (Paris, 1891); A. Renaudet, *Préréforme et humanisme à Paris* (2nd edn, Paris, 1953), 163, 208; and *Sermons choisis de Michel Ménot*, ed. J. Nève (Paris, 1924).
[36] L. Dacheux, *Un Réformateur Catholique à la fin du XVe siècle, Jean Geiler de Kaysersberg 1478–1510* (Paris, 1876); M. Chrisman, *Strasbourg and the Reform* (New Haven, Conn., 1967), 69ff.; Geiler, 'Concerning power fools', in G. Strauss (ed.), *Manifestations of Discontent on the Eve of the Reformation* (Bloomington, 1971), 97ff.

unconscionable length – up to three, four and even five hours. They added poems, songs and jokes (probably more than the three per sermon to which fourteenth-century friars were supposedly limited); they encouraged participation by the congregation, for instance through the *Ruf* or *Leis*; and in general, like Luther later on, they avoided erudite style and abstruse doctrine, although nothing human was alien to them. Geiler delivered over a hundred homilies on the wide range of folly and vices reflected in the famous *Ship of Fools* composed by his fellow citizen Sebastian Brant. Guillaume Pepin, preaching in the late fifteenth century, hunted even more dangerous game, criticizing not only indulgences and the cult of the Virgin but also do-nothing princes and prelates.[37] Equally rash was the Strasbourg satirist Thomas Murner, although he later turned his ill-temper against Luther. Geneva was periodically plagued by subversive preachers, such as the notorious Frère Thomas, who rode into the city in 1517, proclaiming the imminent coming of God and attacking the privileged clergy.

Well before the period of 'reformation', then, the professional – and the freelance – preacher was a familiar figure on the public scene. Traditionally, according to Sargant, the qualifications for this office were two: clerical status and a proper vocation, and to these may be added the occasional requirement of travelling. But reality as usual was a little different. A generation earlier Gabriel Biel, a man of some experience in the matter, distinguished three sorts of preachers: the show-offs, whose aim was to promote themselves; the lazy ones, who lacked even command of their authorities; and subversives, who criticized to the point of inciting disobedience.[38] The last category was large and well publicized. In the free city of Strasbourg, for example, Geiler did not hesitate to use his cathedral pulpit to question the highest authorities, and he often harped upon the theme that 'kings and popes do not have the right to make laws against the laws of God'.[39] For him the preacher had many roles – prophet, watchdog, fisherman, divine archer – and in all of them his function was to talk, not to listen, to lay down the law, not to hear it. It was not a function that encouraged obedience; and it is perhaps not surprising that Geiler's attitude, if not his theology, was subversive. His unruliness seems to have been contagious. One of his disciples was Thomas Murner, who had established a great reputation through preaching and poetry before becoming Luther's neme-

---

[37] See Méray, *La Vie*, 98. Cf. B. Smalley, *The English Friars and Antiquity* (Oxford, 1960), 42.
[38] H. Oberman, *The Harvest of Medieval Theology* (Cambridge, Mass., 1963), 21.
[39] Méray, *La Vie*, 86.

sis.[40] Another was the reformer Jacob Sturm, who remarked that if he was a heretic he owed it all to Geiler, whose work indeed found a place on the Index of forbidden books. Menot's work, though likewise tolerated in his lifetime, escaped this fate but was later bowdlerized for public consumption. In any case the lesson learned by apprentice preachers was not so much specific doctrine as the habits of defiance and denunciation exemplified by men like Geiler and Menot.

This was a lesson that a whole generation of young men were in the process of learning, and not surprisingly most of them were products of, or cast-offs from, the old ecclesiastical system. Luther was himself first represented as a 'certain monk' notable for the degree but not the quality of his protest, and indeed there were sympathetic responses within his order not only in Germany but also in France and the Netherlands. Two of the first Protestant martyrs, though they were guilty largely by association and not technically Lutherans, were Augustinians of Antwerp, Hendrich Voes and Jan van Essen; and others of this order provoked official reactions for their sermonizing in Paris (1523), Toulouse (1526), Nîmes (1532), and elsewhere. Evangelical agitation was also evident within the Franciscan order, in which the strict observants, the so-called *reformati*, had finally, after a two-century struggle, triumphed over the conventuals, *deformati* as their enemies called them, in the very year of Luther's Ninety-Five Theses.[41] Normandy, Berry and Vivarais were among the provinces to be evangelized by Franciscan friars, as in fact was the city of Geneva; and of course France's first declared reformer, François Lambert, had been a Franciscan and had more extensive experience of monastic life than even Luther. Despite the virulent attacks of Lambert and Luther upon their former profession, it seems clear that both drew inspiration generally from the monastic ideal. The pattern was so common that one bitter ex-Protestant characterized the Reformation as in large part the work of monks who took up the cause of the Devil. 'In the order of St Augustine he raised up Luther', wrote Florimond de Raemond; 'in that of St Dominic he brought Bucer; in that of St Francis he brought Conrad Pelican; in that of the Carmelites he shows Viret and Pierre Richer; in that of St Brigid he chooses Oecolampadius . . .', etc.[42]

The volume of preaching – in terms of impact if not of absolute quantity – reached remarkable proportions in the years of Luther's

---

[40] M. Gravier, *Luther et l'opinion publique* (Paris, 1942), 61ff.
[41] J. Moorman, *A History of the Franciscan Order* (Oxford, 1968), 581.
[42] Raemond, 28.

early notoriety and the contemporary emergence of Zwingli, who began his public ministry on New Year's Day 1519 from the pulpit of Grossmünster. In Strasbourg two years later Matthias Zell began to preach on that incendiary work, Paul's epistles to the Romans; and although he was prevented from speaking from the great pulpit of St Thomas used by Geiler, he gained renown before being joined by Bucer, Hedio and Capito in 1523. The publication of sermons in Strasbourg reached unprecedented heights in this decade (1512–24), Catholic as well as Protestant, before entering into decline. In 1522 Jacques Praepositus began preaching in Lutheran, which is to say anti-papal, fashion until forced to flee the persecutions begun by the Emperor Charles V in the implementation of his ban on Luther. In France, too, the spoken transmission of the gospel reached unprecedented heights, especially through the circle established at Meaux by the Bishop Guillaume Briçonnet, who himself set the example with his weekly sermons attacking ecclesiastical vices. All of this vocalizing of the Word seemed for a time to be fulfilling the hope expressed by Lefèvre d'Etaples in the spring of 1522, referring particularly to the seminary of Meaux, that the light of the gospel would transform the world and restore the primitive church.

THE EVANGELICAL REVOLUTION

The early 1520s saw a great wave of missionary preaching. It was a heroic age, a time of unbridled enthusiasm, crucial conversions, pilgrimages to Wittemberg, Zurich and other centers of the 'pure word of God'. It was also a time before confessional lines were drawn and official campaigns of suppression were launched, when Erasmian reformers and Lutheran transformers could still regard themselves as part of a common front with some hopes of maintaining unity. This coalition of moderate and radical reform was illustrated clearly in the reform-minded circle in Meaux under the protection of Bishop Guillaume Briçonnet. Here came not only Lefèvre, the acknowledged leader of French evangelism, but a host of other 'new evangelists' who hoped to preach the world into a state of perfection.[43] Among them were Gerard Roussel and Michel

[43] Among many detailed surveys, E. Arnaud, *Histoire des Protestants du Dauphiné*, 1 (Paris, 1875) and *Histoire des Protestants du Vivarais et du Vélay* (Paris, 1888); R. Collinet, *La Réformation en Belgique du XVIe siècle* (Brussels, 1958); Louis Raynal, *Histoire du Berry* (Bourges, 1847), III; H. Stohl, *Le Protestantisme en Alsace* (Strasbourg, 1950); J. Vienot, *Histoire de la Réforme dans les pays de Montbéliard* (Montbéliard, 1900); H. Vuilleumier, *Histoire de l'église réformée du pays de Vaud* (Lausanne, 1927); Léon Ménard, *Histoire . . . de la Ville de Nîmes*, IV (Nîmes, 1874); H. Morembert, *La Réforme à Metz*, 1 (Nancy, 1969); and innumerable articles in *BSHPF*. The phrase 'révolution evangelique' is from the classic work by P. Imbart de la Tour, *Les Origines de la Réforme* (Paris, 1905–35; 2nd edn, 1944–8).

d'Arande, later preachers to the royal family of Navarre; Calvin's future rival Pierre Caroli and future collaborator Guillaume Farel; Antoine Mazurier, François Vatable and Jean de la Croix. Contemporaneously the ex-Dominican Aimé Maigret was preaching scandalously in Lyon and Grenoble, while in Bourges Jean Michel was trying to gain the ears of Christians until he was shouted down and driven out. The militancy of these men was typified by Pierre de Sebiville, who dropped the 'Ave Maria' from his sermons; preached against images, the principle of clerical celibacy and the prohibition against eating meat (encouraging his fellow monks to break this rule); and in general rejected the 'human traditions' embodied in canon law and papal practices. A similar iconoclasm was displayed by Michel d'Arande in sermons not only in Lyon, Bourges and Alençon but even at court, and by Caroli, who likewise caused scandal in Paris after leaving Meaux.

Reality could not be subdued verbally, however, and this period of revivalism was short-lived. The hyperbole of pulpit oratory became increasingly dangerous, as the target of attacks on materialism and abuse shifted from ecclesiastical to sacramental ground, and in particular to the mass. To threaten this symbol of 'immanence' seemed more fundamentally seditious than attacks on the papal hierarchy; and it drew down upon the new evangelists the entire force of the French ecclesiastical establishment – the Sorbonne, the Parlement of Paris and the crown. When Briçonnet himself, favoring preaching but not 'disputation', reversed his course, the popular front of evangelism collapsed. Michel d'Arande was intimidated into returning to orthodoxy, while Sebiville was forced to make public abjuration of his statements. By the end of 1524 the members of the Meaux circle were scattered, their voices muted.

Yet the 'evangelical revolution' was not defeated, only deflected into other channels. In France there were other lesser currents of missionary preaching, for example in Paris in the 1530s – scandalous sermons by various Augustinians, by Roussel in the Louvre, to crowds of up to 5000 as well as the Queen of Navarre, and by Nicholas Cop at the university, an address which Calvin himself helped to compose. In general these were minor agitations made possible by the French–Lutheran *rapprochement* of these years but soon curbed by the backlash of public opinion following the affair of the placards. The fact is that after 1524 the reform movement was defused in France, and the major course of the gospel passed into exile. The first great refuge was Strasbourg, the 'new Jerusalem' before Geneva, just then in the process of discarding Roman forms under the leadership of Bucer and Capito. Assembled here for a time were Lefèvre, Roussel, Arande, Farel and Lambert, marking not only the beginning of a significant French colony in Strasbourg but also the establishment of a permanent link with international Protestantism, although eventually only Farel and Lambert remained in the Protestant camp in any confessional sense.

It may be that the most significant result of this brief period of rampant Lutheran influence and anti-Lutheran fear was the opening up of the great exile circuit to religious refugees and especially to missionary preaching. From Provence and Dauphiné in southern France to western and southern Switzerland, Franche-Comté, Lorraine and indeed through the entire Rhine Valley through the Palatinate north to the Netherlands, evangelizing preachers travelled – called to this city and expelled from that, settling only when satisfactory Reformation had been accomplished. The earliest pioneer was François Lambert, and his was also the archetypal itinerary.[44] Having begun a career as 'apostolic preacher' for his Franciscan monastery in Avignon in the year of the Ninety-Five Theses, Lambert was dedicated to the apostolic model (*exemplum apostolorum* in the conventional formula); but growing disaffection threw him into disfavor with his superiors. Pushed by conscience and pulled by Lutheran reform, he left his monastery in May 1522 to begin a fantastic voyage. He preached that summer in Geneva, Lausanne, Bern, Zurich, and Basel; the next year he visited Luther and even matriculated at the University of Wittenberg while publicizing his reasons for rejecting monasticism. His next stop was Metz, where he arrived in time to witness the execution of an Augustinian monk, Jean Chastellain, and to write a description of it; and after that he came to Strasbourg in time to encounter the remains of the Meaux group. He ended his career as the reformer of Hesse and died in 1530, when the French reform movement was still in embryonic form.

The great figure in this early age of itinerant evangelism was Guillaume Farel, whose career spanned almost three generations of reform but who ideologically seems never to have grown old.[45] Farel's missionary activity began in the summer of 1521 in Meaux, and thereafter his movements were as extensive as Lambert's. He tried unsuccessfully to preach in his native Gap and later went to Basel, where he published a parody of the Sorbonne's condemnation of Luther that was soon banned in France; and he caused more local trouble by offering for public defense thirteen controversial

[44] R. Winters, *Francis Lambert of Avignon* (Philadelphia, 1938).
[45] Anthoine Fromment, *Les Actes et gestes merveilleux de la cité de Genève*, ed. G. Revilliod (Geneva, 1854); *Guillaume Farel*; Vuilleumier, *Histoire*, 45ff.

theses, which university persons were forbidden to hear. He preached three sermons but soon was ordered to be silent, perhaps at the instigation of Erasmus, who was beginning to repudiate such radicalism. So he took up his travelling again. In Montbéliard, through the recommendation of the reformer of Basel, Oecolampadius, he was given permission to preach and welcomed by people who were, he reported, 'thirsty for the gospel'. After this he moved on to Strasbourg, where he rejoined his friends from Meaux and became, in 1525, the first pastor of the French community. For Farel, this was only the beginning. The reaction in France led him to choose a life of exile, and his heroic voyages on behalf of his mission went on until his death forty years later.

Farel was a representative of a fairly new species, the lay preacher, an office which itself had a certain transforming effect upon religious consciousness. It was in Montbéliard that Farel was assured of his vocation, and he took his reception by the people as a form of consecration. His sponsor Oecolampadius agreed. 'It is easy to instill dogma in people's ears', he told Farel, 'but to change hearts is a divine work.'[46] Obviously the concept of popular ordination was highly debatable, but it was a common assumption of the anti-clerical preachers of his generation. 'It is true that a man without a law degree cannot be an advocate in the Parlement', Caroli had remarked, '. . . but a man can preach the holy scriptures whether or not he is a doctor or bachelor.' On such grounds Farel claimed to be 'bishop' in Aigle in 1526. The principle of 'liberty of preaching', if not of conscience, was useful also to secular governments; and so Bern, after its reformation in 1528 and after the dispute which Farel attended, supported Farel's right to preach within its territories. The following year he received 'an open letter for the free preaching of God's word in the lands of "Messieurs de Bern"'.[47] The same principle was accepted in Lausanne, although orthodox resistance prevented Farel from carrying out missionary work there until its conquest by Bern in 1536. In Neuchâtel, too, according to the city council, 'The gospel is preached and denounced freely and daily at appropriate hours and in places permitted by the government. And those who please can go to hear it for their salvation, and those who prefer to go to mass or other service may likewise do so, without anyone saying, "I am better than you or have more faith", or anything such. So both parties want to live in peace together, as Jesus Christ commanded us.'[48]

In reality such free enterprise in preaching was productive rather of

---

[46] Herminjard, I, 254 (2 Aug. 1524): 'Facile enim est aliquot dogmata instillare auribus; animum autem immatare divinum opus est.'
[47] Argentré, II, 27.   [48] *Guillaume Farel*, 221.

conflict than of peaceful coexistence, violating as it did the old ecclesiastical monopoly and threatening to establish a new ideological elite. For several years after his commission from Bern, Farel travelled through the Vaud, preaching, provoking reactions, gaining disciples and dangerous notoriety. Often he was boycotted and sometimes physically attacked, while on the other hand his partisans indulged in the popular sacramentarian sport of image-breaking. In Orbe he was screamed down by women in church, heckled by children and forced to speak in the market-place. In Grandson he again preached in the open air and again provoked violence. 'Give thanks to Our Lady!', his critics shouted in one village; 'I give thanks to God and none other', he replied.[49] In Lausanne he was prevented from speaking altogether. Yet Farel's pioneering efforts had enduring results. In 1530 he established connections with the Waldensians, who consulted him (as well as Bucer, Capito and Oecolampadius) and who later came to count themselves among Calvin's flocks. He made many key converts and, equally important, propelled a number of hesitant young men into missionary careers. Most notable among these were Viret, who began to preach in Lausanne in 1536, and of course Calvin, who was persuaded to begin his active evangelizing in Geneva the following year. Other protégés of Farel's carried on his work in the Vaud, which continued to provide a market for ministers.

These ideological pioneers established the pattern of evangelical colonization for generations to come. They established the pattern also of ecclesiastical controversy, since their work involved the violation of cultural and linguistic as well as religious and political frontiers. In Bern conflict was unavoidable because of the rivalry between the French- and German-speaking groups, and in fact the Calvinist colony in Lausanne led by Viret eventually found it impossible to put up with the Zwinglian pressure from the Bernese government. Yet there was no stopping the missionary impulse. In Strasbourg there was a similar intercultural problem, but Bucer insisted 'that approved evangelists must be sent out to all parts of the realm' in order to 'announce assiduously, zealously, and in timely fashion to people everywhere the good news of the kingdom'. In time a division arose here, too, between the German and French communities. The pattern was repeated on an even larger scale by Calvin, the disciple of Bucer as well as Farel, after his permanent installation in Geneva. Calvin's field of colonial operations included much of European society – German, Netherlandish,

[49] Fromment, *Actes*, 11.

and English areas – and so the disruptive effects of his labors were many times greater.

It was in this context that the sermon became an agent of explosive force, increasingly important despite the equally explosive advent of print culture.[50] Farel had a remarkable success even though his manner was dogmatic, repetitive and not impressive to most auditors. Much more eloquent and effective was his younger colleague Viret, who attracted great crowds to his sermons in Lausanne and later on his travels in France. In Lausanne in particular the political significance of preaching became apparent. One illustration of this was the practice of 'publication from the pulpit' (*publication du haut de la chaire*), as when, for instance, Viret announced to the people an ordinance of 1537 regarding taxes and another prohibiting the export of grain from the town.[51] More spectacular was the use of sermons to identify and to denounce enemies from without. About the preachers of Lausanne in the 1550s Cathelan remarked, 'Their sermons serve only to call the Pope antichrist, the cardinals gluttons, priests and monks vermine . . . and kings and princes tyrants of the Pope.' Within France such vocal propaganda was also familiar. In the 1530s the Lenten sermons of Roussel in Paris, Jean Michel in Bourges and others in Nîmes, Caen and elsewhere attracted crowds and reportedly converts. The authorities responded in kind. In 1543 Francis I published an edict on 'our faith and form of preaching', complaining about the disturbances provoked by unorthodox preachers and setting down articles of faith as guidelines for all sermons.[52] Other royal legislation urged prelates, including archbishops, not to endanger the spiritual welfare of their flocks by neglecting their teaching duties, while orthodox counter-ceremonies were organized against the 'diabolical Lutheran spirits'.[53]

The grounds for excitement on both sides became increasingly obvious as the wars of religion approached. Inflammatory preaching could be heard everywhere, it seemed.[54] In Nîmes Viret addressed

[50] J. Ainslie, *The Doctrine of Ministerial Order in the Reformed Churches of the 16th and 17th Centuries* (Edinburgh, 1940). There is now an interesting discussion of 'the consciousness of the reformed clergy' in Phyllis Mack Crew, *Calvinist Preaching and Iconoclasm in the Netherlands 1544–1569* (Cambridge, 1978), 107–39, taking its starting point from the view of Weber (see above, p. 104, n. 23).

[51] Vuilleumier, *Histoire*, 352.

[52] *Edict du roy sur les articles faictz par la faculté de theologie de l'université de Paris, concernans nostre Foy et forme de prescher*, 23 July 1543 (Paris, 1552; BN F. 47021).

[53] *Lettres patentes . . .* (Paris, 1557; BN F. 46815.1); cf. *Le Cry et proclamation publique pour iouer le Mystere des Actes des Apostres* (Paris, 1541).

[54] R. Linder, *The Political Ideas of Pierre Viret* (Geneva, 1964), 21ff.; Ménard, *Nîmes*, IV, 285; Pithou, 78, 103; B. Palissy, *Les Oeuvres*, ed. A. France (Paris, 1880); L. Canet, *L'Aunis et la Santonge* (La Rochelle, 1933), 206; Baie, *Le Siècle des Gueux*, II, 244; Beuzart, *Les Hérésies*, 233; Cordeweiner, 'Prêche calviniste à Boeschepe', BSHPF, CXII (1966), 105–20; Ch. Paillard, *Histoire des troubles réligieux de Valenciennes 1560–1567* (Paris, 1874), I, 36ff.

crowds of 8000 and more, and made many converts, especially among lawyers and magistrates, as later he did among the medical scholars at Montpellier. In Lyon he preached daily to huge crowds, and his words were frequently followed by outbreaks of iconoclasm. In Caen in the spring of 1560 (in the wake of the conspiracy of Amboise), a congregation went on a rampage after a sermon, throwing stones, breaking windows and committing other crimes; and later there were violent clashes and even murders under such circumstances.[55] In Troyes, too, preachers from Paris incited the inhabitants of the neighborhood called 'little Geneva' and were blamed for various destructive and seditious acts. In Valence, according to one contemporary, the preaching was so effective that all the monks had left to join evangelical congregations by 1560. At the same time the preachers of Saintes were enjoying remarkable success, as described by Bernard Palissy.[56] So it was also in the Netherlands a few years later, for example in Antwerp, where up to 20,000 people reportedly gathered in the streets and marched outside the city walls to hear the preaching of Guy de Brès, Pierre Dathenus or François du Jon, and often causing disturbances afterwards.

In Paris the ideological commotion mounted with the political crisis after the death of Henry II in 1559 and especially from 1561, the year of debate and religious parleying. Of course both parties were involved. Even before the king's death, according to Crespin, 'The [Catholic] preachers never stopped inciting people to massacre all the Lutherans they could find without waiting for the punishment of the magistrate.'[57] The orthodox professed to be no less shocked. In 1561 Gentien Hervet was astounded to hear two monks preaching heresy to his own flock, which he had sworn to defend against such wolves; and he responded the next Sunday with a refutation of the 'lies of Calvin, Melanchthon, Bucer and other new evangelists'.[58] In October the air was filled with much talk at cross-purposes at the Colloquy of Poissy: Claude d'Espence and the Cardinal of Lorraine taking the Gallican line, including the recent *rapprochement* with Lutheranism; Beza and Peter Martyr maintaining the purity of the Calvinist position; neither side willing to make any significant concession. The art of preaching sermons was reaching a high point,

[55] Floquet, *Histoire du Parlement de Normandie*, II, 310.
[56] Palissy, *Oeuvres*, 128–55.
[57] *Iuste complainte des fideles de France, contre leurs adversaires Papistes* (Avignon, 1560; BN Ld[176].6), 221; Crespin, II, 639ff.
[58] *Recueil d'aucunes mensonges de Calvin, Melancthon, Bucer et autres nouveaux Evangelistes de ce temps* (Paris, 1561).

but the art of listening to them, or learning from them, seemed forgotten.

The confrontation was symbolized by an incident that occurred at the newly founded church in Vassy, which was situated in the territories of the house of Guise.[59] A week before Christmas 1561 the Cardinal of Lorraine sent a representative, the Bishop of Châlons, to investigate the goings-on in this little town of Champagne and the reports of growing religious enthusiasm. He tried several times to interrupt the preaching of the minister Granvelle, who held his ground. 'I am in the pulpit first, so I should speak first', he insisted. 'If you have anything to say, you may speak afterwards.' The bishop argued that he had the king's commission and that, in any case, Granvelle was not ordained. Granvelle then took the Protestant position that spiritual calling and not superstitious ordination determined competency for the ministry and asked the bishop if he preached to his own people. 'Oh, I preach through my vicars', he answered. 'You must be joking', said Granvelle. 'Did the apostles . . . preach through vicars?' Obviously no resolution could emerge from this or any such debate, going as it did to the heart of the 'so-called reformed religion'. The congregation at Vassy continued to prosper on the frontiers of legitimacy, and the suspicions of the Cardinal and his brother, the Duke of Guise, continued to grow. The upshot was the 'massacre of Vassy', which occurred a little over two months later when the Duke, with a band of his armed men, tried to interrupt another service, and fighting broke out between the soldiers and the psalm-singing people. Most observers took this as the opening phase of the civil wars, which almost no one had doubted would come.

But still the time for talk had not ended. After the Colloquy of Poissy Beza had remained in Paris and enjoyed spectacular success in his sermons. Crowds of more than twenty thousand came to hear, to pray, to sing, and to demonstrate. On Palm Sunday he preached in the morning, held baptisms ('according to the new and old traditions', reported a witness), and preached again in the afternoon in the house of Admiral Coligny. In the streets the Catholics walked about carrying branches; the Huguenots, in a minority, with empty hands. The following Friday services were held in the conventional place by the Porte St Jacques, but the next day the Cardinal of Lorraine told the Huguenots that they could worship there on Easter morning only 'at the risk of their heads'. On Monday came a confrontation at Popincourt between a group of Huguenots,

---

[59] G. Herelle, *La Réforme et la Ligue en Champagne* (Paris, n.d.), 22ff., citing Pithou.

who had come for a sermon, and Catholics, who had come for confession. 'They looked at each other without saying a word', wrote the chronicler; but hostility was mounting.[60] The next Sunday stones were thrown, as at Vassy, and a few people were beaten and killed. Most Huguenots were forced to leave the city, many journeying to Condé's headquarters in Orleans, where Beza was continuing his preaching.

Throughout the religious wars the chorus of sermons continued antiphonically, and the mutual vilification became increasingly unrestrained. The growing partisanship can be seen by comparing the funeral sermon for Claude de Lorraine given in 1550 with that for his successor François de Guise, whose murder thirteen years later gave rise to a wave of denunciations from the pulpits of the Catholic party and its leaders – and then with the still greater outpouring after the assassination of Claude's grandson, Henry of Guise, a quarter of a century after that. One defector from the Huguenot cause, Pierre Charpentier, told of two ministers of Toulouse who 'from preachers of peace became trumpets of war' after the massacre of St Bartholomew.[61] A decade later another royalist lamented the inflammatory preachers who exerted themselves against the three fundamentals of monarchy – religion, justice and 'police' (as the institutions of social order were called in the sixteenth century). Preachers of both parties were assaulted. Calvinists were charged with corrupt morals and libertinism, Catholics with superstition and brutality, and both with inciting to violence. The theorist of predication Panigarole denounced the heretic as a Judas, a devil and a traitor, and on these grounds justified the royal action taken on St Bartholomew's day.[62] Sorbin raged against Henry III for not carrying on the policy of exterminating Huguenots. Indeed the political potential of the sermon may have reached its highest point in the preaching of the supporters of the League in the latter stages of the religious wars; but that is another story.

SEED OF THE CHURCH

Bearing witness to the true faith – this was the point of all the sermonizing, singing and more violent demonstrating that accom-

---

[60] P. Paschal, *Journal de ce qui s'est passé en France devant l'annee 1562*, ed. M. François (Paris, 1950), 11ff.
[61] *Advertissement sainct et chrestien touchant le port des armes* (Paris, 1575; BN Lb^{34}.97).
[62] F. Panigarole, *Cent Sermons* (Paris, 1586), 343ff. Cf. Ch. Labitte, *De la Démocratie chez les prédicateurs de la Ligue* (Paris, 1885), 86ff.

panied Protestant worship, and it was a central impulse to the more conventional forms of publicity and propaganda. But the ultimate and perhaps most effective kind of testimony and publication was a more traditional, yet more sensational, expression of religious commitment. Martyrdom, that most extreme ideological gesture, is not a theme that has attracted broad-minded judgments, and even today it is difficult to find examinations of the phenomenon that are not implicitly hagiographical.[63] Yet martyrdom, that 'willingness to die for the indemonstrable' which pagans found so puzzling among early Christians, surely represents a most promising field for some sort of psychohistorical exploration – and, what is more, certain evidence that would make such exploration more than speculative. Nor is it a pattern of behavior limited to religious movements: it has characterized secular as well as sacred enthusiasms and so deserves to be considered in a general context and in a long perspective. It deserves to be considered, that is, within the framework of ideology historically understood.

In these terms it is clear that martyrdom, the theory as well as the practice, long antedated Christianity. As early as the fifth century, B.C. for example, Athenians killed in war were assured of deification; and the notion of dying in battle for a just cause has always been associated with martyrdom. This was especially the case with militant evangelicals. According to Antoine de la Roche Chandieu, martyrologist and pastor of the Huguenot church of Paris, 'We are in the world not to rest but to fight.'[64] Yet the Christian martyr was by no means a mere casualty of persecution, and in the spirit of Biblical humanism evangelicals rejected such corrupt medieval usage. Originally, they insisted, 'martyr' referred not to a victim but to one who 'testified' to the faith. Through such testimony even the most inarticulate could help to spread the word, such as the first victim of persecution in Troyes, who (according to the Protestant chronicler) 'preached only through his martyrdom'.[65]

Protestantism certainly had no monopoly on martyrs even in the sixteenth century, but it did seem to take a proprietary attitude

---

[63] E. R. Dodds, *Paganism and Christianity in an Age of Anxiety* (Cambridge, 1965), 121. In general, E. Kantorowicz, 'Pro patria mori in medieval political thought', in his *Select Studies* (Locust Valley, New York, 1965), 308; W. H. C. Frend, *Martyrdom and Persecution in the Early Church* (New York, 1967); H. A. M. Hoppenbrouwers, *Recherches sur la terminologie du martyre de Tertullien à Lactance* (Nijmegen, 1961); F. A. Norwood, *Strangers and Exiles, A History of Religious Refugees* (New York, 1969); and general bibliographical discussion in D. R. Kelley, 'Martyrs, myths and the Massacre: the background of St Bartholomew', *American Historical Review*, LXXVII (1972), 1323–52, and repr. in *The Massacre of St Bartholomew*, ed. A. Soman (The Hague, 1974), 181–202.

[64] Chandieu, *Histoire des persecutions*, xxviii. [65] Pithou, 5.

toward the martyrological tradition. In a sense the martyrly attitude which became so central to Protestant self-expression and self-advertisement was inherent in the attitude of the Reformation from the beginning; for Luther's stand at Worms, itself reminiscent of Hus's a century before, was potentially that of a martyr. A generation later this attitude was more generally broadcast through the co-operative enterprise of a remarkable collection of men who laid the foundations of modern martyrology. The works of Sleidan, Flacius Illyricus, Chandieu, Crespin, Ludwig Rabe and John Foxe were not only sustained by mutual borrowings but drew upon a common fund of experience, a common ideological commitment and common historical perspective. The international character of modern martyrology is especially evident in Crespin's *History of the Martyrs*, which attempted to be universal not only chronologically but also socially, admitting into its compass 'all conditions, ages, sexes and nations'.[66] There is no more comprehensive view of this aspect of the Protestant conscience than appears in this massive documentation of the persecution complex which shaped Protestant self-consciousness.

Most remarkable in the tradition of martyrdom is the sense of community with the past, even of recapitulating the experiences of earlier martyrs. The basic theme of Crespin's work was 'the conformity of the modern history of the martyrs with that of antiquity'. Another of his colleagues referred more specifically to early martyrs as precursors – 'proto-martyrs'[67] – and Lefèvre d'Etaples may also have had such an analogy in mind when he began his 'Agonies of the Martyrs' in 1519. The martyrly tradition represented not only a psychological link with the 'primitive church' but also the most concrete manifestation of 'true history' from apostolic times on. 'The blood of the martyrs is the seed of the church' is the invariably quoted maxim from Tertullian, and its life-giving force was continuous over the centuries.[68] The orthodox Catholic view, in keeping with the principle of ecclesiastical 'immanence', equated Christian history with the story of 'human traditions', especially of canon law, and of course was totally rejected by evangelical reformers, beginning with Luther. For them the shape of Christian history was the

---

[66] Crespin, I, preface; cf. G. Moreau, 'Contribution à l'histoire du livre des martyrs', *BSHPF*, CIII (1957), 173–99, and 'La Saint-Barthélemy, le martyrologie de Jean Crespin et Simon Goulart', in *Divers aspects de la Réforme au XVIe et XVIIe siècles* (Paris, 1975), 11–36; and W. Haller, *Foxe's Book of Martyrs and the Elect Nation* (London, 1963).

[67] Ludwig Rabe, *Der heiligen aus erwohlten Gottes Zeugen Bekennen und Martyren* (Strasbourg, 1552).

[68] Chandieu, *Histoire des persecutions*, lxii; Crespin, I, 1.

preservation of true doctrine through a tenuous series of 'witnesses to the truth', in the phrase of Flacius Illyricus.[69] It was precisely this doctrinal line (*successio doctrinae*, as contrasted by Melanchthon with the papal *successio personarum*) that was reflected in the history of the martyrs, assigned by retrospective judgment to the extended confessional family, especially of the 'communion of saints', established by sixteenth-century reformers. In contrast to papal interpretation, martyrology was purportedly concerned not with idolatrous relics but with the spiritual legacy of the faithful. In a sense it was the original 'Whig history'.

In many ways, like the humanist view of history to which it was indebted, martyrology was frankly pedagogical. In some ways the 'agonals' of the sixteenth century resembled more the *de viris illustribus* of classical inspiration than the *vitae sanctorum* of the medieval church. 'The memory of the first persecutions', wrote Chandieu, 'is a school that teaches how to remain true to one's calling.'[70] Crespin was even more specific about his didactic intentions. The stories he spent much of his life collecting provided 'consolation', a treasury of *exempla* for imitation and a kind of moral and anagogical mirror, reflecting for posterity the 'deeds and words' of a long line of Christian protagonists. The purpose was mimesis – *imitatio Christi* with a vengeance, for as Crespin recalled, Christ was indeed 'captain of the martyrs' – and thereby 'the restoration of the ruins of the church of the Lord'.[71] As a result of such ambitions martyrology was at least in part a myth-making enterprise. Crespin for one did not hesitate to improve upon his materials for the sake of his higher 'cause'; and he admitted that he wanted his stories not only to 'profit' his brethren but also to demonstrate the justice of the movement to the 'poor ignorant ones' outside it. There was hardly a more effective form of publicity and propaganda in the sixteenth century than the record of the increasing, and increasingly vocal, throng of martyrs.

In psychological terms the martyr was the very model of the true Christian, the true saint, and in the sixteenth century became a stereotype. This was evident in the first place in the martyrologies of Rabe, Foxe and especially of Crespin, who established 'ten marks of the martyr' as the Protestant equivalent of canonization.[72] The proper style of behavior was established by Calvin himself in his role of 'director of souls', the 'conscience of the Reformation'. The 'Nicodemites' he warned about represented the very opposite of the

---

[69] *Catalogus testium veritatis* (Basel, 1556).
[70] Chandieu, *Histoire des persecutions*, xiii.   [71] Crespin, I, 297.   [72] *Ibid.*, 364.

ideal; and much of his correspondence was devoted to urging the faithful, individually and in groups, to observe their religion openly even in the face of persecution. Achieving martyrdom, moreover, entailed a heavy weight of ritual, rhetoric, etiquette and symbolism, as reflected in interrogations, confessions of faith, execution scenes, crowd reactions and contemporary graphic representations. Whether burned in effigy like Beza or in fact like Du Bourg, the behavior of victims as well as officials and onlookers was in many ways predetermined.

The result was the fixing and even institutionalizing of martyrdom. On the one side were the official reactions conditioned by generations of legislation which determined the legal 'style and form' of procedure against 'horrible blasphemy' and which set schedules of punishment ranging from the ceremonious 'honorable amend' and money payment to degradation (in the case of clerics) and execution. Modes of physical punishment were also stereotyped and included the painfully symbolic cutting off of the right hand and cutting out of the tongue (which Crespin mistakenly thought was an innovation in his day) as well as strangulation and burning.[73] On the other side the behavior seems to have been equally structured, at least as reflected in the descriptions and language of the martyrologists. Not only did the condemned display the same virtues (*constance, perseverance, patience,* etc.) but they defended themselves, and attacked their enemies, in the same terms. They stood for 'pure doctrine'; their enemies – from that 'man without conscience or God' Morin, who pursued the men of the placards, to the bloody Lizet and the Cardinal of Lorraine – were all evil and hypocritical 'Sorbonistes', 'Louvainists', 'papists'.

The roll of martyrs grew steadily from the 1520s and was celebrated in song, spectacle, sermon, history and public outcry. They ranged from renowned intellectuals like Berquin to the simplest laborers, but all tended to be idealized through the martyrological process. Of one poor man from Dauphiné named Etienne Brun, Crespin wrote: 'In truth this person presents us with an example of the ancient integrity of rustic life and the first workers, who cultivated and improved not only their land but also their spirits and manners.' Many are named, but many others, thrown into the Seine or Rhine, went unrecorded. Death in these terms became commonplace. In Paris in particular, citizens became accustomed to the sight of executions in conventional places in the city, such as the Place Maubert near the university bookshop section, and the Place de

---

[73] *Ibid.*, 285; cf. Frederick II's *Liber Augustalis,* trans. J. Powell (Syracuse, 1969), 169.

Grève, especially in 1549 with the establishment of the notorious 'burning chamber' (*Chambre ardente*) of the Parlement which, Pierre Lizet presiding, sent down more than five hundred sentences against alleged 'Lutherans' in less than three years, including more than sixty executions. Such official action, paralleled in the Netherlands under Charles V's Inquisition and a little later in Mary Tudor's England, contributed directly to the beginnings of martyrological protest in these years as well as to the rise in emigration from all of these areas to free Protestant cities of the Rhineland, Switzerland and the Netherlands.[74]

The creation of martyrs seriatim was shocking enough; far worse was their mass production, although this too had ancient precedent. According to a famous distinction of the Huguenot historian Agrippa d'Aubigné, massacre victims constituted a second type of martyr, probably even more disturbing to the Protestant conscience.[75] The first sensational episode in France was the persecution of the Waldensians in Mérindole, which Crespin called 'as memorable as anything within the memory of man'. In 1545 a veritable campaign of extermination was waged in which 22 villages were destroyed and hundreds of persons killed; others fled underground (sometimes literally), and many ended up in Geneva. This event, together with the work of the *Chambre ardente*, threatened Protestants with the prospect either of martyrdom or its political equivalent, which was exile. There were other newsworthy atrocities, as Protestants regarded them in these years – the 'fourteen of Meaux', the 'six of Chambéry', the 'four of Lille', and especially the 'five of Lyon', which became truly an international incident.[76] In 1551 five students of Beza and Hotman, returning from the academy of Lausanne to reformed congregations in southern France, were arrested and charged with heresy. Despite intervention from various Swiss governments and appeals to Henry II, they were condemned and, one by one, like 'little soldiers', perished at the stake. Political repercussions, widely publicized letters of support from Calvin, Farel and Viret, and the soon-to-be-published martyrology of Crespin made this hardly unprecedented episode a *cause célèbre* throughout Europe.

In the late 1550s persecution and martyrdom seemed to reach a

---

[74] J. Vienot, *Promenades à travers le Paris des martyrs 1523–1559* (Paris, 1913); L. Halkin, *La Réforme en Belgique* (Brussels, 1957); Paillard, *Histoire des troubles religieux de Valenciennes*.

[75] *Histoire universelle*, ed. A. de Ruble (Paris, 1886–1909), I, 227.

[76] Crespin, I, 493, 595; II, 201, 405; Ménard, *Nîmes*, IV, 217; and cf. L. Bertrando and B. Ely, 'La Grotte de la Berigard, dernier refuge de Vaudois du Libernon en 1545', *BSHPF*, cxviii (1972), 345–53.

crescendo, and so did religious enthusiasm on both sides. In Troyes the head of the Virgin disappeared, and crowds gathered to accuse the Huguenots until the head was secretly – miraculously! – replaced. Other such episodes illustrating an active sort of 'immanence' further widened ideological divisions. These divisions were certified by a series of official pronouncements, especially what Hotman referred to as the 'atrocious' Edict of Compiègne (24 July 1557), and impressed upon the popular mind by a series of encounters, especially the affair of the rue St Jacques, which occurred just six weeks after this legislation fixing the death penalty for heresy.[77] As so often before, official efforts were rather a measure of than a deterrent to the spread of unorthodox opinions. Within two years the first national synod was meeting in Paris. In that same year (1559) there also occurred the execution of the most famous of all the Huguenot martyrs before the civil wars. The *parlementaire* Anne du Bourg was charged and imprisoned just before the death of Henry II and burned in December by the regency government, a fate which was hastened by the murder – counter-martyrdom – of one of his judges.

The distinction between martyrdom and religious massacre was not qualitative but quantitative, certainly as far as the psychology of persecution was concerned; and even before the advent of war, expectations of larger-scale reprisals were growing, if only because larger scale resistance was already in the making. Brewing at the same time as Du Bourg's case was that complex set of uprisings which came to be known as the conspiracy of Amboise and to be regarded by Huguenots, especially accomplices like Beza and Hotman, as the opening phase of the wars of religion. In the wake of this fiasco, which was designed to break the power of the Catholic faction by gaining possession of the person of the under-age King Francis II, came the most notable of the 'massacres' up to that time (March 1560). Of the 'rebels' captured at Amboise some were hanged from the parapets of the château, others were decapitated and others were pursued for months afterwards. The leader, La Renaudie, was hanged from a tree with a sign on his back designating him as 'chief of the rebels'. Another conspirator and old friend of Calvin and Hotman, the Sieur de Villemongis, was represented in a contemporary engraving, accompanying a journalistic account by Hotman, as crying out for vengeance for his fellows just as his own head was about to be cut off.[78] Both joined the growing

---

[77] See below, p. 200, n.57.
[78] D. R. Kelley, *François Hotman: A Revolutionary's Ordeal* (Princeton, 1973), 105ff.

martyrological canon and so helped to publicize their cause. So, a few weeks later, did Hotman's publisher Martin Lhommet, who was arrested and executed for possession of some of the printed propaganda issuing from the conspiracy.

The civil wars themselves were set off by one of the most widely publicized of all 'massacres', that of Vassy, which was precipitated by a confrontation between the Duke of Guise and a congregation within his territories. For some months the Huguenots of Vassy had been holding public services in violation of the law, and on this particular Sunday in March Guise and his men may well have been looking for trouble. They found it: there were over a thousand in the church singing psalms; and after the clash (who started the fighting was and still is debated) seventy-four Huguenots had, according to partisan accounts, been killed. In the view of one of its historians Vassy was 'the signal for a general massacre being prepared by our enemies in all parts of the kingdom'.[79] However improbable, this view was widely accepted among Protestants, and indeed over the next generation became a permanent dread. During the wars themselves other 'massacres' did occur, on both sides, and the fear of a general slaughter seemed to be borne out a decade later in the most celebrated of all the massacres, that of St Bartholomew, which succeeded the most notorious of all martyrdoms, that of the Huguenot leader, Admiral Coligny.

In the wake of these headline stories came one of the most remarkable outbursts of propaganda in modern history. Publicity ranged from lamentations for the victims to atrocity stories and to the most bloodthirsty cries for vengeance. Aside from such emotional appeals there were also objections framed in purely quantitative (if not entirely objective) terms. One prolific Huguenot author calling himself 'N. Froumenteau' – responsible also for the notorious *Alarm Bell* of 1573 and, as such, usually identified with Nicolas Barnaud – compiled two extraordinary works devoted to the question of the social costs of religious conflict. In one of these, *The Secret of Finances*, we are provided with listings not only of the exorbitant taxes and expenditures over the previous generation (down to 1581) but also of the loss of human lives, divided according to sex, status (ecclesiastics, nobles, soldiers, criminals), and other sorts of destruction (houses destroyed, villages burned and razed and 'women violated').[80] In all he estimated that about 765,000 persons had perished in the wars, of whom 76,010 were civilian casualties and

[79] [Hotman], *L'Histoire du tumulte d'Amboyse* (Strasbourg, 1560; BN Lb^{32}.15–16); also in MC, I, 320ff.
[80] *Le Secret des finances de France* (n.p., 1587), 407 and *passim*.

36,000 technically 'massacred'; 4500 bodies had passed Paris on the Seine, and 6000 more had been carried by the Loire; and at least 12,000 women and girls had been raped (probably twice as many since that sort of thing so often went unreported). In another work of that year, *The Mirror of the French*, which was also allegedly founded on archival sources (*preuves*), the author describes in great statistical detail the three precious 'pearls' in the royal treasury, namely, religion, the nobility and the third estate, and how all were being squandered. In the first category, said Barnaud, 'Four hundred ambassadors [that is, martyrs] were sent to the king to announce that most precious pearl in his cabinet' which was 'the word of God'. This was down to 1561; over the next two decades he estimated that 4150 more were added to this honor roll. One of the unnoticed results of St Bartholomew, it seems, was to add statistics to the already substantial arsenal of professional propaganda.

But truth is not beauty for most propagandists, and more effective than such prosaic enumerations were the more lyrical appeals which stirred consciences and sentiments. One Huguenot song dramatized the massacres in the most direct terms:

> In their places of hiding the murderers lay in wait,
> And springing upon us, discharged all their hate.
> 'Kill all!' was their cry. 'Let them remember this date!'[81]

Remember they did, and the memory of 24 August 1572 was the most productive source of propaganda of the entire century.

[81] Bordier, 288;

> Toutes nos voix, faictes plaintes
> Toutes nos lampes esteintes,
> Tous nos temples demolis
> Nos eglises dissipées
> Nos unions desliées
> Et nos presches abolis;
> Toutes nos maisons volées,
> Toutes nos loix violées,
> Tous nos hostels abbatus;
> Tous nos livres mis en cendre,
> Tous nos coeurs prestes à se rendre,
> Tous nos esprits combattus. . .
> Sortans comme de leurs ruches
> Ils ont dressé des embusches;
> Puis en leurs coeurs ils ont dit:
> 'Tuons tout! C'est la journée
> Qui nous estoit destinée
> Pour tuer tout dans le lict.'

> Our lights all extinguished, our temples demolished,
> Our brothers all scattered, our worship abolished.

Yet according to the verse at the head of Crespin's martyrology, even such persecution constituted victory; and in this victory there was displayed another version of that ever-present theme of evangelical revivalism:

> The Phoenix, they say, rises up from the fire,
>   Taking death, and then life, from the very same pyre;
> And so it will be with the martyrs we mourn:
>   You burn them in vain, for they all are reborn.[82]

It must be kept in mind that martyrdom was by no means a necessarily passive or mournful activity. Not only was the experience conventionally envisaged as personally joyful, but it was also potentially productive in a secular way. In the aftermath of St Bartholomew, martyrdom was explicitly politicized by none other than Beza himself. 'And this I conclude', he wrote in his *Right of Magistrates*, 'that we must honor as martyrs not only those who have conquered without resistance, and by patience only, against tyrants who have persecuted the truth, but those also who, authorized by law and by competent authorities, devoted their strength to the defense of the true religion.'[83] So we are back not only to the pagan notion of the honorable sacrifice but also to the Christian concept of the just war, which represents one of the most powerful of all generators of ideological movements. What is more, many contemporaries of Beza were well aware of the historical and ideological functions of martyrdom, so that one Catholic polemicist saw fit to compile a formal 'anti-martyrology'. The Christian God was not alone in benefiting from total commitment, for as Raemond put it, 'The Devil has need of his martyrs.'[84] So, in its most intense manifestations, does ideology.

A state of mind closely related to the martyr complex was the exile mentality, for flight was often the only alternative to death. Moreover, it better suited the growing activism of Protestants, for whom, especially in a time of crisis, Calvin's (and Luther's) theory of 'passive resistance' might be a denial of the Christian duty 'not to rest but to fight'. Contributing to the suspicions of all parties was the growing significance of international connections, especially through

---

[82] Crespin, I, xxxi.
[83] *Du Droit des magistrats*, ed. R. Kingdon (Geneva, 1970; 1st edn, 1574), 67, trans. in J. Franklin, *Constitutionalism and Resistance in the Sixteenth Century* (New York, 1969), 135. See below, pp. 301–6.
[84] Raemond, 870. Jacques Severt, *L'anti-Martyrologie* (Lyon, 1562).

the exile communities, which preserved ties with French congregations and in various ways became the vanguard of militant Protestantism. The same factors which, on a local level, accounted for congregational morale and coherence went into the making also of the international network of 'those of the religion'. Even more than the martyr complex, the exile mentality, dependent upon ideological attraction at a distance and spiritual kinship, transformed religious commitment into group awareness and political consciousness on a world-wide basis. This was the 'flock' (*congregatio fidelium* in an Augustinian and apostolic sense) in its most extended and threatening secular form. Perhaps it was of these sheep, threatening to transform themselves into wolves, that Catherine de Médicis's astrologer Nostradamus prophesied:

> The exiles by anger, secret hate,
> Together will conspire against the king's
> state.[85]

Religion obviously represents not merely a stage but a whole dimension of experience in ideological terms. However the consciousness of religious commitment comes, whether through sudden conversion or gradual enlightenment, and however it is expressed, in private devotion or public demonstration, it parallels other aspects of human life. One of these aspects is particularly essential to the realization of religious goals. If the psychological basis of religious commitment is an inherited or adopted faith, its conscious formulation, justification and perhaps communication to others presumes a more intellectualized structure with another sort of institutional base and with another sort of ideological significance. As the magisterial reformers in particular realized, religious enthusiasm could be fleeting; what was needed to make it enduring over generations was education. Let us turn now from the organization and propagation of religion to the rationalization and in a sense acculturation of religious life – from preaching to teaching.

---

[85] Nostradamus, *Les Propheties*, I, 13:

> Les exiles, par ire, hains intestine
> Feront au Roy grand conjuration,
> Secret mettront ennemies par la mine,
> Et les vieux siene, contre eux sedition.

iv · Academy:
Indoctrination and disputation

Wherein hath Ramus been so offensious?
. . . I say, Ramus shall die:
How answer you that?

Christopher Marlowe

iv · Academy:
Indoctrination and disputation

APOLOGUE: PETER RAMUS AND HIS MESSAGE
(1543)

In 1536 a young student at the University of Paris, defending his master's thesis before the faculty of liberal arts, tried to persuade his mentors that 'everything said by Aristotle is false'.[1] Such at least was the story later told, and given the later career of Ramus, there does not seem to be any reason to doubt it even if some of his disciples blew it up out of proportion. Not in any case that such a proposition would necessarily have shocked academic convention, which was used to toying with the most outlandish hypotheses with impunity and which conceded to reason only slightly less weight than authority. The trouble was that to question Aristotle was to question reason itself, or at least that dialectical brand of reasoning accepted in the schools for three centuries and more; and carried too far, such a challenge would shake the foundations of the highly rationalized faith of scholasticism as well as the structure of education. It was Ramus's misfortune – posthumously his fortune – that he did carry this thesis too far, to the point eventually of establishing himself as a surrogate Aristotle for Protestants who wanted to provide a rational and unencumbered basis for their reformed faith.

Distressing as Ramus's attitudes proved to be, the man himself was by no means a revolutionary type. On the contrary he appeared on the scene as an utterly conventional academic careerist. Five years younger than Calvin and likewise a Picard by birth, Ramus also was drawn to Paris to complete his education; and so he did after unusually prolonged struggles with the authoritarian curriculum of the University, which was as yet barely touched by the graces of humanistic learning. After receiving his master's degree at the relatively advanced age of twenty-one, Ramus went on to a traditional career as a teacher of liberal arts and especially of rhetoric and mathematics. At this lowly – 'trivial' and 'quadrivial' – level beneath

---

[1] General discussion in Walter J. Ong, *Ramus, Method and the Decay of Dialogue* (Cambridge, Mass., 1958), 36ff.

philosophy and the more exalted sciences, Ramus was at liberty to indulge his eccentric anti-Aristotelian views; and it was in these years that he began his more considered assault upon the academic establishment. This time, however, since he intended to publish his views, it would not be with impunity.

Seven years after the notorious if not mythical master's thesis Ramus published two works which really upset the philosophers and theologians of the Sorbonne – his *Institutions of Dialectic* and *Animadversions on Aristotle*, dedicated respectively to the university community and to the future Cardinal of Lorraine. The first was an elementary textbook of logic, the second a free-wheeling critique of Aristotle's *Organon*. Natural dialectic is the very image of God, Ramus declared, though much distorted by reflection in the Aristotelian mirror. Two sorts of men were devoted to its study: the one seeks a single truth through the critical study of authority; the other identifies a single authority with all truth. Aristotelianism not only contradicted nature, he went on to argue, it transformed the Christian religion into a form of idolatry and was an expression rather of the devil. Let us leave the Aristotelian chaos, Ramus concluded; let us go out into the light of true reason, that is, of Ramist dialectic and (by implication) true religion.

The upshot of these publications was the sort of pedantic squabble that Rabelais loved to satirize, specifically a disputation between a university commission drawn from the various faculties and Ramus and his representatives. The confrontation might have been dismissed as a more or less comic episode in the long history of inter-faculty rivalry, except that the king himself was drawn into the matter as arbiter. It was an unfortunate time for controversial works – Calvin's own *Institution of Christianity* had been condemned less than two years earlier – and the decision went against Ramus. A royal edict of 1 March 1544 charged him with having 'the audacity, arrogance, and impudence to reject the art of logic accepted by all nations'.[2] The faults attributed to Ramus were ignorance and bad faith; the religious question was not hinted at, although it was surely not far from official thoughts. In any case there followed the usual 'prohibition to all printers and booksellers and other subjects . . . from printing, selling, and distributing . . . the said books under threat of corporal punishment'. As usual, too, this edict, an authoritarian expression of an authoritarian philosophy, did not discourage Ramus from broadcasting his message.

[2] *Sentence donnee par le Roy contre maistre Pierre Ramus et ses livres* . . . (Paris, 1544; BN rés, F. 2085).

For Ramus this rebuke was only a temporary set-back. His teaching career advanced, and three years later Francis I's successor Henry II revoked the ban on his discussion of philosophical topics. Four years after that, in 1551, Ramus was appointed regius professor in that humanist 'College of Three Languages' which was still in the process of formation. From this eminence he carried on his campaign for a purer form of reasoning for the remaining two decades of his life. By 1561, moreover, he had abandoned religious orthodoxy and championed a reformed religion as well as a reformed dialectic. It was this decision that led to his final rebuke, that is, a martyr's death during the massacre of St Bartholomew's Day, 1572. This fate further dramatized Ramus's ideas, which by then had acquired an international force.

In the sixteenth century Ramus's world, the academy, was not a retreat for contemplation, it was a forum for debate and an arena for combat, sometimes physical as well as doctrinal. As a meeting-point of various generations, nations and disciplines, the university was a microcosm of the Reformation itself, and its pattern of strife was equally kaleidoscopic. Faculties and students, philosophical schools and religious sects, churchmen and laymen, ancients and moderns, gown and town, university administration and secular government – all these contributed to inter- and intra-mural conflicts that foreshadowed the religious and political disturbances which were beginning to divide Europe as a whole. The Reformation had started out as a scholars' quarrel, and in many ways it continued to receive sustenance and direction from the community of masters and pupils. If it was not as profoundly formative as the family in establishing basic assumptions and patterns of behavior, the academy was surely more significant in the conscious formulation, and even the socialization, of such attitudes.

In Ramus's time, then, confessional ferment did not create, it only intensified the long-standing warfare of inflated egos and intrenched groups. Scholarly routine, punctuated by power struggles, law suits, public scandals, and endless attempts to 'reform' curriculum and morals, was diverted increasingly into ideological channels. The student body, with its privileged foreign contingents, especially in the German nation, and a large number of unregistered hangers-on, seemed more than usually unruly, largely because they had the new religious (as well as the old academic) issues to worry about. In July 1534, just four months before the affair of the placards, a statute was passed to prevent students from carrying arms, frequenting taverns and theaters, fighting in the streets, neglecting to wear academic garb and especially reading unauthorized literature. After the treasonable eruption of October 1534, the affair of the placards, the king made a personal appeal to the university community, which he praised conventionally as the direct heir of Athens. 'Some evil blasphemers, people of low estate and lower understanding, have conspired against the holy sacraments . . . and used terms forbidden by all nations . . .', Francis I declared. 'I pray and admonish you and all my subjects to guard themselves, but especially their families and children, to see that they are well instructed and indoctrinated so that they do not fall into these evil opinions.'[3]

The structure of learning too seemed in disarray, and in fact the first concern of the statute of July 1534 was to reinforce the scholastic curriculum and respect for the authority of Aristotle, especially against the innovative pretensions of the teachers of grammar and rhetoric. Three years before, the theologians had criticized the liberal arts faculty for neglecting Aristotle and preferring the upstart Rudolph Agricola. They were perhaps more jealous than usual because of the recent establishment of three regius professors of classical languages, who seemed to threaten the Sorbonne's monopoly; and one of their number, Noel Beda, launched an attack upon this humanist institution, fearing that they would intrude upon the field of Biblical studies and so 'disseminate things favorable to the Lutheran sect'. Eight years later this statute was reissued in another attempt to reinforce Aristotelianism, religious orthodoxy, and academic order, which seemed to represent co-ordinate value-systems. It was just six months after this that Ramus emerged as one of the most obstinate violators of this official ideal, and so as a leader of the party of 'moderns' within the university.

By its very nature, of course, the academy was a dangerous institution, and in later years Ramus had to defend it from charges of sedition and rebellion. Its *raison d'être* was disputation, and its career had never been free of battles among the arts and sciences. In the three centuries before Ramus's subversive activities assaults had been launched against the traditional hierarchy of learning first by the terminist school, in various forms, and then by humanism, according to various styles, especially that of Lorenzo Valla. It was largely from the latter that Ramus derived his method and the quality and intensity of his anti-Aristotelianism. Although he drew significantly on the 'topical' logic of scholasticism, Ramus was concerned mostly with the task of reforming dialectic in terms of the traditionally subordinate art of rhetoric. Like the 'eloquence' of

[3] Bulaeus, VI, 247, 377; Crevier, V, 286.

humanists, the 'method' of Ramus aimed at a more persuasive and public-spirited form of discourse, pedagogical rather than philosophical – not law-given dogma, as Bucer put it, but the art of persuasion.[4] For Ramus reasoning was not the mechanical or tautological exercise of the syllogism but a creative process of 'finding' the 'arguments' located in the commonplaces of eloquent language and arranging them so as (in the Platonic conceit adopted by Ramus in 1543) to lead to divine illumination. Put simply, Ramist method was designed to urge men to conviction, to convert them to another way of thinking, to teach, or preach to them; and from here it was not very far to that more intensive sort of discourse we call (and sixteenth-century writers called) indoctrination.

In an age of print and heightened partisanship Ramus's ideas amounted to no less than a theory of propaganda. Ironically but perhaps not surprisingly, the result of his and other like attempts to reform logic was to re-establish a kind of scholasticism, though on a different basis, and especially to reaffirm the habits and techniques of disputation. Despite his humanistic source of inspiration, Ramus's fixation on the idea of an inalterable topical system made him still more argumentative and dogmatic than his scholastic nemeses; and his attitudes reinforced more piecemeal assaults on authority, political and religious as well as pedagogical. In these as well as in more academic ways Ramus fulfilled the humanist ideal of combining wisdom and eloquence, thought and action. In 1551 this ideal received institutional sanction when Ramus joined the 'Trilingual' college, later College Royal, as 'Professor of Eloquence and Philosophy'. This title indicated the force if not the substance of Ramus's message – just as his martyr's fate suggested its subversive implications.

---

[4] Bucer, *De Regno Christi*, II, 4; in *Melanchthon and Bucer*, ed. Wilhem Pauck (Philadelphia, 1969).

THE OLD STUDIUM AND THE NEW LEARNING

In Ramus's day the world of learning represented not only a social and intellectual elite but in many ways a separate culture. Its members were expected to speak and presumably to think in Latin and so to commit themselves to the heritage and habits of scholastic if not classical tradition. In large part Protestantism preserved this ideal; and among many others Melanchthon, the 'Preceptor of Germany', insisted on Latin to the exclusion of Luther's beloved vernacular, which he regarded as a distraction in the education of youth.[5] From the age of five or so children were to be drilled in conversation and grammar from authors ancient and modern, ranging from Cato and Donatus to Matthurin Cordier and Ramus himself, and sometimes they suffered punishment for vernacular lapses. The aim of this training was clear thinking as well as eloquence – for humanists like Valla and Ramus the two were identical – but of course there were more practical advantages. Mastery of Latin was the gateway to the higher sciences, the ladder to lucrative careers and positions of spiritual and worldly influence, whether in the formation of policy or in the shaping of public opinion. In France, for example, a third of all benefices went to university graduates, and similar preferment was enjoyed by jurists. Latin discourse also entailed a great cargo of attitudes, assumptions, issues and modes of expression independent of religious or political predilection; and many of these carried over into vernacular parlance as well. In many intangible ways the emergence of modern ideology took place in the context of neo-scholastic and neo-classical Latin.

In theory sixteenth-century education was extraordinarily conservative and backward-looking. Though aimed at individual improvement and even perfection, socially it was static and oriented toward traditional ideas of classes, ranks, offices and vocations. One of the most comprehensive expressions of conventional wisdom was a treatise published in 1559 by François Corlieu devoted to the 'education for all estates'.[6] For Corlieu everybody had a vocation which, ideally at least, was determined by his talents and which fixed his position in society. Among the social conditions he de-

---

[5] K. Hartfelder, *Philip Melanchthon als Praceptor Germaniae* (Berlin, 1889), esp. 197, 250ff.; and more generally G. Coulton, *Europe's Apprenticeship* (London, 1940). University history may still be usefully approached through such old classics as Rashdall and D'Irsay, though they are much better informed about the medieval period; all too few works deal with questions of the organization of knowledge and the relation of ideas and institutional arrangements, one exception being G. Leff, *Paris and Oxford Universities in the Thirteenth and Fourteenth Centuries* (New York, 1968).

[6] *Instruction pour tous estats* (Paris, 1559).

scribed were princes, magistrates, lords, merchants, artisans, pastors, doctors, scholars, the police, fathers, mothers, children, servants, widows, the sick and the aged. It was his purpose to establish norms for each of these roles, describing the ideal pastor, for example, who expounds 'true religion' to his fellows, and the ideal wife, who serves her husband and nurtures her children, and exhorting all to maintain the overall social balance. Even educational reformers like Erasmus and Ramus regarded education as dynamic only in moral terms, a way of instilling the patterns and ideals of Latin culture for individual excellence.

On the highest level the preservation of this culture was the business of the university, which was the pedagogical aspect of the ecclesiastical establishment. From the beginning the model was the University of Paris – 'Parent of the Sciences', according to a founding bull of 1231 – which indeed had pretensions as universal as those of pope and emperor. Within France this 'university of masters and scholars' was a world to itself, 'une sommaire de tous etats', Charles IX called it in 1568.[7] Internationally it claimed to be the central repository of the European cultural inheritance, a view reinforced by legend as well as tradition. The most revered story was that the university was the product of a 'translation of studies' (parallel to the more famous 'translation of empire') from Greece to Rome; it was, as Louis XII said on his succession in 1498, 'the fountain of moral and political sciences, which had first been among the Greeks, then among the Italians and now is in our kingdom'. The associated Gallican myth that it was a foundation of Charlemagne (hence another agent of the 'translation of empire') also persisted, though it was exploded later in the sixteenth century. In fact, observed Antoine Loisel, it was an ecclesiastical creation of the twelfth century and its designation as 'daughter of the king' merely poetic. Yet the university had accumulated an impressive collection of privileges, precedents and doctrinal victories which made it an imposing force in sixteenth-century controversies. The faculty of theology was especially intimidating: the Sorbonne was regarded by the orthodox as an authority hardly less final – and by the unorthodox as hardly less tyrannical – than Rome itself.

In theory the Parisian *Studium* was a virtually totalitarian structure intended not only for 'indoctrination' but also for the moral and physical control of its members, especially its younger charges. The curriculum was represented as a ladder of learning rising up out of

[7] Isambert, XI, 11; cf. Pierre Rebuffi, *Commentarii in constitutiones seu ordinationes regias* (Lyon, 1554), 1, and Antoine Loisel, *De l'Université de Paris* (Paris, 1587).

the liberal arts into the 'sciences' of theology, philosophy, law and medicine, and under the guardianship at successive levels of professional 'masters' and 'doctors' of these disciplines, who acted in many ways as surrogate fathers, seeing to it that students went to class (and paid their fees), attended religious services regularly, prayed for the king and behaved themselves in the city. Naturally, they had to set a good example by their own regularity in teaching, seemliness of dress and appearance and obedience to higher authorities, especially in religious matters. Collectively, they also determined the content of the courses, the pace and progress of teaching, the granting of degrees and to a large extent the professional future of their disciples. The statutes of the university formed a continuous and repetitive tradition regulating the privileges of the particular faculties, nations and colleges, determining the method of government and office-holding, and setting down rules for extra-curricular behavior and punishment for misbehavior.

The intellectual basis of this institution in the sixteenth century was still 'scholasticism', that old dialectical method which provided the structure not only of the learning process but also many of the published forms of scholarship. The artificial (and some critics would say, superficial) approach to knowledge taken by the *scholasticus*, or teacher of logic, permeated the faculties both of the self-proclaimed sciences and of the arts situated lower in the scale of learning, including grammar and rhetoric, which made up the bottom two-thirds of the so-called *trivium* and the basis of the humanities (the *studia humanitatis*). Theology continued to be 'queen of sciences' as in the days of St Thomas; and classroom instruction still protected students from original sources through summaries, commentaries, 'questions to be disputed' and 'whatever' (*quodlibeta*). Of course such substitution of a 'barbarous' language for the 'pure words' of ancient authors was lamented by humanists from Petrarch to Erasmus; but before the sixteenth century such criticism remained largely extramural. Although some of the assigned 'authors' might change, the Studium itself remained intact, and the forms and substance of scholasticism kept their grip on learned discourse.

Yet resistance there was, even intermurally; and in general it came from below, in particular from the arts faculty. Here 'humanists', or 'artists', had long struggled for parity with the arrogant scientists. As always there was a material as well as an ideological side to the debate; and in 1507, for example, the *artisti* of Paris agitated for a fairer share of the endowment to enhance their dignity as well as their life-style.[8] Intellectually, the central question was still, as it had been for three centuries, the value of Aristotle, 'the Philosopher'. The classic expression of Renaissance anti-Aristotelianism had been given by the iconoclastic scholar who was a major source of inspiration for Luther as well as for Erasmus and Ramus. Lorenzo Valla presented his critique implicitly in his best-selling textbook, the *Elegancies of Latin*, and explicitly in his attempt to begin a 'reform of dialectic' (*repastinatio dialecticae*), the *Dialectical Disputations*. Valla's final authority was no single figure but rather antiquity as a whole (*auctoritas antiquitatis* was his phrase), and the Aristotelians in particular he condemned as obscurantist and anti-social.[9] 'O that peripatetic tribe!', he lamented, 'destroyer of natural meaning.' In opposition to its empty categories and imaginary problems Valla set the ideals of his own 'profession'. The basis of his 'humanistic method' (*usus humanitatis*) was not dialectic but grammar; and this, he argued, 'depends not on reason but on example . . ., not on law but on custom'. Moreover, he declared, 'philosophy and dialectic should not depart from the most common custom', which is to say civil discourse. One of the axioms of Valla, and indeed of the whole humanist tradition, was the inseparability of eloquence and wisdom, that is, of the liberal arts and philosophy, of language and thought, and in a sense of the human community and learning.

This line of argument established a direct bridge not only between the 'arts' and the 'sciences' but also between Italian humanism and the Reformation. After Valla, the most important travellers on this bridge were Rudolph Agricola, whom Erasmus honored as the first agent of humanism in Germany (and to some orthodox folk suspect on this ground alone); Melanchthon, who reasserted Valla's position; Johann Sturm, a Parisian 'artist' who founded the academy of Strasbourg; and of course Erasmus, of whom one Protestant friend remarked, 'He is a grammarian not a philosopher, a rhetorician not a lawyer, an orator not a theologian.' It was this 'unscientific' attitude, indeed, that led Erasmus to defend Valla's apparently 'intolerable act of temerity' in criticizing scriptures as a grammarian and made him suspect in the eyes of orthodox scholars.[10] Luther shared not only the fundamentalism but also the anti-Aristotelianism of this tradition, though he was worried more about the infidel views of

---

[8] Crevier, v, 69.
[9] *Dialecticae disputationes*, in *Opera omnia* (Basel, 1540), I, 673ff. Cf. Kelley, *Foundations of Modern Historical Scholarship* (New York, 1970), chapter I.
[10] Letter to B. Amerbach, 31 Aug. 1518, in Allen, III, 384.

immortality than about the fallacious logic of the Philosopher; and in 1520 he succeeded in getting Aristotelian logic, physics and metaphysics as well as canon law dropped from the curriculum of the University of Wittenberg. But the most direct continuation of Valla's campaign was that of Ramus, who thereby took over leadership in the many-sided sixteenth-century debate over correct 'method', which underlay so many aspects of religious and political ideology as well as modern scientific philosophy.

The doctrinal pedigree and associations of the 'new learning' (*nova doctrina*) were not lost on its orthodox critics, who from the beginning recognized its subversive tendencies. At the University of Paris, for example, authorities looked with dismay at the increasing popularity of Agricolan logic, especially among the younger masters; and from the 1520s a series of statutes were issued to resist such *avant-garde* ideas and to restore the hegemony of 'scholastic' method. As always first priority was given to mastery of Aristotelian dialectic and to the disputations which developed 'alacrity in argument'; then to advanced logic and physics, again with the customary *quaestiones disputata*.[11] Throughout, the role of grammarians was to be strictly limited, and they were forbidden either to usurp the function of the *scholasticus* or to poach on the profession of philosophy. 'Dialectics for the dialecticians' was the motto of this 'reform' program designed to keep the *studia humanitatis* in their ancillary position:

With regard to many members of the younger generation it was a losing battle. Ramus himself described the beginnings of Aristotle's eclipse and his own fall from academic grace.

Since the fair days of Greece and Rome, Rudolph Agricola is the first to recover the image of logic and to invite youth to search the poets and orators, not only as masters of style and eloquence, but as masters of reasoning and the art of thinking. Formed in the school of Agricola, Johannes Sturm first made Paris recognize these splendid fruits and excited in the university an incredible ardor for the art of which he revealed the utility. It was in the lessons of this great master that I first learned the art of logic and then taught it to the youth . . .[12]

(Nor was Ramus's own reputation as 'corrupter of youth' diminished by his association with the Protestant Sturm.) And there were more general signs of the insubordination of the *studia humanitatis* in the years when Ramus was preparing his academic subversion. In 1535 grammar and rhetoric were finally recognized as 'liberal arts', and

---

[11] Bulaeus, VI, 11; Crevier, V, 248.
[12] Cited in F. Graves, *Peter Ramus and the Educational Reformation of the Sixteenth Century* (New York, 1912), 17.

more significantly, from 1530 Francis I began to assemble that humanist academy of 'Three Languages' which so affronted Sorbonists.

It is in such a context that we should understand the rise of the new learning. It was a 'trivial revolution', a reaction from the lowly abode of the humanities against the professionalism of the upper faculties. As Ramus put it,

The grammarians and the rhetoricians were the first to uncover the trickery and corruption of the scholastics: having expelled the stupid barbarism of such persons and substituted the poets, historians and orators, they showed that there was no better way to become a master of eloquence [*maitre de bien dire*] than through the style acquired by the reading and imitation of remarkable authors . . .[13]

The aim was a fundamental change of priorities, the transformation of a hierarchy of disciplines into a 'circle' of learning, an 'encyclopedia' embracing human culture in all of its richness and concreteness and organized for persuasive transmission to society as a whole. This was the rationale of Ramist method, which accordingly emphasized mnemonics and pedagogical technique at the expense of discovery and the advancement of learning. On the individual level the model was grammar, which classically was divided into two parts, 'history' and 'method', that is, substance and structure (words and syntax). In social terms the basic discipline was rhetoric, which resolved the problem of how most effectively to communicate knowledge and to join it to action.

The intellectual and social implications of the new learning are profound, and at least two of them require attention in the present connection. The first is the attendant belief in the primacy and autonomy of the Word, a kind of intransigent fundamentalism establishing a bond between the critical methods of humanist scholars and the uncompromising Biblicism of evangelical reformers. From the *sacra pagina* of medieval grammarians to the *sola scriptura* of Luther, Biblical humanists have assumed that knowledge and perhaps salvation come only from the direct and literal understanding of original and authoritative texts; and preserving this attitude through charges of triviality and literalism, they contributed much to the style of modern propaganda. A by-product was the prominence given to the dangerous knowledge contained in Greek, that 'language of

---

[13] *Prooemium reformandi Parisiensis Academiae* (n.p., 1562), trans. *Advertissements sur la reformation de l'université de Paris au Roy* (1562), in *AC*, v, 118: 'Comme naturellement la viellesse est avare et rechigné, ainsi la ieunesse est dereglée et abandonne a son plaisir.'

heresy'; and indeed one of the propositions officially condemned was the humanist assumption that 'Holy scripture cannot be well understood without Greek, Hebrew and other such languages.'[14]

The second implication of humanist attitudes is more invidious and harder to demonstrate. This is the belief that orators, whose business was to reach out and to persuade people, had a concern for social welfare lacking in school philosophers. While dialecticians dealt with private arguments and irrelevant issues, rhetoricians had human and even humanitarian aims. They also had more effective methods, moving people by example, as Valla explained the purpose of his profession, not instructing them by precept. So rhetoric had a kind of built-in social conscience, and this claim to public utility was carried over into the ecclesiastical and proselytizing program of religious reform.

For such reasons, aside from specific associations with heresy, the new learning constituted an innovative force, disruptive of conventional attitudes and productive of effective methods of indoctrination. That Renaissance rhetoric in particular contained both a theory and a technique of propaganda is suggested by contrasting it with Aristotelian dialectic. Formally what occurred was the replacement of scholastic categories by rhetorical 'topics', of general species by 'commonplaces'; and the result was to establish as the basic units of discourse invention and arrangement (*inventio* and *judicium*), and so in a sense to give verbal strategy priority over rationality.[15] The aim was to choose a proper (and pre-established) topic and then to devise a pattern of discourse to give it maximum memorability and effectiveness, emphasizing not only logic and consistency but also persuasiveness, impact and usefulness. The key word was 'faith' (*fides*) in the sense not of fidelity to truth as its usage was in formal logic, but rather of persuasiveness and human certitude and contribution to some worthy public purpose. Such was the epistemological thrust of Valla's activist conception of rhetoric, that it not only furnished the best means of understanding the world but that it was also the best means of shaping it. This was the implication of his view that the rhetorician was not only the best philosopher but also the 'leader of the people' (*dux populi*) – not only an ideologue but a mover and shaker of history. Montaigne's observation, though not very complimentary , may be most apt: 'A rhetorician of times past said that to make little things appear great was his profession.'[16] By

---

[14] Argentré, II, 78: 'La Sainte Escriture ne se peut bonnement entendre sans la langue grecque, hebraique et autres semblables.'

[15] P. Joachimsen, 'Loci communes', *Luther Jahrbuch*, VIII (1926), 27–97; J. Lechner, *Renaissance Concepts of the Commonplaces* (New York, 1962).

[16] Montaigne, *Essais*, I, li, 'De la vanité des parolles'.

extension the business of the propagandist in the sixteenth century was to make great things appear incomparably and transcendently great.

SIC ET NON

Universities had always been an intimidating force in intellectual life. Oriented toward the past, they were nevertheless, because of their function and methods, in the vanguard of intellectual change. By design the university was an arena of debate and competition, preparing youth for adulthood, and of necessity it reflected the divisions and conflicts of that same adult world. Envisaged as a bridge between family and society, it shared some of the worst as well as the best features of each. Perhaps most fundamental was the discipular relationship which in some ways recapitulated as well as replaced that between father and son; for normally, intellectual identity and status were achieved either by inheritance of or rebellion against the doctrines of the Magister: Magisterism and anti-magisterism, whether in a favorable or a pejorative sense, were crucial stages in the emergence of self-consciousness. And as intellectual offspring squabbled over and sometimes squandered the magisterial inheritance, so various ideological families feuded over several generations, with distant cousins sometimes taking up the cause of their intellectual progenitors. Every discipline, it seems, had its eponymous heroes and villains; and the posthumous battles of these legendary giants ring through the intellectual life of modern European institutions of higher learning. Similarly, 'moderns' were always rising up to challenge the 'ancients' and so to give impetus to a generational cycle that reinforced the pattern of discipular deviation. Added to this doctrinal pandemonium, of course, were uncounted disputes between the disciplines: law versus medicine, theology versus philosophy, and the liberal arts in general versus the higher sciences.[17]

In the context of sixteenth-century religious schism this doctrinal belligerence contributed to a number of ideological explosions. The age of Reformation was the seed-time of 'isms', and this concept or speech habit was born of university allegiances and commitments.

[17] The battle of the arts has been discussed in the Italian context by E. Garin, *La Disputa delle arti nel Quattrocento* (Florence, 1947), and L. Thorndike, *Science and Thought in the Fifteenth Century* (New York, 1929), 24–58; the academic battles of ancients and moderns have hardly been treated at all in social or intellectual terms, except for later periods.

The suffix itself was a 'Hellenism' of ancient origin and was familiar in such forms as 'sophista' and (in Roman law) 'Papinianista'. Christian tradition made use of it in terms largely of religious connotation, including Christianism, atheism, paganism (from the eighth century) and Judaism, although the active form (-ize, from *izein*) was more common. University jargon added the usage '-ist' (*ista*), applying it in the first instance to students in particular fields or phases of study: *artista* or *umanista*, in the arts faculty, *canonista* or *decretista* in canon law and *legista* and even *feudista* in civil law.[18] More emotive forms referred to doctrinal allegiances, such as Thomist, Averroist, terminist, Bartolist ('Bartolo-Baldism', in the pejorative coinage of the law student Beza), and the like. In the sixteenth century such coinages proliferated to include Ramist, Machiavellist, and a wide range of eponymous religious sects. Behind each of these '-ists', moreover, there lurked at least potentially a more or less coherent '-ism'; and each of these in its own way tended to attract allegiance and to generate a certain amount of self-expression. In some ways this may seem to be a trivial point; but the explosion of '-isms' in this period represents a rough linguistic measure of the expansion of ideology, of which the university continued to be the leading spawning ground.

In these terms too the University of Paris was a leader of academic fashion. Four centuries before Peter Ramus, another humanistic 'corrupter of youth', Peter Abelard, had begun to establish the reputation of Paris as a center of disputatious learning. A poet and champion of the inner life and the primacy of 'conscience' as well as a virtuoso of dialectics, Abelard also posed dangerous questions which, 'yes or no', were essential to conventional doctrine. The subsequent more formal organization of the Studium at Paris gave institutional form to the dialectical and eristic learning which dominated academic thought into the sixteenth century and beyond. Always a leader of academic fashion, the university was, behind its façade of orthodoxy, continuously a cockpit of doctrinal war and generational conflict, a hotbed of intrigue and careerism, and a planting ground for innumerable 'reformations', revivals and radicalisms. From the thirteenth century the central issue of scholarship was the accommodation of Aristotle to Christian theology; and it was largely the positions taken on his philosophy that determined relationships to the various academic families, a spectrum running from quasi-official Thomism to officially condemned Averroism, and

[18] Cf. A. Campana, 'The origin of the word "humanist"', *Journal of the Warburg and Courtauld Institutes,* IX (1945), 60–73.

which established also the form of debate and particular questions
on a wide range of intellectual, religious and social issues.

Whether it was a consequence of training in dialectic or a reflection of institutionalism, such academic partisanship was ingrained
and by the sixteenth century had become a standing joke as well as a
traditional target of criticism. The *kis-kis, kan-kan* controversy (how
to pronounce properly the Latin *quisquis and quamquam*), satirized by
Rabelais and others, became a symbol for the extremes to which
academic frivolity might go. That even such pedantic nonsense
could stir emotions and attract converts was suggested by Ramus,
who in one passage mentions the condemnation of a scholar for
'grammatical heresy'. But Ramus himself fell in perfectly with the
pattern, carrying on one of the storied quarrels of the century with
Jacques Charpentier, defender of Aristotle and (some said) murderer of Ramus during the St Bartholomew massacres. In any case
the argument over Ramist dialectic – 'Petromachy', contemporaries
called it – lay at the very center of debates over not only pre-
Cartesian 'method' but also true (and literally pre-'Methodist')
religion.

From the beginning the University of Paris had been a center of
turmoil that was not only intellectual but also social and even
political, especially in times of crisis or schism. Over many generations placards had been posted in the quarter, and illegal assemblies
and rioting had disturbed academic tranquility. The Sorbonne itself
had created a tradition of schismatic potential, that is, the Gallican
program of a national clergy and a conciliarist church; and these
ideas continued to generate dissent in confrontation both with king
and with pope. One of the most serious disputes arose from the
Concordat of 1516, by which patronage of the French church was
placed largely in the king's hands, striking directly at the privileges
of university graduates, whose degrees put them in line for lucrative
benefices. In 1518 disorderly meetings were held to voice objections.
The king reacted angrily, issuing 'prohibitions to rectors, doyens of
the faculty and other university persons of this city to assemble to
discuss matters of the king, his government and his laws, and things
which are none of the university's business'.[19] Even before the
problem of organized heresy, then, the dissenting habits of the
university community and the repressive habits of officialdom were
firmly established: the form if not the content of ideological warfare
was set.

This turmoil found a focus during the 1520s through the 'Lutherist'

---

[19] De Thou, I, chapter 8; cf. Bulaeus, vi, 88.

issue, which was identified in the popular as well as the official mind with radicalism of all sorts and threats from Germany (since this was during the first stage of the Habsburg–Valois conflict). In a sense the Sorbonne had fixed its position in 1514, when it pronounced against Reuchlin in his struggle against scholastic critics of the humanist *avant-garde*, and its reaction to Luther seven years later was wholly predictable. A commission of the faculty of theology condemned his views even before the pope issued his bull and the Emperor his imperial ban. From then on the university community was increasingly factionalized, ranging from the most intemperate sacramentarians and iconoclasts through Erasmians of various persuasions to orthodox intransigence. The latter was personified by Noel Beda, who from 1516 had been in conflict with Reuchlin, Erasmus, Lefèvre d'Etaples and others over a series of technical theological issues; and he had no scruples about locating Luther in the same nest.[20] For the next thirty years in fact 'Lutheranism' became a catch-all term for almost any heresy short of anabaptism. For Beda, moreover, neither the popularization of scriptures nor philological criticism was to be tolerated without strict ecclesiastical controls, and he became opposed both to the work of Berquin and the Trilingual college. Beda appeared to be an archetypal Sorbonist, a symbol of everything that evangelical reform hated.

The convulsive state of the academic community was increased by its cosmopolitanism in these years; and the cultural shock inherent in university education was intensified by the mixture of nationalities as well as the disparities of ages and social backgrounds of the students. Young men like Valentine Tschudi and Franciscus Dryander, who had been exposed to German ideas of reform, found the antiquated scholasticism of Paris both ludicrous and impious; and of course French Protestants found it totally evil. Dryander came expecting marvels. 'Unfortunately, once arrived', he wrote, 'when I realized the ignorance, pride and arrogance ruling there, I cursed my luck. Small preceptors, small masters . . ., small instruction . . . Neither the rhetoricians nor the philosophers nor even the theologians . . . had any concern for public welfare but only their private interest.'[21] Complaints were registered by the faculty, too. George Buchanan, who was rector during the 1530s, wrote a Latin poem describing 'How miserable is the condition of the teachers of humanities in Paris.'[22] Calvin vividly described the troubles at the

---

[20] W. F. Bense, 'Noel Beda and the Humanist Reformation at Paris' (unpublished Ph.D. thesis, Harvard University, 1967).
[21] J. Le Coultre, *Mathurin Cordier* (Neuchâtel, 1926), 2–3.
[22] *Opera omnia* (Paris, 1725), II, 301: 'Quam misera sit conditio docentium literas humaniores Lutetiae.'

university in the months before he took flight. Severest of all, of course, were victims of the Sorbonne like Luther, who called it 'the mother of all errors in Christendom, the greatest spiritual whore the sun shines on, and the real backdoor to hell', and this opinion was current in Paris as well, especially in the privileged German nation.

From the 1520s students' misbehavior seemed to be on the rise, and this was obviously related to contemporary acts of religious dissidence, demonstrations and vandalism, including the outbreak of iconoclasm in 1528 and of course the affair of the placards six years later. Increasingly, university legislation tried to curb excesses inspired by religious enthusiasm, including the singing of psalms and other unconventional actions at the traditional 'tumultuous celebrations', notably the May Day rites in the fields of St Germain-des-Prés; and culprits were threatened with loss of academic privilege. It was in the fall of 1533 that the rector Nicolas Cop gave the scandalous address which sent his collaborator (and recent convert) Calvin into exile. This was a year before the reforming statute of 1534. This declaration, which had reaffirmed scholastic method, directed itself also to the morals and religious opinions of students (*etudians* included masters as well as pupils), ordering them to mind their classes and chapel attendance instead of the popular and increasingly impertinent dramatic presentations, and forbidding young masters to sport beards (*prolixa barba*), which were apparently becoming symbols of defiance and perhaps of unorthodoxy.[23] Special warnings were given about unmatriculated troublemakers, who swelled the academic community to 20,000, as the Venetian ambassador estimated in 1546, about money-lenders and unlicensed booksellers, and especially about the 'impudent books of the heretics'. Instructors were supposed to reprimand students found with such books and report any second offenses.

Such efforts at control seemed to be largely in vain. Heresy remained on the rise, and so did the 'fetes tumultueuses' of the students, such as the May Day celebrations of 1539, which got more than usually out of hand.[24] Three years later the 'edict of the beards', as Beza liked to refer to it, had to be repeated. It was in such an effervescent environment that numerous future ideologists – not only Calvin, Mathurin Cordier and other earlier exiles, but also younger men like Beza, Hotman, Du Bourg, Sleidan and Sturm – spent their formative years. This was the period too, it should be remembered, of the condemnations of the iconoclastic views both of

---

[23] Crevier, v, 267; Beza, *Le Passavant*, trans. I. Liseaux (Paris, 1875), 23.
[24] Crevier, v, 342.

Ramus and of Calvin. Within the faculty the result was a decision to establish a theological code; and in July 1543 twenty-five articles of faith were issued under the seal of the Parlement of Paris.[25] This pamphlet, issued to all prelates, reasserted the value of the sacraments, the invocation of Mary and the saints, monastic vows and other items of dogma which would soon be re-endorsed at the Council of Trent. But like that assembly, which was to convene within two years, the Sorbonne and its profession of faith reflected less the unity than the doctrinal polarization of the intellectual community.

Such conditioned belligerence contributed very directly to the religious conflicts which formed the ideological context of Ramus's entire academic career. In the 1550s these conflicts reached a new height as religious enthusiasm converged with traditional university rivalry: on the one hand the students, especially foreigners and 'externals', who unlike the 'martinets' lived in the houses of citizens, many of them exercising their right to bear arms, and sometimes using them; and on the other hand the 'new evangelicals', whose practices of psalm-singing, marching and 'going to sermon' exhibited a similar tendency to public disorder. Together, in the spring of 1557 several weeks before the turmoil in the rue St Jacques, they created a major crisis for the university.[26] As usual the scene was the Pré-aux-clercs, a student gathering place for generations, though bitterly disputed with the monks of St Germain, and since September 1555 a favorite spot also for Protestant services. In May, the usual month for student unrest, even as the university was discussing another 'reform', there was rioting in protest against the erection of buildings in these fields. In the ensuing clashes one student was killed, another arrested and imprisoned, while his supporters staged further demonstrations against interference from civil authorities, especially the Châtelet, the municipal court, which had been trying to extend its jurisdiction over the unruly university community. The result was that the Parlement of Paris, after confiscating the Pré-aux-clercs, issued a severe edict to control the problem. A six o'clock curfew was imposed, windows were ordered to be kept closed and rooms checked, and all weapons to be confiscated. The most seditious of the students, Baptiste Coquastre, was condemned to be hanged and then burned, after which his supporters responded by the old practice of posting 'seditious and menacing' placards. They shouted down the rector when he tried to read the

---

[25] *Edict du Roy sur les articles faictz par la faculté de theologie de l'université de Paris concernans nostre Foy et forme de prescher* (Paris, 1562; BN F.47621.3 and 46803.5); also in Isambert, XII, 367, 374. Cf. Crespin, II, 365.

[26] Crespin, II, 586.

edict in assembly and threatened to start fires. Some threw stones at the police, killing one of them. Finally the king himself took charge of the problem, ordering classes to be suspended, more arrests to be made and foreign students to be expelled.

This upheaval threatened the privileges and the very foundations of the university and threw a scare into faculties, which for once acted in a unified fashion. A commission was appointed to appeal to the king, including among others Peter Ramus, who had been appointed regius professor in 1551 despite his unpopular views. In an address in defense of the university community Ramus suggested that the trouble was not political or religious but merely a manifestation of the age-old conflict of generations, which afflicted schools as well as families. 'The university should not be called seditious and rebellious', he argued. 'Old age is naturally illiberal [*avare*] and ill-humored', he pleaded, 'while youth is disorderly and given over to pleasure.'[27] In the end the king relented, and academic privileges were restored. Yet the pattern of conflict continued and in fact increased, as the religious question became ever more pressing. Two years later degree-holders were denied their traditional right to preach in Parisian pulpits without permission of the bishop, but this practice continued, as did the posting of placards.

In this growing chorus of dissent the familiar voice of Ramus continued to be prominent. He had the sort of career that encouraged legends and anecdotes – many of them exaggerated, to say the least, beginning with the notorious master's thesis of 1536 and ending with the circumstances of his murder in 1572 – and it is often difficult to distinguish fact from fable. One story pertains to the months just preceding the outbreak of civil war. Having for many years displayed what one historian has called 'a kind of inner iconoclasm',[28] Ramus apparently decided to go in for the real thing; and in his own College of Presles he either had removed, or had destroyed, some religious statues, remarking that he had no need for such deaf and dumb auditors. Thus he helped to provoke the extensive dispute during the spring of 1562 over the worship of images, a dispute that would be carried on more violently in the real fighting a few months later. In this same period Ramus delivered an extraordinarily ill-timed address to King Charles IX on the old question of 'the reformation of the university of Paris'.[29] After his

---

[27] *Harangue touchant ce qu'on faict les deputez de l'Université de Paris envers le roy* (Paris, 1557). See above, p. 141, n. 13.

[28] F. Yates, *The Art of Memory* (London, 1966), 235.

[29] Argentré, II, 399, request (3 June 1568) followed by an *arrêt* of the Parlement of Paris against Ramus.

usual defense of grammar and rhetoric over conventional philosophy, he set out a program of practical reform including higher salaries for teachers and a more rigorous schedule for students. He went on also to support the practice of allowing theology students to give sermons in order to help 'spread the gospel'. Bad as his timing was, his choice of words was worse. They reeked of heresy, and in fact Ramus admitted that his final decision to join the evangelical religion came in the fall of 1561 in the wake of the Colloquy of Poissy.

So Ramus fled from Paris just after the outbreak of war and just before he would have had to sign the oath modeled on that of 1543, and establishing *de facto* what would be legally binding six years later, that is, the exclusion of all Calvinists from the University of Paris.[30] This marked the final polarization of the academy, and it was endorsed in a later statute giving absolute priority to that symbol of immanence which had been the major object of contention since the affair of the placards had disturbed academic tranquility – celebration of the mass. Ramus himself, returning to Paris after spending some time teaching his 'method' in the Protestant centers of Basel, Zurich, Bern, Strasbourg and Heidelberg, never escaped his reputation for academic subversion. Directly or indirectly he paid the price for this in 1572 – a casualty not only of the massacres of St Bartholomew but also of that 'Petromachy' that had started out as a scholastic dispute. Ramism (unlike Ramus himself) survived the massacres, but not in the context of the old Studium. When Abelard's old dialectical game of *sic et non* was carried to such ideological extremes, the old university could no longer contain it. When the 'new learning' took such a revolutionary form and acquired such heretical associations, it had to find a home in another part of the European academy.

PROTESTANT *PAIDEIA*

Although European schools were reverberating with the new learning, there were few that provided instruction in the 'pure word of God' during the first generation of evangelical reform. Yet educational reform was fundamental to such purification, and indeed for Luther the two processes were practically the same. On the individual level the problem could be reduced to the turning of a young person away from his animal nature to things of the mind and spirit – *paideia*, the Greek term for education and culture, which we have already seen associated with 'conversion'. Christian humanists like

---

[30] *Arrestz de la Court de Parlement . . . pour le Reglement et Reformation de l'université de Paris* (Paris, 1577; Harvard).

Erasmus and Ramus regarded this process not only as the fulfillment of the new learning but as a first step in the regeneration of
society as a whole. Most crucial in this indoctrination was the
so-called 'third childhood', roughly from five to fifteen but including the early years of university training, when the pedagogue
succeeded the mother as 'conscience' to the child.[31] The master
had only two things to work with, nature and reason; and to these
he added a third ingredient, practice (*exercitatio*), by example and
repetition. It was a battle, but Erasmus was characteristically optimistic about the outcome. He told a story concerning Lycurgus to
show the contrast between an unruly and a highly trained dog:
'Nature may be strong', remarked the Greek legislator, 'yet education is more powerful still.'[32]

The educational psychology of the new learning, like its approach
to knowledge in general, was grounded in the *trivium* and not on
interpretations of Aristotle's *De Anima*. The earliest stages of de-
velopment could be formulated in roughly curricular terms: first an
empirical stage of Latin conversation, next a practical stage of written
discourse, and then a theoretical phase of thoughtful argument.
According to the 'Preceptor of Germany', Greek was even more
important to Protestant *paideia* than Latin. 'Of the Greek language',
declared Melanchthon, 'we say that it is the mistress and fountain
not only of holy doctrine but of the rest of the arts and . . . as
necessary to life as air or fire.' Among the arts special emphasis was
placed on history, 'without which', as Melachthon put it, 'one
remains a child'.[33] But of course the destination of this pedagogical
pilgrimage was always religion, as educators like Melanchthon
urged and as the statutes of Sturm's academy of Strasbourg laid
down. The ideal remained that Erasmian combination of piety,
eloquence and learning – *sapiens et eloquens pietas*, in Sturm's phrase,
or *pietas litterata* – the Christian orator, in the style of Jerome or
Augustine.[34]

Where could one go to find 'the light of the gospel'? From the
early 1520s reform-minded young Frenchmen looked to Germany
and then to Switzerland; the first center was naturally Luther's own

---

31 P. Ariès, *Centuries of Childhood*, trans. R. Baldick (London, 1962), 21, and D. Hunt,
   Parents and Children in History (New York, 1970), 47.
32 W. Woodward, *Desiderius Erasmus concerning the Aim and Method of Education* (New
   York, 1964), 4, 184, and critical edition by J.-C. Margolin, *Declamatio de pueris statim
   ac liberaliter instituendis* (Geneva, 1966); Graves, *Ramus*, 109.
33 K. Hartfelder, *Philip Melanchthon als Praeceptor Germaniae*, and E. C. Scherer,
   Geschichte und Kirchengeschichte an den deutschen Universitäten (Freiberg, 1927).
34 P. Mesnard, 'La pietas litterata de Jean Sturm', *BSHPF*, CXI (1965), 281–302, and
   'The pedagogy of Jean Sturm', *Studies in the Renaissance*, XIII (1966), 200–19.

University of Wittenberg, founded by the Elector Friedrich of Saxony in 1505 and modeled generally on the University of Paris. One of Luther's greatest achievements was to transform and to establish doctrinal hegemony over this school, which always remained his principal headquarters. Before the imperial ban enrollment had increased spectacularly, reaching a total of 552 in 1520; and Luther's and Melanchthon's lectures attracted even greater numbers. From 1523 on, when Luther's academic reforms were put into effect, the University became the ideological center of Lutheranism and attracted a stream of foreign students, including Lambert and De Coct. From it extended an academic network which was strengthened above all by the efforts of the educational reformer Melanchthon. Some ten institutions of higher learning, including those of Heidelberg, Marburg and Tübingen, reorganized along Lutheran lines, constituted the doctrinal nerve-centers of German Protestantism and a refuge for many foreign enthusiasts. For Luther education had a social as well as a religious function, which was to disseminate the word over all classes and many generations; and so, as he argued in a sermon of 1530 'on the duty of sending children to school', civil authorities should make education compulsory.[35] Out of this educational ideal emerged concepts and practices of modern state education.

If evangelical education performed a conservative and reinforcing function in safely reformed areas like the Lutheran states and cities, it could obviously be adapted to more radical and upsetting purposes in orthodox areas. From the 1520s individual teachers like Wolmar and Cordier worked more or less deliberately to make their teaching an instrument of religious transformation as well as of literary enlightenment. To the extent that the educational process tended, even inadvertently, to encourage conversion, it posed a threat to society as well as to the ecclesiastical establishment. In the first place it threatened the stability of the family, usurping the traditional paternal right to control upbringing and religious choice. Secondly, it disrupted the balance of estates by giving members of social and professional groups values and loyalties incompatible with those of their fellows. This happened in various trades, such as printing and bookselling, and within the professions of law and medicine. Finally, though more indirectly, unorthodox education became a political threat, especially through clandestine schools and unlicensed tutoring; and this became a

---

[35] F. Painter, *Luther on Education* (Philadelphia, 1889), 210–71; cf. G. Strauss, *Luther's House of Learning* (Baltimore, 1978), Farel's educational writings in *Anthologie Protestante Française* (n.p., n.d.) and R. Henderson, *The Teaching Office in the Reformed Tradition* (Philadelphia, 1962).

major target of repressive legislation. The very first woman martyr in France, a schoolmistress, was a victim of this.[36]

In general it was in the free territories of Switzerland and the Rhineland that the ideals of what may be called missionary teaching were most effective for international evangelical movements. Of seminal importance was the Academy of Strasbourg, which from its founding in 1538 was an institutional model as well as a major attraction for students all over Europe, eastern and western. Surprisingly, there had been no permanent educational institution in this center of printing, *avant-garde* culture and interconfessional contact. From the late fifteenth century there had been concern for educational reform in Strasbourg, especially among humanists like Wimpheling and Brant and clerics like Geiler and Murner, who formed a loose sodality devoted to good letters and German nationality. Several petitions were presented to the city council to support lay education, and in 1504 Wimpheling even urged the use of ecclesiastical benefices to subsidize such a program. Little came of these efforts, however; educational innovation had to wait for the religious transformations of the 1520s. From 1523 there were regular public lectures and sermons given by Bucer and other reformers for the edification of adult citizens – first in presumably innocuous Latin, but then in the vernacular and announced by church bells. The next year, barely a week after formal permission to preach the gospel (as the official euphemism went), the council was forced, prodded by the newly enfranchised ministers, to turn its attention to educational reform. The year after that a commission of public instruction was formed, soon to be placed under the supervision of officials called 'scholarchs'.[37]

It was in this way that education became a public monopoly in Strasbourg; and indeed from the start the purpose of reform was as much civic as religious, aimed, that is, at the moral and social improvement of the city and the establishment thus of a firm basis for the perpetuation of the Reformation in general. After 1530 this movement went beyond adult education, necessarily, to the longer-range task of instructing the young, especially through the new Latin schools attached to the cathedral of St Thomas, the most notable being that directed by Otto Brunfels. Most essential was training of ministers; and for the next few years attempts were made to found, and to fund, such a seminary, with the particular support of Bucer. In 1534 a 'college of preachers', housed in the old Dominican monastery, was opened for Strasbourg and five sur-

---

[36] H. Meylan, *Silhouettes du XVIe siècle* (n.p., n.d.), 5.
[37] Fournier, IV, nos. 1962ff.; cf. Ch. Schmidt, *La Vie et les travaux de Jean Sturm* (Strasbourg, 1855), W. Sohm, *Die Schule Johann Sturms und die Kirche Strassburgs* (Munich, 1912), and especially A. Schindler, *Humanistische Hochschule und freie Reichstadt* (Wiesbaden, 1977).

rounding villages. Soon a number of French refugees came to study as well, even before the short period of Calvin's residence. Four years later the gymnasium of Strasbourg published its statutes, opened its doors, and began a career hardly surpassed by any educational institution in modern times.

From the start the guiding spirit of this pedagogical enterprise was Johann Sturm, who had been the mentor of Ramus in the University of Paris. Sturm's own views had been shaped by Erasmian pedagogy, the educational experience he had enjoyed at the school of St Jerome in Liège (founded in 1496 by the Brothers of the Common Life), and no doubt by the intellectual excitement at Paris, where he had taught rhetoric and dialectic from 1529 to 1535. In 1537 Sturm was invited to Strasbourg to take over the foundation of the academy and three years later was given a benefice from St Thomas's.[38] He oversaw the first half-century of the school's life, watching its spectacular growth from a local gymnasium to an international 'academy', as it was designated in 1565. In 1546 the school had an enrollment of 646 and was in the process of building a multi-national faculty of unprecedented distinction and influence. Besides Calvin, who worked with Sturm for a time during the early 1540s, the faculty included at various times Bucer, Peter Martyr, Hotman, Baudouin, Jerome Zanchi and the official Lutheran historian Sleidan. Yet it was an excruciatingly difficult time as well. The civil wars in Germany, the hated Interim, the conflicts between the German and French (and later English) congregations, the stream of refugees from France and Marian England, the persecution of Protestants in nearby towns such as Metz, and then a generation of civil war in France: all of these troubles made the position of this 'free' city increasingly ambivalent and precarious. Equally uneasy was the situation of Sturm, all the more so because he remained politically and religiously an Erasmian, a man in the middle in an age in which there was no middle.

Sharing honors and travails with Strasbourg as an original Protestant educational foundation was the Academy of Lausanne, the oldest in the French-speaking world, having been established in 1537, three weeks after the edicts of reformation published by the conquering Bernese, following the famous Disputation.[39] From the thirteenth century there had been a tradition of lay education in the Vaud. One product of it was Pierre Viret, who before his conversion had studied in Orbe with a reform-minded schoolmaster, Marc Romain. Ultimately, Viret became professor of New Testament

---

[38] Fournier, IV, no. 1976.
[39] Le Coultre, *Mathurin Cordier*, and Vuilleumier, *Histoire de l'eglise réformée du Pays de Vaud* (Paris, 1870). See above, p. 102.

theology at the academy as well as pastor of Lausanne. The pedagogical counterpart of Sturm, however, was Mathurin Cordier, a friend of Calvin who had also taught at the University of Paris and had also been one of the refugees of the year of the placards, as had his distinguished colleague Conrad Gesner. It was to this school, which opened its doors in 1540, that Beza and Hotman came to begin their careers as promoters of Protestant *paideia*. Lausanne, too, became a center of turmoil, interconfessional as well as international, and, like Strasbourg, increasingly uncomfortable for most of its Calvinist inhabitants.[40]

In the academies of Strasbourg and Lausanne we can see the institutional embodiment of the new learning as it was adapted to evangelical organization and proselytism. The overall pattern of indoctrination and intellectual conflict was remarkably similar in the two schools. Ideological commitment was reinforced by ambitious attempts to regulate the moral behavior of students in all phases of their lives. Like their Parisian counterparts the students at Strasbourg and Lausanne were compelled to speak Latin and to dress properly and forbidden to haunt taverns and other scandalous places, but practical supervision was evidently more intense. In Strasbourg, to minimize conflicts between town and gown, they were forbidden also to take up residence with citizens and to indulge in what were euphemistically called 'nocturnal ambulations'. At Lausanne younger students were assigned to the households of married professors like Beza and Hotman, where they received moral guidance as well as room and board. Students were also involved in the policing of their own community, not only as 'sub-doctors' tutoring younger pupils but also as informers. Games were strictly regulated, and to judge from the statutes more time was taken up with prayers and psalm-singing. Like the Protestant congregation, then, the Protestant academy seemed to revitalize old institutions of learning through participation and communal consciousness.

The Protestant pedagogical ideal received early expression in the work of Mathurin Cordier, older statesman of the Calvinist educational network, who was at least sixty-five when he came to Lausanne to teach in 1545. His textbook *On the Correction of Corrupt Language* of 1530, which echoed some of the naive evangelism of the Meaux circle, carried to a more elementary level the sort of remedial philology expressed most famously in Lorenzo Valla's *Elegances of Latin*, except that Cordier was characteristically concerned with morals and piety as well as eloquence. The same combination is

---

[40] Kelley, *Hotman*, 53ff.

displayed in his extraordinarily popular *Colloquies*, which were designed to introduce young boys to Latin conversation but which also afford a glimpse into school life in sixteenth-century Lausanne. In these dialogues students discussed a variety of commonplace topics: not only books, classes and the 'monthly victors' in the disputations but also problems of parents, the need for money, food and permission to visit the market, the attractions of the big city (Lyon), games and 'singing psalms in the shade'. But more than counterbalancing flashes of humor is the high moral tone of the discussion: emphasis on duty (*officium*) and punishment ('For a boy correction' – i.e., beatings – 'is as necessary as meat') and the superiority of virtue and knowledge to riches. The three main rules were to pray very often, always to be heedful, and to be charitable. The school was like a family, and members had at all times to 'love their brothers' and 'do good' (*benefacito*). Throughout was the intimidating presence, at least morally, of the Magister. 'It is not proper to be idle and prattle here while waiting for the master', says one pupil. 'What do you mean, "not proper"?', asks the other. 'We *must* not, or else be beaten' (*volpulare*).[41] This was another way of reinforcing communal consciousness.

One of the most distinctive and innovative devices of Protestant *paideia* was the system of 'classes' and 'promotions', though there were precedents in the schools of the Modern Devotion and the College of Guyenne, where Cordier had taught. According to the influential view of Sturm, the practice was to follow a concentration of subjects starting with grammar and rhetoric, Greek as well as Latin, through a graded series of the best authors, on to a more theoretical level of literary and dialectical studies, philology and finally theology.[42] At Strasbourg this program was arranged in an ascending order of yearly classes, from the eighth (elements of reading and writing) to the first; at Lausanne there were seven. At both schools periodic examinations were required for 'promotion', which became a kind of certification of as well as check on successful indoctrination. At Lausanne there were bi-weekly disputations on subjects set by the arts professors, and from these came not only the 'Saturday champions' but also, twice a year, promotions from class to class, elaborately celebrated and attended by notable scholars, including Calvin himself.[43] In all phases of study, of course, religion

[41] Cordier, *Colloquiorum centuria selecta*, ed. and trans. J. Clarke (London, 1751), 3.
[42] Fournier, IV, no. 1977, and Sturm, *De Litterarum ludis recte aperiendis* (Strasbourg, 1543). On classes see also Ariès, *Centuries of Childhood*, M. Gaufrès, *Claude Baduel* (Paris, 1880), 40, and P. Bourchenin, *Etude sur les Académies protestantes en France* (Paris, 1882).
[43] Le Coultre, *Mathurin Cordier*, 203ff.

had priority. At Strasbourg even in the teaching of jurisprudence the connection with divine law was to be maintained 'by precept and by example'. For such, according to the original statutes, was always the end of the educational sequence ('Das End volkummenes studirens ist die Religion Gottis und göttlicher Ding erkanntnüss').[44]

Because of this religious orientation and the ideological commitments of Protestant education, it would be wrong to insist too much on the novelty of Protestant *paideia*. Similar changes can be seen in orthodox views of pedagogy, especially as exemplified a little later in the work of the Jesuits. Despite humanist innovations, moreover, Protestant education in some ways seemed to revert to medieval patterns of indoctrination. This is apparent especially in the re-emergence, or perhaps covertly continuous influence, of Aristotle, even among promoters of the new learning like Valla and Ramus. The truth is that their purpose was not to reject the 'true' Aristotle but to discover him behind the 'false' creation of scholastic commentators assailed by Ramus. Among others who supported this enterprise were Agricola, Lefèvre, Melanchthon and Sturm. The curriculum of Strasbourg in particular, despite Sturm's efforts to construct an alternative to Aristotelian dialectic, leaned heavily upon the *Organon* and Aristotle's work in natural philosophy, as did Lutheran curricula, despite Luther's fulminations. In their constructive efforts, in other words, Protestant educators like Melanchthon, Bucer and Sturm turned away from unstructured humanism and fundamentalism back to a kind of organized learning suitable for the exposition and defense of established doctrine. In some ways the demands of militant Protestant indoctrination and propaganda were no less dogmatic than those of an embattled orthodoxy, and the inevitable result was a sort of closing of the circle of *paideia*, a hardening of ideology.

Yet these same ideological demands encouraged innovation in other parts of the Protestant Studium, and two disciplines in particular illustrate this. One was the study of history, for which Strasbourg had perhaps the first appointed chair (that is, ecclesiastical history and not the literary reading of classical historians). Protestant fascination with history is perhaps best illustrated by Melanchthon, both in his publications (especially the Lutheran chronicle of Johann Carion) and in his university reforms, and by Johann Sleidan, official Lutheran historiographer. History was taught at other Protestant schools, including Heidelberg and later the Academy of Nîmes, where the books of Sleidan and Carion were reportedly used as texts; and it furnished a dominant – some would argue the dominant –

---

[44] Fournier, IV, no. 1980.

mode of Protestant propaganda.[45] In general 'tradition' was an emotive term both for Catholics, for whom it was on a par with scriptures, especially after the conclusions of the Tridentine fathers, and for Protestants, who regarded it in the human sense as almost obscene. History itself in that human sense was suspect: 'The pagans called history the mistress of life', Calvin remarked, 'but . . . scripture alone deserves that high position.'[46] Yet in a more spiritual sense Protestants appealed massively to history both to discredit their rivals and to reconstruct their own past in a way to make themselves seem, morally at least, the culmination of the historical process.

The other field was that of law, for which Sturm succeeded in getting a chair established in Strasbourg in the early 1550s. Offered first to Charles Dumoulin (who never claimed it), the chair was held successively by his younger protégés Baudouin and Hotman.[47] Implicitly, Protestants were gaining new respect for a profession of which, because of their hatred of Italianate legalism, they had originally been suspicious on principle; and in fact their increasing appeal to legal precedent led them to begin seeking their own 'human traditions', and so to appropriate the legacy of Christian culture. In general, emphasis on this field, as on history, represents an aspect of that phenomenon which has been called the 'politicization of Protestantism', the transmutation of religious propaganda into secular and potentially revolutionary form. This phenomenon also has its roots in the academy, and (as we shall see in the next chapter) it contributed very directly to the drawing of lines and defining of resentments underlying the civil wars.

THE WARS OF ACADEME

As the university was an agent of intellectual subversion even in peaceful times, so in a period of upheaval it could become a dangerously divisive force; and indeed the patterns of conflict within the French universities as well as the Protestant academies not only anticipated but in some ways prepared the ground for the wars of religion in Europe. The University of Paris characteristically set the

---

[45] Léon Ménard, *Histoire . . . de la Ville de Nîmes*, v (Nîmes, 1875), 179. In general see Scherer, *Geschichte und Kirchengeschichte*; P. Polman, *L'Elément historique dans la controverse religieuse du XVIe siècle* (Gembloux, 1932); P. Fraenkel, *Testimonia Patrum* (Geneva, 1961).

[46] 'Commentarius in Epistolam Pauli ad Romanos' (1539), *CO*, LXXVII, col. 86.

[47] J. Duquesne, *Les Débuts de l'enseignement du droit à Strasbourg du XVIe siècle* (Strasbourg, 1922), 20.

style; but though dominant, it was not alone in its revolutionary potential. The other 'famous universities' of France – that is, those subject to the Concordat of 1516 – had their own traditions of violence and division.[48] This was reflected in the boisterous student fraternities as well as in various doctrinal squabbles that got out of hand. Besides the 'crotez' of Paris, for example, there were the 'bragards' of Angers, the 'danseurs' of Orleans and the 'fluteurs et joueurs' of Poitiers. The institutional horseplay of such groups was much intensified by the psalm-singing iconoclasm inspired by religious enthusiasm.

Closest to Paris, the University of Orleans had a special importance in that it provided the law faculty for its sister university, where the teaching of civil law had been forbidden for over two centuries.[49] The Parlement of Paris, as the supreme organ of the legal profession in France, took a particular interest in this law school, requiring graduates to argue before the assembled advocates. In 1538 the Parlement proposed to improve academic order by legislation, and among the first targets were the student nations, in which (as in their Parisian counterparts) alien ideas as well as persons enjoyed special protection. Troubles had erupted as early as 1524, when a few German students were imprisoned, and continued intermittently thereafter; and for this reason the number of these nations was reduced from ten to four. Here many future Protestants came to pursue a legal education – which in most cases amounted to little more than an extension of the liberal arts program in a secular rather than an ecclesiastical direction – and encountered ferment similar to that in Paris. In the late 1520s Calvin himself arrived to study with the faculty's main attraction, Pierre de l'Estoile, and in fact became embroiled in his first academic controversy by defending this eminent jurist against his Italian rival, Andrea Alciato (with whom Calvin had also studied at the University of Bourges). Among Calvin's protégés who likewise studied at Orleans were Beza, Hotman and the future martyr Anne du Bourg. Throughout the period before the wars of religion Orleans kept its reputation for dissident ideas and behavior. In 1546 and again in 1554 there were rock-throwing incidents between the German and French students. An especially violent outburst of iconoclasm ushered in the civil wars in 1562, when Orleans became the headquarters of the Huguenot forces under the Prince of Condé.

Even more tumultuous was the University of Toulouse. The

---

[48] E. Bimbenet, *Histoire de la ville d'Orléans*, III (Orleans, 1887), 139; Bourchenin, *Etude sur les Académies*, 27.
[49] Bimbenet, *Histoire de l'université des lois d'Orléans* (Orleans, 1853).

Parlement and the Estates of Languedoc had tried again and again to impose order on the students and faculty, beginning well before the injection of religious issues. In August 1517 the 'excesses of scholars and regents' had to be punished by the Estates, and two years later the Parlement of Toulouse forbade the carrying of arms and the holding of illicit assemblies. Such legislation was repeated many times over the rest of the century.[50] Students had to be restrained from carrying swords, wearing masks, interrupting lectures and (in 1531) even from grouping themselves into nations. As at Paris, members of the university were forbidden to wear beards or to display 'scandalous habits', and as at Paris the ban seemed largely ineffectual. In 1532 one member of the law faculty, Jean de Caturce, was executed for heresy and another, Jean de Boyssoné, fled.[51] The following year the young Etienne Dolet gave a scandalous (unfortunately not extant) oration attacking the legendary intolerance of Toulouse, especially of its Parlement; and after this he too was banished. In 1540 there was another uprising of students; and the school of two famous professors, Jean de Coras and Arnaud Ferrier, was burned. This was followed by another 'reformation', but the incidence of violence continued to mount over the next two decades. Among the young scholars exposed to the law faculty of Toulouse in these disturbing times were Jacques Cujas, Jean Bodin and Louis le Roy, though all left before religious troubles merged with civil war. In May 1562 the school had to be closed because of the 'sedition' going on 'day and night'.

The pattern was similar in other universities, especially in the law schools, perhaps because the students were a bit older and the faculty a bit less inclined to orthodoxy than their theological colleagues. The University of Poitiers reportedly contained Protestants in its law faculty.[52] Another center of trouble was the University of Valence, which was disturbed by the nocturnal services of Protestants in the late 1550s and then by the establishment of a clandestine elementary school by a man from Geneva bringing with him a manual for the 'education of small children'. The students in general were unmanageable and always, as Cujas remarked, preferred to play tennis rather than attend to their studies.[53] In this same period they demonstrated against a jubilee planned by the bishop of Valence, Jean de Monluc, and tore down the placards issued by

---

[50] R. Gadave, *Les documents sur l'histoire de l'université de Toulouse* (Toulouse, 1910), 126ff.; J.B. Dubédat, *Histoire du Parlement de Toulouse* (Paris, 1885), i, 363.

[51] Gadave, *Documents*, 143ff.

[52] Prosper Boissonade et al., *Histoire de l'université de Poitiers* (Poitiers, 1930), 111.

[53] Joseph-Cyprien Nadal, *Histoire de l'université de Valence* (Valence, 1861), 49.

him. In May 1560 classes had to be suspended, and remained so until the end of the first civil war. Even then religious tensions were unabated. After Cujas left, Calvinist intrigues blocked the appointment of Baudouin (recently returned to Catholicism), and in his place Calvin's protégé Hotman came to teach law. But the Catholic majority made life impossible for him and his family, and in 1566 he was forced to flee. Unfortunately Bourges, his next stop, proved even less hospitable.

By mid-century the University of Bourges had surpassed Toulouse as the outstanding center of legal studies in France, perhaps in Europe; certainly it was the most controversial. Bourges's major claim to fame was its reputation as the first home of that academic movement which later came to be called 'legal humanism', introduced first by Alciato in the late 1520s and resumed a decade or so later by his French epigones, especially Eguinaire Baron and François le Douaren. Increasingly this 'reformed jurisprudence', to which Calvin himself had been exposed, was associated with the reformed religion as part of a grand social ideal; and both became targets of orthodox criticism. Parallel and almost contemporaneous with Alciato's innovations in jurisprudence were the missionary activities of Jean Michel, who gave his first sermons in 1525 and his last ones shortly before his martyrdom in 1539.[54] In the next decade there was further evangelizing (for example, by the Franciscan Abel Pepin), and more conversions (for example, the Colladon family, who joined Calvin in Geneva). By the mid-point of the century these two disruptive movements were converging in the academic community, establishing it in the eyes of many citizens as a nest of troublemakers, and contributing directly to the divisions leading to civil war.

The University of Bourges furnishes a classic example of petty academic squabbling erupting into full-fledged ideological war. The origin of the factionalism was apparently a personal rivalry between the two principal law professors, Baron and Le Douaren, ostensibly over the legal doctrine of sovereignty (that is, the *imperium*) but sustained by professional jealousy.[55] Le Douaren found it expedient to absent himself from the University, returning only in 1550 after Baron's death; but the conflict continued when the young François Baudouin, recently secretary to Calvin, took over both Baron's place and his rivalry with 'the partisans of Le Douaren', who were also Calvinist sympathizers. Aligned with the feuding professors were

---

[54] Raynal, *Histoire du Berry* (Bourges, 1844), III, 405.
[55] For much of what follows see Kelley, *Hotman*, 53ff.

factions in the notoriously unruly student body, especially the German nation and the quasi-feudal fraternities called 'morphes'. In the ensuing disorders a student of Le Douaren, Daniel Schleicher, was killed. At the same time personal animosity was being replaced by the religious question, and Baudouin was progressively alienated from the Calvinists in a manner already described. Charged at first with the private faults of disloyalty and neglect, academic as well as religious, he ended by being denounced for his public position on the questions of toleration and conciliation.

The immediate upshot was that Baudouin had to flee Bourges, going first to Strasbourg and then to Heidelberg, from which he launched his anti-Calvinistic 'irenical' campaign. His alleged defection in these years (1555–61) involved him in controversies first with Le Douaren and Hotman and finally with Beza and Calvin himself. Meanwhile Baudouin's successor at Bourges, Jacques Cujas, who inherited the hostility of Le Douaren as well as Baudouin's chair, also had to flee in 1559. After Le Douaren's death two years later the Calvinist faction was represented by his protégé Hugues Doneau and later Hotman, but increasingly they found themselves under fire and indeed barely escaped with their lives in the massacres of 1572. It is interesting that every one of these men was involved in the upsurge of propaganda in the later sixteenth century, including even the usually serene scholar Cujas, who was finally persuaded to take up his pen against the Huguenots (his professional rival Doneau in particular) after St Bartholomew. So the Catholic University of Bourges represented a sort of training ground not only for humanist jurists but also for the professional ideologists of the next generation.

In the world of the Protestant academy conflicts were hardly less violent, and again the pattern was one of personal rivalries reinforced by national and confessional differences. In Strasbourg the divergence between the French and German contingents in the University, always latent, became alarming during the 1550s, when Calvin's influence (mainly through his old comrade Sturm) started to become disruptive, and when the split between moderate and ultra-Lutherans further fragmented the community. Melanchthon's moderating influence was to no avail against the intransigence of the Calvinists, represented by Peter Martyr and Jerome Zanchi, and the so-called 'miso-Philipists', headed by Marbach.[56] An early victim of this split was Baudouin, who, having been forced out of Bourges in

---

[56] J. Kittelson, 'Marbach vs Zanchi', *Sixteenth Century Journal*, VIII (1977), 31–44, and N. Paulus, *Die Strasburger Reformation und dir Gewissensfreiheit* (Strasbourg, 1895).

1555, suffered the same fate a year later at Strasbourg as a result of Calvinist intrigues. With the support not only of Sturm and Calvin but also of a group of students who got together a petition for him, Hotman managed to oust his rival and take over the single chair of law, while Baudouin went down a road that took him into the Lutheran camp and finally back to Tridentine Catholicism. After-wards Sturm may have repented his acts and certainly he disap-proved of Hotman's conspiratorial activities against the French government (that is, the controlling party of the Guise family), and wanted no part of the Huguenot 'conspiracy of Amboise' of 1559 which contributed so directly to civil war.

In Strasbourg the split between the French and German congrega-tions came more specifically through another more academic episode of that same year. The students of the theology professor, Jerome Zanchi, complained about his unorthodox views on communion, in which he, like Sturm himself, followed Calvin. The ultra-Lutheran authorities reacted by forbidding Zanchi to discuss the subject in his lectures, and he responded by refusing to continue his course and demanding, on Biblical grounds, 'liberty of teaching'. The controv-ersy over this administrative 'tyranny' went on for several years, but the growing *rapprochement* between Catholics and Lutherans (spon-sored by the Guise party) made resistance by the Calvinists in Strasbourg hopeless. Peter Martyr fled to Zurich, while Zanchi and Sturm eventually surrendered and in October 1561 signed a confes-sion of faith agreeable to the Lutheran authorities. In German territories Heidelberg (after the conversion of the Elector in 1559) replaced Strasbourg as a Calvinist refuge.

Events in the Academy of Lausanne followed a similar pattern, that is, a steady divergence between the French faculty and students, who inclined towards Calvinist doctrines, and the German and Zwinglian Council of Bern. Disagreements arose over the eucharist and then over predestination, and partisanship infected the students as well as their mentors.[57] One of them, Louis Corbeil, joined with André Zébédée to discredit the Calvinist clique, which in 1548 included Beza and Hotman as well as Viret and Cordier. The result was an investigation of the school by the Bernese administra-tion. Viret was obliged to submit a confession of faith, but he could not prevent the coming conflict. The conventional weekly colloquies were suppressed despite petitions by the faculty carried to Bern by Beza. In 1551 the Zwinglian liturgy was imposed, and the preaching of Calvinist doctrine in the Vaud was prohibited. Suspicions of

---

[57] J. Barnaud, *Pierre Viret* (Saint-Aman, 1911), 335ff.

Calvin grew despite the pleas of Viret and Beza. In the debate over predestination Bern supported Bolsec against Calvin and in 1555 prohibited further discussion of the question in its territories. This was another violation of the freedom of teaching, and thereafter relations degenerated rapidly until the violent outbreak of 1558, which sent the remaining members of the Calvinist faction into exile.

At just about the time that the Calvinists lost their foothold in the two principal Protestant academies (and none too soon for the educational needs of international Calvinism), Calvin finally realized his dream of a university in his own republican stronghold. The Academy of Geneva opened its doors and published its statutes in 1559, and two years later Beza was established as its first rector.[58] This institution was prefigured in the Ecclesiastical Ordinances of 1541, which designated the 'doctors' as second only to the ministers in 'the instruction of the faithful in true doctrine', and indeed in Calvin's *Institutes*, which in a sense was the embodiment of Protestant education; and of course it was indebted to the academies both of Strasbourg, where Calvin had taught, and of Lausanne, where so many of his protégés had gone. For years he had talked about the idea, for example in 1550 with Claude Baduel, who was still trying to make a success of his school in Nîmes; but Genevan authorities were reluctant to subsidize the project. From the beginning the career of the academy was watched with interest – with jealousy by competitors and with high hopes by friends like Peter Martyr, especially after having to leave Strasbourg. 'I pray God . . .', he wrote to Calvin in the fall of 1559, 'that it fulfills your hopes and becomes rich in men for the service of religion and the state.'[59] And so it did, at least in its early years, attracting men from German, English and Italian as well as French-speaking areas, and growing to an enrollment of 1500 or more students by 1564, the year of Calvin's death. The most influential members of this seminary were the so-called 'alumni', who were foreign students come for theological training with the intention of returning as missionaries.

In the later sixteenth century the Genevan academy was a major nerve-center of the Calvinist republic of letters, a training ground for the shock-troops of the religious wars. Matriculated students took an oath that required them to undertake 'true worship of God, to live piously and to abjure all papal superstitions'. As at Strasbourg and Lausanne there were periodic and very popular disputations, but now deliberately open, so that even Catholics, it was said, were

[58] C. Borgeaud, *Histoire de l'université de Genève* (Geneva, 1900).
[59] *CO*, XVIII, no. 653.

permitted to speak freely. Although theology still had first priority, the study of law was introduced in 1565; and three of the first teachers of this subject in Geneva were among the most vocal publicists of the age. The first was Pierre Charpentier, who gained considerable notoriety as a critic of the Calvinist 'Cause' after St Bartholomew; and the other two were leading advocates – and almost victims – of that cause, Hotman and Doneau.[60] Hotman reacted with particular bitterness to the charges of Charpentier, both because of his former sympathy with the Huguenots and because he had the temerity to trade on the name of one of the most famous martyrs of 1572, Petrus Ramus. Largely because of this legalistic approach each of these authors contributed conspicuously to the increasingly secular tone of public controversy.

Despite simple beginnings, the Genevan academy soon established itself as a Studium hardly less international than Paris itself. From the start it received students of Polish, Spanish, English and Italian as well as French and German background; and so it came to supplement the Genevan pastorate as center of an international network. In France, moreover, other Huguenot academies emerged to extend this network: establishments at Nîmes and Orthez in the 1560s and later others in Montpellier, Montauban, Puylaurens, Saumur and Die (as well as places outside, such as Orange and Sedan) joined Geneva, and likewise continued the pattern set by Sturm, Cordier, Baduel and Calvin himself.[61]

Once again it must be recalled that Protestants were not alone in trying to renovate education and place it directly in the service of religion, nor indeed in operating in an international arena. Catholic pedagogical efforts paralleled and indeed counterbalanced these in various ways. In the vanguard was the Society of Jesus founded by Ignatius Loyola – along with Calvin, Sturm and other educational pioneers a product of the University of Paris in the first decade of Lutheran influence. In 1551 the Jesuits had been given permission to open a college in Paris just after a papal bull granted them license to teach theology and then to award degrees. From the first, both the Parlement and the University frowned upon this alien institution that could hardly be fitted into a French corporate structure subject to royal control. In 1554 the Sorbonne attacked this 'new society' as a threat to faith as well as to the institution of monasticism, thus beginning a struggle that would last for two centuries and more.[62] One of the lesser known results of the Colloquy of Poissy was the

---

[60] See below, pp. 290–1, 308–14.   [61] Bourchenin, *Etude sur les Académies*.
[62] Pasquier, *Recherches de la France* (Paris, 1621), book III, chapter 43 and *Les Lettres* (Paris, 1619), IV, 24; also Kelley, *Foundations*, 275.

giving of recognition to the Jesuits, but Gallican opposition continued. In 1564 Etienne Pasquier represented the University in a lawsuit against the Jesuits argued in the Parlement, and for another half-century he carried on this campaign personally and vindictively. This was one subject on which Gallicans and Protestants were in complete accord. For this reason the Society of Jesus, even before it began to become involved in high political issues, became a prime generator of and target for polemic throughout the century.

In general, however, Protestant educational reform was mounted earlier than Catholic and concerned more with promoting public indoctrination. Beyond confessional boundaries the international character of this education, higher education at least, was maintained in many ways throughout the wars of the sixteenth century. In particular the professoriate continued to be strikingly mobile. The most renowned and highest salaried professors moved about through the universities of Europe like the vagrant, less amply subsidized humanists of old. Interchange between such institutions as Basel, Geneva, Strasbourg, Heidelberg, Oxford and later Leiden was never broken off; and the professional odysseys of Baudouin, Hotman, Doneau, Cujas and even Ramus (to mention only a few of the familiar figures) were international and interconfessional to an extraordinary degree, resembling in some ways the trails of the missionary preachers of the early part of the century. And traditional rivalries over plagiarism, salaries, students, religion and politics seemed only to reinforce academic interconnectedness. Through such channels passed not only ideas and intellectual fashions but also intelligence, intrigues and various currents of ideology. In these and other ways the academy contributed to the religious and political divisions of sixteenth-century European society.

The Academy was in many ways a prime vehicle of ideology – instilling attitudes, teaching methods, and in general providing the training-ground for intellectuals and all sorts of propagandists. But normally it was only upon leaving the Academy, or at least addressing oneself to a wider public, that one could have much impact on society at large. One of the major bridges between the classroom and the world of larger hopes and needs is represented by the professions (medicine, law and theology in particular), which all led from books and academic discussion to careers and perhaps public action. The law, as an extension of the liberal arts program in general and a professional adaptation of the techniques of rhetoric in particular, was by its very nature bound up with ideological questions – especially in a period of polarization and politicization. It is this threshold of public life that we now approach.

v · Forum:
The profession of law and
the political man

Juristen, böse Christen.

Luther (proverb)

Jurisconsultus . . . homo politicus.

François Baudouin

v · Forum:
The profession of law and
the political man

APOLOGUE: CONFRONTATION IN THE
PARLEMENT OF PARIS (1559)

On the last Wednesday of April 1559 a special assembly – a
Mercuriale, so-called for over a century – of all the chambers of the
sovereign court of the Parlement of Paris was convened to discuss
the problem of heresy and more consistent ways of dealing with it.
The 'Grand' Chambre' had been proceeding with all the rigors of
medieval criminal law, while the 'Tournelle', the specifically criminal section, had been inclining to the milder practice of banishment;
and indeed the tendency of judges to act 'according to their
consciences' instead of the royal will had led to the present meeting.
The President of the Tournelle, Pierre Seguier, had been repri-
manded bitterly by the Cardinal of Lorraine for laxity toward
heretics.[1] 'You have assisted them by sending them back to their
bishops. What a nice trip that is!', he complained sarcastically,
turning a deaf ear to Seguier's plea that some had had a change of
heart. 'No, no Mr President', he went on. 'It is your fault that not
only Poitiers but all of Poitou as far as Bordeaux and Provence and
France in general has been covered with their vermin, which grows
and prospers with your help.' So the members of the entire court
were called to account for their professional behavior and implicitly
for their religious opinions. This scene was played out just a month
before an even more dramatic assembly gathered just a few blocks
away in the faubourg St Germain, commonly referred to as 'Little
Geneva': this was the first, highly secret, national synod of the
French reformed church.

In the Palais, principal seat of the French legal elite, opinion was
divided about how to handle the growing menace to public order
posed by these new opinions, Lutheran and worse. A few voices
were raised on behalf of leniency, or at least a suspension of
punishment until a national council could be called. Although the
deliberations of the advocates were supposed to be secret, these
dangerous views were passed on to King Henry II by two of the

[1] Crespin, II, 644ff.

171

presidents, Minard and Le Maistre, along with alarming reports of the personal unorthodoxy of certain *parlementaires*. The result was that the king allowed himself to be persuaded to appear before the Mercuriale – in effect to stage a traditional *lit de justice* – to see for himself the extent of this infection. Since the Palais was pre-empted by the marriage of Philip of Spain and Elizabeth of Valois agreed upon at the treaty of Cateau-Cambrésis earlier this year, this festive meeting of the lawyers took place in the monastery of the Augustinians; and the atmosphere must have been electric. The king set the tone by inquiring why his Parlement had not yet registered his recent edict against the Lutherans, and then he sat back to listen to what amounted to a series of professions of faith.

An august and intimidating scene, and yet several of the jurists did not scruple to offer counsels of moderation which they surely knew would irritate the king. Paul de Foix, later advocate to the king of Navarre and supporter of Baudouin's Erasmian plan to reconcile religious parties in 1561, was one of those who made bold to instruct the king in his duties. Most outspoken of all was Anne du Bourg, son of a former chancellor, who took his title of 'counsellor of the king' all the more seriously, he said, because of the royal presence, though he was well aware of the risks. Then he raised his eyes to thank God for his good fortune and, in good evangelical style, launched into a sermon of some hour-and-a-half's length.[2] Those called Lutherans or new evangelists, he declared, though derided in France as heretics, in fact believed the pure word of God and followed the practice of the primitive church. On the other side was the Roman church and its notorious abuses. Here the First President Le Maistre interrupted to say that this was irrelevant to the Mercuriale, but the king irritably ordered Du Bourg to have his say. With such encouragement Du Bourg went on literally to hang himself. He criticized the severity of the edicts both of Henry II and of Francis I which 'have made you, Sire, at once accuser, condemner, judge and party, and your court the executors, although it is not proper to make laws concerning religious affairs'. At the same time, while defending the words of Luther as conforming to the Bible, he denounced 'Anabaptists, Servetists and other heretics'. In conclusion, he hoped that he had not gone too far, but had felt it necessary to 'discharge his conscience'.

All this only confirmed the king's suspicions, for he had no intention of postponing the 'pursuits' against heresy, let alone adopting a sympathetic attitude. He was quite in accord with the

---

[2] *Ibid.*, 678, reciting, 'Allez et preschez ceste Evangile par tout le monde.'

opinions of men like the presidents Christofle de Thou, Minard, and Le Maistre, who argued that the royal edicts must be enforced and the so-called reformers treated like the heretics of old. Le Maistre recalled in particular how Philip Augustus had burned 600 Waldensians in their houses and places of work. So the king, having obtained the opinions of the court in writing, began the process of purging. Eight of the contumacious counsellors were arrested and given over to the captain of the guards, the Comte de Montgomery, and taken to the Bastille. The worst culprit by far was Du Bourg, and Henry added that he wanted to see him burn with his own eyes.

That pleasure the king did not enjoy. Exactly a month later he was accidentally injured jousting with this same Montgomery at the marriage celebration of his children, and ten days after that he was dead. Nevertheless, the persecutions were continued by his son Francis II, and so more particularly was the process against the advocates begun in the Mercuriale. A few of those imprisoned managed to escape. Others, including Paul de Foix, Louis du Faur and Adam Fumée, were suspended and forced to recant; but Du Bourg remained adamant. Within two weeks after the Mercuriale he had been interrogated three times and had managed to incriminate himself even further. While denying charges of sedition, contumacy and rebellion, he could not conceal his religious convictions in the responses he gave to his judges, who in effect led him back through his catechism. Did he believe in the traditions of the church? Not that provided recently by the Council of Trent, he answered, for the Bible was the sole source of tradition; and on this basis he went on to reject all but two sacraments. He was especially hostile in his opposition to the Roman mass and to canon law. Specifically, he admitted 'that he had read some of Calvin, but not Luther, and had bought his books from the colporteurs who travel about in this country'. So Du Bourg sealed his own fate, and no talk of conscience could change it.

Despite appeals to the Parlement and to the archbishop of Lyon, Du Bourg remained in prison and five months later received a sentence of degradation. On 17 December one of his judges, President Minard, was attacked by ten armed horsemen and shot to death. As usual, Protestant culpability for the murder was widely assumed. Whatever the connection, Du Bourg was executed four days later; and the French evangelical movement had its first distinguished martyr since the death of Berquin, also a lawyer, thirty years before.

The Mercuriale of 1559 dramatized a phenomenon that was

shortly to have massive ideological and social significance, namely, subversion of the legal profession. The result was that by the outbreak of the religious wars not only the government, along with the Guises who controlled it, but also the opposition party, even before they found a leader in the Prince of Condé, had legal counsel and expert apologists. On the one hand were the royal legists, who could trace their heritage back at least to the lawyers of the last Capetians and who had over two centuries of precedents as well as the riches of Roman law to defend the monarchy and the principle of Gallican unity. On the other hand were the radicals, renegade Gallicans as their critics regarded them, who sympathized with, if they did not actively support, the evangelical movement, and who likewise had traditional arguments as well as reformist attitudes to draw upon. On the one hand, in short, was machinery of legislation and enforcement that laid claim to pre-historical tradition and orthodoxy, on the other an opposition party that rested upon an assumption of transcendent truth and a legitimacy which drew upon the same tradition, though a different construction of it. Much of the ideological production of the rest of the country, not only the polar extremes of absolutism and limited government but also the conciliatory program of the 'politiques', was the creation of the professional conflicts between juristic rivals and professional brethren.

From the beginning the Parlement of Paris had joined with the University of Paris in opposing Lutheran doctrines, and so had the various provincial parlements connected to it. The members of the court were sworn to uphold orthodoxy and to maintain a high standard of professional ethics. The institution of the Mercuriale itself, regularized in 1520, was a way of ensuring that the advocates minded their manners.[3] The rules included public propriety in the smallest matters, including dress and attendance at religious services. In 1540 they were even forbidden to wear beards, which were associated in the Palais as in the universities with the new religious opinions. At this same time the Parlement was charged directly by the king with the 'pursuit' of these opinions, and heresy was identified not only with 'scandale public et sedition' but even with lese-majesty. Yet the legal profession, of which the Parlement represented the upper echelon, was increasingly and notoriously infected with the new ideas, beginning with Berquin and including at least one in the affair of the placards. Evangelical religion claimed many members of the generation that was coming of age before mid-century and who followed the vocation of law – including Calvin

[3] R. Delachenal, *Histoire des avocats au parlement de Paris 1300–1600* (Paris, 1885).

himself, Beza, Hotman, Baudouin and Dumoulin, and not a few royal officers.

With the execution of Du Bourg the French public had irrefutable evidence that heresy had infiltrated the highest court in the land. His *cause* was the most *célèbre* of all up to that time; and publicized in sermon, song and history, it shortly assumed the status of a legend. During his imprisonment he had spent his time singing psalms and writing his confession of faith, later widely circulated. He received letters of support from many quarters, including Calvin and the Elector Palatine, who offered him a chair of jurisprudence at his University of Heidelberg, where Baudouin was teaching. But Du Bourg was doomed, virtually self-condemned. His stand on conscience and his demeanor made a tremendous impression on contemporaries. One of the most famous of them, though converted back to Catholicism, recalled many years later the constancy of the man. 'As we returned to our colleges from the execution', wrote Florimond de Raemond, 'we were melted in tears; and we pleaded his cause after his death, anathematizing those unjust judges who had justly condemned him. His sermon at the gallows and upon the funeral pyre did more harm than a hundred ministers could have done.'[4] As others had 'preached through their martyrdom', so Du Bourg pleaded his 'cause' thereby more eloquently and effectively than he could have done through any professional effort.

Appeals were of course made to Du Bourg in terms of his professional duty. He was 'reminded that he was a conseiller of the king, hence a man of letters and one who understood the constraints of the law'; but he would listen to no such arguments. He was unrepentant about his allegiance to the new religion, and in his defense he took a position that was at once reminiscent of Luther's stand at Worms and predictive of the line eventually taken by his 'Huguenot' comrades, as they soon would be called. 'They say we disobey princes because we offer nothing to false gods . . .', he said of his Gallican critics, but this was blasphemy.[5] 'Is it disobedience to our prince', he asked, 'for us to pray God for his prosperity in order that his country should be governed in peace and that all superstitions and idolatry should be banished from his kingdom?' Duty required the contrary. 'Is it not rather disobedience to dishonor God, to offend Him by all sorts of impieties so that one transfers His glory to material things and generally surrenders to the inventions of man, which are only lies?' As Calvin had taught in the *Institutes* and as Beza would teach in his more politically-minded statement of the

[4] Raemond, 1051.   [5] Crespin, II, 675.

principle of resistance, a subject's obligation to his ruler was always tempered by a prior responsibility to God.

Between the execution of Du Bourg and the formal outbreak of civil war, that is, a space of little more than two years, the convergence of heresy with the legal profession was striking and in some respects explosive. This convergence also coincided with and intensified the constitutional issue which the premature death of Henry II provoked. Although technically involving the minority of Henry's sons, the problem in reality hinged upon the power struggle between the Catholic party, headed by the Duke of Guise and his brother the Cardinal of Lorraine, and the opposition, presumably led by the princes of the blood, especially the house of Bourbon. Neither side had a clear legal position. The Guises controlled the person of the king and hence the government, but their legitimacy was in question because of their 'foreign' origins. On the other hand the opposition party was compromised by its associations with the reformed religion, its lack both of leadership and of a clear-cut justification for opposing Guise influence. Much of the public controversy for the next generation consisted of attempts by each side to legitimize itself and to discredit its enemies. The ideological beginnings of the civil wars in France may be understood in many ways as a clash between the king's lawyers and those of the Huguenot opposition.

From a more general point of view the problem that emerged in the years before the outbreak of war was that old medieval question of the two swords, though in a transmuted modern form. The distinction was now between the *Question de religion* and the *Question politique*, whether expressed as a conflict of jurisdiction or as different levels of human experience. The principle of Gallican unity implied a fusion of the two – 'Un roi, une loi, une foi' – and a confusion of the offenses of heresy and civil crime, that is, sedition. This took the form of an edict in 1554 that bestowed jurisdiction over heresy jointly on the Parlement and the Inquisitor of Faith. To many *parlementaires*, however, this step violated not only the separation of civil and ecclesiastical jurisdiction but also the professional frontier between law and theology. On this point at least the Huguenots were in agreement, and they never ceased trying to keep the religious and political questions separate. But force of circumstances in the end made this impossible. To separate out religion was unrealistic; to separate out politics was immoral – hence the invidious distinction between 'Huguenots of religion' and 'Huguenots of policy', or Malcontents, and that pejorative use of 'politique' which would later be associated with Machiavelli. Nevertheless, the urgency of political questions was becoming obvious and irresistible, and so the role of lawyers increasingly outweighed that of theologians in the generation of ideology. This is another fundamental characteristic of the 'politicization of Protestantism'.

THE FOURTH ESTATE

'A lawyer's a bad Christian', Luther remarked when the subject came up at his dinner table. An old proverb – 'And it's true', he added.[6] Calvin, who had studied with representatives both of the old and the new humanistic jurisprudence, had a similarly low opinion of the legal profession, its trickery and chicanery. 'If you have fought the jurisconsults', he wrote in 1562, no doubt thinking of Baudouin among others, 'you know that almost everywhere they are enemies of Christ's ministers because they do not think they can have first rank where ecclesiastical authority is well founded.' As one admirer of Luther, Henry Cornelius Agrippa, argued in his assault on 'the vanity of learning', law was the most degenerate embodiment of 'human traditions', depending as it did upon the wills of sinful men. Lawyers were members of a mercenary trade – 'pragmatici', in the derogatory Ciceronian term – and were taught literally to be 'duplicitous' in their methods (*duplex interpretatio* was the academic term).[7] At their worst, it was assumed, lawyers were liars out for hire. Satirists and social critics echoed these views in poetry and prose over many generations and attributed to the legal mind extremism in the directions both of tyranny and of disobedience. Such in their own ways were the scholastic *Bartolisti* of humanist criticism, the pettifoggers (*Chicanourrois*) derided by Rabelais and the Roman variety (*rabulae*) attacked by Hotman. Juvenal's often-quoted charge that Gaul was 'nursing mother of lawyers' (*nutricula causidicorum*) was never truer than in the sixteenth century, when the possibilities of employment and requirements of propaganda put a premium on the talents of qualified advocates.

The profession of law in this period was an imposing force. It was not only an academic discipline but a power structure, or set of power structures, that extended beyond national boundaries and even then formed what one eighteenth-century jurist called a 'republic of jurisconsults'.[8] On the continent all members of this community were university-trained, drew upon a common intellectual tradition, and spoke the same language even when serving

---

[6] Luther, *Table Talk*, ed. and trans. Theodore G. Tappert in *Luther's Works*, LIV (Philadelphia, 1967), 474. Cf. R. Stintzing, *Das Sprichwort 'Juristen böse Christen'* (Bonn, 1875), and C. Kenny, 'Bonus Jurista, Malus Christa', *Law Quarterly Review*, XIX (1903), 326ff. Calvin to Glareanus, 27 Oct. 1562, CO, XIX, 565.

[7] Agrippa, *De Incertitudine et vanitate scientiarum declamatio invectiva* (n.p., 1531), chapter 91. Cf. J. V. Alter, *Les Origines de la satire anti-bourgeois en France* (Geneva, 1966), 166ff., and R. Marichal, 'Rabelais et la réforme de la justice', *BHR*, XIV (1952), 176–92.

[8] G. Gennaro, *Respublica Jurisconsultorum* (Leipzig, 1733).

different causes. Their underlying, and sometimes overriding, professionalism bound them together despite fundamental and publicly more conspicuous divisions. Civilians fought canonists, yet their common allegiance to a Romanist tradition and the fact that many took their degree *utriusque* gave them common ground. There were also social differences (academics versus practicing members of the bar) and national ones ('ultramontanes' versus 'citramontanes'); but again difference served rather to increase than to cut off communication. The most publicized of all breaches in the sixteenth century was the methodological war between the humanists and the scholastics (*mos gallicus* versus *mos italicus*); but even here professionalism triumphed, as is shown by the case of Alciato, a founder of the humanist school who nevertheless prized the technical learning of Bartolus above the literary elegance of Valla. The significant thing was that they looked at the world through the same spectacles and shared what Justice Holmes was to call 'inarticulate major premises'. So the *Respublica Jurisconsultorum* provided a great training-ground for intellectual mercenaries and an inexhaustible source of argumentation and means of legitimization on which governments and interest groups of all sorts could draw. It was perhaps the primary agent of secular ideology in modern times.

In France the legal profession dated from the late thirteenth century, when a royal ordinance (1274) established the oath and rules of the lawyers' guild.[9] This 'Confrérie de Saint-Nicolas et communauté des advocats et procureurs' was a quasi-religious fraternity whose members swore a lifelong oath to uphold standards of truth, to remain orthodox and never to cheat or to overcharge clients. If they fell short of these goals, it was not for lack of good intentions. They heard mass every day and attached extraordinary significance to ceremonial, as on the 'day of oaths', when they swore on tablets bearing images of Jesus and John, and the phrase 'In the beginning was the Word', in the solemn pronouncements of parlementary declarations (the *arrêts*), and in the Mercuriales. They frowned upon the practice of defending 'bad causes'; but this was at least an open question, upheld by some on the analogy of a doctor bound to treat a hopelessly sick patient. By the end of the fifteenth century in any case they had built up a formidable legend, pretend-

---

[9] In general Delachenal, *Histoire des avocats*, 29ff., 296, etc; E. Maugis, *Histoire du Parlement de Paris* (Paris, 1913–16); and J. P. Dawson, *A History of Lay Judges* (Cambridge, Mass., 1960) and *The Oracles of the Law* (Ann Arbor, 1968); L. Romier, *Le Royaume de Catherine de Médicis* (Paris, 1921), II, 22ff.; and again the fundamental work of Weber, *Sociology of Law*, trans. E. Fischoff, in Weber, *Economy and Society*, II (New York, 1968), 641ff.

ing to a tradition of eloquence and service going back to the Carolingian *missi dominici* and more generally with the revived splendor of classical oratory. They even claimed inherent nobility through their office.

The coherence and self-consciousness of the legal profession were intensified by connections with that parallel and in some ways overlapping corporation, the university, which provided academic apprenticeship and licensing for the vocation of jurisprudence. That the 'republic of jurisconsults' was a power-base as well as an intellectual ideal was no less evident in the academy than it was in the forum. The hierarchical and monopolistic view of a professional elite has never been expressed better than by the jurist Barthélemy de Chasseneux, explaining from a cosmic perspective the best way to rank professors of law.[10] 'Those doctors are to be preferred', he wrote: (1) who actively teach, (2) who have the largest salary (*majora stipendia*), (3) who put together or write books (*libros composuerunt seu scripserunt*), (4) who have seniority (*antiquior*), (5) who are appointed by the higher authority (pope or emperor), (6) who have several degrees (*plures habent gradus*), (7) who teach in the larger, more famous and better university (*in majori famosiori et digniori universitate*), and (8) who have other honors. Here is as concrete a measure of authority as can be imagined, certainly more regular than the corresponding criteria for practicing lawyers. Many jurists of course lived in both worlds, although others affected to scorn their colleagues in the other camp, on grounds respectively of irrelevance and of greed. But in their own way both contributed to the generation and secularization of ideology.

On a number of grounds, then, and certainly in the popular mind, the professional lawyers had become literally a 'Fourth Estate'. As such its fortunes were bound up especially with those of the Parlement of Paris, that highest of 'sovereign courts' which also took shape in the age of the last Capetians. It was above all in relation with the Parlement that advocates achieved public identity, fame, influence and, needless to say, wealth. Again ceremony served as a measure. By the sixteenth century procedure and the professional hierarchy were both fixed. The ranking of lawyers at the bar (*barreau*) was reflected in the seating arrangement in the *Grand' Chambre* of the Parlement, the benches on the right for members and on the left for the pleaders, all of them located behind the decorated 'high benches' reserved for presidents, *conseillers, gens du roi* and other judges. One of the most prized attainments of the advocates was

---

[10] *Catalogus gloriae mundi* (Lyon, 1529), 220.

freedom of speech (*liberté de la parole*), which derived from the hard-won privilege of pleading against one's lord in the royal court – and indeed against the king himself, except in matters which directly touched his sovereignty (*majesté*). That parlementary offices became increasingly hereditary further strengthened the independence of the court and the legal profession. Like the larger guild of lawyers, of course, the Parlement accumulated its own body of legends as well as precedents, which likewise gave it a Carolingian and even classical pedigree and a quasi-religious character. This was reflected in a distinctive genre of legal treatises, such as those of Jean de Montaigne and Nicolas Bohier, celebrating the virtue and authority of this extension of the king's Great Council (*magnum concilium*) and reincarnation of the Roman Senate.

By the sixteenth century the Parlement was an impressive and abundantly privileged body – a 'mystical body' according to Bohier and indeed a veritable 'republic', as another advocate argued in 1527 – represented in the provinces as well as Paris.[11] It was the basis of a 'kingdom of the lawyers' lamented in Gaul since antiquity, a seven-headed monster that displayed growth in both a demographic and an institutional sense. To the four chambers of the fifteenth century eight more, some temporary, were added. The number of advocates was supposed to be fixed at 100 in imitation of the Roman Senate, but this was far exceeded; and by the outbreak of civil war there were over 400 members of the court, a growth paralleling that of offices in general, which was the object of universal lament. At the same time the authority of the Parlement – 'sovereign court', as it was proud to call itself – had expanded into the political realm, at least implicitly. Not only did it issue *arrêts* for the policing of the city of Paris and the University and other guilds, but it had also come to claim the rights of enregistering royal legislation and presenting 'remonstrances'. Nobody denied that the king was the sole source of law – it would be lese-majesty to suggest anything different – but the proper form of law-making was for the ordinances to be 'read, published and registered' in the court of the Parlement, a process that often took weeks or months. Technically, the source of this legislation was the royal Chancellerie, which contemporaries regarded as a direct extension of the royal council and a direct link between it and other parts of the bureaucracy. This body was also bound up closely with

---

[11] Bohier, *Tractatus de auctoritate magni concilii et parlamentorum Franciae*, in *Stilus Parlamenti* (Paris, 1542); Montaigne, *De Auctoritate et praeeminentia magni concilii et parlamentorum*, in *Tractatus*, XVI; Isambert, XI, 145. Cf. R. Doucet, *Etudes sur le gouvernement de François Ier* (Paris, 1921), I, chapter 1.

the legal profession and in this period was headed by a succession of distinguished jurists.

There was another corporate body, attached to the Chancellerie and to the Parlement as well as to other courts, which had an even more direct association with the production of legislation and statements of policy, namely, the college of royal notaries and secretaries. This *confrérie* was established in 1352 with a membership of 59 (in fact about 120 because of the conventional venal process of doubling), and in the course of the sixteenth century it grew to over 200. Like the advocates these secretaries took an oath of loyalty and followed a quasi-religious regimen, modelling themselves self-consciously on the apostles whom they called the 'notaries of Christ'.[12] They occupied a somewhat lower level on the social scale and also in literary achievement, but they were in effect 'intellectuals' and some of them published authors. A few were distinguished scholars, most notably Guillaume Budé, who held one of these charges before becoming *maître des requêtes* in the Parlement, Jean du Tillet, archivist and pioneering antiquarian, and Bernard Girard du Haillan, later royal historiographer. Their principal accomplishment was drawing up the great body of official acts for the king and *arrêts* for the various sovereign courts, including the Parlement of Paris. To what extent they were official ideologues and even policy-makers as well as official scriveners can only be guessed; but certainly they were significant as purveyors and popularizers of political thought on a certain, often ignored, level, contributing in particular to royalist, Gallican and parlementary doctrines.

It was above all the advocates of the Parlement of Paris, together with their more anonymous notarial colleagues, who constituted the ideological shock-troops of the monarchy. They fashioned the official image of French kingship and justified, beforehand or retrospectively, the expansion of its power. This 'legist tradition', whose history (including its hagiography and mythology) was written by Antoine Loisel in the early seventeenth century, began with such Capetian lawyers as Guillaume de Nogaret and Pierre de Cugnières and ended with Loisel himself and such colleagues as Charles Dumoulin, Pierre Pithou and Etienne Pasquier.[13] Despite extensive and indeed methodological reliance on Roman and canon law, these royalist *gens de plume* had always assumed an aggressively anti-Roman stance. Indeed the dual theme of Loisel's book was the excellence of French tradition and the pernicious influence of

[12] Isambert, XI, 34 (Feb. 1484); cf. H. Michaud, *La Grande Chancellerie* (Paris, 1967).
[13] *Pasquier, ou dialogue des advocats du Parlement de Paris*, ed. A. Dupin (Paris, 1844). Cf. R. Génestal, *Les Origines de l'appel comme d'abus* (Paris, 1951).

Romanism, which had first raised its ugly head during the Babylonian Captivity of the fourteenth century. 'It was from that time', he remarked, 'that we began to learn chicanery.' It was from that period of ecclesiastical chaos, too, that the Parlement took occasion to extend its jurisdiction over the church, especially during the time of divided allegiance created by the Great Schism after 1378, and to devise such remedies as the *appel comme d'abus*, which permitted appeals from ecclesiastical courts to the Parlement, to the detriment of the former. Characteristically, this process was represented as a restoration to an original and better condition (*reducere ad statum pristinum*), and 'Parlementary Gallicanism' in general was seen as a program to 'revive the ancient liberties' of the French church.

Such attitudes survived despite the triumph of 'royal gallicanism' in the Concordat of 1516, which indeed the Parlement refused to register for several years. Around mid-century they reappeared in the guise of a radical and even schismatic kind of Gallican reform which not only made a *rapprochement* with evangelical religion but also urged the monarchy to sever ties with Rome and establish a national church on the Anglican model. This was the position taken in particular by the 'prince of legists', Charles Dumoulin; but when King Henry II withdrew his support in 1552, this cause was doomed to failure – and of course the chasm between new-fangled 'reform' and old-fashioned Gallicanism was made virtually impassable. Although in a longer perspective the legal profession in France preserved loyalties both to some sort of reform and to the monarchy, the more immediate result was to pose a most difficult ideological dilemma. Most jurists remained in the orthodox Gallican fold or, like Dumoulin and Baudouin, returned to it, but a growing minority subordinated the ideal of national unity to the higher goals of evangelical religion. The case of Anne du Bourg symbolized this mounting threat to social and political stability.

The affinity between law and heresy had been evident for many years in the law schools, going back at least to the famous case of Jean de Caturce in 1532. A law candidate at Toulouse, Caturce was charged with refusing to drink the king's health, among other things, since evidently he took this secular ceremony to be as abominable as the mass. 'O palace of iniquity!', he is supposed to have cried before his execution, referring to the chambers of the Parlement; 'O seat of injustice!'[14] Among the elite of the legal profession, too, contamination was apparent long before the Du

---

[14] Crespin, I, 284; C. Devic and J. Vaissèle, *Histoire générale de Languedoc*, XII (Toulouse, 1889), 237; cf. R. Fédou, *Les Hommes de loi lyonnais à la fin du moyen âge* (Paris, 1964), 443.

Bourg affair. In 1539, two years after the ceremony of expiation held in the Parlement of Bordeaux, a resolution was passed to 'extirpate' heresy as a species of lese-majesty. In 1551 the Parlement of Normandy held its own Mercuriale, and five advocates of heresy were expelled. The Parisian Mercuriale of 1559 simply gave national prominence to a very long-standing and widespread phenomenon.[15]

The culmination of this, as of the division within French society as a whole, came in the spring of 1562. At this time a sort of blacklist of suspected heretics was drawn up, including sixty-three names, virtually all of them lawyers.[16] Among them were Paul de Foix, Adam de Fumée, Claude Violle and Louis du Faur, who had been arrested in the *mercuriale* three years before, and other eminent jurists such as Barthélemy de Faye (who had recently edited the posthumous works of Calvin's old school-friend François Connan), Pierre de la Place (a pioneering Huguenot chronicler as well as president of Parlement), Adrien du Thou, Achille Harlay and one of François Hotman's brothers. All these men were under suspicion – 'fort suspect de la nouvelle religion' was the phrase – on grounds ranging from attendance at unauthorized sermons, to association with those of the religion, to suspicions about wives, brothers or other relatives, to simple hearsay ('le bruict commun') and story remarks that so-and-so 'they say to be an atheist'. On 10 June 1562 the division was complete. All the advocates of the Parlement of Paris were required to sign a profession of faith – on the traditional tablets of the 'day of oaths' – that was in effect an oath of allegiance to the Catholic party.[17] At that time 367 signatures were obtained by the *procureur royal*, two days later another 32 lawyers added their names, and a month after that 4 more came into the fold. These lawyers were also forbidden to have heretics in their domestic service, and were of course required to report any suspects. Six years later this requirement of orthodoxy was reinforced by threat of deprivation of office and imprisonment, and there is evidence to show that this edict was put into effect.

Like the academy, then, the legal profession had a divided soul, and its public image declined accordingly. On the one hand there was the lawyer as nemesis of true religion, symbolized in the popular mind by Pierre Lizet; but of course he was supported in his efforts by hordes of lesser minions, such as Hotman's father and

---

[15] C. Boscheron des Portes, *Histoire du Parlement de Bordeaux* (Bordeaux, 1877), 50; A. Floquet, *Histoire du Parlement de Normandie* (Rouen, 1840), II, 274.

[16] Text in Haag, IV, 57.

[17] *Le Proces verbal faict par ordonnance de la Court de Parlement . . . touchant les articles et la profession de foy d'icelle Court* (Paris, 1562; BN Lb33.84).

later brother and cousins. On the other hand there was the lawyer as heretic, illustrated by Du Bourg and Hotman himself. For both parties the old proverb seemed to hold true: 'Bon jurisconsulte, mauvais Chrestien', wrote Brantôme, endorsing Luther's opinion – 'A lawyer's a bad Christian.'

TRUE PHILOSOPHY AND THE HUMAN CONDITION

'It is impossible for a good jurist to be a heretic', declared one civil lawyer, citing the famous phrase that celebrated jurisconsults as veritable 'priests of the laws' (*sacerdotes legum*).[18] Here we encounter a totally different face of the legal profession, one which took cognizance of the nature of society and the means of understanding and improving it. In the sixteenth century legal scholars and practitioners formed a unique lay class analogous to the clergy, a sort of secular intellectual corporation whose vocation was the analysis and regulation of human relations – the cure, in a sense, not of souls but of citizens. They were devotees not of 'sacred' but of 'civil science', and as such they played a number of roles that would later be distributed among a number of specialisms. They were not only legislators, administrators and apologists for particular causes, but also critics of tradition, social arbiters and reformers, lay defenders of the faith, political theorists and, finally, philosophers with the most exalted claims. More than any other group they provided the intellectual framework for the emergence of modern ideological movements, and to understand this it is necessary to consider their perceptions of and judgments about their world.

Among jurists of every sort it was the commonest of commonplaces that 'jurisprudence is true philosophy' (*vera philosophia*). This formula appeared in the very first sentence of the chief collection of civil law, the Digest (indeed in the same sentence as that characterizing jurists as priests of the laws); and it became a central theme of Renaissance jurisprudence. Defending this thesis, Claude de Seyssel went on to argue that 'jurisprudence . . . is to be preferred to all other fields of knowledge because of its purpose'.[19] This claim rested on three propositions: first, that law, which was defined classically as 'the knowledge of things divine and human', was

---

[18] A. Favre, *Iurisprudentiae Papinianae scientia* (Cologne, 1631), 16: 'Bonum Iurisconsultorum haereticum esse nullo modo posse.'

[19] *In VI [Diges]torum partes* (n.p., n.d.), 1; and in general D. R. Kelley, 'Vera philosophia: the philosophical significance of renaissance jurisprudence', *Journal of the History of Philosophy*, XIV (1976), 267–79.

equivalent to wisdom (*sapientia*); second, that, because it treated the true causes of things and was universal in application, law was a true science; and third, that, because it 'consisted in action and not contemplation', it was joined to that highest philosophic value, justice, and to the welfare of humanity in general. The point was perhaps made best by one of the pioneers of the new jurisprudence who was at the same time an active promoter of religious reform. 'For the welfare of humanity', wrote François Baudouin, 'Socrates said that either philosophers should rule over kings or kings should be philosophers, and if this is true, philosophy should be expressed not in words but in actions . . . But since public actions are more potent than private, the true and supreme philosophy [*vera et summa philosophia*] is contained in the laws which pertain to public actions.'[20]

That jurisprudence was a law unto itself had been made clear in various medieval disputes with other disciplines, including medicine and even theology. Was theology really necessary for lawyers? ran one conventional *quaestio*. 'I answer no', asserted the author of the thirteenth-century legal Gloss, 'because everything is included in the civil law.'[21] Nor did the humanist movement transform the profession of law in any fundamental way. Andrea Alciato may have introduced literary methods into the teaching of legal texts, but he rejected entirely the view of such radical classicists as Valla that would subordinate law to the *studia humanitatis*. The point was that for professional jurists their science 'belonged' neither to the humanities nor even to philosophy; it subsumed them all along with other disciplines. In sum, the study of law, more than any other field, represented an encyclopedia, a total *Weltanschauung*, expressed concretely in various philosophic systems modelled on classical jurisprudence. Its horizons ultimately encompassed such large questions as the problem of knowledge, the process of cause and effect, the nature of man and his place in the universe, and the ideals of social and political organization – epistemology, methodology, cosmology and sociology, as it may be anachronistically summarized. Even more significant in the present context, jurisprudence took upon itself the task of transforming the world, whether in a positive or a negative way, through reformation or repression, with a vision of the future (often disguised as a passion for the past). Not that law constituted an ideology; rather, it was the source of many ideologies, and contained the means for legitimizing many more.

In the republic of jurists there were many provinces and parties, but

[20] Baudouin, *Commentarius in quattuor libros Institutionum* (Paris, 1554), *ad tit.*
[21] Accursius, *ad tit.*

beneath the clash of opinions there was a fairly consistent perception of the human condition. In the disparate forms of sixteenth-century jurisprudence – ranging from polemic to pedantic exegesis, from technical monographs to the grandest systems, from the most fanciful flights of oratory to the most utilitarian collections of precedents – we can see in the most direct fashion the intersection of the ideal and the real, that is, of institutions and social groups on the one hand and the norms and goals of society on the other. Of course social analysis in this period was an infant and indeed embryonic discipline, proceeding by analogy and often by wishful thinking, and proposing rather to justify than to criticize legal and political arrangements. These tendencies by no means precluded lamentations about social ills; but to most lawyers sixteenth-century society seemed to be a static and well-balanced, if not always well-regulated, creation, marred by sin and weakness rather than by institutional failings, except perhaps those of foreign import. The dominant metaphors were those of organism, of hierarchy, of biological function and ceremonial rank. Typical is the view expressed in the late fifteenth century by Octavien de Saint Gelais.[22] For him the republic (*la chose publique*) was an organism in which the prince represented the head, the priesthood and royal administration (*senechaux*) the ears, the counsellors the heart, the nobles the hands, and the working class the feet. Such, argued the author of this contribution to the mirrors-of-the-prince tradition (he calls his book a 'lunette'), was the social basis of true wisdom (*sapience*).

In these terms society appeared as a great web of estates, corporate bodies, offices and less formal establishments held together by tradition, natural affinity and such moral factors as love, deference and especially fidelity; and individual behavior was determined largely by the habits, rules and privileges of membership in such groups. From this point of view law was seen rather as a reflection of social structure than as a means of changing it. 'History teaches us', wrote one advocate of Parlement, 'that the ancients who were devoted to the public good abhorred the introduction of new laws into a republic and that they were very dubious about any who wanted to introduce such laws.'[23] So custom was regarded as prior in a legal as well as a historical sense. 'Custom interprets law', wrote Calvin's friend François Connan, 'and judgment confirms custom.'[24] Not that society was immutable; indeed, its delicate balance was

---

[22] *Le Tresor de noblesse* (n.p., 1506), A.
[23] Jean de la Madeleine, *Discours de l'estat et office d'un bon Roy* (Paris, 1575), 34; cf. Montaigne, *Essais*, I, xxii.
[24] Connan, *Commentariorum Iuris Civilis libri X* (Paris, 1553), 43.

evident in various polarities which lawyers either emphasized or not, according to the particular cause at stake. Public welfare counterbalanced private privilege, 'absolute' sovereignty counterbalanced 'mixed' government, and 'interest' or 'reason of state' counterbalanced corporate 'liberty'. On the one hand the government continuously guaranteed the privileges of special groups, such as guilds or universities; on the other hand it had ready a formula for dealing with any 'rebels' forming a 'party' contrary to the interests of the monarchy, and in particular for recalcitrant towns.

Yet the social ideal transcended such apparent paradoxes. Lawyers managed to argue that limitations on government also enhanced it, that the public good was really the sum of private interests (a kind of juristic prefiguring of *laissez-faire*), and that 'liberty' was of benefit to the whole commonwealth. All was for the best in that (the lawyers') best of all possible worlds, and so particular causes could be promoted without much strain on individual consciences. At least this was the case as long as the old Gallican ideal continued to dominate popular opinion. As formulated by its most fervent supporters, the ideal was one of almost monolithic unity: 'Un dieu, un roy, une foi, une loy', recited Antoine Loisel in an oration of 1582. Or as Guillaume Postel put it in his still more inflated celebration of 'true concord', 'A single world under a single God, and under a single king and sovereign bishop, one faith, one law and one single common agreement' (*commun consentement*).[25]

In political and social terms this comforting ideal was first and most authoritatively described by Seyssel – ironically on the very eve of that Reformation which would make it obsolete. In his comprehensive portrait of the 'grand monarchy of France' Seyssel combined formal legal training with an extensive career in practical politics. In a sense he moved from an academic concern with legal norms to an almost Machiavellian interest in policy-making – from the 'mirror of feudal law' (*Speculum feudorum*) of his university days to the 'mirror of the prince', one aspect of his *Monarchy of France* reflecting his experience as diplomat, royal counsellor and Gallican prelate. For Seyssel the key to social stability (equivalent to national unity and political strength) was a trinity of forces he called 'bridles' (*freins*) – religion, justice and police.[26] These bridles he associated not only with the 'conservation' but also with the 'augmentation' of the monarchy. The religious basis of society was to be reinforced by

---

[25] Postel, *Les Raisons de la Monarchie* (Paris, 1551), iii, and Loisel, *La Guyenne* (Paris, 1605), 99, 'Amnestie' (1577), dedicated to Montaigne.

[26] Seyssel, *La Monarchie de France*, ed. J. Poujol (Paris, 1961), I, 9–11; English trans., *The Monarchy of France*, by J. H. Hexter, ed. D. R. Kelley (New Haven, Conn., 1981).

obedience to the pope, continuous 'reformation' of ecclesiastical abuses and rejection of heresy (*toutes heresies et sectes reprouvees*); and in fact, as bishop of Turin, Seyssel himself spent his last years trying to root out remnants of the Waldensian sect. The 'second great treasure' of a nation was justice, and Seyssel celebrated in particular the legal profession, whose qualities determined the fairness and speed of the judicial process and the wisdom of royal counsel. Here his own experience as adviser to the king gave his speculations a practical basis.

Much more complex was the notion of 'police', a term which already had a rich history in the context of royal legislation. For Seyssel 'la police' corresponded to the 'many ordinances made by the king and confirmed later by time, tending to the conservation of the kingdom in general and in particular'; and it included as well what would later be called 'fundamental law', especially the principle of non-alienability of the domain, and the structures of royal government and social classes. Of the latter Seyssel recognized three, not including the church, which was common to all – for 'Religion', as the jurist André Tiraqueau put it, 'knows neither persons nor classes of men.'[27] The three classes were the nobility and the 'people', divided in Italianate fashion into wealthy and mean (*peuple gras et menu*); and Seyssel emphasized the social mobility of France – 'how one moves from the third estate to the second, and from the second to the first', especially through religious calling, education or the accumulation of wealth.[28] This too was a major source of political 'force'.

A generation later another jurist and historian, Guillaume de la Perrière, offered a more complex, if more static, reconstruction of French society in a book that also affected to be a 'mirror' and also concentrated on the 'conservation' of the monarchy. La Perrière's *Political Mirror* pictured the world as a forest, with individual trees standing for various social arrangements such as marriage, justice and the republic itself. For him, as for Seyssel, monarchy was ideally a 'mixed' government, and in this context he referred not only to Machiavelli but also to Nicholas of Cusa, whose 'conciliarist' thesis, which (though officially condemned) was still popular with French lawyers. Like Seyssel, La Perrière preserved an essentially feudal model; but his arrangement was more elaborately hierarchical, including as it did administrative and economic functions as well as social strata (priests, magistrates, nobles, bourgeois, artisans and

---

[27] Tiraqueau, *Commentarii de Nobilitate et iure primigeniorum* (Lyon, 1566), 159: 'Religio nescit personas nec conditones hominum.'
[28] Seyssel, *Monarchie*, I, 17.

laborers).[29] Nor did he envisage the sort of mobility permitted by Seyssel; for to him it was nature, which is to say birth, that destined one to these roles, training that fitted one for them (as Corlieu had also argued), and fidelity, whether in the sense of loyalty or of religious calling, that confirmed the whole structure.

Seyssel's three categories continued to dominate political assumptions during the religious wars (although at least one deliberately 'Machiavellian' author joined 'arms', instead of the more neutral conception of 'police', to religion and justice). They were appealed to not only by orthodox scholars like Pasquier, Le Roy and the royal historiographer Du Haillan but also by Protestant observers, whose perceptions were not radically different except for their greater emphasis on the flaws which offended their reformed sensibilities. Thus Nicolas Barnaud praised the estates as three precious 'pearls' in the royal treasury, and Du Laurier likewise celebrated Seyssel's three 'bridles' while calling for their reforming and strengthening.[30] Most famous of all was Innocent Gentillet's *Anti-Machiavel*, which employed demonology to give a new edge to the old Seysselian tradition. Gentillet offered remedies for the supposed advice of the old Florentine 'politique', reformulated through a series of maxims neatly distributed under three rubrics: counsel (this Machiavellian topic being substituted for the Seysselian 'justice'), religion and police.[31] Despite the pose of outraged religious and national sensibilities, Gentillet offered at least by implication a political and social ideal that served as a corrective to the 'atheistic' and 'tyrannical' views of Machiavelli, who betrayed a deplorable lack of social conscience. The contrasting French ideal was based on independent and institutionally guaranteed (instead of individually calculated) 'counsel', which indeed was one of the 'fundamental laws' of the French monarchy, and a proper system of 'police' to provide a social context allegedly ignored by Machiavelli and his like. Gentillet's Huguenot colleague Henri Estienne, likewise scornful of 'Machiavellists', contrasted this moral view with the uncivilized Italian *polizza*. His view coincided in fact with that of La Perrière, who in good humanist fashion associated 'police' with 'the Greek word *politeia*, which we translate

---

[29] *Le Miroir politique* (Paris, 1567), 20ff., 102ff.

[30] Barnaud, *Le Cabinet du Roy* (Paris, 1567), and Du Laurier, *De l'estat present de ce Royaume quant a la religion, justice, et police* (Paris, 1583; BN Lb34.213). Cf. *Discours politique*, ME, III, fol. 162, and for influence on Le Roy and Du Haillan, see Seyssel, *Monarchie*, appendices. Barnaud's section on the clergy has been published separately as *La Polygamie sacrée au XVIe siècle*, ed. J. Hervez (Paris, 1908).

[31] Gentillet, *Discours contre Machiavel* (1576), critical edn. by A. D'Andrea and P. D. Stewart (Florence, 1974).

as "civility". What the Greeks called political government the Latins called republican or civil society.'[32]

The Protestant conception of calling reinforced these conservative views of social structure. One Huguenot *parlementaire* who was also a pioneering historian of the first phase of religious conflict in France expressed this elaborately in a treatise on 'vocation' in the sense not only of 'interior' but also of 'exterior', which is to say social, calling.[33] Pierre de la Place argued that the members of a commonwealth, though it was governed by laws, were more immediately subject to individual feelings of duty toward all of their functions, toward their domestic as well as ecclesiastical offices and charges. Nor were they permitted to undertake functions for which they had no specific charge. Those not directly 'called' (*appellez*), for example, could not take it upon themselves to preach the gospel. Admittedly, this celebration of vocation might in some circumstances cast doubt upon other more traditional sources of authority, and indeed La Place was himself called to chronicle such circumstances during the time of civil war. But even conflicts between vocation and law were covered by La Place's principle; for – in line with Calvin's own position – resistance itself could be undertaken only by those who were 'called' to it, that is, by magistrates. Like 'conscience', then, 'calling' remained within the rule of law, and so, of course, did various Protestant conceptions of reform, political and ecclesiastical.

In general, and in marked contrast to the civic view taken by many Italian observers, French lawyers, Protestants as well as Catholics, maintained a conservative, legalistic amd moralistic vision of society and the political structure which depended on it. Among orthodox jurists, Pierre Grégoire de Toulouse and Louis le Caron both defended the notion of France as a 'mixed constitution', though during the civil wars such an argument verged on treason. Grégoire's ideal, in contrast to that of 'the most pernicious Machiavelli', was the republic as 'a communal society of property and life constituting a civil body composed of divers parts which are its members, under one head and spirit . . .', for well-being in this life as well as preparation for the next.[34] Despite heretical overtones he did not scruple to identify this scholastic ideal with the 'Francogallia' described in Hotman's notorious and inflammatory survey of French institutional history. Le Caron, who had been a student of Baudouin

---

[32] Henri Estienne, *Deux dialogues du nouveau langage François italianizé*, ed. I. Liseaux (Paris, 1883), 97.

[33] Pierre de la Place, *Traitté de la vocation et maniere di vivre a laquelle chacun est appellé* (Paris, 1578).

[34] Pierre Grégoire de Toulouse, *De Republica* (Frankfurt, 1609), XIII, 21.

at Bourges, followed the same line, though with a Platonic rather than Aristotelian slant, and went on to identify the French legal (as well as political) tradition with 'harmonic justice' and the highest form of philosophy. 'I find the customs of French very *politique*', he wrote, 'and quite in accord with the opinion of our Plato.'[35] Le Caron's major achievement was a Romanoid legal system based on native customary materials. 'French law', he declared in this vernacular 'digest' (1587), 'is composed of all parts of universal law, the science of which is called jurisprudence, civil science or a wisdom which some refer to as "royal". It is the major part of moral as well as political philosophy, which is most useful to human society.'

Conservatism remained the keynote of the legal profession for all parties. Yet behind the rhetoric of social stasis there were provisions which accommodated change and even promoted improvement. There were, for example, the devices of 'desuetude' and 'evil customs' which could be overridden, various kinds of 'interpretation' which medieval jurists had raised to the level of a systematic science, and above all the flexible idea of 'reformation' in a specifically legal sense, which underlay the great sixteenth-century campaign to regularize and to unify feudal customs. In accordance with organistic assumptions, legislators likened their role to that of doctors, whose business was to diagnose disorders and to prescribe remedies. This medical imagery was applied to Machiavelli, whose first French translator (more sympathetic than later readers) compared the Florentine secretary's counsel to the unusually strong medicine necessary for a patient in a crisis condition. It was used also by Michel de l'Hôpital in his treatise on the general 'reformation of justice', and by Hotman in his reform-minded *Antitribonian*, which was dedicated to L'Hôpital.[36] Obviously the hopes and ideals of authors like Hotman were closely allied to ecclesiastical reform, and in fact it is often difficult to keep separate secular and spiritual reforming enterprises, especially in ideological terms.

In any case, these are some of the attitudes which went into the making of early modern social consciousness and especially of modern 'political science'. This new, or renewed, discipline emerged in recognizable form in the sixteenth century as a sort of conflation of two older disciplines which until then had, philosophi-

---

[35] Louis Le Caron, *Les Dialogues* (Paris, 1555), 29; and see Kelley, 'Louis Le Caron philosophe', in *Philosophy and Humanism, Renaissance Essays in Honor of Paul Oskar Kristeller* (New York, 1976), 30–49.

[36] L'Hôpital, *Oeuvres inédites*, ed. P. Duféy (Paris, 1825), I, 23; Hotman, *Antitribonian* (Paris, 1603), 6; Denys Janot in A. Gerber, *Niccolò Machiavelli, Die Handschriften, Ausgaben und Übersetzungen seiner Werke im 16. und 17. Jahrhundert* (Turin, 1962), III, 21.

cally but perhaps unreasonably, been kept apart. One was the 'science' of jurisprudence (the jurists' *legitima* or *civilis scientia*) and the other that of the ancient 'politiques', as L'Hôpital characterized Plato and Aristotle. The term 'science of politics' (*la science de politiques*) was introduced in the fourteenth century, but it was in the sixteenth century that this conception (*la science politique*), elaborated by humanists beginning with Budé and culminating in the work of his disciples Louis le Roy and Louis le Caron, came to maturity.[37] A graduate of the law school of Toulouse, Le Roy applied not only to law and to classical philosophic tradition but also to such modern experts as Seyssel and Machiavelli in his effort to restore 'la politique' to its rightful position as 'the worthiest, most useful and most necessary of all' disciplines. Le Caron pursued this ideal even more single-mindedly and systematically and took the very same point of departure. 'The divine Plato has elegantly declared that true philosophy concerns itself with the life and customs of men', he wrote. And furthermore it 'is contained in the books of law, not in the useless and inarticulate libraries of the philosophers . . ., so that' – once again the theme sounds – 'jurisprudence may indeed be called the true philosophy'.[38]

WHAT PLEASES THE PRINCE

'The true philosophy' of jurisprudence not only held up an ideal of social order, it also provided means of establishing and preserving this order and of punishing deviations from it. In his celebration of the civilizing force of French law, for example, Louis le Caron did not mind endorsing the rigorous views of Pierre Lizet on criminal law, and in particular the conditions and uses of confiscations to maintain social order.[39] Here we move from jurisprudence back to politics, since the law-making power was increasingly identified by jurists with expressions of the royal command: 'For such is our will', as the legislative formula had it (*car tel est notre plaisir*). 'Qui veut le Roy, si veut la loy' was the French equivalent of the Roman *lex regia*, and

---

[37] Budé, *De l'Institution du prince* (Paris, 1547), and Le Roy, *De l'Origine, antiquité, progres, excellence et utilité de l'art politique* (Paris, 1567), prefacing his translation of Aristotle's *Politics*, which appeared the next year. Cf. N. Oresme, *Le Livre de politiques d'Aristote* (Paris, 1489), 44, 'la science de politiques'. A locus classicus is Cicero, *De Oratore*, 28, 109: 'Illi olim, propter eximiam rerum maximarum scientiam, a Graecis politici philosophi appellati.'

[38] *La Claire, ou de la prudence du droit* (Paris, 1554), 23; cf. *Pandectes ou Digestes du droict françois* (Paris, 1587), 1, 3.

[39] Preface to Pierre Lizet, *Brieve et succincte maniere de proceder tant a l'institution et decisions des causes criminelles que civiles* (Paris, 1555).

specifically the opening clause, *Quod principi placuit*, 'What pleases the prince has the force of law.'[40] By the sixteenth century even private law, traditionally immune from legislative tampering, became subject at least indirectly to royal will, and so to lawyerly meddling, through the movement to 'reform' the customs of Paris and of the provinces, while the range of matters treated by ordinances, edicts and *arrêts* continued to grow. This expansion of governmental ambitions, if not power, was accompanied by an inflation of royalist rhetoric and of judicial and bureaucratic activity; and the whole process seemed to reflect an almost totalitarian view of social control. In this age of religious turmoil, the tendency to influence and intrude into the innermost recesses of private conscience – and private property – reinforced the recurring off-with-their-heads attitude toward dissent. The result was to make the will of the prince, together with the wills of his spokesmen and enforcers, a major factor in the generation of ideology.

Most important in the expression of royal will was the sovereign court of the Parlement and the Chancellerie. In general the legislative tradition of the monarchy went back, at least in terms of the mythical but legally valid juridical tradition recognized by the lawyers, to the Carolingian capitularies. From the thirteenth century there were the ordinances, increasingly in the vernacular as well as in Latin, which in later times were interpreted as constitutions or edicts on the imperial model – for the king indeed, according to the celebrated canonist formula, was 'emperor in his kingdom'. Here is one of the most visible expressions of that majesty, or sovereignty, whose form would be reconstructed and rationalized by philosophical jurists like Le Caron and Bodin. At the same time his official 'actes' – legal hyperbole for what were after all verbal declarations – constituted one of the most conspicuous manifestations of ideology.[41]

As always there was a considerable distance between rhetoric and reality – between legislative intent and administrative accomplishment. In his various pronouncements the French king addressed himself to all classes of society and to most aspects of life; and as the occasion demanded he adopted tones of complacency, conciliation,

[40] Hotman, *Francogallia*, ed. R. Giesey and trans. J. Salmon (Cambridge, 1973), chapter 14; Loisel, *Institutes coustumiers* (Paris, 1611), 19; and in general P. Schramm, *Der König von Frankreich* (Weimer, 1939), 251ff., and D. R. Kelley, *Foundations of Modern Historical Scholarship* (New York, 1970), 197ff.

[41] The ordinances will normally be cited in their original printed form, listed conveniently in Isnard and, more sporadically, in LN, but reference may also be made to Isambert and other modern collections, perhaps most conveniently in the topically organized publications of Brisson, Rebuffi, Fontanon and others. On the edicts of pacification see now N. Sutherland, *The Huguenot Struggle for Recognition* (New Haven, 1980), and the convenient collection, *Edicts des guerres de religion*, ed. A. Stegmann (Paris, 1979).

national pride, righteous indignation or uncontrollable fury. Dispensing privileges, sustaining monopolies, overseeing the church, curbing personal excesses, confiscating goods, fixing prices, regulating dress and exhorting to duty or to 'reform', the king affected to assess and to supervise all ranks of the social, military and administrative hierarchy at whose apex he was situated. Most of the ordinances dealt with the formal structures of government and society – the courts, the system of fiscal and administrative offices, the church, the army, the guilds and commercial organizations, schools and so on. Reorganizing and 'reforming' such institutions was relatively easy; problems arose in the need to control, to enforce and if necessary to punish. In general the imposition of new taxes (in the name of urgency), changes in customs (in the name of uniformity), enforcement of sumptuary and other legislation (in the name of public welfare) and urging of university 'indoctrination' (in the name of orthodoxy) all assumed a condition of social malleability reflecting either extreme optimism or an unrealistic moralism quite at odds with the machinery of enforcement. In any case, the king's pleasure and displeasure were extending into the furthest reaches of society.

The contrast between legislative ambition and the most threatening kinds of anti-social behavior was striking in the sixteenth century. It was, certainly to judge from complaints and legal efforts, an age of rising civil violence. Over and over again, and patently in vain, men were forbidden to carry arms – 'arcs, arbaletes, hallegardes, piques, ronges, epees, dagues et autres batons invasifs' – although nobles as well as royal officers were exempt until the more stringent measures taken by Henry II. In the 1520s the Habsburg–Valois conflict, bringing transients (*oisifs*) and trouble-makers (*mauvais garçons*), intensified the disorders, and in the fall of 1523 an edict condemned such 'adventurers, pillagers and devourers of the people' who raped, stole and started fires.[42] Taking a high moral tone, Francis I blamed much of the 'evil and serpentine seed' of crime on his imperial enemies, who had provoked war without cause and so had disturbed domestic peace as well; and he urged that they be killed and cut to pieces, if not chased from the country. Paris was in a constant state of anxiety, fearful especially of incendiaries, who the next year burned a large part of Troyes; and more than one suspect was imprisoned or executed, sometimes apparently by being thrown into the Seine without trial. In 1526 a new officer, a 'lieutenant of police', was commissioned 'to visit the streets, taverns and public

---

[42] Isambert, XII, 115; cf. *Le Guidon de secretaires* (n.p., 1516; Columbia), and *Chronique du roy Françoys*, ed. G. Giuffrey (Paris, 1860), 34.

places to seize vagabonds and persons without identification'.[43] Measures had to be taken, too, against 'illicit assemblies', in which armed and ill-intentioned men gathered against the king's interests, and against the wearing not only of masks but (again) of beards, in this case because of the disguising effect, though again nobles and gendarmes were exempted. It should be recalled that this was also the time of the Constable Bourbon's scandal, which set a frightful precedent of defiance and, according to the charges, 'lese-majesty, rebellion and felony'.

Crime was an increasingly conspicuous part of city life in particular, and it was vividly depicted in a publication of 1541 devoted to criminal law. In what passed for contemporary journalistic illustration, a series of woodcuts showed in somewhat idealized form the commission of a street crime, the apprehension of the perpetrator, his charging before the court, his 'interrogation' and final condemnation.[44] Appended to this illustrated *Praxis criminis* was a short treatise by the young François Hotman which discussed violent crime in a more systematic way – and which foreshadowed some of Hotman's own later partisan involvements in illegal agitation. He distinguished between private and public offenses, capital and non-capital, and arranged them in an ascending scale ranging from theft and physical injury to crimes of 'tumult, that is, perturbation and sedition'. High on the list was the crime of conspiracy (*conjuratio*), which was precisely the offense with which Hotman was himself associated in the Amboise uprisings of 1559–60. At this point, however, Hotman, who had recently received his license in law from the University of Orleans, was expressing the utterly conventional abhorrence of violence and approval of the severe penalties which a peaceful society demanded of violators.

Despite such attitudes and despite the continuing legislation, the crime-rate seemed to be increasing visibly during the next reign: 'for daily', Henry II declared in an edict of 1548, 'there are countless murders and crimes by those who go about armed with arquebuses and pistols'.[45] So this king took a still harsher and more punitive line, shifting emphasis from the fruits of civil peace to the horrors of punishment on the wheel, and from alien to domestic 'murderers and assassins'. He urged citizens to band together against the threat and to cry, 'A la porte, à la porte!' when a crime had been

---

[43] *Registre des delibérations du Bureau de la Ville de Paris*, I, ed. F. Bonnardot (Paris, 1883), 225, and *Lettres patentes de François Premier Du Septième May 1526* (BN F. 23610).

[44] Ioannes Millaeus, *Praxis criminis* (Paris, 1541), with Hotman's *Tabulae de criminibus*.

[45] Isambert, XIII, 74. Cf. D. Richet, 'Aspects socio-culturels des conflits religieux à Paris dans la seconde moitié du XVIe siècle', *Annales*, XXXII (1977), 764–83.

committed, to ring church bells, to block exits and gang up on the culprits.[46] This legislation had to be repeated almost yearly and even monthly, during the religious wars under his successors. Yet it was largely in vain, as Francis II admitted in an edict of 17 December 1559, complaining that 'great and execrable murders are committed daily by the carrying of pistols'. Like his father he urged public outcry – 'aux traitres, aux boutefeux!' – against criminals, and like his father he had to admit failure.[47] The very next day one of the most sensational crimes of the century occurred, the murder of President Minard, and of course the conspiracy of Amboise was already brewing. In general there was a very thin line between individual crime and public offenses loosely referred to as 'rebellion', 'sedition', 'conjuration' and 'lese-majesty'.

That line was passed as mounting violence merged with military confrontation in the spring of 1562 and as a generation of civil war succeeded a generation of more sporadic conflict. Although the wars themselves were intermittent, religiously based crime was apparently continuous and certainly more variously motivated. One Parisian family that had more than its share of violence was that of the jurist Charles Dumoulin, elder colleague of Hotman and Baudouin. Dumoulin himself suffered exile, imprisonment and destruction of property for religious opinions, but he left to his offspring even greater troubles, characteristically bound up with problems of inheritance.[48] Although Dumoulin originally gave up his patrimony for scholarly celibacy, he later changed his mind and reclaimed it, so passing on a bitter feud with his brother Ferry as well as the disputed property itself. In the spring of 1572 Dumoulin's daughter, along with two of her children (actually three, since she was pregnant) were 'massacred', and his niece Anne, daughter of Ferry, and her husband were charged with the atrocious deed. The result – just three months before the massacres of St Bartholomew – was one of the headline cases of the century. The prosecutor was none other than the famous jurist Barnabé Brisson, who two decades later, as President of the Parlement, would be the last of the famous martyrs of the religious wars, hanged by the Catholic League. In the course of his harangue he lamented passionately 'the misfortune of our century, which is seeing every day the appearance of new criminal

---

[46] *Edict . . . contre tous meurdres et assassinements qui se committent journellement en ce royaume*, 15 July 1547 (BN F. 47021. 4). Publication of the *Catalogue des actes de Henri II* was begun in 1979.

[47] *Lettres patentes du Roy contenant reiteratives defenses a toutes personnes . . . de porter harquebuses, pistoles . . .* (Paris, 1559; F. 46818. 21; LN 151); cf. other legislation of that autumn in Isnard and LN.

[48] *Recueil des plaidoyez notables* (Paris, 1611), 246–64; and see below, pp. 207–10.

monstrosities'. Such private feuding was overshadowed by more publicized assassinations and casualties of war, but it shows that problems of 'police' and social stability were not limited to public affairs.

It was in the efforts both to maintain control over that social 'force' celebrated by Seyssel and to suppress threats to legal order that the king extended his will into the private sphere, a sphere which was theoretically immune from political meddling. Through arguments of varying degrees of ingenuity his lawyers interjected his sovereign claims into the most fundamental areas of individuality and potential defiance, into the very ground-level of ideological disorder. Royal attempts to maintain family integrity and especially paternal power have already been noticed in connection with the law concerning 'clandestine marriages', which was issued precisely in the tumultuous decade before the civil wars. Even more striking was the king's presumption in the educational sphere, where he took very literally his parental role in relation to the universities. His responsibility was that of sponsor and protector of 'true and salutary doctrine' (*vera et sana doctrina*) and 'the purity of faith among the French' (*fidei puritas in Galliis*); and in fulfillment of this he intervened not only in academic politics but also in scholastic dispute. In a famous edict of 1474, for example, Louis XI took it upon himself to chastise the realists and 'terminists' for their unseemly battles.[49] This was only one precedent for the various interventions made by the monarchy in the following centuries, when the wars of '-isms' became so much more explosive and when 'indoctrination' became so much more socially significant.

It was of course the religious question that brought such efforts at ideological control to a head in the sixteenth century. For intrusions into matters of conscience the French monarch had political justification in his title 'Most Christian King' (itself one of the recognized 'marks of sovereignty');[50] and he found specific legal precedent in older legislation against individual acts of blasphemy and iconoclasm, which fell under the purview of the Parlement in particular. Typical was the act of Charles VIII in 1487 that 'prohibited anyone from denying, blaspheming or cursing the name of God, the glorious Virgin Mary His Mother or the saints . . .', and that set down the scale of punishment, starting out with 'pecuniary amends' and then moving successively to the pillory, piercing the tongue with a hot iron and, on the fifth occasion, something unspecified but still more

[49] Isambert, x, 664–72 (1 Mar. 1574).
[50] Jean de Pange, *Le Roi trèschrétien* (Paris, 1949).

horrible.[51] The most authoritative of the edicts against blasphemy was that of 1510, repeated four years later on the succession of Francis I. The growing seriousness of the problem is suggested by the growing elaboration of the schedule of punishment: pecuniary amends stipulated for the first four convictions, then exposure in the pillory – from eight until one in the afternoon 'subject to the villanies and insults anyone might want to give' – and again various degrees of mutilation down to the eighth conviction; 'and if, which God forbid, they by some desperate will commit the same enormous crimes, we order that they have the tongue cut off, so that they do not continue to speak and to spread their evil demands and blasphemies against God or His glorious Mother'.

In legal terms, therefore, the French monarchy was well prepared to deal with the Lutheran menace, condemned in 1521 by the University and then by the Parlement. In fact all Francis I had to do was to revive the blasphemy legislation already on the parlementary registers; and in the next few years he did precisely this, endorsing the papal bull condemning Luther and expressing the intention, repeated many times over the rest of the century, 'to extirpate, extinguish and abolish this miserable and damned sect and heresy'.[52] In the wake of the placards the campaign was vigorously renewed. In June 1540 Francis officially bestowed on the Parlement and his judiciary the chief responsibility for rooting out the heresy; and a month later, not coincidentally, he issued the first of the edicts forbidding emigration without cause.[53] Subsequent legislation urged the conscientious pursuit of Lutherans as rebels – 'seditieux, perturbateurs de la paix publique, et conspirateurs contre la sureté de l'etat' – and in July 1543 prescribed those articles of faith that represented in effect an oath of loyalty to the monarchy. A parallel campaign was waged by Francis's imperial rival, Charles V, in his territories, especially the Netherlands and Germany.[54]

In France some jurists were disturbed at this tendency to assimilate religious to civil matters, or rather to confound the two. According to an anecdote set down in the parlementary registers of

[51] Isambert, xi, 171–3 (3 Dec. 1587).
[52] *Catalogue des actes de François ler*, I (Paris, 1887), 359 (25 Sept. 1523); 'lesd. blasphemateurs execrables, avant que suffrir mort, ayent la gorge ouverte avec ung fer chault, et la langue tire et couppee par le desoubz, et ce fait penduz et attachez au gibet ou potences, et etranglez, selon leurs demirites . . .'. Cf. R. Doucet, *Les Institutions de la France au XVIe siècle* (Paris, 1948), I, 331.
[53] *Edict du Roy . . . contre les heretiques et seminateurs des heresies et faulces doctrines de Luther et autres adherans et complices . . .* (Paris, 1540; BN Rés. F. 1906); in Isambert, XII, 305; cf. 309; cf. p. 79 above.
[54] *Ordonnance et edict de lempereur Charles le Quint . . . pour l'extirpation des sectes et conservation de nostre saincte foy catholique*, 25 Sept. 1550 (BM 618.b.43).

1542, one of the two royal spokesmen, the *procureur royal* Noel Brulart, complained to the sovereign court about the scandalous preaching going on in some of the parishes in Paris and urged that steps be taken to have it stopped.[55] Pierre Lizet, the last one to favor such preaching, raised an objection. 'This is the office and charge of the bishop of Paris', he argued; 'I do not find it right that this court should take over this office.' Yet just a few years later, presiding over the 'burning chamber' which assumed responsibility for heresy cases from the *tournelle*, Lizet took over such duties with a vengeance, compiling an unprecedented record of some 450 *arrêts* in two years (1547–9).

In this activity we can see another factor in the progressive 'politicization of Protestantism'. Yet the effort was obviously inadequate, and in November 1549 Henry II expressed the fear that heresy 'would be fed like fire under the coals . . . and secretly inflame a great number of simple people'.[56] So the legal remedies continued, first in the legislative landmark two years later, the Edict of Chateaubriand, which forbade all further emigration and established a more rigorous system of police controls, and then the Edict of Compiègne of 1557.[57] By this time the Parlement had become accustomed to the expansion of its jurisdiction. After the conspiracy of Amboise in 1560, in fact, the court bitterly objected when the king gave to the prelates cognizance of the crime of heresy; and the king had to relent.[58] He issued a declaration reassuring the Parlement about its jurisdiction over 'illicit assemblies', participation in which became a capital crime, and the growing split in the legal profession was endorsed.

The invasion of religious life by the king's judicial and legislative will was accompanied by a more fundamental phenomenon, which was the unmistakable (if not always demonstrable) convergence of religious disaffection with the growing civil disorder already discussed. These aforesaid 'illicit assemblies', fighting in the streets, rioting by students, strikes by workers, 'rebellion' by nobles and

---

[55] In fly-leaf of *Ordonnances . . .* (vol. in Harvard Library cited below, p. 241, n.71); cf. N. Weiss, *La Chambre Ardente* (Paris, 1889).

[56] *Edict du Roy sur le faict du jugement des Lutheriens*, 19 Nov., publ. 31 Dec. (Paris, 1549; F. 46805. 8; 35149); in Isambert, xiii, 103: 'Comme le fier soubs le cendre, ilz se seroient nourriz et continuez soubs couvertes palliations et dissimulations en leurs erreurs et damnees opinions, dont descretement ilz aurioent infecte et seduict un nombre infiny de personnes simples . . .'

[57] *Edict du Roy touchant la cognoissance, jurisdiction et jugement des proces des Lutheriens et heretiques* (Paris, 1551; F. 46807.5–7; LN 36) and *Edict du Roy portant la peine contre les perseverns en leurs mauvaises opinions contre la foy* (Paris, 1558; BN Rés. F. 1956).

[58] *Deux remonstrances de la cour de Parlement a Paris* (n.p., 1561; BN Lb33.11); in Isambert, xiv, 27, May 1560.

towns, and iconoclasm all violated the 'police' of the kingdom; and all had various direct and indirect connections with the 'religious question', and hence unavoidably with the 'political question' which loomed in 1559.[59] The murder of President Minard, which precipitated the execution of Du Bourg, was itself used as a threat against the Guise the next year. 'Beware, Cardinal', said one Protestant lyric, 'that you are not treated à la Minard by a Stuart.'[60] A series of edicts reiterated the ban on hand weapons, yet the king's own men, and later on loyal Parisians, were permitted to arm themselves against the 'rebels'. At the same time murder was itself becoming politicized; and the word 'assassination' – killing 'Italian style', as one Huguenot propagandist put it in 1566[61] – had to be imported for this unspeakable practice (in fact it was a common term of legislative rhetoric), which was so shamefully replacing the honorable art of duelling. In many ways, then, the civil wars were simply amplified continuations of social violence which passed beyond legal control.

At all times the government seemed to be as worried about verbal agitation as it was about physical violence, and again political considerations became increasingly prominent. One reason for this was the important distinction drawn by the *Chambre ardente* between simple, that is private, offensive opinions (*delit commun*) and public preaching of condemned doctrines (*cas priviligié*), which called for more drastic measures.[62] The offical theory of rebellion was clearly expressed in the Edict of Compiègne, directed against those 'heresies which, belonging first to the mind and spirit, [constitute] sedition by the open declaration of follies and audacious opinions not only in secret conventicles but also in many scandalous acts and armed public assemblies, inducing and seducing the poor people to their opinions . . . which move from heresy to blasphemy, scandal, sedition and the crime of lese-majesty, both divine and human . . .' Royal obsession with the power of the spoken word was also demonstrated in attempts to suppress verbal abuse. In 1561, for example, what Chancellor L'Hôpital had politely requested of Frenchmen (in his famous address to the Estates General of Orleans) the government tried to impose as legislation, that is, to forbid anyone from calling others by these words 'Papist' or 'Huguenot'. Unfortunately, the only way of enforcing this ban seemed to be to answer the libeller 'in corporal terms', as the edict euphemistically put it;

---

[59] *Edict du Roy sur la prohibition et defense de faire conventicules et rasement des maisons ou se feront lesdicts conventicules et assemblees*, 4 Sept. 1559 (BN F. 46818. 5 and 12).

[60] J. Pineaux, *La Poésie des protestants de langue française* (Paris, 1971), 103.

[61] H. Estienne, *Apologie pour Hérodote*, ed. P. Ristelhuber (Paris, 1879), I, 353.

[62] Weiss, *La Chambre Ardente*.

and so even in legal terms libel entailed violence.[63] The implied ideal of ideological uniformity, always inherent in Gallicanism and often prominent in legislative rhetoric, received its most explicit formulation in an edict of 1568, which declared baldly that only the Catholic religion would be tolerated in France.

Official violence, physical punishment, was not the only or indeed the most threatening means of policing the hearts and minds of French subjects. Perhaps the most ominous acts, which appeared first in that edict of 1535 provoked by the affair of the placards, was the confiscation of the property of heretics and their protectors. Added to this was an insidious provision granting a quarter of the confiscated property to informers, a reward previously made in cases of lese-majesty.[64] Again at the outset of the first war of religion – on 19 March 1562, just as the Duke of Guise was entering and the Prince of Condé leaving Paris – the government provided for the confiscation of the goods of all those who took up arms against the crown, and later of those who refused to return to Paris. In succeeding years this threat was elevated to the level of public policy. Later edicts order the sale of confiscated property, some of it designated for the Catholic clergy for reparations but most of it for the king. Legislation banning Huguenots from all offices, fiscal as well as judicial, would have much the same effect. It is hard to estimate how effective such measures were in the long run, though certainly they generated considerable litigation over the next generation; but in any case they posed the heaviest of all threats to the 'so-called reformed religion', even worse than death. Although it may thrive on martyrdom for a time, no ideological movement can long endure without a material base and a human legacy.

Yet such a final solution – 'extirpation and extermination', in normal legislative rhetoric – was indeed 'What pleased the king'. So the Huguenots assumed, at any rate, and their interpretation seemed to be confirmed in the notorious edict in which Charles IX, referring somewhat ambiguously to the events of St Bartholomew, declared that 'What has been done has been done by my will.'[65] This particular application of a familiar legal fiction represented, at least for the Huguenots, not only the final debasement of sovereignty but also the catalyst for the greatest outburst of ideological protest of

---

[63] *Les Defenses a toutes personnes de porter dagues ny espees, ou autres armes, ne faire sedition* (Paris, 1561; LN 234): '. . . n'appeller par ces motz de Papiste ou Huguenot, sur peine d'on respondre eux mesmes corporellement'.

[64] Cf. J. Sambuc, 'Documents sur la réforme dans le Comtat et en Provence', *BSHPF*, CXVII (1971), 629ff.

[65] See below, p. 291.

modern times. And that, too, we may assign in large part to the lawyers.

HOMO POLITICUS

'The jurisconsult is the political man' (*Jurisconsultus hoc est Homo Politicus*).[66] So remarked one sixteenth-century lawyer who was unusually active in the ecclesiastical politics of the period before the civil wars. In this phrase, François Baudouin not only summed up the activist view of jurisprudence endorsed by many humanists as well as scholastics but also suggested the significance of the legal profession for the generation of ideology in this vociferous and argumentative age. Indeed this conception of the jurist's role is part of the ideal of law as 'true philosophy' as well as the reality of legal practice in the service of particular 'parties and causes'. In many minds 'the political man' represented that compound Renaissance ideal of scholarship and social utility, of private learning and public virtue. This was the ideal, for example, of Baudouin's disciple Louis le Caron, who praised law as 'la vraye philosophie' because it combined the Platonic goal of abstract justice with practical services to the community. Taking issue with his colleague Montaigne, Le Caron argued that 'the excessive pursuit of one's self is vain and useless curiosity'.[67] The old formula 'Cognoy toy-mesme' was the key to but not the end of wisdom. So it was that 'true philosophy' was turned into 'political science' – and the *philosophe* into the *politique*.

A similar view was taken by Le Caron's friend Etienne Pasquier. On the eve of the religious wars he published a *Dialogue on the Prince* in which the dominant speaker was 'le Politic', a broad-minded observer who tried to maintain a reasonable balance between the narrower views of a courtier, an academic philosopher and a scholar.[68] In later years Pasquier was himself taken as an embodiment of legal wisdom, when another of his friends, Antoine Loisel, gave the title 'Pasquier' to his historical (or hagiographical) survey of the grand tradition of French advocates. This general concept of the political man was also shared by Protestants, though with a greater emphasis on the religious dimension of social life. In

[66] François Baudouin, *Commentarius de jurisprudentia Muciana* (1559), 20. In general see K.-H. Mulagk, *Phänomene des politischen Menschen im 17. Jahrhundert* (Berlin, 1973).
[67] *La Philosophie* (Paris, 1555), 15.
[68] Pasquier, *Pourparler du prince*, in his *Recherches de la France* (Paris, 1621); cf. p. 182 above, n.13.

the famous *Reveille-Matin* (attributed to Nicolas Barnaud) the major interlocutor was again called the 'Politique', this time in the company of 'Alithie' and 'Philalithie' (the Truth and her friend) and a 'Historiographe', who rehearsed the background of the religious wars culminating in the massacres of St Bartholomew.[69] The result was that the Politique was converted both to the 'light of the gospel' and to the Protestant party. Similar sentiments were expressed a few years later in the same author's *Mirror of the French*, in which good citizens (*bons politiques*) are identified directly with the reformers (*nouveaux reformateurs*). The elevated conception of 'political' consciousness maintained at least a tenuous existence during the wars of religion.

Yet at the same time a more ambivalent and finally pejorative view of the 'politique' mentality was emerging, a view that focussed on the apparent divergence between the theory and practice of politics and the moral and especially religious values that society required. Although this divergence came to be associated above all with the attitudes of Machiavelli (or at least a popular distortion thereof), the syndrome was at first identified and designated by the term 'politique' in a derogatory sense implying immorality and impiety. It was applied in particular to any who seemed to place party or even national interest above religion, and in France the first targets were the so-called Malcontents, distinguished from the 'Huguenots of religion' by their political ambition and self-interest. In such terms, for example, Cardinal Granvelle stigmatized Admiral Coligny in 1564. During the first decade of the wars the term became increasingly common – as in the definition of one Catholic author, '"Politiques" . . . are those who give more to men than to God.'[70] According to the historian De Thou the usage originated in a professorial controversy at the University of Paris. The debate was between Jacques Charpentier, lifelong nemesis of Ramus (whose death in the massacres some thought to have been at Charpentier's instigation), and Ramus's friend Denis Lambin (who feared a similar fate). Once again the academy had its contribution to make to the wars of words.

But it was in the wake of St Bartholomew that the epithet came into its own, first as a term of journalistic abuse applied by Protestants and Catholics alike, and then as a party label. It was in this context that the 'political' cast of mind was associated with the

[69] See below, pp. 301–5.
[70] Ch. Waddington, *Ramus* (Paris, 1855), 270, and F. De Crue, *Le Parti des Politiques* (Paris, 1892); D. R. Kelley, *François Hotman: A Revolutionary's Ordeal* (Princeton, 1973), 250, and cf. De Thou, IV, 593, and J. de Serres, *The Three partes of Commentary* (London, 1574), 59.

supposedly amoral, 'atheistic' and 'tyrannical counsels of Machiavelli'.[71] The influence of Machiavelli had been felt for over a generation in France, but the specifically demonic image was a product of the passions and prejudices which boiled over after the massacres of August 1572. Mythology aside, Machiavelli's *Prince* and *Discourses* constituted ideologically useful symbols of a particular kind of political attitude and analytical method and of the generalized anti-social behavior of 'libertinism'. 'There are the Machiavellisms of which the world was delivered before Machiavel was born', as Pasquier put it, 'and there be a great many Machiavels among us at this day, who never read his books.'[72] Pasquier tended to distrust these 'Machiavellistes' (and indeed was one of the inventors of this eponym), and yet Pasquier's own *politique* views were evident not only in his attitudes toward the religious wars but also in his social thought, which was founded on the belief in 'political proofs no less certain than those of mathematics'. The main difference between the science of politics as conceived by Machiavelli and by Pasquier was that Pasquier did not presume to set down universal maxims but rather embraced deliberately the limitations of historical perspective, social and institutional context, and cultural tradition. His mathematics was one of probability, it seems, not of certainty.

At the time that the term 'Machiavellism' was receiving currency, the conception of the 'Politique' was in the process of becoming a party label, being applied to a sort of emerging common front consisting of a few Huguenots as well as moderate Catholics. The origins of this attitude may be traced back to the disillusioning confrontation at the Colloquy of Poissy in the fall of 1561. There certain 'moderatores' and neo-Erasmian 'mediators' attempted to reconcile the Huguenot and Catholic extremes on the basis of a broadly based (which was to say a Melanchthonian) religious formula, but the only result of this fiasco was to make it clear once and for all that no religious solution was feasible.[73] The only answer was 'political'. This attitude, implicit in the long series of edicts of 'pacification' and explicit in various liberal Gallican writings, was developed above all by the lawyers; but it took over a generation of

---

[71] Kelley, 'Murd'rous Machiavel in France', *Political Science Quarterly*, LXXXV (1970), 545–59, and references there cited; also G. Schneider, *Der Libertin* (Stuttgart, 1970), R. Pintard, *Le Libertinage érudit* . . . (Paris, 1943), and J. Charbonnel, *La Pensée italienne en France au XVIe siècle* . . . (Paris, 1919) and *XVII Colloque internat. de Tours*, *Théorie et practique politique à la Renaissance* (Paris, 1977), esp. the articles of Gaeta, Mastellone, Stegman and Jouanne.

[72] Pasquier (trans. as) *The Jesuites Catechisme* (London, 1602), 64, and see A. Cherel, *La Pensée de Machiavel en France* (Paris, 1935).

[73] See above, p. 102, n. 21, and below, pp. 328–36.

civil strife before it gained wide acceptance and, finally, a power base. By the late 1580s exhaustion of alternatives (among other things) established the credit of this view, and 'politiques' began to return to the attitudes of compromise of the pre-war 'moderatores', or 'moyenneurs'.

In more general terms, 'political' consciousness in this age, heightened by the contradiction between religious ideals and social reality, reflected intense partisanship; but beyond that it implied also a broader and more flexible conception of social structure and change and the limits of policy and legislation. To doctrinaires of either party such an attitude might seem a secular version of the religious 'vacillation' and duplicity denounced by Calvin, more suitable to lawyers than to theologians; and indeed a sense of relativism, religious as well as historical and geographical, was common to French legists. Montaigne is only the most celebrated example. According to Michel de l'Hôpital, justice is like the sun, which shines on Rome and Constantinople alike; but laws had to be accommodated to national and cultural differences.[74] What is just in one time and clime, remarked another Gallican jurist, Pierre Ayrault, is unjust in another, depending on the condition of the people and their civilization. 'In republics one must consider not only what is just in itself', he concluded, 'but also what is appropriate to the state, which preserves itself here in one way and there in another.'[75] Among other things this was a way of exalting judicial interpretation above legislative declaration, and indeed in another work defending his profession, Ayrault argued that in fact law was the sum of individual judgments (*res judicatae*). But there was a larger point: 'As things unjust and unreasonable in themselves may be done for reasons of necessity that one cannot define, so one can do just and good things outside the law.' More bluntly, reason of state – 'utilité publique' in the euphemism more conventionally employed by Ayrault – existed apart from private morality. This was another condition of sixteenth-century ideology.

Another feature of the lawyerly mentality in the sixteenth century was a curious eclecticism in method and argument which permitted recourse to a wide range of (sometimes conflicting) traditions. The famous debate between humanist and scholastic jurists – between the *mores gallicus* and *italicus*, as they were later dubbed, that is, between a literary–historical approach and the Bartolist dialectical–authoritarian method – was limited largely to pedagogy.[76] Practice

---

[74] L'Hôpital, *Traite de la réformation de la justice*, in *Oeuvres*, I, 6.

[75] *De l'Ordre et instruction judiciaire* (Paris, 1576), 29; cf. his *Liber singularis de origine et auctoritate rerum judicatum* (Paris, 1573).

[76] See D. R. Kelley, 'Civil science in the Renaissance: jurisprudence Italian style', *Historical Journal*, XXII (1979), 777–94. On Cujas see below, pp. 289–90.

was something else, as is clear even in the work of that most detached of 'grammarians', Jacques Cujas, when he condescended to enter into political controversy. 'Legal humanism' was a luxury; and even at Bourges, where students stamped their feet at any attempt to depart from this style, the municipal authorities frowned on it. 'Are you wiser than the Parlement of Paris', the city fathers asked the law faculty, 'that you prescribe this [humanistic] method?'[77] In practice jurists exhibited an indiscriminate conflation of methods that included literary sources and legal authorities, historical examples and juridical precedents, conventional formulas and logical reasoning. Evangelical religion might rely on scripture alone, but evangelical lawyers like Hotman were grateful for support from any quarter. Who knows, he asked, what might persuade some people? After all, persuasion was more important than methodological consistency for pleading a cause.

Partisanship remained the very essence of the legal profession – 'party' and 'cause' were primordially legal concepts and terms. The argumentative conditioning grounded in liberal arts education was professionalized in the law curriculum and perfected in the forum – whether in the sense of courtroom oratory or published discourse for some particular interest. Lawyers were always in the employ of some client or other, and it was unavoidable that their notion of truth should be in a sense dialectical, not to say duplicitous. 'Truth' was multi-dimensional, myriad-formed. For François Hotman, for example, truth could mean agreement with either fact or law (*de facto* or *de jure*), divine endorsement, or simply the correctness of a particular point of view – at one point he went so far as to speak of 'French truth'.[78] Indeed the very notion of a 'true philosophy' of law whose ultimate standard is less rationality than the 'common good' implies (in a modern sense) an 'ideological' rather than a philosophical view. Not that jurists had the inclination (even if they had the self-consciousness) to entertain such criticism, but certainly observers of their 'chicanery' did not let it pass unnoticed. In this pejorative sense too – that is, that they were hired ideologues – lawyers could be regarded as 'politiques'.

No one better illustrates the professional world of the lawyer in this extended sense than Charles Dumoulin, who lashed out against Protestants as well as Catholics in the course of his extraordinarily litigious career. Dumoulin was the arch-ideologist – the 'prince of legists' – who drew upon both humanist and Bartolist interpretations but who identified above all with Pierre de Cugnières and other

[77] L. Raynal, *Histoire du Berry* (Bourges, 1844), III, 395.
[78] Kelley, *Hotman*, 300, and in general, R. Schnur, *Die französischen Juristen im konfessionellen Bürgerkrieg des 16. Jahrhunderts* (Berlin, 1962).

'lawyers of the last Capetians'.[79] Having studied at the University of Orleans, he was a master of all varieties of continental law, and he had practical experience in both the municipal court of the Châtelet and the Parlement of Paris. The targets of his professional commentaries show the unparalleled range of his expertise: not only civil and canon law but also the work of modern scholars like Budé, Alciato, Filippo Decio and Jean Ferrault, royal legislation (including the reforming ordinance of 1539), the authoritative *Style of Parlement*, and especially the provincial customs of France. Dumoulin's method, though it exhibited both humanistic and scholastic qualities, was more pointedly argumentative, and he preferred to characterize it as 'analytical'. His debating talents, erudition and professional reputation drew him into many of the crucial controversies of his day – to the extent indeed that his career seems almost a history in miniature of French ideology during the second generation of the Reformation.

Dumoulin's first campaign was waged against feudal law, both because it was an obstacle to national unity and because it implied acceptance of imperial jurisdiction. In general it was his purpose to exalt native 'Franci-Germanic' tradition, especially the Parisian custom, above the 'Emperor's law'. In this same spirit he accepted a commission from Philip of Hesse to defend him in the interminable suit with Charles V.[80] Dumoulin's consultation for this Protestant leader (appearing in 1552) reflected not only his affection for German 'liberties' but also the policy of Henry II, who had recently been declared protector of these same liberties in the Parlement. Thus Dumoulin could at the same time defend French foreign policy and 'Reformatores' like Calvin and Bullinger, with whom he sympathized first privately and then publicly: thus he could simultaneously attack the abuses of feudal and of canon law. Like Luther he began with a small canonist issue, specifically that of usury, and from that was led to larger doubts about papal supremacy. What prompted his assault on canon law was a commission from King Henry II himself to examine the suspect practice of post-dating the assignment of benefices.[81] After his commentary on Henry's edict against these 'little dates', Dumoulin went on to a general critique of the Corpus Juris Canonici; but while Luther had only burned the collection,

[79] Fuller treatment by Kelley in *Traditio*, xxii (1966), 347–402, and *Hotman, passim*. And see now Jean-Louis Thireau, *Charles Du Moulin (1500–1566)* (Geneva, 1980).

[80] *Consilia quattour* (Paris, 1552).

[81] *Commentarius ad edictum Henrici Secundi contra parvas datas* (Lyon, 1552), also a French translation, and *Annotationes ad jus canonicum*, in *Opera omnia*, I (Paris, 1681). Another Protestant gloss on canon law is Ch. Leopard, *Le Glaive du geant Goliath, philistin et ennemy de eglise de Dieu* (n.p., 1579; LN 970).

Dumoulin undertook an unprecedented and sometimes vitriolic Protestant gloss, throwing in for good measure denunciation of the deceitful 'Sorbonists' whom Luther too detested.

For his pains, or rather for his excessive zeal, Dumoulin was called before the Parlement to answer for his opinions. His book was condemned as 'the most pernicious, scandalous, schismatic, impious, blasphemous . . . [etc.] in the whole Christian world'.[82] This was one case which Dumoulin could not hope to win, and so even before his trial was over he fled into exile, first in Switzerland and then in Germany. Though an elderly man by sixteenth-century standards (he was over fifty), his spirits were in no way damped by this experience. Returning to France (and to royal favor) in 1557, he continued his lawyerly attacks and indeed increased the range of his targets. Exile taught him to despise all Protestant sects, Zwinglians, Lutherans and especially the Calvinists, who represented a 'foreign' and 'seditious' threat to the French monarchy. In 1563, when accused of having written a defense of the Huguenots, he replied with the denial that he had never, in a lifetime of royal service, supported such 'evil and illicit liberty'.[83] Yet he by no means changed his attitude toward the Roman church; and the very next year he wrote two classic briefs against its most objectionable expressions, namely, the Society of Jesus, then in the process of infiltrating the University of Paris (which had instituted a suit against it), and the canons and decrees of the Council of Trent, which Dumoulin found irreconcilable with French law.[84] All these represented threats to the sort of reformed Gallicanism which Dumoulin spent his life trying to formulate and to protect.

Dumoulin offers a striking example of the modern propagandist, following to be sure the traces of magisterial reformers like Luther, who in fact had begun the war on canon law, but translating the arguments into secular terms. And his impact was hardly less striking than his example. His dominating influence over the sixteenth-century 'reformation of customs', and indeed the whole codification movement down to the revolution, was unmatched. So it was too with his attacks on Romanism. His assault on the canonist

---

[82] Argentré, 205.

[83] *Apologie . . . contre un Livret intitulé, La deffense civile et militaire des innocens et de l'eglise de Christ* (Lyon, 1563), and *Opera omnia*, v, 621 (1565); also *HE*, III, 244; Argentré, II, 205; R. Kingdon, *Geneva and the Consolidation of the French Protestant Movement 1564–1572* (Geneva, 1967), 138–48; A. Cartier in *Revue des livres anciens*, II (1917), 200–4; and M. Reulos in *BSHPF*, C (1954), 1–12.

[84] *Consultation . . . sur l'utilité ou les inconveniens de la nouvelle secte ou espece d'ordre religieux des Jesuites* (n.p., n.d.) and *Conseil sur le faict du Concile de Trente* (Lyon, 1564), both in Latin as well as French.

doctrine was mentioned earlier. Of his consultation against the Council of Trent one historian has remarked that it 'remained the arsenal from which the Politiques, in their turn, took the weapons with which to attack the new [i.e., the Catholic] reform'.[85] Among his disciples, moreover, were scholars of various religious and political positions. On the Catholic side were included Le Caron (who carried on the project of bringing some uniformity to French law) and those two *gens du roi* Pierre Pithou and Antoine Loisel. On the Protestant side there were, most notably, François Hotman, the most prolific of all Huguenot propagandists, and François Baudouin, who followed Dumoulin in returning to (at least what passed for) orthodoxy, when civil war seemed to give precedence to the 'Question politique'. For these men and for many others Dumoulin represented, peerlessly, the pleader of causes (*causidicus*) and the *homo politicus*.

In the sixteenth century the 'republic of jurisconsults', like Europe itself, was fundamentally divided; and as Dumoulin's career illustrates, the lawyerly mentality lay at the very heart of ideological conflict. Although traditionally regarded as champions of legitimacy and royalism, lawyers were soon drawn into the service of Protestant resistance and soon adapted their professional heritage to the new cause. As the Lutheran movement became increasingly political during the late 1520s, appeals were made to the 'doctors of law' to provide justifications for the Protestant party that came to include rebellious princes and cities as well as Luther's confessional following; and Luther himself consciously yielded to the expertise of lawyers in circumstances of internal war. So it happened also with French reformers in the constitutional crisis that befell in 1559: they, too, turned from the theologians to the 'doctors of law' (Hotman perhaps most prominent among them) for advice on secular matters, and specifically 'the political question'.[86] From this point of view the role of the lawyers seems absolutely pivotal in the 'beginning of ideology'.

The theory and practice of law represented a major arena of ideological activity, and lawyers themselves were prototypes of the ideologue. On the one hand there was the lawyer as nemesis of heresy, Pierre Lizet, who seemed to Protestants the very embodiment of tyranny – red not only with drink, in Beza's caustic description, but also with the blood of many martyrs – followed by hordes of lesser minions, such as Hotman's father, who bore similar

[85] V. Martin, *Le Gallicanisme et la Reforme* (Paris, 1919), 73.
[86] See below, pp. 261–9.

guilt. On the other hand there was the lawyer as rebel, symbolized by Du Bourg and by Hotman himself, who in more than one way carried religious reform over into political resistance. But of course lawyers had often, in medieval as well as ancient times, been at the center of controversy. It was only in conjunction with another institution that the law could become an effective voice of propaganda in broadly social terms. Taking over ideological leadership from theologians, lawyers likewise made use of the device of printing to gather popular support. Let us look more directly at this new technological vehicle of ideology, the medium of print.

VI · Publicity: Propagating the faith

Tolle lege, tolle lege.

Augustine

C'est n'avoir pas de Religion . . . de mettre es mains du peuple tous les mysteres et secrets de Dieu.

Florimond de Raemond

VI · Publicity: Propagating the faith

APOLOGUE: THE BURNING OF ETIENNE DOLET (1546)

On 2 August 1546 Etienne Dolet, printer and author of Lyon, faced sentence by Pierre Lizet, First President of the Parlement of Paris, on charges of blasphemy, sedition and selling banned books. Dolet had been in prison for almost two years and most of the last four, and he was not optimistic about his trial. Just before this, he had written his last verse, the 'doleful' song of a caged bird:

> Sooner or later the body returns to earth,
> For nature demands her due.
> This is exacted from all those given birth:
> Every one must die.[1]

But it was the French government, not nature, that was collecting this tribute from him. Dolet was put to the torture to name his accomplices and warned that further blasphemy would result in the cutting out of his tongue. The next day he was to be taken to the Place Maubert, the customary scene of execution in the university quarter, and put to death in prescribed fashion. Dolet was only one of many victims in these years, the most repressive so far in France; but he was one of the few not attached to the so-called reformed religion as well as the first intellectual of international renown to die in this way since Berquin seventeen years earlier.

A pyrotechnical end to a spectacular life. Outwardly Dolet's short career – he was not yet 39 – seemed a typical success story of the sixteenth-century world of letters. From Orleans he had come to Paris, like Beza as a very young student, and had acquired an even stronger passion for classical literature. Although he came in 1520, just as Lutheranism was making its first inroads, his intellectual enthusiasms were unfettered by any particular religious inclination. He studied also at Venice and Padua, centers of philosophical radicalism, and at Toulouse, bastion of Gallican orthodoxy, before settling down in Lyon to follow a career in the thriving publishing

---

[1] R. C. Christie, *Etienne Dolet, the Martyr of the Renaissance* (London, 1880), 475.

business. He began his apprenticeship in the year of the placards (which he disapproved of) and within four years, with the help of a wealthy partner, managed to move into the select ranks of the masters. By then, too (1538), he had gained distinction as a poet and scholar, enhancing his reputation by printing such prestigious authors as Valla, Erasmus (in Berquin's translation) and Marot as well as Cicero, Vergil and other classics. Of his own works the most influential was perhaps his *Commentary on the Latin Language*, called by one authority a 'manifesto of the new pedagogy'.[2] By the age of 31 he was an established scholar-printer, married, with a young son, and looking forward to a bright future unclouded by association with the new religious opinions. How could such an efficient careerist have come to such a bad end?

In part it was because of Dolet's personality, which was unusually abrasive, unstable and self-advertising even in that heroic age of self-advertisement. He clashed with contemporaries, including Rabelais and the elder Scaliger, over Latin grammar and plagiarism. At one point his rashness and fear of enemies, real and imaginary, went beyond literary aggressiveness, and he killed another man in a street brawl (and in fact was never acquitted of this charge). His extremism is reflected, too, perhaps, in his Ciceronianist excesses, his fondness for pagan ideas and conceits, and his irresponsible treatment of such dangerous topics as fate and immortality, which gave him the reputation of 'atheist' among Protestants as well as Catholics. It is impossible to say what traumas, deprivations, and pressures shaped this volatile character; but the overall pattern seems common to many uprooted, overreaching intellectuals beginning with those first 'gladiators of the Renaissance', Valla and Poggio.[3] The syndrome might include inflated ego, compulsive drive for personal fame, literary exhibitionism, hypersensitivity on questions of style and taste, a tendency toward paranoia, irreverence to authority and exaggerated faith in the power of persuasion. The collection of traits reads like a pathology of the intellectual temper over the ages but especially since the beginning of print culture and publicity.

The most direct source of Dolet's tragedy was professional rather than personal, since his role as printer magnified his flaws and made him a public threat. His colleagues at Lyon sensed this before the government did. During the short period of his success (1539–43) labor problems arose between the elite of master printers and the

---

[2] F. Buisson, *Répertoire des ouvrages pédagogiques du XVIe siècle* (Paris, 1886), VIII.
[3] Ch. Nisard, *Les Gladiateurs de la Renaissance* (Paris, 1860).

journeymen, who wanted better pay and easier hours.[4] The upshot was a strike and considerable violence. For whatever reason, Dolet sided with the workers, and the results he described to the king himself from his prison cell. Out of jealousy, he was convinced, 'arose a great and mortal hatred on the part of the members of my own trade, and in the place of the ridicule which they had been accustomed to use, they at the end plotted my death'. Of course the masters won, and in July 1542 the workmen's appeal was rejected by the Parlement. Less than two weeks later Dolet was arrested for the first time. He assumed that it was at the instigation of his enemies, and under the circumstances it seems a case of justifiable paranoia.

There was another less tangible dimension to these troubles. Dolet professed to believe that 'Vertue' had the power to overcome that 'imbecile' Fortune, but events were too overpowering at this juncture. It was just during Dolet's imprisonment that official attempts to control the printing trade reached a peak. In July 1542, during Dolet's first incarceration, the Parlement had published an ordinance 'against the new and heretical doctrines', naming Calvin in particular and forbidding booksellers to distribute books of such authors 'sur peine de la harte', while at the same time a catalogue of prohibited books was being prepared.[5] This catalogue, printed in 1545, included publications of Dolet, notably Berquin's translation of Erasmus's *Enchiridion* and Marot's of the Psalms, and shows clearly that Dolet was at least in part victim of the same indiscriminate heresy-hunting that resulted in the contemporary condemnation of Ramus (March 1544).

So Dolet spent his last four years in jail. Released in 1543, he was arrested again when a packet of books, some from his press and others from Geneva, was seized. He managed to escape for a few months, time at least to compose his pathetic 'Second Inferno' (named after Marot's confessional poem), but his original captor caught up with him in Lyon and returned him to Paris. His record convicted him, and on 3 August he met his end. He agreed to invoke the Virigin Mary and St Stephen, and as a reward he was hanged before burning. Although his fellow poet Beza wrote an ode in his memory, even most Calvinists thought it good riddance; and if Dolet was a 'martyr', it was for no determinable cause, except perhaps free enterprise in the printing industry. According to one contemporary admirer:

[4] P. Mellottée, *Histoire économique de l'imprimerie* (Paris, 1905), I, 324.
[5] See below, p. 241, n. 71.

Dolet is dead, consumed by the fire.
The loss is great, the tragedy dire.
But such today is often the fate
Our heroes and saints must fear and await.

His face turned upward, he spoke at the end:
'To heaven on high my soul will ascend;
My ashes will spread, and so will my name,
Over the earth, insuring my fame.'[6]

At least part of the prophecy was accurate, for on the spot where Dolet's gallows once stood there remained (at least until the late 1970s) the statue erected to honor his involuntary contribution to the liberty of thought.

The burning of Dolet was at once symbolic of and crucial for the art of printing as an issue of sixteenth-century controversy. For Dolet was not a mere purveyor of radicalism but a distinguished scholar in the classic humanist mold; no colporteur or fly-by-night publicist but a master printer; no suspect foreigner but a patriotic enthusiast for French culture and the monarchy. With his execution the printing trade was served notice that it was expected to co-operate with the government in the new regimen of censorship and thought control. Gallican purity was to be protected from foreign ideologies, whether heresy from Germany or paganism from Italy, and the printed page was to be the battleground for this crusade. By the time of Dolet's death the lines were drawn: on the one hand an outpouring of subversive literature and on the other a persistent stream of legislation to suppress dissidence; behind this a conflict between an establishment based on an old alliance of church, law courts, and university, and a new intelligentsia not organized but increasingly identifiable through official pressure on authors, printers, and distributors. Dolet personified this intelligentsia – as symbol and as scapegoat – all the more clearly because he did not serve a particular cause, except that of publicity.

By Dolet's time, then, the printing trade had become the art of an intellectual elite as well as a commercial network. Over this growing and tightening web ideas and books moved quickly, and so did their human conveyors – journeymen printers, small peddlers, agents of great houses, itinerant scholars looking for temporary work as editors or proofreaders, and finally, in times of persecution, great printers seeking refuge and freedom of action. Through such channels printing created a cosmopolitan republic of letters, a grand

[6] Christie, *Etienne Dolet*, 477. Cf. Dolet, *Le Second Enfer*, ed. C. Longeon (Geneva, 1978).

arena of cultural interplay and confessional crossfire. It was a world
filled with many unprecedented opportunities and endless intellectual excitement, a Babel of many tongues, an elaborate society
ranging from (proto-) Grub Street hacks and Fleet Street sensational-
ists to princely houses that built their reputations on knowing what
was fit to print. It was also, as Dolet had reason to know, a world of
troubles – of conflicts between labor and management, authors and
censors, and danger to limb, liberty, and life.

The most spectacular services performed by the printed book
were to the world of learning, not only to the older recognized
sciences but to a variety of new fields which uniform type made
feasible. Literary scholarship, the critical study of history and various
branches of natural science were all established upon solid foundations during the first century of printing; all were given a degree of
self-consciousness and a kind of social organization which would not
have been possible in manuscript culture. Medieval as well as
classical studies advanced through the publication of texts and
synthetic modern works. Print made possible not only large-scale
co-operation but also scholarly controversy which likewise led at
some points to the exposure of frauds, the explosion of myths, and a
broader scholarly consensus than could have been attained before.
Only through the printed book could scholars like Henri Estienne,
the younger Scaliger and Isaac Casaubon have laid the foundations
of modern 'Criticism'.[7] Needless to say, print also made possible,
and in some ways provoked, quarrels, scholarly pen-wars and
academic vendettas on a scale unknown in earlier ages; and it is this
eristic aspect of print that is most relevant here.

To Protestants and Catholics alike, at least at the beginning, the art
of printing appeared as a providential gift through which the world
could be renewed. In general the sixteenth century was a great age
of public eloquence, secular as well as sacred, and printing served a
vital function in amplifying and accelerating the processes of communication, education, persuasion and command.[8] Having been employed for a half-century in the dissemination of orthodox devotional
material, the technology of print was exploited even more insistently by Protestants, especially Calvinists, who could draw on
Lutheran experience as well as ideas, and who, as we have seen,

---

[7] J. Jehasse, *La Renaissance de la Critique* (Saint-Etienne, 1976), on the heroic generation of the late sixteenth century; most recently on the earlier work of Reformation
criticism, J. P. Massaut, *Critique et tradition à la veille de la réforme en France* (Paris,
1974).
[8] See now the comprehensive book of Elizabeth Eisenstein, *The Printing Press as an
Agent of Change* (Cambridge, 1978).

attached so much importance to the public witnessing of faith, as opposed to dissembling Nicodemitism. Printing provided the most conspicuous as well as the most reprehensible means of testifying to and publicizing the faith. Prior to this, of course, governments had been making use of printing for their own purposes of public notification, legislation and social persuasion and control. So the putative reading public was confronted by a variety of official and unofficial efforts to gain its approval or shape its actions.

Obviously, the printed book was potentially a threat as well as a promise, a source of inflammatory declamation as well as enlightened discussion, and within a half-century of Gutenberg's invention it was the menacing aspect that was attracting the most attention. Official censure, officially assigned attacks, censorship, condemned books and lists thereof, and ceremonial burnings were also products of what has been called the 'typographical revolution', and most of the controversies of this age were carried out in the shadow of inquisitors of the faith and censors of the book. Modern ideological movements were shaped and extended in many ways by this complex dialectic of authority-and-criticism, institutional as well as intellectual, which the printed book expressed and intensified. So were other social vehicles of consciousness – the family, the church, the academy, and the legal and other professions. It is impossible to understand the politicization of these institutions as well as of religious groups without appreciating printed publicity not only as evidence but also as a social phenomenon in its own right.

PRINT AND PROTO-JOURNALISM

Western civilization has been obsessed with the metaphor, and sometimes with the reality, of the book. Not only the Bible but Homer and other less authoritative 'classics' have become the basis of a canon, generating reverence or scorn, conflicting interpretations, standards of judgment and perhaps of behavior, and offering a basis for history, science, philosophy and especially religion. The world is envisioned as a book, as Ernst Curtius says, and some books – Dante's *Divine Comedy*, Montaigne's *Essays* – as a world. If words are magical, sacred, illuminating, life-giving, destructive, the textual cosmos of the written book is a more-than-human creation. Appropriate reverence was exhibited by medieval commentators on the 'sacred page', by humanist scholars of the Renaissance (in their own egocentric style) and certainly by the magisterial reformers, whose fundamentalism reflected a transcendent faith in the value of the word. Their motto was indeed Augustine's *tolle lege*, for their conversions were almost without exception the product of struggles with the Biblical text. And the writing of texts was no less essential than the reading of them, for faith required not only the private 'witnessing' of true religion but also the 'publishing' thereof.[9]

In many ways the sixteenth century was the age of the book, but in all the recent celebration of the 'typographical revolution' the bibliographical prominence of the luxury book should not be allowed to obstruct the appreciation of lower, but arguably more widely effective, forms of communication. The story of printing is almost always told by authors who, professionally committed to the medium, overlook the continuing (and often reinforcing) influence of oral and scribal culture.[10] The effectiveness of the sermon in the 'evangelical revolution' shows that the spoken word continued to be a major factor in mass communication. Moreover, it acted as a spur and a model for printed propaganda. So it was for example with Geiler of Strasbourg's disciple Thomas Murner, who turned – like Luther, and second only to him in impact – to print in order to broadcast and to amplify his preaching.[11] And as sermons offered material for the printed book, so books of model sermons, prayers and manuals for preachers contributed to the production (as well as

[9] B. Faÿ, *Naissance d'un monstre, l'Opinion publique* (Paris, 1965).

[10] N. Davis, *Society and Culture in Early Modern France* (Stanford, 1975), 213; G. Le Hardy, *Histoire du protestantisme en Normandie* (Caen, 1869), 11; Ch. Nisard, *Histoire des livres populaires* (Paris, 1864); R. Engelsing, *Analphabetentum und Lektüre* (Stuttgart, 1973).

[11] M. Gravier, *Luther et l'opinion publique* (Paris, 1942).

to the standardization) of sermons. So it was, too, with songs, dramatizations, orations and disputations, and various kinds of ceremonial.

Like the spoken word, handwriting preserved at least a marginal significance in the period of ascendant print culture. This is evident not only for wealthy collectors of books who continued to assign priority to manuscripts, especially for ceremonial uses and presentation copies (to the extent indeed that there are cases of manuscripts being copied from printed books), but also for more immediate purposes of publicity. The placards posted in the university quarter objecting to the Concordat of 1516 were probably handwritten, for example, and so were those posted during Luther's well-publicized journeys to the disputation of Leipzig and to Worms.[12] Many other forms of propaganda were circulated in manuscript form in the later part of the century, such as the ill-fated 'Livret de Strasbourg' smuggled into France by Beza in 1560, the texts both of the Huguenot 'treaty of association' and of the later Catholic League, and items on surviving lists of confiscated books. Moreover, the vast quantities of diplomatic correspondence, often supplemented by printed matter, functioned as publicity and propaganda as well as intelligence (just as diplomats served as agents for all of these). Any assessment of the impact of print should take into account such outmoded but surviving means of communication.

The institution of 'publication', it may be recalled, was itself pre-typographical. For books it meant the release of multiple manuscripts at a given time, and formally it resembled the ceremonial occasion observed by printers. In France there was an analogous process of 'publishing' official acts which included an oral as well as a scribal stage.[13] So the royal ordinances were regularly 'read, published and registered' (*lecta, publicata et registrata*) before the assembled Parlement of Paris, or other provinces, whose members were specially enjoined to attend.[14] This normally occurred on the 'day of oaths' after an oration by the Premier President. There were ordinances, too, for the 'publication' of provincial customs (*publier et faire publier* is the conventional phrase), involving distribution as well as redaction for purposes of official notification. Manuscript volumes of these ordinances included topically arranged 'books' as well as

---

[12] Raemond, 79; Bulaeus, VI, 99. In general see G. Weill, *Le Journal* (Paris, 1934), 7–14; J. Kleinpaul, *Die Nachrichtendienst der deutschen Fürsten im 16. und 17. Jahrhundert* (Leipzig, 1930), esp. 147ff.; and F. Fatorello, *Il Giornalismo italiano* (Udine, 1932).

[13] E. Maugis, *Histoire du Parlement de Paris* (Paris, 1913–16), I, 522, regarding the famous ordinance on royal majority (see below, p. 268, at n. 27).

[14] E.g., Isambert, XI, 11 (31 Aug. 1498).

chronological registers. One interesting ceremony inherited from medieval times and continued for two centuries and more after the advent of printing was the 'crying' of edicts and official publications in the street (*a la criee*) and announcement at the sound of trumpets (*a son des trompes*). The form of publication was organized in a highly specialized and professional way. On 27 August 1561, for example, 'Letters patent of the king on the matter of religion' were 'read, cried and published by public cry by me, Paris Chrestien, sworn crier of our lord the king . . . in Paris, accompanied by Claude Malaseigne, sworn trumpeter, and other trumpeters of the said lord.'[15] Geneva also had 'public criers' to announce official edicts to the accompaniment of trumpets. Printing enhanced but for generations did not replace such primitive mechanisms for attracting public attention.

The institutional base of printing too, at least in France, long antedated the invention itself. The publishing elite was located in the booksellers' guilds, most notably the Parisian *Confrérie des libraires jurés de l'Université*, an organization which dated from the late thirteenth century and which came under municipal jursdiction. Besides maintaining the quality of manuscript books, this corporation preserved a professional monopoly, especially by forbidding the sale of books by other merchants (such as the *merciers* and *porteurs de balles*). From 1302 an oath was required of all twenty-four members (four of them styled 'grands libraires jurés'), who were thereby not only protected from competition but also were exempted from the *taille*.[16] In 1316 the guild was incorporated into the University, thus separating the booksellers from the menial 'mechanical arts' and trades and allying them with academic intellectuals and authors. In 1488 they were joined in this professional condition by the paper manufacturers, and of course the whole arrangement was confirmed by royal privilege.

It was into this medieval corporate framework that the art of printing, introduced into the University of Paris in 1470, was fitted and soon given similar monopolistic and privileged status. The printing trade as a whole flourished and grew into a sizeable community. In Paris during the sixteenth century there were at least 1400 identifiable publishers and workers, ranging from poor transients to the elite of book-making and book-selling. To judge from intermarriage, professional co-operation and succession, and the emergence of large and often subdividing dynasties, the wealthiest

---

[15] *Les defenses a toutes personnes de porter dagues ny espees, ou aultres armes, ne faire sedition* (Paris, 1561; LN 234); cf. A. Cartier, *Mémoires et documents publiés par la Société d'Histoire et d'archéologie de Genève*, XXIII (1888–94), 364.

[16] *Code de la librairie et imprimerie de Paris* (Paris, 1744), 5ff.

class represented a sort of neo-feudal aristocracy that must have exercised enormous influence on the book-writing intelligentsia as well as the book-buying public. Their principal locations were in the university quarter, especially the rue St Jacques, and around the Palais, where official materials were distributed. Ties with the government were strong from the beginning and increased with time. The office of royal printer was created as early as 1488, though apparently it was informal until the appointment of Robert Estienne, the seventh to enjoy this title, in 1539.[17] The alliance between the printing establishment and the monarchy was illustrated both by official rhetoric, which regarded printing as a mark and a vehicle of national glory, and by the symbolism of printers. In 1501 one of them chose as his device the old royalist slogan, 'Ungne Foy, un Dieu, ung Roy, ungne Loy.'

Though some historians have tried, it is hard to overestimate the impact of this new business even in simple numerical terms – 'la multiplicateur de l'écrit', as a recent scholar puts it.[18] Estimating this quantity can never be done in more than the most conjectural fashion. Square miles of paper, thousands of barrels of ink, millions of man-hours went into the attempt to reach the purses, if not the hearts and minds, of literate Europeans in the first century-and-a-half of printing. The incunabular period (up to 1501) unquestionably marks a threshold in the history of modern publicity and popular culture. Over 40,000 editions (perhaps 10,000,000 copies) have been tabulated, and the count goes on. During the second half-century of the printed book (1500–50) the figures surpass 100,000 editions (50,000,000 copies?), and this total will never be as accurate as that for the fifteenth century even in terms of extant literature. But even these statistics are misleading, since they apply mostly to highbrow books and easily identifiable titles. Beyond this there was a rising wave of popular literature – 'little books', pamphlets and single sheets (placards or, in German, *Einblattsdrücke*) – which, despite the random pattern of survival, must have reached blizzard proportions in the latter part of the sixteenth century (perhaps 2,000,000 copies by 1600).[19] The remains of this material represent perhaps the most concrete expression of the ideological upheavals of the early modern age, and as such it deserves qualitative as well as quantitative appreciation.

[17] G. Le Preux, *Gallia Typographia*, I (Paris, 1911), 50ff.; cf. E. Armstrong, *Robert Estienne, Royal Printer* (Cambridge, 1954), and Ph. Renouard, *Imprimeurs parisiens* (Paris, 1898), 56.
[18] P. Chaunu, 'Niveaux de culture et Réforme', *BSHPF*, cxviii (1972), 320; C. Bellanger *et al.*, *Histoire générale de la Presse française*, I (Paris, 1969); J.-P. Séguin, *L'Information en France avant la périodique* (Paris, 1964); D. Pottinger, *The French Book Trade in the Old Regime* (Cambridge, Mass., 1958); and E. Weller, *Die ersten deutschen Zeitungen* (Stuttgart, 1872).
[19] Some of the earliest of such fragments are collected in BM C.18.e.2, but there is no easy way to control this material, so essential to the study of modern propaganda.

The first phase of this stream of ephemeral and largely anonymous literature, scarce for the incunabular period but rapidly increasing thereafter, may be regarded as the earliest form of modern journalism. In sensationalism if not in impact such vernacular literature, especially the German 'tidings' (*Zeitungen*), rivalled the yellow journalism of more recent times, advertising its wares variously as 'wonderful', 'marvellous', 'terrible' (*erschröcklich*) or 'terrible but true'. At first such horror was reserved largely for natural disasters, monsters and foreign threats, particularly the Turks; but soon it was extended to ideological dangers as well, especially the anabaptists.

In France some 200 such 'occasional' publications have survived for the period before 1530, and these 'canards' seem to vary even more than their German and English counterparts, ranging from the most sensational to the most humdrum items. They dealt variously with prodigies, prophecies and miracles; with fires, floods and assorted scandals; with more fictional entertainments, poetry and prose; with devotional literature, calendars, almanacs and other everyday matters.[20] Others reported great events, such as Columbus's discoveries, the advance of the Turks, high crimes, major battles, diplomatic agreements, and especially ceremonies – royal births, marriages, funerals, processions, jousts, banquets, entries into cities, 'joyous' and otherwise. Probably the first big headline story was Charles VIII's invasion of Italy; and a steady stream of 'news' (*nouvelles*) reported his advance, his entries into Rome and Naples and his 'manner of dining there', some employing poetic forms and illustrations.[21] This pattern of news reporting, legal justification, public relations statements and more outrageous propaganda, together with other features familiar to modern newspaper readers (including horoscopes and comics, or the equivalent), was permanently fixed by the adoption of print as a support and enhancement of political action.

Almost from the beginning print was conscripted into government service.[22] As early as 1476 printers were set to work turning out

---

[20] See *CHF* (BN collection) with supplement, esp. the series Lb (history); unfortunately the legal series was never reached; also J.-P. Séguin, *L'Information en France de Louis XII à Henri II* (Paris, 1961).

[21] Cf. J. de la Pilorgerie, *Campagne et bulletins de la Grande Armée d'Italie* (Paris, 1866), and W. Herde, *Die älteste gedruckte Zeitung* (Mainz, 1931).

[22] Besides Isnard and the BM catalogue see J. Jenny, 'L'Imprimerie à Bourges jusqu'en 1562 environ', *Bulletin philologique et historique* (1967), 867–90, and 'Libraires et imprimeurs de Bourges au XVIe siècle', in *L'Humanisme français au début de la Renaissance* (Paris, 1973), 193–202; M. Besson, *L'Eglise et l'imprimerie de Lausanne* (Geneva, 1938), II, 10, 18; and A. Claudin, *Histoire de l'imprimerie en France* (Paris, 1900), II, 22. *Traité de paix entre Louis XI et Maximilien d'Autriche*, 14 Dec. 1482 (n.p., n.d.; BN rés. Lg⁶.2), and *Oratio reverendissimorum dominorum oratorum Christianissimi Francorum regis ad sanctissimum D. Innocentiam papam VIII* (n.p., 1485; BN rés. Lg⁶.3).

synodal constitutions, papal bulls, legal titles, imperial acts and especially diplomatic documents, one of the earliest being the treaty of peace between King Louis XI and the Emperor Maximilian in 1482. Municipal governments also turned to the new form of publicity, and in 1507 one proud city celebrated its 'liberties and franchises' in these lyrical terms:

> Glory be to the trinity,
> Peace, honor and stability
> Be to Geneva, and good unity
> To the People, church and nobility.[23]

Such chamber-of-commerce statements continued to form an important part of early modern publicity, though it would be drowned out – and above all in Geneva! – by more urgent issues.

In France the printing press became especially significant as an adjunct to legislation. From 1488 that charter of Gallican liberties, the Pragmatic Sanction of Bourges, appeared, along with its anti-Romanist commentary, in a series of editions. From about this time, too, royal ordinances and *arrêts* were distributed 'in front of the Palais' in printed form as well as by public cry. One of the earliest of these was the collection of Languedoc customs, printed in Toulouse in 1490.[24] Italian printers chipped in by printing foreign news and even legislation, such as the Milanese statutes reformed by Louis XII. Regularly at the beginning of each reign collections appeared to assist magistrates with a variety of professional problems – fiscal (taxes, duties), economic (prices, monopolies, guild regulation), judicial (reforming litigation, defining criminal penalties), ecclesiastical (benefices, preaching, morals), military and, endlessly, 'police'. Under Francis I and his son Henry II the printing of this material was increasingly concentrated in the hands of a few printing houses, notably those of Jean André, Jean Dallier, Guillaume Nyverd, Galliot du Pré, Charles Estienne and especially his brother Robert (II), who published at least 100 government pamphlets during the seminal years of the early civil wars (1563–8). This published legislation became itself, as has been apparent, a deliberate sort of propaganda.

A major factor in sixteenth-century publicity was the extraordi-

---

[23] E. H. Gallieur, *Etudes sur la typographie genevois* (Geneva, 1865), 96.

[24] *Les Ordonnances faictes par le Roy nostre Sir touchant le faict de la justice du Pays de Languedoc* (Paris, c. 1496); cf. Bellanger, *Histoire générale de la Presse française*, I, 20; *S'ensuyvent les nouvelles Ordonnances faictes par le roy nostre sire Françoys premier* ([Paris], 1519; BN rés. F. 1501.2); cf. E. Armstrong, 'The publication of the royal edicts and ordinances under Charles IX', *Proceedings of the Royal Society*, XIX[2] (1959), 41–59. *Statuta iurisdictionum et extraordinarium reformata a Ludovico rege Francorum Mediolanum* (1502), in G. Sapori, *La Cinquecentine dell'università di Milano*, 1 (Milan, 1969), no. 13.

narily widespread practice of translation, though it is a phenomenon
which has hardly been explored except in terms of famous texts and
authors.[25] Unlike authorship, translatorship seldom seemed important enough to credit; and the personnel and organization involved,
sometimes even the motives and the market, have left little trace.
Yet in the course of the century it became an international craft, first
for official and then for more informal purposes. As early as 1507
there was a German version of a French account of Louis XII's entry
into Genoa, and in 1515 an Italian translation of a report of Francis I's
entry into Milan. Diplomacy, coronations and royal and noble
marriages attracted similar attention, as did certain legal questions,
such as Charles V's claims over the Duchy of Guelders, translated
from Latin into French as well as Dutch. But by far the most popular
topic for jounalistic translators was war news. Such headline stories
as the battle of Pavia, Henry II's invasion of German territories in
1553, and the various laws and treaties as well as murders and
massacres of the religious wars were quickly reported in many
languages. When Coligny was condemned in 1569, the parlementary *arrêt* was translated into *eight* languages to achieve maximum
publicity. A striking example on another level is that of the official
Lutheran historiographer, Johann Sleidan, who himself translated
Seyssel, Commines and Froissart from French into Latin; he published his own contemporary history in Latin in 1556, and within
five years this mighty compendium of Reformation history, plun-
dered by martyrologists and pamphleteers as well as historians, was
translated into French, German, Italian and English. This sort of
information flow adds further substance to the view that modern
journalism was a product of the earliest stage of print culture,
however primitive the economic and technological conditions.

Paralleling this flood of primitive newsprint was the emergence of
a new class of publicists, some of them printers, most of them
professing some literary, legal or scholarly speciality, but all drawn
together by what was potentially a common readership. One of the
first major names is that of Claude de Seyssel, diplomat, churchman,
translator and councillor to Louis XII. Underlying his most famous
work, the *Grand Monarchy of France*, was not only extensive political
experience and knowledge of ancient and modern history but also
(something that sets him apart from his rival Machiavelli, to whom
he has so often been compared) an apprenticeship as a royal
propagandist. One of his orations, originally delivered at the court of

---

[25] See Séguin (cited n. 18), 131; Charles V's *Assertio juris* over Guelders (Latin with
French and Dutch trans.) is cited in B. Sanchez Alonso, *Fuentes de la historia española*,
II (Madrid, 1952), no. 5618, and on Coligny see below, p. 286, n. 79.

Henry VIII in defense of his master's policy, was published in Latin and in French and then expanded into a panegyrical account of Louis XII's reign, his virtues, political achievements and general superiority to his predecessors. Contemporaneously, Seyssel also published a pamphlet on the king's victory over the Venetians, typifying one sort of sixteenth-century 'campaign literature'.[26] These enhancements of the Most Christian King's public image appeared in the midst of a gush of patriotic publicity which drew upon the most varied literary and journalistic forms. Nor was the monarchy the only beneficiary of this sort of publicity. Later the house of Guise was also honored with quantities of public praise, such as the eulogy for Claude de Lorraine published by Dallier in 1550 and subsequent celebrations of the military victories by his son Francis.[27] The sixteenth century was also the first age of the public-relations expert.

The dominant secular theme of official French propaganda in the first half of the century was the controversy with the Empire, stemming in public terms from the rivalry between Charles VIII and the Emperor Maximilian for the hand of Anne of Brittany (who married the former in 1491). In response to the apologetic 'news' about Charles's invasion of 1494 and his Italian claims, spokesmen for Maximilian issued attacks 'against the false publications of the French', denouncing their 'perfidy' and 'frauds' and claiming the principle of the 'just war' for the imperial cause.[28] Later imperial broadsheets were distributed to discourage mercenaries from joining the French armies. In more general terms French legists had for at least two centuries argued the superiority of French kingship to the Empire in terms of a variety of formulas, notably the canonist rule that 'the King of France recognizes no superior in temporal things'. In the early sixteenth century these pretensions, put forward by legists like Jean Ferrault and Charles de Grassaille, were extended to support the candidacy of Francis I during the imperial election of 1519. With the renewal of war between France and the Empire, especially after Francis I went back on his word and refused to honor the Treaty of Madrid of 1525, this ideological conflict

26 Seyssel, *Les Louanges du roy Louis XIIe de ce nom* (Paris, 1508) and *La Victoire du roy contre les venitiens* (Paris, 1510), also J. Lemaire de Belges, *La Légende des venitiens* (Paris, 1509); cf. M. Sherman, 'The Selling of Louis XII' (unpublished Ph.D. thesis, University of Chicago, 1974), B. Rave, *Venise dans la littérature française* (Paris, 1916), 234ff., and P. Jodogne, *Jean Lemaire de Belges* (Brussels, 1972).
27 *Le Discours de la guerre de Metz en Lorraine* (Lyon, 1553; BN Lb31.44).
28 *Plusieurs nouvelles envoyees de Naples Par le Roy nostre sire a monseigneur de Bourbon* (n.p., 1495; BN rés. Lb28.24); *AC*, I and II, and generally *Recueil des pieces du temps* (BN rés. Lb28.1). *Contra falsas francorum literas* (n. p., [1492]; BN Lb28.1), complaining about 'ipsa versipellis ac detestanda francorum perfidia' and 'francorum fraudes', and BM D. C.5. (State Papers).

228

became more public; and there was a talk of a duel between the two. In 1528 this story was dramatized in a 'defense of the Most Christian King', which in form was a reported dispute between Francis and an ambassador of Charles. In this pamphlet the imperial herald 'blamed the king for breaking faith and using insulting words which touched his honor'. Interrupting, Francis asked the man for his credentials. 'Your master cannot make laws in France', he snapped, and the interview (though not the dispute) was over.[29]

It was an international incident, and the pamphlet reads like a news dispatch or an eyewitness report. Later publications took a more critical and editorializing approach to the continuing quarrel, even appealing to the princes and cities against their master's presumptions, calumnies and violations of 'liberty'. Some complained about war atrocities, and all questioned the legality of Charles's position. In 1534, a few months before the affair of the placards, Francis had his own placards published against the emperor.[30] In 1536 the imperial publisher, appropriately named Martin Lempereur (Keyser), printed letters purporting to show that the whole blame for the war belonged with the French king; and it was in response to this that Robert Estienne published a famous collection – *The Texts of Letters by which Francis, Most Christian King of France, is Defended against the Slander of his Enemies* – which has been described as one of the earliest 'white papers' of European history.[31]

It is interesting to see how external and internal threats competed for public attention in these years. Just nine days after the public condemnation of Calvin (1 July 1542) the 'cry of war' was again raised against Charles V for great offenses and injuries – in both cases at the sound of trumpets – and the Emperor's spokesmen responded in kind, and in French.[32] Under Henry II both threats seemed to reach new heights, and so did the propaganda surrounding them. While intensifying his father's campaign against 'Lutheranism' at home, Henry moved from diplomatic flirtation with the Lutheran powers in

---

[29] *La Deffense du roy treschrestien contre lesleu en emperor delayant le combat dentre eulx* (Paris, 1528; BN rés. Lb30.51). Cf. *Apologie contre le traicté de Madric* [sic] (Paris, 1526; Chantilly, 100 bis).

[30] *Epistre ou voirement Oraison tresparfaicte dung quidam Aleman bonne scavant et de la liberté Germanique trestudieux* (n.p., n.d.; BN rés. Lb30.67); Herminjard, III, 249. *Double d'un lettre escripte par ung serviteur du Roy* (n.p., n.d.; BN rés. Lb30.65); *Lettres du roy treschrestien aux souverains estats du S. Empire* (Lyon, 1553; BN Lb31.53).

[31] *Exemplaria literarum quibus et Christianissimus Gallorum Rex Franciscus ab adversarium maledictis defenditu . . .* (Paris, 1538), and Chantilly (Musée), *Le Cabinet des livres* (Paris, 1905), no. 414. Armstrong, *Robert Estienne*, 142.

[32] *Cry de guerre ouvert entre le Roy de France et empereur . . .*, 10 July 1542 (BN Lb31.29); *L'Excuse et response du trèsillustre et très redoubte empereur* (Antwerp, 1542); *Apologie pour le Roy, contre les calomnies des Imperialz* (Paris, 1550; BN Lb31.29) and *Second Apologie . . .* (Paris, 1553; BN Lb31.32); Herminjard, I, 120.

Germany to political alliance; and the shift was reflected in the productions of the Estienne press. Although Robert Estienne was forced into exile for his publishing indiscretions, his brother Charles continued to serve the king. Among his publications was a widely circulated series of 'apologies', in both French and Latin, objecting to the continuing calumnies by the Emperor. This was just about the time that Henry II decided to proclaim himself 'protector of German liberties' – and implicitly to become an accomplice in lese-majesty – against the Emperor.

By this time, around mid-century, the convergence of political and religious questions was acting to change the quantity as well as the quality of journalism and propaganda. What was in effect religious propaganda had long focussed on the problematic relationship between France and the papacy, but internal criticism of royal policy was at best marginal. Heresy with its subversive implications, not the schismatic potential of the national church, was the main catalyst. In a most direct sense the 'typographical revolution' was a function of the 'evangelical revolution' of the 1520s, when itinerant preachers and teachers were joined by itinerant printers to publish the gospel to all nations. 'I want France to be filled with evangelical books', wrote one member of this pioneering generation, Farel's friend Anemond de Coct.[33] And so it seemed to be – to critics and enthusiasts alike. 'The whole world is filled with books', lamented the disillusioned Bishop of Meaux in 1523. 'The common people, enamored of novelty and seduced by the vivacity of [Luther's] style, seem to be giving themselves over to his imaginary and fallacious liberty.' It was a refrain that generations of religious conflict would not still.

A WORLD FILLED WITH BOOKS

The power of the press has always seemed to strike awe into the hearts at least of the literate, and its intimidating force was well recognized by those who hoped to control public opinion. In a model ordinance of 1513 King Louis XII declared that 'the invention of printing seems to be more divine than human' because of its value in propagating 'the holy Catholic faith'.[34] The supernatural quality of

[33] Herminjard, I, 282 (to Farel, 2 Sept. 1524), 155 (G. Briçonnet to the faithful of his diocese, 15 Oct. 1523).

[34] 'Declaration en faveur de l'imprimerie nouvellement inventee', 9 April 1513 (Isambert, XI, 113); cf. *Code de la Librairie*, 7. The standard survey is L. Febvre and H. Martin, *L'Appariton du livre* (Paris, 1958); cf. R. Hirsch, *Printing, Selling and Reading 1450–1550* (Wiesbaden, 1967), and H. J. Martin, *Livres, Pouvoirs et Société* (Geneva, 1969).

typography was expressed in a variety of ways. At least until the seventeenth century the invention of printing was associated with the legend of Faust, arising from a confusion about the name of Johann Fust, who had capitalized on Gutenberg's device.[35] On the other hand, it was revered as a divine gift – the 'tenth muse', proclaimed the poet Du Bellay. Printers were worshipped as veritable 'gods' for their ability to confer or to revive life and in a sense to insure immortality. From the beginning, then, the view that printing was more than human was standard: from the commercial rhetoric of the first printers and their authors to the meliorist arguments of Bacon and Condorcet, and from the Faustian interpretations of German idealists to the pronouncements of Marshall McLuhan and Elizabeth Eisenstein. It is true that the hyperbole has been secularized a bit, imputations of divinity being replaced by talk of 'revolution' and various sorts of psychic and social distress, but the claims for its powers continued to be transcendent and earthshaking, if not heavenstorming.

The mythical aspect of printing is closely bound up with the mystique of Renaissance humanism and the classical revival. As Guillaume Budé declared (in a work which ironically he never saw in print), 'The invention of printing is the restitution and perpetuation of antiquity'; and according to his disciple Le Roy, who wrote a generation later, it was a 'miracle' that printing emerged just in time to secure the unprecedented achievement of the humanist movement.[36] The goal of this miraculous, though admittedly German, art was perhaps best described by Budé's chief rival Erasmus, writing in praise of Aldo Manuzio. 'By God', he exclaimed, 'it is a Herculean task and one worthy of a princely mind to restore to the world something which has almost foundered, to reconstruct passages which have been mutilated, and to emend others distorted in countless ways . . .'[37] This scholarly process of reconstruction (*restitutio* and *emendatio* being the technical terms) was extended from textual matters to the cultural arena in general, and the significance of printing was correspondingly enhanced. 'Movable type is the symbol of humanism', as Egon Friedell put it.[38]

So typography became the chief vehicle of the 'prodigious effort of anamnesis' which Mircea Eliade regards as a distinguishing trait of

35 Pasquier, *Recherches de la France* (Paris, 1621), IX, 29; cf. A. Firmin-Didot, *Alde Manuce et l'hellenisme à Venise* (Paris, 1875), 218.

36 Budé, *De l'Institution du prince* (Paris, 1547), 63; cf. Louis le Roy, *De la vicissitude ou varieté des choses en l'univers* (Paris, 1575), fol. 215.

37 Cited by D. Geanakoplos, *Greek Scholars in Venice* (Cambridge, Mass., 1962), 271.

38 *A Cultural History of the Modern Age*, trans. C. Atkinson (New York, 1920), I, 210.

western civilization.[39] From the sixteenth century it also became associated with the highest attributes of human nature and indeed with that central theme of the humanist movement, 'the excellence and dignity of man', which represented the culmination of the art of writing, that most graphic boundary between men and animals.[40] In the humanist canon of achievement, then, the invention of printing came to hold first rank. It was rivalled only by that of artillery, but that, according to one author, related not to the dignity of man but rather to the obverse thesis, the 'misery of man'. Along with the marine compass these inventions constituted the great trinity of transforming factors celebrated by Louis le Roy, Francis Bacon and other pioneering historians of civilization. 'Printing alone', Bodin wrote, 'can easily vie with all the discoveries of the ancients.'[41] Thus, as an essential piece of evidence for the Moderns in their long 'quarrel' with the Ancients, the myth of printing became one of the essential ingredients of the modern idea of Progress.

If printing seemed divine to its scholarly, commercial and political exploiters, it struck evangelical-minded dissenters as literally miraculous, especially in its timing. To a religion of the Book the 'sacred page' seemed the very embodiment of fundamentalist truth, the dissemination of this Word the very life-principle of the faith. This was perhaps the most spectacular aspect of the Lutheran 'revolution', for out of it came a veritable tidal wave of polemic and popular literature, and the sheer physical measurements of this wave are impressive even to scholars unconcerned with the size of readership.[42] The popular 'newspaper' (*Zeitung*) was well established as a means of communication, but the Lutheran *Flugschriften* were unprecedented in quantity as well as speed of flight. By 1520 some 300,000 copies of Lutheran books had issued from the presses of Wittenberg, Strasbourg, Basel and other cities friendly to his cause. It was said that in that year 4000 copies of his 'Address to the Christian Nobility of the German Nation' were sold.[43] Over the next decade there were at least 630 German editions (not counting Murner's works), over half by Luther; and by the time of his death there had been 430 editions, complete or partial, of the most

[39] *Myth and Reality*, trans W. Trask (New York, 1963), 134.
[40] Pierre Boaistuau, *Le Theatre du Monde* (Antwerp, 1575).
[41] Bodin, *Method for the Easy Comprehension of History*, trans. B. Reynolds (New York, 1945), 302.
[42] H. Buchli, *6000 Jahre Werbung*, II (Berlin, 1962), 18; C. Kortpeter, 'German Zeitung literature in the sixteenth century', *Sixteenth Century Texts*, ed. R. Schoeck (Toronto, 1966); W. G. Moore, *La Réforme allemande et la littérature française* (Strasbourg, 1930).
[43] Gravier, *Luther et l'opinion publique* (Paris, 1942), 32ff.

effective *Flugschrift* of them all, the Lutheran Bible. It was on this rising tide of books, perhaps even more than in public spectacles and disputations, that Luther emerged as one of the dominant voices of modern history.

The winds of Lutheran doctrine were felt almost immediately, outside as well as inside Germany, because of the printed page. From 1519 his books were circulating from Avignon to Antwerp, which was soon 'burning with the books of Herr Doctor Martin Luther'.[44] In 1520, a young Swiss student wrote to Zwingli, a shipment of 1400 copies had arrived from the Frankfurt fair and were being sold under the very noses of the Sorbonists.[45] Through placards, pamphlets and *petits livres* this contagion spread into academic, professional and urban communities. Propagandizing became a significant new calling, as did the ancillary art of translation, one of the most trafficked 'roads to heresy'. As early as 1519 Luther appeared in Flemish, while the first French translation dates from 1523.[46] Thanks to the industry of such scholars as Berquin, Lambert and Farel, Frenchmen had early access not only to Luther (at least a dozen works by 1535) but also to Erasmus, Melanchthon, Bucer, Hutten, Sleidan and others. And thanks to the risky ventures not only of various freelance and fly-by-night printers but also of major figures like Simon Dubois, Wygand Köln, Pierre de Vingle and Antoine Marcourt, texts were published that otherwise would never have seen the light of day. This was an age of book-making as well as of teaching and preaching missionaries.

The German wave itself crested in 1524–5, but elsewhere the flow continued and in some channels reached flood proportions. The necessary condition for this was the extraordinary geographic extension and interconnections of the book trade. By the sixteenth century, printing had become internationalized as well as industrialized, the basis of a network of intellectual and commercial intercourse that gave further coherence to the European community of scholars which had earlier maintained itself largely through the universities and courts.[47] Originally printing had moved down the

---

44 *Chronijk der Stadt Antwerpen Nolaris Geerard Bertrijn*, ed. G. Havre (Antwerp, 1879), 71 (13 July 1521).

45 Herminjard, I, 62 (Glareanus to Zwingli, 1 Nov. 1520).

46 E. Baie, *Le Siècle des Gueux*, II (Brussels, 1932), 228.

47 In the enormous bibliography on this subject, reference here should be made to *Aspects*; Moore, *La Réforme allemande*; E. Droz, *Chemins de l'hérésie* (Geneva, 1970–6); A. Parent, *Les Métiers du livre à Paris au XVIe siècle* (Geneva, 1974); G. Berthoud, *Antoine Marcourt*; J. Pineaux, *La Poésie des protestants de langue française* (Paris, 1971); F. Charbonnier, *La Poésie française et les guerres de religion* (Paris, 1919); and the continuing B. Moreau, *Inventaire chronologique des éditions parisiennes du XVIe siècle*, I (Paris, 1972–   ), and Ph. Renouard, *Imprimeurs et libraires parisiens au XVIe siècle*, I–II (Paris, 1964–   ).

Rhine from Mainz to Frankfurt, Strasbourg, Basel and across the Alps to Venice and then south; and this route (travelled also by scholars and preachers) remained one of the major axes of exchange. In the Francophone world Lyon and Antwerp as well as Paris maintained ties with this Rhine axis; but of course there was a proliferation of smaller presses in smaller towns that filled the interstices, at least forty locations in France before mid-century. Of increasing and finally crucial importance were the émigré communities in Basel, Strasbourg (sixty families by 1560) and especially Geneva. This communications network was strengthened by a number of interrelated factors: the transporation, legitimate or covert, of books by colporteurs, small tradesmen and such organizations as the Hansa, which carried books to Antwerp, London and other places; the great book fairs, including those of Antwerp and Frankfurt; and a widening circle of commercial and scholarly contacts between printers, authors, research helpers and book-hunters, which formed not only a cornerstone of the European 'republic of letters' but also part of the expanding network of international Protestantism.

As contraband, Lutheran propaganda was naturally diverted from orthodox areas, and this circumstance also contributed to the international diffusion of the printing trade. In Protestant centers the upsurge began in the 1520s. In Basel the number of books nearly tripled between 1520 and 1550.[48] In Antwerp there were 35 presses in 1525 and 50 more in 1540, accounting for over half of the 2221 titles listed for the first four decades of the century. Increasingly important, too, was Strasbourg, which began to publish French as well as German and Latin books as Francophone émigrés began to arrive. By mid-century Geneva was joining these older centers as a prime generator of publicity.[49] The production of reformed presses rose from an average of 5 a year before 1540 to over 32 a year after 1550. By this time three extraordinary publishers had come to Geneva to ply their trade: Robert Estienne, who came with two of his sons, Henri and François, leaving two others to run the family firm in Paris

[48] P. Bietenholz, *Basel and France in the Sixteenth Century* (Toronto, 1971), 51, and *Die italienische Humanismus und die Blützeit des Buchdrucks in Basel* (Basel, 1959); Baie, *Siècle*, II; Hauser; W. Knuttel, *Catalogus van de Pamfletten-verzameling berustende in de koniklijke Bibliotheek* (The Hague, 1899), as well as the listings of Dutch pamphlets by L. Petit; J. van Somern; J. Van der Wulp and W. Nijhoff.
[49] P. Chaix, *Recherches sur l'imprimerie à Genève de 1550 à 1561* (Geneva, 1954) and, with A. Dufour and G. Moeckli, *Les Livres imprimés à Genève de 1550 à 1600* (Geneva, 1966); H. Bremme, *Buchdrucker und Buchhändler zu Zeit des Glaubenskämpfe* (Geneva, 1969); Th. Dufour, *Notes bibliographiques sur le catechisme et la confession de foi de Calvin (1537)* (Geneva, 1878); H. L. Schlaepfer, 'Laurent de Normandie', in *Aspects*, 176–83.

after his publishing policy had made him unwelcome; Laurent de Normandie, a relative of Calvin who had fled under a charge of lese-majesty; and the great martyrologist Jean Crespin, who had fled from the persecution of Charles V in the company of François Baudouin. Before Calvin's death in 1564 the Genevan printing industry had expanded to include 34 firms employing 170 master printers and workers. The quantity of production increased proportionately, and so did the distribution throughout Europe. Calvin himself accounted for 160 editions. The number of copies per edition is usually guesswork – perhaps two thousand. In 1562 one printing of Estienne's Bible comprised 9000 copies; one edition of Erasmus's *Colloquies* reportedly totalled 20,000; but the record surely belongs to Beza's translation of the Psalms, which reached over 30,000 that same year.[50]

In the Francophone world in general it is difficult to give quantitative estimates for the production of pamphlets, especially for unofficial publications, since the number depends on the survival, which may be three-quarters of the total. To judge in particular by the incomparable Parisian collections (supplemented by the American aggregate) the pattern of production is one of striking, if irregular, increase. Altogether there are more than 10,000 identifiable pamphlets, more than for other European nationalities, at least if Latin publications, especially common early in the century, are included. Roughly half of these are official in character. A minority have survived in multiple editions and/or copies. Up to the beginning of Francis I's reign, unofficial pamphlets seem to have outstripped acts (numbering 77 and 14 respectively in the Bibliothèque Nationale collections, which were themselves started at this time), and thereafter their increase was proportionate (over 100 for that reign). For the acts the take-off period begins in 1539, largely because of the great reforming edict of that year, which appeared in at least 18 editions. During the reign of Henry II the average number of acts per year is 15, compared to 11 for pamphlets. The threshold for the latter can be located just on the eve of the civil wars, specifically in 1558. Over the next comparable period, from the death of Henry II (1559) to the Massacre of St Bartholomew (1572), the average is 36 for acts and (much more irregularly distributed) 32 for pamphlets. After this seminal period the increase is both more moderate and more regular.

Other measures of the expansion of ideology are even harder to

---

[50] P. Pidoux, *Le Psautier huguenot du XVIe siècle* (Basel, 1962), II, 30; cf. B. Latimer, 'Pamphleteering in France during the Wars of Religion' (unpublished Ph.D. thesis, Duke University, 1976).

determine, but for the circulation of ideas movement may be as important as mass – quality as quantity. The shipping of books was certainly not the business only of the large producers; the colporteurs, who were becoming the proletariat of printing, operated in countryside and town and often at considerable risk. Raemond lamented the swarms of peddlers of 'little books' with illustrations and the illiterate booksellers ('ces libraires idiots') who dared to dispute theological questions with university experts.[51] Nicolas Pithou, in his account of the beginnings of Protestantism in Champaign, mentions the scandal caused – and the tragedy suffered – by one of Laurent de Normandie's colporteurs who came to Troyes with his books.[52] In 1563 a colporteur returning from the book fair in Frankfurt was captured in Antwerp, and out of a total of almost 100 books confiscated, the majority were by Calvin, Farel, Viret, Beza and other Swiss reformers. The threat posed by this book trade is reflected in a contemporary verse:

> They have eaten up the gospel
> and all of St Paul.
> The Devil take these printers
> and their books in the vulgar tongue.[53]

On the other hand the martyrologies rank the printers high on the list of the holy propagators of the word.

What about the impact of the printed page? Did people read these books and pamphlets, and were they moved? Were they at least impressed by the illustrations, some of them the crudest, most obvious and most offensive kind of religious and political cartooning? These questions always arise, but it seems unlikely that stray testimony or retrospective literacy-tests will provide satisfactory answers about reading-patterns. Clearly, contemporaries thought that books were read and had a mighty influence on belief and behavior, but then of course these contemporaries were themselves readers and usually writers of books. Besides reports of conversions, public readings were common practice and supplemented the sermon as a communal experience, and sometimes 'little books' were distributed after services. The Huguenot Bernard de Palissy tells how the poor, proselytizing monks of Saintonge spread their faith to children by reading to them out of evangelical books; and there are other such stories.[54] Certainly the published edicts, especially those

---

[51] Raemond, 874.   [52] Pithou, 10. See below, p. 242, n. 78.   [53] Pamphlet reference lost.
[54] B. Palissy, *Les Oeuvres*, ed. A. France (Paris, 1880), 139; Floquet, *Histoire du Parlement de Normandie* (Rouen, 1840), II, 233.

concerning the religious question, had a substantial effect, for instance in the correspondence of Protestants. François Hotman alerted his Swiss colleagues to the threat of the Edict of Compiègne of 1557, which prescribed death and confiscation for heresy but which significantly, and as he thought maliciously, exempted Lutherans and concentrated on Calvinists and Zwinglians.[55] Nicolas Pithou refers to the alarm caused by royal edicts in Troyes, and the confusing legislation published in Paris during the spring of 1562 noticeably inflamed the citizens, according to a contemporary chronicler.

The impression made by the printed word will always be subject to question, but its physical presence cannot be doubted – not only its production and distribution but also its possession by a variety of social types. The number and size of libraries, private as well as public, were on the rise in the sixteenth century, especially among lay readers. Particularly striking were the libraries assembled by jurists and royal magistrates – who were also, as has been remarked, the most prolific composers of books.[56] Before 1493 there were few collections among the lawyers and they were small; by 1550 in Paris there were a dozen with a 100 or more volumes and a few approaching 1000, including those of President Lizet and Guillaume Budé's brother Dreux. This is based on a small sampling, made possible by surviving testaments. Other records, such as those of Amiens, suggest a generally similar pattern, which is that the larger collections were those of lawyers, though religious books and collections still predominated. None of this seems very surprising, but at least it seems compatible with the character of modern ideology as reflected in the proto-journalism and propaganda of the early modern age.

What is undeniable in this age is the presence, and in Protestant communities even the omnipresence, of the book, if not of the Word. Protestant publicists like Crespin and John Foxe were convinced that the printed book was a divine gift which promised fulfillment of a divine mission. Catholic critics, though they would not put the matter that way, had similar suspicions about the supernatural potential of printing, especially when it was directed at the mass of people. The threat was not only to traditional religion

---

[55] Kelley, *Hotman*, 100; Pithou, 87; P. Paschal, *Journal de ce qui s'est passé en France devant l'année 1562*, ed. M. François (Paris, 1950),11.

[56] R. Doucet, *Les Bibliothèques parisiennes au XVIe siècle* (Paris, 1956); A. Labarre, *Le Livre dans la vie amienoise* (Paris, 1971); H. J. Martin, 'What Parisians read in the sixteenth century', *French Humanism*, ed. W. Gundersheimer (London, 1969), 131–45; A. H. Schutz, *Vernacular Books in Parisian Private Libraries in the Sixteenth Century according to the Notarial Archives* (Chapel Hill, Virginia, 1955).

but also to the intellectuals' monopoly over ideas. In either sense, according to one Catholic convert from Calvinism, referring to the elitist and perhaps obscurantist view attributed to Hermes Trismegistus, 'It is not religious to place in the hands of the people all the mysteries and secrets of God.'[57] Nor, as many suspected, was it even political.

BANNING AND BURNING

Or was the book – as distinct from the Word – the Devil's invention? Certainly it came from Germany, had 'Faustian' connotations and often seemed to become a purveyor of forbidden knowledge. The first graphic representation of the printing press, which appeared in Lyon in 1499, showed two of its operators being dragged off, presumably to hell. If the first Hebrew book appeared in 1475, as historians have pointed out, so too did the first anti-Semitic publication. If the printed book brought enlightenment to good citizens, as many thought, it might also enflame those whose allegiance was less stable. In France Louis XII indeed declared that 'impression' was a divine invention, but less than a generation later his successor Francis I, despite the proudly-worn title 'father of letters', had become so disillusioned that (as has been remarked) he attempted, implausibly, to suppress it altogether.[58] Here is one of the paradoxes of the 'typographical revolution', that it laid the foundations not only for the modern age of publicity but also for its ideological obverse, preventive censorship.

Censorship and attempts at thought control were also part of the scribal heritage and especially of university discipline, which conventionally required that 'reason' be subordinated to 'authority', though to be sure the definition of this authority changed in the course of generations. Between the thirteenth and the sixteenth century, for example, Aristotelianism was transformed from the embodiment of intellectual radicalism to the symbol of the most impervious orthodoxy. One face of the whole history of Christian philosophy, and theology as well, was the record of errors which arose and were either accommodated or more or less successfully suppressed. Protestants as well as Catholics had their histories of heresies, such as Bullinger's comprehensive *Origins of Errors*, and adopted similar ways of trying to suppress them. From the late fifteenth century there were attempts, imperial as well as papal, to

[57] Raemond, 585. [58] François Ier, *Catalogue des Actes*, VI, 686, 23 Feb. 1535.

censor printed books – in 1501 one such edict intended for the Empire was defended 'as a duty of conscience' – and before the emergence of Luther the Reuchlin affair had become the scandalous focus of this policy, which was directed at confiscating the books written by those of Reuchlin's party.[59] In 1515 Pope Leo X issued an important constitution 'concerning the impression of books', and so in general the institutional defenses were well prepared for the Lutheran onslaught, which soon overshadowed the problem of Reuchlin.

Despite talk of the 'new errors' of Luther, his doctrines in fact were treated no differently from those of Hus, Wycliffe or any of the older innovators, for Luther's 'newness' was of a very traditional sort to most critics. Their reaction, too, was traditional. Luther was interrogated, his work was analyzed and reduced to debatable propositions, he was judged by academic and ecclesiastical authorities, and finally he was condemned by the secular arm.[60] The very first public act of the young Emperor Charles V in Germany – written in French and published in Antwerp in 1521 – was an attack on the false and 'cretinous' ideas of Luther.[61] Eight years later he followed this with a famous 'Placard' establishing permanent censorship with extreme but again traditional penalties of burning, tongue-piercing and confiscation of property. Characteristically, Luther was lumped together with Hus, Wycliffe, Marsilius of Padua and Jan Pupper von Goch, whose work on 'Christian liberty', though independent of Luther's views, seemed to reinforce them.[62] In some areas this legislation was effective. In 1525, according to one of Farel's friends, two booksellers were expelled from Metz; and in the territories of Lorraine in general, where printing had been flourishing in 1521, 'the great voice of the Reformation was silenced', as one historian put it, from 1527 to 1550.[63] Imperial policy continued unchanged, and again in 1550 an edict was published against 'books made or composed by Martin Luther, Johann Oecolampadius, Ulrich Zwingli, Martin Bucer, Jean Calvin or other heresiarchs and members of their sects'. 'And do not be surprised', the reader was

---

[59] Argentré, I, 353; H. Reusch, *Die Indices librorum prohibitorum des sechszehnten Jahrhunderts* (Tübingen, 1886); cf. M. Leber, *De l'état réel de la presse et des pamphlets* (Paris, 1854).

[60] *Eyn Urteyl der Theologen zu Paris über die lere Doctor Luthers* (n.p., 1522; Harvard).

[61] O. Droszt, *Les premiers imprimés en France de Vienne (1521–1538)* (Szeged, Hungary, 1934), 7.

[62] *De Libertate christiana* (1521), in *BRN*, VI, ed. S. Cramer and F. Pijper (The Hague, 1910).

[63] J. Beaupré, *Recherches historiques et bibliographiques sur les commencements de l'imprimerie en Lorraine* (St. Nicolas-de-Port, 1845), 99.

warned by a catalogue of prohibited books put out by the University of Louvain in 1550, 'that this catalogue contains so many disapproved Bibles and New Testaments, because heresiarchs arise from there.'[64]

In France the official response was just the same and no less prompt. There, too, censorship had become a conventional practice. In 1514 the Sorbonne had supported the imperial campaign against Reuchlin, and within two years Noel Beda had begun his assault on the heterodox Christian humanists and evangelicals of all varieties. Such issues as the Council of Pisa and especially the Concordat of 1516 provoked 'a great number of writings', according to De Thou, and official action to prevent their circulation.[65] There was little question, then, about the sort of welcome Luther's ideas would receive. The reception began with the Sorbonne's 'Determination' against him in the spring of 1521, which presented a defense of 'scholasticism' and a reassertion of the value of the sacraments against Luther's errors.[66] In June the secular arm, that is, the Parlement of Paris, followed suit first by endorsing the requirement that no book could be published without the imprimatur of the faculty of theology and then (several weeks before the edict of Charles V) by forbidding altogether the printing of Lutheran literature. On 1 August this edict was read, 'at the sound of trumpets', and all such books were ordered to be surrendered to the authorities.[67] This was the first in a long line of specifically anti-Lutheran acts aimed at suppressing printed publicity.

In a sense the style of dealing with offensive literature was set by Luther himself, for he was the one who celebrated his rejection of Romanism late in 1520 by casting into the flames that bookish embodiment of papal tradition, the corpus of canon law. For centuries, he argued, holy men had so treated evil books – and indeed there was classical as well as ecclesiastical precedent for this practice, the works of Abelard among others having been burned. Many of Luther's own publications would suffer the same fate in succeeding years: in 1521, 400 copies were burned in Antwerp, more in Ghent the next year, and in August 1523 fires were lit in Paris for the so-called *publica combustio* of books belonging to Louis Berquin and filled with 'many errors and damned heresies'.[68] Among the titles were 'On the Abrogation of the Mass', 'Debates between Piety and

[64] *Le Catalogue des livres reprouvez* (Louvain, 1550; BM 618.b.43); L. Halkin, *Histoire religieuse des règnes de Corneille de Berghen et de Georges d'Autriche, Princes-Evêques de Liège 1538–1557* (Paris, 1936), 117.

[65] De Thou, I, 40; Isambert, XI, 111.   [66] Argentré, I, 365.

[67] R. Doucet, *Etudes sur le gouvernement de François Ier* (Paris, 1921), I, 331; cf. *Journal d'un bourgeois de Paris*, ed. L. Lalanne (Paris, 1854), 169.

[68] Argentré, I, 406.

Superstition', a response to Henry VIII's critique of Luther and apparently a copy of (Erasmus's anonymous) 'Julius Excluded'.[69] As Erasmus himself remarked to Beda, book-burning tended to be followed by people-burning; and indeed a week later the first 'Lutheran' martyr in France, Jean Vallière, followed Berquin's volumes into the fire for his 'blasphemies and monstrous words'. Six years later he was joined by the irrepressible Berquin himself.

After the affair of the placards of 1534 the pursuit of heretical publications was intensified. In June of the next year Francis I established a special commission of the Parlement to oversee the censorship of books.[70] The great humanist Budé defended this policy in an attack which he published that year on the sacramentarians; and it was at least partly in response to this that Calvin made his appeal to Francis I in his dedicatory letter to the first edition of his *Institutes*, appearing the year after that. The censorship campaign became fiercer, and in this heated atmosphere Calvin and Ramus were honored with personal legislative attacks. In 1542 the Parlement, in an ordinance which was in effect a pioneering piece of anti-Protestant propaganda, identified the *Institution of Christian Religion* and its author 'Alcuin' (a Latin anagram for Calvin) as a particularly pernicious source of error.[71] The book was condemned, as would be any bookseller who continued to sell it twenty-four hours after notification. Indeed they were forbidden to sell any such books – 'French or Latin, large or small' – and the faculties of law, medicine and theology were assigned the task of examining new publications, even in grammar, for signs of heresy. By a parlementary *arrêt* of 14 February 1543 books of Erasmus and Melanchthon as well as Luther and Calvin were ordered to be burnt in front of Nôtre Dame at the sound not only of trumpets but of the great bell of the cathedral.[72] The culmination of this campaign came the next year with the publication of the Sorbonne's *Catalogue of Censured Books*, which, in its successive versions, constituted a sort of best-seller list of Protestant literature. Among the works of 'evil doctrine' were included not only known heretics but also Rabelais and Dolet and, in later expanded editions, the New Testament of Robert Estienne.[73]

[69] P. Feret, *La Faculté de théologie de Paris*, I (Paris, 1900), 100ff.
[70] See above, p. 238, n. 58.
[71] *Ordonnances faictes par la court de Parlement contre les livres contenantz doctrines nouvelles et heretiques et aussi touchant le faict et estat des libraires et Imprimeurs. Publiees a son des trompes par les carrefours de la ville de Paris*, 1 July 1542 (Harvard and BN F.35149).
[72] *Argentré*, II, 134ff.
[73] *Edict faict par le Roy tres chrestien Henry, deuxieme de ce nom. Sur les livres censurés par la Faculté de theologie de Paris* (Paris, 19 Dec. 1547; BN F. 46804.15); in Isambert, XIII, 34.

These efforts to manage public opinion were not limited to direct censorship, of course; they were part of a more general attempt to establish control over the flourishing industry. This was carried out through a stream of legislation prescribing rules for master printers and workers as it did for all guilds.[74] In general the purpose was to maintain standards of literary merchandise and to make publishers responsible for their products. From 1539 printers were prohibited from issuing anonymous or pseudonymous books, and from 1537 they were to send copies to be deposited in the royal library in Blois. Except for edicts, books were to be sold only in the university quarter. The famous Edict of Chateaubriand of 1551 required printers to keep the original manuscripts and to display on each printed book their own true name.[75] Such legislation also covered problems of defamation and blasphemy and so reinforced practices of censorship. Of course it was largely in vain. The *Chambre ardente* was more successful in publicizing than in suppressing heretical literature, and the Edict of 1551, which tried to stem the flow of emigration as well as the influx of foreign books, admitted as much: 'These errors have become a plague so contagious that they have contaminated many towns and territories of our kingdom, including even children.' Ideological ferment was becoming a social problem due in part to the book trade.

Contemporaneously, the printing business was experiencing its own difficulties, and while these were certainly not independent of religious ferment, the precise connections are not always discernible.[76] The main problem stemmed from the increasingly unmanageable force of apprentices, colporteurs and lower forms of labor; and these too became the object of legislative attention.[77] From 1539 the master printers of Paris and Lyon were confronted by strikes (*trics*) by workers discontented over low wages and slow (or no) advancement. Two years later Francis I issued an edict forbidding such behavior and even assemblies of more than five men. In labor troubles throughout the century printing-workers were found, or suspected, to be in alliance with vagrants, beggars and worse. Unlicensed colporteurs were widely regarded as thieves, drunkards and 'seducers of girls', and their religious and political opinions were distrusted accordingly.[78] To establish some control, later legislation

[74] *Conference des statuts accordez par le Roy a la communauté des imprimeurs et libraires de Paris* (Paris, 1684).

[75] See above, p. 200, n. 57.

[76] Mellottée, *Histoire économique de l'imprimerie*, P. Chauvet, *Les Ouvriers du livre* (Paris, 1959), and H. Hauser, *Les Ouvriers du temps passé* (Paris, 1927).

[77] *Code de la Librairie*, 161ff.

[78] P. Brochon, *Le Livre de colportage en France* (Paris, 1954), 12; G. Moreau, 'Un Colporteur Calviniste en 1563', in *BSHPF*, cxviii (1973), 1–31; Pithou, 10.

demanded that these men be apprenticed and possess a minimum standard of literacy, while blasphemers and other recalcitrants could be fired immediately.

Protestants did not deny the ideological threat of printing, and indeed the Huguenot historian D'Aubigné pointed with pride to 'the great quantity of books circulated by the constancy of martyrs'.[79] Printers were always getting into trouble. At least a dozen were executed in France in the course of the century, and of course many more suffered lesser penalties or went into exile. One victim was the Parisian printer Martin Lhommet, who was involved in the very first wave of Huguenot propaganda in the wake of the conspiracy of Amboise in the summer of 1560. While investigating a murder, it seems, Parisian police entered his house and came across certain anti-Guise writings that had been circulated in the city, including the notorious attack on the Cardinal of Lorraine, the *Tiger of France*, later recognized as the work of François Hotman. A month later Lhommet was executed at one of the customary sites, the Place Maubert in the university quarter.[80] There were other such incidents – three colporteurs suffered similar fates in Lyon in these years, for instance – and they continued into the larger-scale violence of the civil wars. So of course did legislative attempts to control the press. Indeed this battle of books became more general because of the growing need of the government to protect itself against contraband literature from foreign centers. Books from Geneva in particular were banned from 1548 but not very effectively. Confiscations and book-burning all through the 1560s could not, any more than censorship, stem the flow of propaganda.

This overall pattern was repeated in various parts of Europe, not only in Catholic areas like the Empire and Savoy, but also in Protestant principalities and cities. In reformed Geneva, for example, the first 'Edict of Printers' was announced 'with sound of trumpet' in May 1539; and the city council was likewise severe in its judgment of alien literature.[81] Among the banned works were those of 'libertines' like Rabelais and Poggio as well as 'papist' productions like the edict published in Savoy calling Geneva a 'den of heretics'. In contrast to France, however, permits to publish were sometimes made only with the proviso that the name of the city and perhaps of the author also did *not* appear. So it was with some of the propaganda produced for the Prince of Condé at the outset of the religious

[79] *Histoire universelle* (Paris, 1616–20), II, 338.   [80] Kelley, *Hotman*, 112.
[81] A. Cartier, 'Arrêts du Conseil de Genève sur le fait de l'imprimerie et de la librairie de 1541 à 1550', *Mémoires et documents publiés par la Société d'histoire et d'archéologie de Genève*, XXIII (1888–94), 361–566; Chaix, *Recherches*, 19.

wars. In any case printing without a license was forbidden. The standards of the city fathers were so high, or rather the caution of the council was so great, that even Calvinist propaganda, such as Beza's *Right of Magistrates*, was at times denied permission to be published, and at one crucial point copies of Hotman's *Francogallia* were confiscated. In the case of politically inflammatory books like Beza's and like the *Reveille-Matin* (which was printed in Geneva, but only surreptitiously), it was not the actual publication that worried city authorities but taking the responsibility.[82] In a sense, then, Geneva was part of the clandestine press that grew up in the early sixteenth century, though within its own territories the government acted as carefully and as selfishly as any other.

The coming of the wars of religion did not change but it intensified and regularized efforts of censorship in France. The distribution of placards which had stirred up so much trouble a generation before was still a central issue, and the circulation of propaganda accompanying the conspiracy was itself denounced as a major cause of the sedition. The Edict of Romorantin of May 1560 condemned not only unlicensed preachers but also 'placards, broadsheets and defamatory books, which can only stir people to sedition, and also printers, sellers and distributors thereof, who are enemies of us and of public repose and guilty of lese-majesty . . .'.[83] In the first month of the civil war the Huguenots were still exhibiting their placards, Catholics publishing counter-statements and receiving replies, and so on – *ad bellum*. After the first war, censorship was tightened up. No book, poetry or prose, could be published without a 'privilege' from the Parlement and a permission from the chancellor, and two of the twenty-four *libraries jurés* were appointed inspectors. But of course such self-regulation did not work either. No more than the civil wars themselves could the battle of books be legislated to an end: pamphlet and sword continued to be brandished together, and the toll of the victims of each continued to mount for another generation.

PATTERNS OF PROPAGANDA

'Propaganda' is a sixteenth-century concept and term (*propaganda fidei*) and a conspicuous product of print culture. In the years after St Bartholomew Pope Gregory XIII convened at various times a 'Commission for the Propagation of the Faith', a gathering that was

---

[82] See below, pp. 301–5; Bremme, *Buchdrucker*, 85.
[83] *Edict du roy sur la residence des evesques*, May 1560 (BN F. 46819.16; LN 193–4); in Isambert, xiv, 27.

institutionalized a half-century later by a bull of Clement VIII, establishing 'The Sacred Congregation for the Propagation of the Faith'. In many ways of course this Counter-Reformation creation emerged very directly in relation to the 'propagations' of Lutheran, Calvinist and other confessions whose dissemination seemed to threaten the unity of Christendom. Modern patterns and techniques of printed propaganda have been in very large measure the product, or at least the by-product, of these ideological wars. The fact that the particular doctrinal context of this early phase of modern propaganda was religious should not blind us to its secular and in some ways global implications. In various ways it fulfilled the requirements which Jacques Ellul has suggested for modern 'total' propaganda: it operated in both a 'horizontal' and a 'vertical' fashion, that is, on the levels both of leadership and of followership; it was not only political but also social, that is, arising not only from political direction but also from social situations and institutional arrangements; it involved not only verbal intimidation but also social agitation; and finally it involved a theory of persuasion that included irrational as well as rational factors.[84] If metaphysics is the ghost of dead theologies, as Auguste Comte suggested, then secular ideologies may well be regarded as the ghosts of dead religious enthusiasms, at least in terms of the patterns of propaganda.

In the sixteenth century the 'roads to heresy' were many and, from a distance of so many generations and cultural changes, difficult for modern observers to uncover and to retrace. This is especially the case with oral modes of communication, but it holds as well for the printed word. Every species of religious discourse from the prayer to the great colloquy contributed to published propaganda, but literature of a more ephemeral type on a lower level of distribution cannot be so directly assessed. Broadsheets, some illustrated, calendars, minor treatises on various sacraments and stray sermons that happen to have survived reflect a process of 'horizontal' propagandizing that for the most part must remain forever obscure.[85] So too with much popular literature, musical and dramatic, that has long since vanished. What the printed book accomplished in general was to project onto a much larger screen a great variety of oral and scribal traditions and modes of discourse: catechisms and confessions of faith, plays, poems, popular songs

---

[84] *Propagande*, trans. K. Kellen (New York, 1965), a trans. of *Les Propagandes*; cf. J. Drirencourt, *La Propagande, nouvelle force politique* (Paris, 1950). Again, most works on this subject pay little if any attention to earlier centuries.

[85] Droz, *Chemins*, and *Aspects*; Latimer (see above, p. 235, n. 50) suggests an interesting, though not exhaustive, typology for French pamphlets.

and proverbs; sermons, harangues and lectures; treatises, textbooks, handbooks and polemics; histories, hagiographies and martyrologies; accounts of great spectacles, conferences and interrogations – not to speak of caricatures, cartoons, 'comic strips' and a whole world of pictorial propaganda which (if only because of the lack of visual aids) cannot be discussed here. These and untold new forms of propaganda gave visual and emotional shape to public opinion on religious and political matters – and of course material for the busy pens and presses of the new printing intelligentsia.

Under the classification of religious propaganda the earliest pamphlets circulating in France were miscellaneous, devotional, often translations or paraphrases of German or Swiss publications, and many, if printed at all, have not survived except as garbled titles in lists of works seized by authorities. The tone ranged from the most quietistic and mystical to the most intransigent and aggressive. On the one hand there were Biblical commentaries, celebrations of 'Christian liberty' and the requirements of conscience, and instructions (by Erasmus, Farel and others) on 'How to Confess'; on the other hand, provocative assaults on the enemies of the faith – papists, Sorbonists and other delegates of the antichrist.[86] Exiles like Lambert, De Coct and Farel in particular adopted the radical evangelical rhetoric popularized by Luther, which in France culminated in the inflammatory placards of 1534.

From the beginning humor was an effective weapon of the 'new iconoclasts', more effective, perhaps, than expressions of outrage and literary temper tantrums. The sarcasm and humor associated with the style of Erasmus, Sebastian Brant and the 'obscure men' and Pierre Gringoire were reflected in lesser known works, such as the anonymous 'Dialogue of an Abbot, a Courtier and the Devil'. The satirical style of attack, though not part of Calvin's own armory, was employed by Beza, most notably in a youthful work ridiculing the notorious Lizet, who retired from a career in the Parlement to an abbacy and – perhaps at the instigation of the Catholic publisher Jean André, later a pamphleteer himself – dedicated himself to libelling those of the religion. Besides Lizet himself and his nose (red as the cardinal's hat he coveted and the rosé wine he drank to excess) Beza continued the assault on the 'latrine' of canon law in terms worthy of Rabelais himself (though Beza would not have appreciated the comparison).[87] During the wars the satirical style was continued, perhaps most famously in the *Satyre Menippée* composed by a

---

[86] Feret, *La Faculté de théologie de Paris*, I, 116; cf. Besson, *L'Eglise et l'imprimerie de Lausanne*, II, 247.
[87] *Le Passavant*, trans. I. Liseaux (Paris, 1875), 11, 106.

number of humanists and lawyers. A related popular genre was the pseudograph, such as the pretended 'Confession of Beda' and Melanchthon's parody of the Sorbonne's 'Determinatío' against Luther, in which it appeared that Mary was superior to God Himself and that canon law and all the popes were heretical. Later in the century such fabrications became more malicious and incriminating, as Huguenots began to attribute to their enemies terrible plans of 'extermination'. In a sense *ad hominem* attacks have always been the front line offensive of propaganda, and certainly the position of Luther insured that this should hold true for his and following generations. In this age of eponymous '-isms' and 'anti-isms' personality seemed to overshadow doctrine, not only in biographical approaches like that of Cochlaeus but also in works laying claim to theological or historical scholarship. Ideas were always targets, but symbols seemed always to be needed to define and to give public visibility to these ideas. In France no really effective symbol of popery was found until the late 1550s, when the Cardinal of Lorraine emerged to claim the principal villain's role, unchallenged until Catherine de Médicis's uncertain public image became sufficiently blackened in Huguenot eyes. The 'tiger of France' and the 'whore' were only two of a number of black legends created in this golden age of libel and vilification. Their reputations, in the process of formation on the eve of the wars, reached their high point a decade later, for example in the 'Legend of the Cardinal of Lorraine' of 1568 and especially in Henri Estienne's polemical biography of Catherine appearing in the wake of St Bartholomew.[88] In the Netherlands the Duke of Alba served as surrogate villain, and only in the 1580s did Philip II himself become a primary target.[89]

Probably the most characteristic mode of early modern propaganda even in religious controversies was the historical. In publicity as in pedagogy the rejection of the old (and the construction of the new) tradition was an item of first priority for Luther and other evangelical reformers. It was a conspicuous theme in Calvin's *Institutes* from the 1543 edition on and in the work of his followers, especially of Hotman and Baudouin. It was evident also in the official histories, including the *Magdeburg Centuries* of Flacius Illyricus and his Lutheran colleagues, the contemporary Lutheran 'court history' by Johann Sleidan and the *Ecclesiastical History* of the French Reformation supervised by Beza. Yet in the Protestant reconstruction of

---

[88] See below, p. 292, n. 96, and in general J. R. Armogathe, *Les Vies de Calvin au XVIe et XVIIe siècles*, in *Historiographie de la Réforme*, ed. P. Joutard (Paris, 1977), 45–59, and G. P. Wolf, *Das Neue französische Lutherbild* (Wiesbaden, 1974).
[89] P. A. Geurts, *De nederlandse Opstand in Pamfletten 1566–1580* (Nijmegen, 1956).

history individual personality continued to figure prominently, as indeed evangelical religious psychology seemed to require. So there was a massive search not only for heroic figures of the past (notable heretics as well as early fathers), as in Flacius's comprehensive *Catalogue of the Witnesses of the Truth*, but also in the systematic recording of the victims of 'false religion', especially Bullinger's inventory of the 'origin of errors' that had plagued true religion. The great martyrological enterprise inaugurated around mid-century by Crespin, Foxe and other members of the international Protestant community, served not only as a memorial to these victims but also as one of the most effective agents of pedagogy and propaganda.[90]

Beyond the partisan reconstruction of a plausible evangelical tradition, historical propaganda of course had other more journalistic functions to perform. Some pamphlets were devoted to simple reporting in the style of accounts of major events, usually military, such as Volcyr's celebration of the victory over the rampaging peasants of 1525, or Crespin's account of the massacres at Mérindole and Cabrières.[91] There also continued to be poetic versions of prosaic narratives, such as the 'Acts of the Colloquy of Poissy' and Hotman's 'Tiger of France'. Other pamphlets were more analytical, explanatory and concerned with the assigning of praise and blame. In the early stages of conflict there were many pieces of propaganda devoted to rehearsing the 'causes' of one problem or another, perhaps the whole Huguenot predicament in the reign of Francis II, and finally the wars themselves. 'Histories' of the execution of Du Bourg, of the conspiracy of Amboise, of the tumult of St Médard, of the massacre of Vassy and of other newsworthy events preceded, and in various ways went into the making of, the larger historical syntheses by La Place, La Popelinière, and others, which themselves constituted propaganda on a higher level.[92] It was above all in such works that broader questions of moral responsibility, war guilt and premeditation were exposed and debated.

Direct and more generalized confrontation of such issues became increasingly common with the approach of armed conflict. As problems of legitimacy and authority, or conversely illegitimacy and tyranny, became unavoidable, the importance of the lawyers be-

[90] See P. Polman, *L'Elément historique dans la controverse religieuse du XVIe siècle* (Gembloux, 1932), and S. Bertelli, *Ribelli, libertini e ortodossi nella storiografia barocca* (Florence, 1973). See above, p. 158, n. 45.

[91] Nicole Volcyr, *L'Histoire et recueil de la triumphante et glorieuse victoire obtenue contre les seduyctz et abusez Lutheriens mescreans du pays daussays* (Paris, 1526), and Crespin, *Histoire memorable de la persecution et saccagement du peuple de Merindole et Cabriers* ([Geneva], 1556).

[92] See Hauser.

came more and more obvious; and with the posing of the 'political question' in the summer of 1559, as we have seen, the need for professional legitimizing became pressing. From this time on legal forms became increasingly important in comparison to theological. The shift was a general one, but in concrete terms it is neatly illustrated in the work of Hotman, who was one of the most active of all lawyer-propagandists during the civil wars. One of his youthful works, the first to be published in his Genevan exile (in 1551), was a little essay on *The State of the Primitive Church*, a typical ecclesiastical utopia based on the Protestant vision as expressed especially in Calvin's *Institutes*.[93] Almost a generation later Hotman published an analogous treatise on the 'primitive constitution' of the French nation, for his *Francogallia* (1573) was indeed a kind of political transmutation of one of the central myths of evangelical religion – as well as a more systematic realization of the political propaganda which Hotman, among others, had begun to fashion on the eve of the civil wars.

From 1560 the flood of propaganda began, and it would be published not in the guise of satires or religious protests but rather of moral and legal pleas and demands – 'requests', 'supplications', 'remonstrances', 'counsels', 'complaints', 'exhortations', 'warnings' (*advertisements*), 'harangues', 'declarations', and, endlessly, 'responses' to all the above and to other responses. On the other side came, besides publications, in French and Latin, of papal pronouncements relating to the Council of Trent, the official declarations, edicts, ordinances and letters which in general represented a monarchy vacillating between the partisan policy of the Guises and an old fashioned Gallicanism that emerged from time to time to appeal to national sentiment.[94] In 1562, after a year of peace-making efforts, the mutual suspicions became overwhelming; and in March the 'massacre of Vassy' confirmed Huguenot fears of conspiracy. From April on they began to issue their own counter-legislation, that is, legal justifications devised by Condé's counsellors for the benefit of the rulers of Europe as well as for the pamphlet-reading public, however extensive this may have been. Within a few weeks during the summer of that year a dozen or more official letters and declarations were published from the headquarters in Orleans. Certain German *Zeitungen* reported from the same source on the

---

[93] *De Statu primitivae ecclesiae* . . . (Geneva, 1553), and see below, pp. 293 and 308.

[94] E. de Barthélemy, *Recueil des Plaquettes historiques champenoises du XVIe siècle* (Paris, 1885); Beaupré, *Pamphlets pour et contre les Guises* (n.p., 1865). In consulting *CHF* the *Supplement* should not be overlooked, especially for German translations; and cf. Emil Weller, *Die ersten deutschen Zeitungen* (Stuttgart, 1872).

plight of the 'Calvinists'. As so often before, all this publicity was further amplified by more poetic expressions of defiance and of Huguenot party unity.

So the opposition press in France came out of hiding. A major figure in this journalistic phenomenon was Eloi Gibier, whose career up to the advent of the civil wars was unremarkably representative of orthodox French publishing.[95] In 1536 he established, or re-established, the art of printing in Orleans, and among his various products were a sermon of the ultra-Catholic Gentien Hervet, a laudatory account of Henry II, an oration of one of his ambassadors, a collection of customs and various royal edicts and parlementary *arrêts*. On the record the first sign of unorthodoxy was the publication of a work by Calvin's old secretary Nicolas des Gallars in 1556 and five years later the rousing oration, favorable to the Huguenots, given at the Estates General of Orleans by Jean Lange, representative of the Third Estate. On the eve of the wars Gibier also printed two pieces of legislation purporting to curb religious debate and releasing Huguenot prisoners. When Orleans became the Huguenot headquarters in the summer of 1562, however, it was his press, in collaboration with that of Robert Estienne in Geneva, that began to pour out Condé's propaganda. Whether or not Gibier's activities were the product of ideological commitment in any significant way is doubtful, since a few years later he resumed publishing official material for the government. For the process of propagandizing this consideration is perhaps not too important; the fact is that propaganda was not only an aspect of party behavior, it was also a thriving (if not necessarily profitable) business.

Another Protestant publisher who illustrates the shift from religious to political propaganda was Barthélemy Berton, who operated from La Rochelle.[96] During the early stages of the religious wars his publications were confined mostly to devotional literature, a volume of prayers and a treatise on the Protestant view of the sacraments, for example, and an edition of Marot's translation of the Psalms; but after the first war he became increasingly involved in more material issues. In 1565 he issued the first substantial historical review of the background of the civil wars, the *Commentaries* of President Pierre de la Place, later to be one of the victims of St Bartholomew. No less interesting, he published in 1568 the first of two 'protestations' of the Huguenots of La Rochelle against Catholic aggression. This and other pieces of Protestant propaganda he sent out with the false

[95] L. Desgraves, *Eloi Gibier, Imprimeur à Orleans (1536–1588)* (Geneva, 1966).
[96] E. Droz, *L'Imprimerie à la Rochelle*, I (Geneva, 1960), 63.

imprint of 'William Hopper, in Heidelberg'. After 1572 such fictive names and addresses would become increasingly common, to the confusion more of later historians, probably, than of contemporaries.

This propaganda – this unprecedented political dialectic of legislation and counter-legislation – demonstrated that the French press, like the legal profession, the academy, the religious community, in some respects the family and in some cases individual souls, was seriously divided. And after a decade of sporadic fighting, three wars and corresponding political exchanges, the division became worse. New extremes of internationalization as well as polarization were also reached, as French debates became entangled in the 'paper war' of the Netherlands. William of Orange rivalled the Prince of Condé as a symbol of Protestant heroism, as the Duke of Alba rivalled the late Duke of Guise as the embodiment of 'tyranny' (such was the message of a certain *Neue tyrannische Zeitung* devoted to Philip II's champion in the struggle against Dutch Protestants).[97] In terms of political journalism if not of the realities of power politics the culmination of these controversies came in the wake of the massacre of St Bartholomew. If the year 1562 marked the first threshold, the year 1572 marked the point at which modern political propaganda came of age.[98]

The significance of print culture has been treated all too briefly and selectively, but of course it has been implied repeatedly in discussions of other aspects of the phenomenon of ideology. For historical investigation the printed page remains the principal medium not only for the communication of information and testimony but also for direct visual contact with bygone ages, although even on this physical level its significance must be mostly speculative. Nevertheless, an effort must be made to interpret on its basis some of the larger configurations of ideological behavior and some of the longer-range consequences. It is time now to turn to the less accessible questions of the mobilization of consciences for action and the realization of an ideological program, that is, to that militant community of mutual interests which constitutes, in however primitive a form, the political party.

[97] Weller, *Zeitungen*, 334, 258ff., *passim*.
[98] On the later period D. Pallier, *Recherches sur l'imprimerie à Paris pendant la ligue* (Geneva, 1975), and A. Soman, 'Press, pulpit and censorship in France before Richelieu', *Proceedings of the American Philosophical Society*, cxx (1976), 439–63.

VII · Party:
Defending the cause

Martyres veros non facit poena, sed causa.

Augustine

Caussae? Nihil aliud respondebant, quam
C'est pour faire un bon coup.

Pierre Charpentier

VII · Party: Defending the cause

APOLOGUE: THE PRINCE OF CONDÉ MAKES A PACT (1562)

On Wednesday 2 April 1562, the Huguenot leader Louis de Bourbon, Prince de Condé, set up headquarters in the city of Orleans. A week earlier he had left Paris, in fact the day after Palm Sunday, when Beza preached a belligerent sermon in the face of growing Catholic hostility. During Easter week he led the Huguenot march south to the accompaniment as usual of psalm-singing. By mid-April some 3000 men had assembled from all parts of France, including members of the highest nobility, and by June the number had grown to more than 20,000. So the social base of Huguenot ideology was gathering itself into a fighting force and indeed, to judge by the propaganda already flooding off the Protestant presses, a political unit. The party was formed; all it needed was a platform, and Condé's publicists constructed this with great haste out of ready-made materials.

It was on 8 April that the first formal declaration was issued.[1] 'Those who take up arms first by their private authority should give reasons for their actions', this pamphlet begins, 'and so the Prince of Condé, faced with so many different judgments in the present commotion and with the need to provide a certain and prompt remedy for the common good, desires, in order to prevent any calumnies, to declare the reasons which have moved him to proceed, along with relatives, friends and servants, to the aid of the king, queen and the whole kingdom in its present need.' The troubles arose out of the religious situation (*le faict de la religion*), the manifesto continued, and specifically from the failure to enforce the liberal edict of the previous January, published throughout all France. Following this had come the immediate precipitant of the present confrontation, which was the massacre at Vassy charged to

---

[1] *Declaration faicte par monsieur le prince de Condé, pour monstre les raisons que l'ont contrainct d'entreprendre la defense de l'authorité du roy, du gouvernement de la royne, et du repos de ce royaume* ([Orleans], 1562; BN Lb33. 64 *et al.*; LN 261); also in *MC*, III, 222ff., and in BN Lb33.49–50, which represents the first version of *MC*, according to Hauser.

the Duke of Guise, who had added fuel to the fires in Paris by entering the city in violation of the king's command. Rumor had it that the Duke was planning 'to exterminate all those belonging to what was called the new religion', and if nothing else, self-defense (*vim vi repellere licet* was the legal formula) justified the present action.

Following this declaration of intent came Condé's specific legal case, his 'Protestation'. This carefully designed brief argued, first, that the Prince was indulging no private interest (*passion particuliere*) but wanted only what was due to God and to the French crown; second, that the enemies of the crown were depleting the resources of the 'poor people'; third, that he acknowledged the seniority of his brother the King of Navarre; and finally, that he was acting out of complete loyalty toward the King and Queen Mother of France. Here we have stated in the most urgent and concrete situation some of the fundamental themes of propaganda over the next decade. Above all was the insistence on the legality of the Huguenot position. Condé was no innovator, certainly no revolutionary, and was operating within the institutional structure of the monarchy and through proper channels, including the order of peers. The 'tyranny' he opposed was not that of the king but rather his evil – foreign and selfish – advisers from Lorraine, who were exploiting the manhood as well as the wealth of the kingdom. Ultimately it was to the welfare of the kingdom, *pro bono publico*, that Condé was dedicating his life and his honor.

Three days later (11 April) Condé gave further legitimacy to these ideals by a feudal-sounding sort of social compact. This was the famous 'Treaty of Association' made by Condé with his immediate followers: ten 'chevaliers' besides himself, including Admiral Coligny and D'Andelot, and 62 lesser 'gentlemen', including the man responsible for Henry II's death, Montgomery.[2] But this compact extended beyond this feudal elite and included, as the text proclaimed, members of 'all estates'. It was furthermore in accord not only with conscience and true religion but also with the 'liberty' of the king and the peace of the kingdom. A similar stand would shortly be taken in the Netherlands by a group of 'allied gentlemen' (*gentilshomme confederez*) under the aegis of

---

[2] *Traité d'association* . . . ([Orleans], 1562; Lb^{33}.66 and 50; LN 271), in *MC*, III, 258; and published with signatories in Beza, *Correspondance*, IV, Appendix VIII. Bordier, 212:

> Sus donc, hommes pleins de vaillance!
> Faisons une sainte alliance
> Obligeons nostre pure foy
> A deffendre de Dieu la loy . . .
> Une cause plus juste et sainte
> Et une bien prudente crainte
> Nous font en cest accord.

William of Orange.[3] This idea of associating liberty and legitimacy with a compact would also be a fundamental theme of later propaganda, indeed of political theory in general; and as usual it would be celebrated in poetry as well as prose:

> Rise up, valiant men, and form a holy alliance.
> Let's defend our faith and offer a holy defiance . . .
> We fight not for gain; we fight because we must,
> Our reason is survival, and our cause is surely just.

The other party to the debate, official and unofficial spokesmen for the government, responded in similar time-honored and usually predictable terms.[4] Besides personal attacks on Condé, Coligny and lesser figures, there were the standard counter-arguments that the opposition was demanding not liberty but license and that they were guilty of sedition, rebellion and lese-majesty. Aside from 'liberty of conscience', in fact, most of the colorful and agitating terms of modern political vocabulary were given currency by established powers, while opposition movements were often reduced to denying their application. It was in these debates, nevertheless, that the terminology of modern revolutionary and reactionary discourse, and to some extent behavior, was established.

Condé stood for constitutional opposition, but the basis of his movement was much broader than the neo-feudal interests of his immediate following. 'The Cause', as this movement came to be called, depended more specifically for its coherence and endurance on its evangelical foundation. For years there had been talk about the 'Calvinist cause', and it was the convergence of this confessional group with men who were politically alienated – the 'Huguenots of religion', in the words of Pierre de la Place, and the 'Huguenots of state' – that produced the opposition party.[5] The origin of the term 'Huguenot' has been long debated. The consensus is that it derives from the word for the resisting Swiss confederates (*Eidgenossen*), but it seems to have emerged during the conspiracy of Amboise, and opponents of the 'foreign' house of Guise construed it as designating their allegiance to the descendants of the royal dynasty of

---

[3] P. A. Geurts, *De nederlandse Opstand in Pamfletten 1566–1580* (Nijmegen, 1956), and cf. *Advertence a tous les inhabitans des Provinces du Pays bas, estantz uniz et confederez pour la deffence de la liberté de leur Religion, personnes, Privileges, et anciennes coustumes, contre la tyrannie des Espagnolz, et leurs adherans* (n.p., 1583; BM 873. g. 26).

[4] MC, III, 271, letters from the Parlement to Condé.

[5] La Place, *Commentaires de l'estat de religion et republique*, in J. Buchon (ed.), *Choix de chroniques et mémoires* (Paris, 1836), 41. Pithou, 21, assigns this term to 1555, but his work was composed later.

'Hughes' Capet. In any case the evangelical movement provided both the ideological incentive and the social base for this party, though its origins were quite separate and its goals not in every way reconcilable. Nevertheless the common ground between the two was substantial enough to keep French society in turmoil for a generation and more.

The transformation of an evangelical movement centering on the charismatic person of Calvin into an international political organization is a dramatic story, an ideological epic whose ostensibly bookish theme, the career of the gospel in the sixteenth century, appears most conspicuously in the mass of printed propaganda generated by opponents, partisans and non-partisans alike. One of the central political issues was posed by Calvin himself at the very beginning of his mission. Charges had been made, he acknowledged in the preface to his *Institutes*, of the 'many disturbances, tumults and contentions the preaching of our doctrine has drawn along with it . . .'. Although Calvin went on to deny these accusations, his and his comrades' reputation for trouble-making continued to grow, and indeed much of the history of his doctrine can be expressed in terms of a series of duels and larger-scale combats. Alciato, Budé, Sadoleto, Castellio, Bolsec, Servetus, Baudouin, various Lutheran and Zwinglian theologians – these and others came under fire from Calvin in the process of forming his opinions, of defining and purging his doctrine, of answering criticism and creating greater coherence among his followers. The mass, baptism, the trinity, astrology, predestination, the problem of tradition, the right of magistrates to punish heresy and of the faithful to resist tyranny – these and other issues inspired him, as well as disciples and enemies, to add to the outpouring of polemic and propaganda in the middle years of the century. Indeed Calvin's image as an agitator and trouble-maker was lamented by fellow Protestants, especially Lutherans, more than by Catholics. 'As is proved by many examples', remarked Christoph von Württemberg, leader of the ultra-Lutherans, 'Calvinism is seditious in spirit, and wherever it enters it is determined to usurp dominion, even over magistrates.'[6]

Internally, on the other hand, 'Calvinismus' – 'Calvinolatry' in Baudouin's term – seemed rigid and dogmatic in the extreme, at least to outsiders. Nor did Calvin try to disguise his passion for order and discipline. Throughout his evangelical career he attacked not only papists and outright hypocrites, 'nicodemites', but also Erasmians and moderate Lutherans, such as supporters of the 'adultero-German Interim' and all of the irenic 'temporizers' and 'media-

---

[6] A. Kluckhohn (ed.), *Briefe Friedrichs des Frommen*, I (Braunschweig, 1868), 271.

tors' (*moderatores; moyenneurs*), as if compromise were on principle a cardinal sin.[7] Baudouin was the worst of these false pacifiers, as his consorting with Lutherans and final defection to Catholicism seemed to demonstrate; indeed he ended up attending the Council of Trent with the Cardinal of Lorraine. As it was put increasingly on the defensive, not only in France but also in Geneva, where it was continually threatened by the house of Savoy, Calvinism adopted an increasingly hard line. The cliquishness of Calvinist rhetoric – the exclusiveness of the confessional 'we' and 'our' – reflected an ideological narrowing as well as proselytizing zeal, and the printed propaganda issuing from Geneva and other centers magnified both tendencies.

The 'Calvinist cause' from the start was both proselytizing and, at least by implication and certainly in the eyes of critics, political. Not only Calvin and younger disciples but elder colleagues like Farel and Viret and sometime friends like Bucer and Bullinger were committed to promoting their faith and publicizing it on a universal scale. Their disciples were all taught to take the offensive: to assert, to answer objections, to criticize errors, to identify and to attack the enemy. Ideally every evangelical was a catechizer, a preacher, a missionary. The pattern of Lutheran propagandizing was duplicated and organized on a larger scale. At the same time there was, in the context of public opinion, a perceptible shift of emphasis from spiritual and individual ideals to worldly and social goals, from the 'pure word of God' to the secular interests of the congregation. Among the factors involved in this shift were the emergence of a new generation that, while looking to Calvin for moral leadership, faced rather different practical problems; the expanding role of publicity and counter-publicity; the infiltration of evangelical ideas into the higher levels of the nobility as well as the intelligentsia; the growing importance of lawyers (over theologians) as spokesmen on social and political issues; and especially the increasingly painful dilemma of irreconcilable religious differences in a society which could tolerate these neither on theological nor on institutional grounds. The result was what has been referred to in several contexts as the 'politicization of Protestantism'.[8]

The Calvinist community itself had certain political experiences that contributed to their attitudes toward authority. At the Academy of

---

[7] *Response a un certain moyenneur ruse*, translation of Calvin's attack on Baudouin in 1562, in *Opuscules* (Geneva, 1567), 1185; cf. D. R. Kelley, *François Hotman: A Revolutionary's Ordeal* (Princeton, 1973), 141ff.

[8] R. Nürnberger, *Die Politisierung des französischen Protestantismus* (Tübingen, 1948), V. de Caprariis, *Propaganda e pensiero politico in Francia durante le guerre di religione* (Naples, 1959), and the works of R. Kingdon cited earlier, *Geneva and the Coming of the Wars of Religion in France* and *Geneva and the French Protestant Movement*.

Lausanne there was conflict with the Council of Bern, and Viret in particular responded angrily to the Zwinglian 'tyranny'. The 'revolutionary innuendos' of some of his writings, it has been suggested, influenced his two younger colleagues, Beza and Hotman; and certainly these early controversies of the 1540s contributed to the general view of resistance that was being generated.[9] The same issue of 'liberty of conscience', and specifically of teaching, arose a little later in Strasbourg; and again the Calvinist community, this time in opposition to the pressure of the ultra-Lutheran party, was forced to take a dissenting stand. Indeed that particular clash, in which Baudouin, Hotman and Sturm were involved, contributed very directly to the definition and coherence (as well as the alienation) of the Calvinist cause. To these experiences may be added, too, the ideas of resistance imported and developed by English Protestants fleeing from Marian persecutions and mingling with their French comrades in Strasbourg, Geneva and elsewhere. Evangelical migrations in general, especially from France to Geneva (some 10,000 in less than two years at mid-century), contributed to the dissolving of national ties and created conditions for the realization of these ideas.

Meanwhile, partisan propaganda continued to issue from the Protestant press, centered increasingly in Geneva. Militant Biblical texts, especially from the Psalms, could be and were easily turned to purposes of defiance of secular authority which, when ungodly, ceased being authoritative. Assaults on Roman institutions – materialist tradition – could be turned against more immediate intimidations from the Sorbonne, the Parlement of Paris and legislative expressions of royal will. Before the coming of the civil wars Calvin, Viret and others had also discussed the problem of resistance directly and seemed to be in general agreement about the way to frame the question, if not entirely about a definitive answer. Certainly it was one of the central questions of the age, a question on almost everyone's mind, especially during the constitutional crisis in France created in 1559. 'We are often asked', wrote Beza that fall, 'whether it is permitted to rise up against those who are enemies not only of religion but also of the realm.'[10] These discussions also contributed to Condé's program and to the alignment of religious and political motives, although the final formulation was, as we have seen, largely the work of lawyers. Such in any case were some of the main ingredients in the formation of one of the earliest approximations of that characteristic modern institution, the political party.

[9] R. Linder, *The Political Ideas of Pierre Viret* (Geneva, 1964), 129.
[10] Beza to Bullinger, 12 Sept. 1559, *Correspondance*, III, no. 150.

THE LINES ARE DRAWN

Ideological differences abounded in France in the 1550s, but the lines did not become hard and fast until the jousting accident that laid Henry II on his death bed in the summer of 1559. It was at this point that the neo-feudal conflict between the Guise faction and that of the house of Bourbon under Antoine of Navarre became a struggle for power centered upon the person of the fourteen-year-old Francis, which is really to say his 'second body', the body politic. When the king died and Francis succeeded, Antoine failed to act decisively; but the Cardinal of Lorraine and the Duke of Guise lost no time in assuming control of the government; and the imbalance in this old rivalry became the center of political attention for the next generation. At the same time religious divisions were intensified and became further politicized by an edict of the young king, the first of his reign, directing bishops to control all preaching in their dioceses, and especially through the continued imprisonment of Anne du Bourg and other *parlementaires* who had been charged in the Mercuriale assembled just a few days before Henry's death.[11] The situation was further agitated by an apparent crime wave, to which several other early pieces of legislation were directed. The events of the next three years produced not only one of the bloodiest conflicts in European history but also a major upsurge of political consciousness and action.

In the latter half of 1559 there was a certain amount of muted verbal opposition to the Guise rule or, as critics thought, usurpation. At the beginning of the reign two written appeals were made to Catherine de Médicis, which may have been printed, though copies have not survived. One, written by a former courtier signing himself 'D.V.', warned the Queen Mother of her enemies, including that 'snake of a Cardinal', and recommended to her 'evangelical truth' in general and Marot's translations of the Psalms in particular[12] The

---

[11] Ordonnances of 23 July, 18 Aug. and 26 Dec. ('reiteratives defenses') 1559 (BN F. 46817. 8, 11, 46818. 21); also banning 'illicit assemblies' 4, 13 and ? Nov. (BN F. 46818. 5, 10, 12), and summoning *gendarmerie* 14 Nov. 1559, 10 Dec. and 8 Jan. 1560 (BN F. 46818. 11, 13, 46819. 1) and later acts concerning the affair of Amboise (LN 132, 135, 139, 140, 145, 146, 151). In general see L. Romier, *La Conjuration d'Amboise* (Paris, 1923), Kelley, *Hotman*, 105ff.; and especially H. Naef, *La Conjuration d'Amboise et Genève* (Geneva, 1922).

[12] *Epistre envoyee a la Royne Mere du Roy . . . En laquelle est sommairement respondu a calomnies on a par cy devant charge malicieusement ceux qui font profession de l'Evangile* (n.p., 1561; Lb32.6), in MC, II, 561, and (published?) *Coppie des lettres envoyees a la Royne Mere par un sien serviteur apres la mort du feu Roy Henri II*, '26 Aug. 1559', in MC II, 531–44.

other was a letter by an evangelical defending 'nostre cause' and a Calvinist confession setting down more specific demands: revocation of the edicts giving bishops secular authority, release of the *parlementaire* prisoners and, in general, freedom of worship, which was being attacked daily in orthodox sermons. The other main theme of Protestant propaganda was the affair of Du Bourg, an emotional issue which assumed legendary quality in the 'True History' and other pamphlet accounts of this martyr's prideful refusal to abjure his faith or even to moderate his language against the 'tyranny' of his enemies, 'miserable vermine' and 'thugs of antichrist' that they were.[13]

While some men were writing and talking, others were planning and acting. In these same months a real conspiracy was being hatched; and this underground movement, with all its attendant confusion and consequences, was to be crucial in the explosion of propaganda in the latter part of the century. The Conspiracy of Amboise, too, acquired the status of a legend and possesses some of the same difficulties of reconstruction. In the absence of a qualified chief, which is to say a prince of the blood, a discontented exile named La Renaudie devoted himself to assembling a force of men to depose the Guises and to 'liberate' the king. Although the plan itself, which came to a head in March 1560, was a dreadful fiasco, the ideological repercussions were immeasurable and, to the extent that they contributed to fundamental issues and trains of thought underlying much of modern political thought, unending. Some of the accompanying propaganda may have been carried by the conspirators themselves before the abortive assault on the château of Amboise, where Francis II was residing; but the largest and most sensational part was the flurry of pamphlets appearing in the wake of the uprising. Enough of the leaders were executed to qualify it as a 'massacre' in the eyes of Huguenots, and some two dozen publications appeared in the course of the next few months lamenting the fate, or justifying the intentions, of these 'martyrs' of Amboise. They were celebrated, too, in a famous contemporary engraving and in songs mourning the dead and the bodies floating down the Loire.[14] A number of other publications, especially official acts,

---

[13] Du Bourg, *Confession sur les principaux points de la religion chrestienne* (n.p., n.d.; Lb³².30), *Oraison Au Senat de Paris pour la cause des chrestiens* (n.p., 1561; BN Lb³².7), *L'Exemplaire et forme du process* (Anvers, 1560; Lb³².8), in *HE*, and *La vraye histoire, contenant l'unique iugement et fausse procedure faite contre le fidele serviteur de Dieu Anne du Bourg* (n.p., 1561; Lb³².9), in *MC*, ed. 1743, I, 217; also *Recueil des choses memorables* (Strasbourg, 1565; Lb³³.50), Crespin, II, 689ff. and Charbonnier, *La Poésie*, 123.

[14] See Henri Bordier, *La Saint Barthélemy et la critique modern* (Geneva, 1879); Kelley, *Hotman*, 70.

appeared in response to this propaganda, and the pattern of political debate was set for many years.

The basic purpose of the Amboise publicity was to give legitimacy to the constitutional opposition to the Guise-dominated government without seeming to question the 'majesty', that is, the sovereignty, of the king. Like war, insurrection could be justified under certain circumstances, or so at least some religious authorities seemed to teach. Calvin himself had provided, if not the final solution, at least the means of finding a temporary answer. He recognized two exceptions to the rule that resistance to established authority was unjustifiable, one religious and one secular. In the first place and most generally, duty to God always had priority over duty to human authority. Secondly, such action might be permitted, according to Calvin, under the authorization of the 'inferior magistrates', which in France could only mean the princes of the blood, namely, Antoine of Navarre. Although Calvin himself did not draw the conclusion that La Renaudie and his followers were justified, Huguenot supporters, and especially the lawyers, felt differently. So it was that the theologically based notion of passive resistance was transformed by men like Hotman and Beza into what amounts to the first expression of the modern idea of revolution.

One of the earliest pamphlets was 'The Estates of France Oppressed by the Tyranny of the Guises', and its purpose was to convey the impression of absolute legality and conformity to tradition as expressed in ordinances as well as historical sources.[15] Despite the superficial appearance of novelty and violence, the participants at Amboise were represented as acting on behalf of the crown. On the contrary, according to this apologist, it was the Guises who were violating the majesty of the king and indeed had designs upon his throne, as shown by their ambition and claims to be descended directly from Charlemagne. Their malicious influence was compounded by their fiscal oppression and corruption of the French legal system, including the Parlement of Paris. Unfortunately the force of this argument was deflected somewhat by the painfully defensive tone of the manifesto, which gave prominence to (while denying the validity of) the charges of 'mutiny and sedition'. Whether those terms were applicable or not was indeed a central issue from this point on.

Efforts were still being made to keep the 'political question' separate from the 'question of religion'. This pamphlet, for example,

---

[15] *Brieve remonstrance des estats de France . . . Sur l'ambition, tyrannie, et oppression du tout intolerable des de Guyse* (Rouen, 1560; BN Ld¹⁷⁶.9; LN 169); in MC, I, 26ff.

concluded by denying that the needs of 'those who desired to live according to the gospel' had anything to do with the protesters of Amboise.[16] Logical as this might appear, however, other pieces of propaganda made it difficult to maintain this distinction. One of these was an appeal from 'The Poor Faithful who have been unjustly defamed' issued to 'everyone who is willing to listen' and prefacing the Huguenot confession of faith presented to the king at Amboise. Again, in the last two of the forty articles of faith, claims of constitutional legitimacy were set forth, but the main thrust of the pamphlet was religious – bold attacks on 'idolatry', the mass and other malpractices of the 'Papists'. Later there were other petitions on these grounds, including two requests on behalf of 'the Faithful of France who want to live according to the reformation of the gospel'.[17] According to this appeal, 'The Jews, though abominable in the sight of God, have been granted temples in many parts of Christendom for the sake of peace and concord. How much more should it be permitted to us, who take Jesus Christ as our only savior and intercessor with God the Father?' Members of the Parlement had an answer for this in a remonstrance of the next year: 'The conversation of a Jew or other infidel is notoriously less dangerous to a Christian than that of a heretic.'

Spokesmen for the government certainly assumed this. 'In the greater part of our kingdom', according to an edict of March 1560, 'we have found great trouble in the religious situation because of the licentiousness of the past wars and through certain preachers coming from Geneva, most of them low and illiterate types, and also through the malicious distribution of books carried from Geneva . . .'[18] Although this legislation was intended to offer amnesty, it specifically exempted Huguenot preachers as well as all who had taken part in the conspiracy of that month. Two months later the official campaign continued in another assault against the 'criminals of lese-majesty', in royal phraseology, who 'rose up to trouble the order and repose of ourselves and our subjects, hoping to implant by force the new opinions which they hold in religion'.[19] Writing to the potential Huguenot leader Antoine of Navarre, Francis II said, or was made to say, that the trouble-makers wanted

---

[16] *MC*, I, 51ff. (printed).
[17] *Deux requestes de la part des fideles de France, qui desirent vivre selon la reformation de l'Evangile* (n.p., 1560; Lb^{32}.21), in *MC*, II, 654ff.; *Remonstrances* of the Parlement (Cambrai, 1561; LN 230), Diii: 'La conversation du Iuif ou autre infidele est notoirement moins dangereuse au chrestien que celle de l'heretique.'
[18] *MC*, ed. 1743, I, 9.
[19] *Edict du Roy sur la residence des evesques*, May (Paris, 1560; F. 46819.16; LN 193); in Isambert, XIV, 27; *MC*, I, 96ff.

'to dip their hands in blood, to break the ordinances of God and to dissolve the ties of human society by introducing licentiousness to evil people, oppressing the good and bringing all things to confusion'.

These events provoked, or intensified, fears about the secret practices of the Huguenot church in Paris. One 'Catholic remonstrance' saw the influence of 'the Protestants' infiltrating all levels of society.[20] They tried to corrupt education, they conspired to fill offices and judicial posts with men of their persuasion, and above all they were subverting the family and the patrimony. The author, Jean de la Vacquerie, thought them capable of all sorts of 'unnatural' acts and 'incests', detrimental to the social as well as the sacramental institution of marriage. 'For after trampling underfoot the honesty of marriage, who can be assured of his true and legitimate heir?' His imagination carried him further, for 'with such great liberty and impurity a father could lie with his daughter and a mother with her son'. Who should be surprised if the Protestants turned their destructiveness on the state itself?

Huguenot publicists did not play down, indeed they insisted upon, the extremism of the charges against them, at least the political charges. The Amboise affair, admitted the author of one 'Christian Response', was regarded in some quarters as 'a detestable conspiracy and unfortunate enterprise, that is, rebellion, disobedience, even insupportable treason against the majesty, honor, state and life of the king, his brother, mother and all the royal line'.[21] Yet such intemperate language, he continued, only betrayed the source of these false charges: talk about 'illicit assemblies' and 'our enemies the rebels' was appropriate not to sober legislation but rather to the spoutings of a propagandist – 'rhetoriqueur' or 'orator' as the Christian responder put it – 'for he has colored his discourse with rhetorical hues, amounting to lies, to make the false appear true'. This was the voice not of the king or his mother but of the Guise faction, which indeed was the real target both of the actors of and spokesmen for Amboise. It was undeniable that, in this period of martial law, power had in fact been given to the Duke of Guise as commander-in-chief.

---

[20] Jean de la Vacquerie, *Catholique remonstrance aux roys . . . touchant l'abolition des heresies, troubles et scismes qui regnent auiourd'huy* (Paris, 1560; BN Ld^{176}.6 and LN 212); cf. G. Desautelz, *Harangue au peuple françois contre la rebellion* (Paris, 1560; Lb^{32}.20). On Catholic propaganda see G. Wylie Sypher in *Sixteenth Century Journal*, XI (1980), 59–84.

[21] *Response chrestienne et defensive* (MC, I, 114ff.) to certain official letters attributed to Guise influence, especially *Lettres du Roy, Contenant les moyens de la destestable Coniuration et Conspiration, entreprinse contre sa maiesté, tendant a la subversion du Royaulme*, 31 Mar. (Poitiers, 1560; Lb^{32}.19); but at this point the official publications become too voluminous to cite.

The primary symbol of and scapegoat for the backlash to Amboise, however, was the Duke's brother, the Cardinal of Lorraine; and the Amboise propaganda reached a crescendo and even lyrical heights in denouncing this Gallican devil. He was assailed as an atheist, personally corrupt and guilty of innumerable cruelties in his own territories, especially Metz (from which a number of evangelical families had in fact been expelled) but also France in general. A supplication to the King of Navarre accused him of a variety of 'incests, violences, cruelties, inhumanities and extortions'.[22] To whom should the miseries of France be attributed?

It is to you, Cardinal, redder with our blood than with any dye, to your disloyalties, to your ambition and avarice . . . It is to you who have divided the forces of this kingdom to make yourself pope and your brother king of Sicily, from whom so many evils have come. It is you who have taken so many millions in gold . . . It is from you that so many widows demand their husbands, so many husbands the virtue of their wives, so many fathers their children, so many orphans their fathers and mothers, crying just vengeance from God against you and yours . . . It is to you that the courts and parlements of France, dishonored and degraded by you, complain; for it is you who have introduced into France this horrible custom of having men executed secretly without even the forms of a trial . . . In short it is you, wretched man, to whom our ancestors complain from their graves . . .

Other publications took up this colorful theme. One was a 'Pasquil de la cour' by 'Cognieres resussité', referring to the fourteenth-century legist Pierre de Cugnières so much admired by Dumoulin, which denounced the Cardinal as 'Lucifer attached to the firmament of the earthly kingdom'.[23] According to one poetic complaint

> Would you care to hear
> Certain news of your fame?
> Just drop the 'i' and
> Reverse the vowels of your name.[24]

---

[22] *Supplication et remonstrance addressee au roy de Navarre* (n.p., 1560; Lb33.9), in MC, 1, 310, cf. 109.

[23] *Le Pasquil de la cour, composé nouvellement par maistre Pierre de Cognieres resussité* (n.p., 1561; Lb33.16) Aiiiv; in MC, ed. 1743, 1.

[24] *Iuste complainte des fideles de France. Contre leurs adversaires Papistes, et autres* (Avignon, 1560; Ld176.6):

> Aux Lorrains,
> Si vous voulez ouyr nouvelles
> Certaines de vostre renom
> Ostez un I, de vostre nom
> Et transportez les deux voyelles.

The Cardinal was a thief, a 'larron', a plunderer of the monarchy. But the shrillest attack of all came in François Hotman's notorious *Tiger of France*, which repeated, in the style of Cicero's denunciation of Catiline, all these charges and added others. 'Will you never put an end to your unlimited ambition, to your impostures, to your thievery?' 'Who does not read in your face the misfortune of our age, the ruin of this kingdom and the death of our King?' 'You kill those who conspire against you . . ., you who have conspired against the crown of France, against the property of widows and orphans, against the blood of the afflicted and the innocent.'[25] For the rest of his life the Cardinal had to put up with this sort of abuse.

Even more than religious enthusiasm, it seems, the public image of the enemy created by this sort of propaganda, and the woes of the 'poor people' of France blamed on them, acted to give coherence to the opposition party. One of the most rousing manifestos was a 'Warning to the People of France' against the house of Guise, which had dared to put itself on a level with the reigning dynasty of Hugues Capet. They were the true enemy. 'For this reason, French people', the pamphleteer continued, 'your duty, for the love you bear toward your prince and Most Christian King, is to strive with all legitimate effort to oppose this evil and unfortunate enterprise and to demand help from God . . . and then from all the Parlements and estates of the Kingdom.'[26] A related 'Complaint to the French People' was even more militant.

French people, the hour has come to show our faith and loyalty toward our good king. The plot is uncovered, the conspiracy is known, the machinations of the house of Guise revealed . . . The enemies of the king have chased the nobility into the sea to be food for the fishes . . . The whole world should know of the misery and calamity of a nation which, simply because of its faith and loyalty toward its prince, is oppressed by the rage and tyranny of its enemies.

From the beginning, however, there was a more fundamental issue than the fact of Guise domination; also at stake was the survival of the French constitution. One early publication, a 'History of the Tumult of Amboise', probably by Hotman, began with a point of law – 'a law in France based upon ancient custom as well as the

[25] *Le Tigre de 1560*, ed. Ch. Reade (Paris, 1575); cf. Kelley, *Hotman*, 113, and J. Poujol, 'Du Bartas et le tyrannicide', *BSHPF*, CI (1955), 33–7.
[26] *Advertissement au Peuple de France* and *Complainte au Peuple François*, published with [Hotman], *L'Histoire du tumulte d'Amboyse* (Strasbourg, 1560; BN Lb^{32}.15 et seq); in *MC*, I, 21ff. and 6ff. These may have been the broadsheets circulated during the conspiracy itself.

agreement and determination of the three estates assembled at Tours in 1484' – that would have placed the government in a council of regency established by a meeting of the Estates General. According to French tradition, too, the members of the council were restricted to peers of the blood, and foreigners were specifically excluded. To support this argument Hotman added not only historical evidence but also points from civil law, notably that the king was under-age until he became twenty-five and so could not, of his immature 'will', choose his own guardians any more than a ward could choose a guardian (tutor) in law. The Guise claims to be descended directly from Charlemagne were irrelevant, even if true. The essential point was 'that the king was not old enough to rule without the council established legitimately according to the aforesaid law'. This was the primary legal issue at the outset of partisan struggle: not the majesty but the minority of the king, and the constitutional arrangement arising from that minority.

The job of refuting these arguments was given to the chief clerk and archivist of the Parlement (*greffier civil*), Jean du Tillet, an old enemy of La Renaudie as well as an advocate for the Guises. As *greffier* he signed virtually all the royal legislation, published as well as unpublished, in these years. In his little treatise on *The Majority of the King*, published in the summer of 1560, Du Tillet argued that the question ought to be settled in terms not of civil but of feudal law and especially French legislation, according to which (an ordinance of 1374) the age of reason was fourteen.[27] For Du Tillet the far-fetched arguments of the 'rebels' were merely part of their deeper subversion, and he went on to reject their entire program with the remark that 'the notorious and seditious writings published by clandestine printing are worthy of neglect because of their lies and impudent insults'. Yet Du Tillet did not hesitate to resume the debate when two Huguenot responses were issued on behalf of the 'cause', protesting 'good conscience' and innocence of the charges of sedition. 'An ignorant counsellor is a great curse to all men', wrote Du Tillet's critic. 'He has as his enemy the truth of the histories of France.' The controversy concluded with a second treatise by Du Tillet, who rejected the errant constitutionalism of the 'rebels'. The Estates General might be 'holy' (by virtue of their status of a 'mystical body'), but they were by no means sovereign. Most of all he objected to his enemies' tendency to rely on the mythical material

---

[27] Du Tillet, *Pour la majorité du Roy tres chrestien, contre les escrites des rebelles* (Paris, 1560; BN Lb³².10 and LN 173) and *Pour l'entiere Maiorité du Roy tres chrestien, Contre le Legitime conseil malicieusement inventé par les rebelles* (Paris, 1560; Lb³².12); *Response* (Amboise, 1560; Lb³².11), in *MC*, I, 169ff., and the *Legitime conseil*, *MC*, I, 225ff.

in French chronicles rather than the documented truth of his own archival sources, that is, the registers of the Parlement of Paris. This contrast between an idealized national and an authorized official tradition would also persist in later stages of these propaganda wars.

At certain points in this early confrontation Huguenot enthusiasm went beyond such legalisms to pose more fundamental questions about the limits of obedience. Hotman's *Tiger*, for example, ventured beyond the bounds of personal vituperation and charges of tyranny to sound the theme of tyrannicide: 'If Caesar was killed for having pretended to the sceptre justly', he asked, 'can we permit you to live who pretend to it unjustly?'[28] And the author of the 'Christian Response' had an even more comprehensive answer to the question of the legitimacy of armed resistance. 'Certainly religion forbids this when the subject does so against his prince, the law and his country', he admitted. 'But the religion of God and all human laws not only excuse but even command subjects to take up arms for the defense of their natural prince, when he is oppressed, for the conservation of law and the preservation of society.' Beneath the legal fictions and strategies this argument represents a primitive version of an idea later, in a time of even greater urgency, more explicitly formulated: this was not merely the constitutional right of resistance but, in the case of royal forfeiture of 'majesty', the divine right of revolution.

VOICES OF REASON AND UNREASON

The spring and summer of 1560 were the seed-time of ideology, and more than one harvest would be gathered over the next generation and more. But if the lines were drawn theoretically, all possibilities of practical accommodation were not exhausted, the connection between ideas and bases of power were not fixed, and leadership and organization were still in doubt. Above all, Catherine de Médicis, with some few supporters, was still making efforts to keep the peace. So open conflict was postponed (though few doubted that it was coming); and for almost two years a variety of proposals for remedies and reform, both political and religious, was discussed. Such mild and diffused propaganda, ranging from vague exhortations to peace and concord to practical legislative and institutional resolutions of differences, preserved some concern for the stability and 'police' of the monarchy. Whether reasonable or merely cynical,

[28] Hotman, *Tigre*.

utopian or duplicitous, these voices represented at least a reluctance to resort to force – until they were drowned out finally by overriding and uncompromising partisanship.

On the Huguenot side there seemed to be a growing suspicion of the emphasis on individual personality which the position of the Guises encouraged – 'as if the pyramid of the French monarchy does not depend on its base', in the mixed metaphor of one petition to Antoine of Navarre, 'but like an old tottering ruin supports itself on a single branch'.[29] The premise of Huguenot propaganda was the concern for the welfare of the 'poor People' of France. It was the People, according to another 'Apology' against Guisard calumnies, who were being accused of rebellion and sedition; it was the evangelicals who were their defenders. Appeals were consequently made not only to the king and queen and the princes of the blood but also 'to all estates'.[30] Such assumptions were linked not only to 'national consciousness' but also to the desire to see a meeting of the Estates General called. It was in anticipation of this that old Seysselian notions of limited and structured monarchy were revived and advertised. Before, during and after the assembly of Estates at Orleans in 1561 there was a flurry of partisan and non-partisan publicity about the vital connection between the three estates and the monarchy, between 'the concord of the people', according to one evangelical spokesman, 'and the grandeur and wealth of their king'.[31]

Beginning in late 1560, attention turned increasingly from threats of resistance to hopes for reform. This was the message of one pamphlet called 'The Way of Ending the Troubles in France Today'.[32] This publication upheld the need for the 'fear of God' and rejection of 'Religion Papale', and it defended the preachers from Geneva as well as the men of Amboise. Yet its major concern was with the practical problems of reforming the clergy and the distribution of benefices, the corresponding abuses in secular offices, the never-ending difficulties in the law courts and in general the condition of the 'Estat Politique'. Why, the author continued, single out the evangelicals? Why not attack the prostitutes instead? Needless to say such reforms could not be expected from a Guise-dominated government. 'This is like expecting drunkenness to be reformed by tavern-keepers, usury by bankers or prostitution by whores.' The

[29] *Supplication et remonstrance* (see p. 266 above, n. 22), Cii (*MC*, I, 288).
[30] *Remonstrances a tous estats* (Paris, 1560; Ld[176].7), in *MC*, II, 839.
[31] *La Harangue du tiers estat de France* (*MC*, II, 660), by M. Bretagne at the estates of St Germain en Laye, 27 Aug. 1561.
[32] *La Maniere d'appaiser les troubles* (*MC*, I, 341, 369).

only hope lay in a purified religion in conjunction with a reconstituted monarchy; and this meant, in the absence of a conventional princely father figure, reliance on the institutions and the law of the land. To some degree these ideals were reflected in the assemblies of Estates meeting at Orleans and later at Pontoise during the year and in some of the edicts of pacification, culminating in that of January 1562. Two months later Condé, who had been charged with conspiracy after Amboise, was released from prison, and the stage seemed set for something pleasanter than the heavy tragedy of civil war.

As the 'political question' seemed to be yielding to counsels of moderation, so the 'question of religion' seemed to some susceptible to compromise; and the institutional solution was very much the same – that is, the calling of a nation-wide assembly to talk over differences. Whether the old institution of the national council or the newer device of the inter-confessional colloquy, such a meeting would at least keep the doors öpen to communication and ward off the continuing threat of the papal-dominated Council of Trent, which in fact began sitting again in the spring of 1561. The opening move had been made in August 1560 in a meeting sponsored by the Queen Mother. Coligny was present; but the most remarkable statement, soon issued in pamphlet form, was that by Jean de Monluc, bishop of Valence.[33] The evangelical doctrine he referred to as 'new doctrine', but his attitude toward it was most conciliatory. 'The doctrine which pleases your subjects, Sire', he told the young king, 'has been disseminated over thirty years, not in two or three days, and it has been brought by three or four hundred learned and diligent ministers with great modesty, seriousness and appearance of holiness, claiming to detest all vices, especially avarice, with risk of dying for their preaching . . .' He approved of the wider 'publication' of the Bible, even the singing of psalms,[34] and in general registered a counsel of toleration. The miseries of the age were not due to religion, he argued, but to violations of law and to corruption. And he, too, hoped that a national council could be called.

During the next year there were other pleas for Frenchmen to live in concord and peace, not only from statesmen like Monluc and L'Hôpital and in published legislation but also in pamphlets written by scholars like Pasquier, Castellio, Louis le Roy and Guy de Brès.[35]

[33] *MC*, I, 324. [34] *Complainte apologique des eglises de France*, 1561 (*MC*, II, 496).

[35] Pasquier, *Exhortation aux princes* (1561), in *Ecrits politiques*, ed. D. Thickett (Geneva, 1966); Brès, *Confession de Foy* (1561), on which see E. M. Braekman, 'La Pensée politique de Guy de Brès', *BSHPF*, cxv (1969), 1–28; Le Roy, *Des differences et troubles advenus entre les hommes par la diversité des opinions en la religion* (Paris, 1562); Castellio (see above, p. 62, n. 13).

The Gallican dilemma had been wrestled with in the public arena by Dumoulin and others for years: how to pursue a program of reform and still avoid the twin menaces of heresy and popery. The old Gallican insistence on 'one faith, one king, one law' was becoming an empty formula, though it was proclaimed at the Estates of Orleans by Chancellor L'Hôpital and many others. In his *Exhortation to the Princes* Pasquier also repeated it in order to reject the extreme parties, but he had no illusions about the feasibility of religious uniformity at this late date. A lifelong foe of the Jesuits in particular, he abhorred the idea of subordination to Rome, but he was no less apprehensive about Geneva. 'Les Protestans' were probably numerically superior, he thought, though he also believed that the nobility 'favored the party of Rome on political grounds' (*vous favorise le party de Romme par esprit politique*). In order to achieve peace in national terms, he concluded, 'there is no more expeditious means than to permit two churches in the kingdom, the one of the Romans and the other of the Protestants', though he immediately added, 'I do not doubt that some of you will be upset by this statement . . .' As the continuing stream of partisan propaganda showed, this was a masterpiece of understatement. Nevertheless it was an opinion that attracted support for a few months of this conciliatory year, 1561.

More serious than this sort of wishful thinking, perhaps, was the emergence at the same time of the so-called 'irenic movement', whose purpose was to reconcile the parties on the basis of a loosely construed Lutheran theology. At least it had a fairly respectable intellectual tradition, being associated with the conciliatory efforts of Melanchthon and the Erasmian theologian George Cassander, and it attracted a certain amount of political support among such 'moderatores' as Catherine de Médicis, Antoine of Navarre, L'Hôpital and even (for his own purposes) the Cardinal of Lorraine. The publicity campaign for this movement was headed by that ex-Calvinist Baudouin, who had already laid some of the foundations in his publications on early Christian legal history and who, in the summer of 1561, began distributing in France the major manifesto, Cassander's *Office of Pious Men*.[36] The overt message was compromise in terms of a broad reformed but 'catholic tradition'; implicitly, however, the movement threatened to isolate if not to undermine the Calvinist extremists and to bring closer together Gallicans and Lutherans (already in political alignment). So at least Huguenots feared, and their suspicions determined their attitude

---

[36] *De Officio pii viri*, in *Opera omnia* (Paris, 1616), 781–97; cf. Kelley, *Foundations*, 134ff.

toward the Colloquy of Poissy, called in October 1561 ostensibly to realize the irenic program but in fact representing only the famous lull before the storm.

The Colloquy of Poissy was a comedy of misunderstanding, a tragedy of cross-purposes.[37] Designed to conciliate, in fact it served only to intensify the polarization of public opinion. Beza, heading the Calvinist delegation, used the occasion to preach to the unconverted for a change. His three orations were given before the royal family and the Cardinal of Lorraine.[38] Significantly, Beza knelt before God to pray but not before the King, whom he addressed in much the same terms as Calvin had done a quarter of a century before in the preface to his *Institutes*. The posture was still defensive. Some say, he admitted, that we set too great conditions upon concord. Some go further and speak (in the contemporary Scots version) 'as though we pretended to overturn the present state of the world, and to make a new world of our own fashioning, and to spoyle a number of theyre goods to enrich our selves withall'. This was not the case, but even further from the truth was the view 'that our disagreeing both stande in no greate matter of importaunce but consisteth in thynges indifferent . . .'. Such laxity – whether Melanchthon's 'adiaphorism' or nicodemitism – was insufferable; and in fact Calvin had given private instructions not to make any concessions in points of theology. The purpose of the colloquy, 'to agree upon a sound doctrine', was laudable; but all the Cardinal offered, Beza complained, was a version of the confession of Augsburg. Through his arguments and especially through his attitude, Beza in effect and indeed consciously shut the door on any possibility of agreement, even if the government seriously contemplated this.

On the other side the Cardinal of Lorraine spoke in apparently diplomatic terms – deviously, the Huguenots preferred to think – but others were more forthright. Theologians such as René Benoist, Gentien Hervet and Claude de Sainctes carried on the campaign against Calvinism and any idea of making concessions at Poissy. They lamented the fashionable indulgence in iconoclasm, and De Sainctes in particular recalled the old canonist doctrine that there

---

[37] *Ample discours des actes de Poissy* (n.p., 1561; Lb33.29 and LN 219), in *MC*, II, 688ff., and poetic version by Tarander, *Les Actes de Poissy* (n.p., n.d.); and see D. Nugent, *Ecumenism in the Age of Reformation* (Cambridge, Mass., 1974), and H. O. Evennett, *The Cardinal of Lorraine and the Council of Trent* (Cambridge, 1930).

[38] Beza's three 'Harangues', published separately, were widely circulated (Paris, 1561): first (BN Lb33.34, 35 and LN 200), second (Lb33.38, 39 and LN 221), third (Lb33.40); cited here is the contemporary English translation, *Ane Oration* (Edinburgh, 1561; STC 2026–7); Cardinal of Lorraine, *Oraison* (n.p., 1561; Lb33.36). Cf. Hauser, 177.

was 'no salvation outside the Catholic church'.[39] Lawyers, including Jean Gay, Julien Tabouet and Jacques de Faye, added the weight of their arguments. It was not long before they were joined by Baudouin, guiding spirit of the irenic movement. Baudouin denounced Beza for his spoiler's role and charged that he had returned to Paris, 'where he was so well-known among the ruffians and troublemakers who usually haunt the houses of gambling, prostitution and drinking', only as an agitator.[40] Although Beza seemed to condemn the Catholic institution of benefices, he had himself enjoyed more than one, Baudouin recalled, and in general had been won over to Calvin's new religion for status and wealth. Baudouin also recalled to mind the responsibility of Beza and Hotman for the part they played in the Amboise uprising the previous year, 'the cruelest and evilest the world has ever seen', as he described it. So the personal, professional and confessional animosities of the previous generation provided fuel for more explosive controversies.

Few episodes of the century were more productive of propaganda than this spectacular confrontation, which served not only as a focus for longer-standing controversies but also as a forum in which the last doubts even of moderates were dispelled. This was unmistakable in the publicity issuing from the assembly itself, especially the harangues of Beza and the address of the Cardinal of Lorraine, which were almost immediately published in pamphlet form and translated – the Cardinal into German and Beza into English and Italian. During the Colloquy an edict was printed calling once again for the 'pursuit' of heresy and sedition.[41] Beyond this there was a continuing stream of publications, especially remonstrances to the Queen Mother attacking the opposition party 'and their great Idol Calvin', as one put it.[42] The spirit of controversy was also reflected in more private ideological duels. One of the most sensational was that between another ex-Calvinist, the Chevalier de Villegagnon, and anonymous critics, who attacked bitterly this 'vain and effeminate' ignoramus, comparable to Catherine de Medicis's astrologer Nostra-

---

[39] Hervet, *Epistre envoyee a un quidam fauteur des nouveaux evangeliques. En laquelle est clairement monstré que hors l'Eglise Catholique n'y a nul salut* (Rheims, 1562; LN 248, 287); cf. *Discours* (Paris, 1563; Lb³³.55 and LN 349–50); Sainctes, *Confession de Foy Catholique* (Paris, 1561; LN 255) and *Discours sur le saccagement des Eglises par les heretiques Anciens* (Verdun, 1562; Lb³³.57). See Hauser, 174–5.

[40] *Defense premier* (Paris, 1562); *Responsio altera* (Paris, 1562).

[41] *Ordinance* of 20 Oct. 1561 (BN F. 46821. 46 and LN 243).

[42] *Discours sur ce qu'aucuns seditieux ont temerairement dit et soustenu que pendant la minorité des Rois de France, leurs meres ne sont capables de la Regence* (Paris, 1579; BN Lb³³.7), dated 19 Mar. 1560.

damus in his credulity.[43] The whole thing had been started by Villegagnon's criticism of a Protestant 'remonstrance' to Catherine by Augustin Mallorat, who attributed to the Queen Mother the provocative admission 'that one need not obey an infidel king'.[44] Now Villegagnon responded to his critics with his own disillusioned kind of bitterness. There were seven different 'sacramentarian' sects, he claimed, all different but all equally dogmatic. They pretended to be legitimate, yet continued to assemble in violation of repeated laws forbidding this. Like Baudouin, Dumoulin, Raemond, Cathelan and others, Villegagnon illustrates a curious characteristic of ideological warfare, that defectors from a movement are often transformed into its harshest and most unforgiving critics.

After the experience of Poissy there was little hope for a general settlement, and there was a marked inclination toward violence. The spirit both of iconoclasm and of martyrdom was in the air.[45] One particularly newsworthy event occurred at the end of the year (27 December), when the parish priests of the church of St Médard tried to interrupt nearby Protestant services, starting a riot in which one Huguenot was killed.[46] Afterwards a crowd of Protestants frolicked in the wake of a procession taking Catholic prisoners to trial. This clash had reverberations for months. On 18 April Huguenots again posted placards around the street-corners of Paris, protesting against the violence they had suffered. This was followed by a Catholic counter-attack on 'blasphemies, sacrileges, pollutions, murders, pillages, inhumanities and carnage' committed by Huguenots, and then another Protestant pamphlet responding to this and condemning again the 'sedition of St Médard'.

By this time (mid-April) the civil wars were already imminent The final straw was the massacre of Vassy, and the arguments over the blame for this outbreak filled works of propaganda and history for generations. War guilt became a central issue, and as usual Huguenots were on the defensive. One of their earliest protests was a 'Discourse on the Rumor that We have brought about War for the

---

[43] Villegagnon, *Responce* (Paris, 1561; Lb33.19) to [Mallorat], *Remonstrance a la Royne Mere de Roy, par ce qui sont persecutez pour la parole de Dieu* (n.p., 1561; Lb33.18); and another pamphlet (Lb33.21) responding to another 'response' by Mallorat (Paris, 1561; LN 254).
[44] *Remonstrance*, Eii.   [45] *MC*, II, 743.
[46] *Histoire Veritable de la Mutinerie, Tumulte et sedition faite par les Prestres Sainct Medard* (n.p., n.d.; Lb33.41); in *MC*, II, 864ff.; *AC*, IV, 77ff.; *Requeste des habitans de Paris, qui soubs la Protection du Roy . . . desirent estre maintenuz es exercices de la Religion reformee selon l'Evangile*, 18 April 1562 (BN Lb33.72), in *MC*, II, 876, the 'placard' attacked by *Remonstrances faictes au Roy, par les Catholiques . . . sur les placars et libelles attachez et semez le 18. de ce present mois d'Avril* (Paris, 1562; Lb33.67); and *Response aux Remonstrances faites contre les Placars . . .* (n.p., 1562; Lb33.68), in *MC*, II, 878. Cf. Edict of 17 Jan. (Isambert, XIV, 44, and many printings).

Sake of Religion', and again the purpose was to deny charges of 'sedition and rebellion'.[47] A pamphlet 'Warning' addressed to Catherine de Médicis complained about that 'race of tigers, the Guises, and their ministers, who are present only to agitate the people and cry, "Kill everyone, strike them all down!"'[48] One Huguenot 'History' of the events of the spring of 1562 exposed the intrigues of the Guises and the reasons for the stand that Condé was taking in Orleans.[49] 'It is not conscience that pushes those who are so fond of the Roman religion', wrote the author, 'for their only goal is to take over the government of the kingdom.' Responding to this 'fabulous History . . . by our new Reformers' was a counter-'Warning' against the lies being spread by the rebels; and so the debate continued. The Malcontents had long been ready for war, and so in their own way were the evangelicals. According to one ominous warning published for the benefit of the Queen, 'the victory of the church has been won not by the force of princes and magistrates but by the blood of martyrs'.[50] In general, the tone of propaganda was changing from ideological maneuvering to belligerent manifestos; religious protest was not only drawn into politics but it was also conscripted into the military; and *homo politicus* was being transformed into *homo bellicus.*

BLOOD AND INK

When the fighting began, the shouting did not cease, and indeed verbal and martial excesses reinforced each other in many ways. Warfare over the next decade (1562–72) was sporadic; but the flow of propaganda was ceaseless, and the polarization of parties relentless and irreversible despite interludes of peace. The variety as well as the quantity of pamphlets and occasional publicity grew apace. Old

---

[47] *Discours sur le bruit qui court que nous aurons la guerre, a cause de Religion* (n.p., 1562; BN Lb33.45), Aiiii (*MC*, III, 73).

[48] *Advertissement a la Royne mere du Roy* (Orleans, 1562; BN Lb33.43), in *MC*, II, 119.

[49] *Histoire comprenant en brief . . .* (Orleans, 1562; BN Lb33.48 and LN 288): '. . . ce n'est le zelle de la conscience, qui pousse ceux qui se monstrent si affectionnez pour la religion Romane, ayans ce principal but proposé devant leurs yeux, de s'emparer du gouvernement du Royaume . . .'. This was answered by *Advertissement sur la faulseté de plusieurs mensonges semez par les Rebelles* (Paris, 1562; BN Lb33.53 and LN 258), B$_2$: 'Nous avons prins les armes au nom du grand Dieu des armes, pour la liberté et delivrance du Roy, nostre Sire, et messeigneurs ses freres, de son Conseil et de tout le Royaume: contre lesquelz par tyrannie, violence, force et privee authorité, se sont saisis et emparez la personne de leurs Maiestez, et de ceux dudict Conseil, de leur pays, forces et finances . . .'.

[50] *Remonstrance a la Royne Mere du Roy, par ceux qui sont persecutez pour la parole de Dieu* (n.p., 1561; BN Lb33.18), 76.

themes were preserved or transformed, new ones introduced; but in general it was in these few years, it would seem, that the pattern of political debate was set for the rest of the century and in some sense long after that.

The launching of this debate was marked especially by the publicity campaign started by the Prince of Condé, opening with the fundamental statements of his 'Declaration and Protestation' and the 'Treaty of Association' as well as a stream of letters, published and unpublished, sent in all directions to gain support or anticipate criticism.[51] 'In order to be understood truly by their majesties', his spokesmen told the young King and Queen Mother, 'the Prince has not wanted to neglect writing down his reasons, publishing them throughout all Christendom and making them known to all princes, potentates, allies, friends and confederates of this crown and all the courts of this kingdom.' In this propaganda the party line was set. Old sores were reopened, new injuries reported in almost day-by-day fashion, conclusions were drawn and the constitutional arguments framed. As always, rebellious intent was denied, and in fact the old convention of pleading that 'evil counsel' and not royal will was to blame was reinforced by the fiction that the king and his mother had lost their freedom to their Guise protectors. 'Now I ask those who published letters patent under the king's name . . . if this young king of 11 or 12 years, surrounded by pistoliers and harquebusiers, accompanied only by his mother and a little brother, is not a captive king . . .?' The ultimate purpose of Condé's association, then, was by force of arms 'to vindicate the liberty of the king and to conserve the authority of the queen'.

In fact such arguments were a poor covering for the ugly reality of civil war, which gave release to fanaticism and targets for long pent-up hostilities. Divine favor was invoked on both sides. On the one hand God's 'miraculous punishment of the Lutherans (now called Huguenots)' was celebrated; on the other hand, and even more indelicately, His 'terrible vengeance for the murders commit-

---

[51] See p. 255 above, n. 1. And among other pamphlets Condé's *Second Declaration* ([Orleans], 1562; BN Lb33.70 and LN 269), in *MC*, III, 249; *Oratio legatorum Principis Condei ad sacra Romani imperii principes electores Francofurti* (Brussels, 1563; BN Lb33.92; French trans. 91), in *MC*, III, 371; *Discours sur la liberté ou captivité du roy* ([Orleans], 1562; BN Lb33.83 and LN 275); *Remonstrances de monseigneur le prince de Condé et ses associez, sur le iugement de rebellion donné contre eux par leur ennemis ses disans estre la cour de Parlement de Paris* ([Orleans], 1562; BN Lb33.87 and LN 267). In general Hauser, and the classic essay of H. G. Koenigsberger, 'The organization of revolutionary parties in France and the Netherlands in the 16th century', *Journal of Modern History*, XXVII (1955), 335–51.

ted by princes' was praised.[52] Private vituperation against the 'tyranny of the papists' ran ahead of official propaganda, but not by much. With the outbreak of sporadic fighting in the summer and the intransigence of the government, the Huguenot party line became harder and more demanding, and once again a jeremiad denounced Paris as the 'new Egypt'. In a pamphlet on the 'Means of pacifying the Troubles in this Kingdom' Condé made three concrete demands: first, that a council be established for the king in his minority; second, that reparations be made for losses suffered by those of the religion; and finally, that the Guises, as those who bore exclusive blame for the predicament, should leave the court and return to their own lands.[53] In a 'Summary Declaration and Confession of Faith' published in July he presented himself as nemesis of the enemies both of God and of the king, again bringing in the religious and political questions.[54] A few days later he launched an assault on the Parlement of Paris, dismissing it as a mere rump assembly. 'The best part of it', he declared, 'the faction and partisans of the Guises have not tolerated or permitted to remain.' He went on to list specific charges against the various presidents, nor did he hesitate to mention the lines of patronage extending to the Guises and other usurpers. And as so often before, Huguenot poetry and song gave lyrical force to the evolving political program.

Official responses were as prompt as they were predictable. The Parlement expressed 'great sadness' at the Prince's words and the 'evil counsel' they betrayed, and the members reminded him that they represented the 'sovereign justice' of the king himself. They denied both the 'calamitous rumor' that the royal family was captive and the charge that the edicts of pacification were ineffective.[55] The Queen Mother, replying to the Prince's demands in the same spirit, also agreed that the edict of January should continue to be observed, that there should be reparations according to the requirements of simple justice, but that there should be no more talk about sending the Guises away. Anyway, she continued, the Huguenots must first lay down their arms. So the stalemate remained. The intensity of the debate paralleled the violence of the first civil war, which increased

---

[52] *Traite dé la iustice de Dieu et horrible vengeance contre les meurtres commis par les Princes et Potentats de la terre* (n.p., 1562; BN Ld[176].17) and *Les miraculeuses punitions divines advenues sur aucuns meschans et malheureux Lutheriens . . . (a present nommez Huguenotz) ennemis de nostre Mere saincte Eglise* (Paris, 1562; BN Ld[176].18); *Dialogus contra Papistarum tyrannidem*, 10 Aug. 1562 (*BSHPF* R. 11410); *La Consommation de l'Idole de Paris suivant la parole du prophete Ieremie* (Lyon, 1562; BN Lb[33].44).

[53] *Les moyens de pacifier le trouble qui est en ce royaume* ([Orleans], 1562; BN Lb[33].77 and LN 265), *MC*, III, 289ff.

[54] *Sommaire declaration et confession de foi* ([Orleans], 1562; BN Lb[33].85 and LN 270), in *MC*, III, 394. And cf. Bordier, 211.

[55] *MC*, III, 274, 278.

from sporadic iconoclasm to major atrocities to pitched battles. One Protestant remonstrance from Maine lamented the decimation of the nobility in particular and listed the provincial victims in a sort of secular martyrology.[56] Hardly easier to bear than the casualties of war were the repeated confiscations of Huguenot property which even more enduringly attacked their honor and their posterity.[57]

Despite such social turmoil, however, personalities continued to dominate propaganda, especially when Francis of Guise was killed in February 1563, a few weeks before the end of the first war. This assassination not only reinforced the feud between the Guise and Bourbon factions but sparked a whole train of eulogies and, on the other hand, attacks on Coligny, who was personally blamed for the crime.[58] Standing at the very center of political controversy, this conflict was productive not only of colorful invective and poetry but also of political legends and, ultimately, political theories. A similar pattern is evident in the Netherlands, where the confrontation likewise began with a personal, yet widely publicized, petition to Philip II. Such clashes resulted in a spectacular process of what the historian of the Dutch pamphlet literature has called *Mythvorming*.[59]

With peace came a diminution of violence but not of verbal assaults. The flow of propaganda continued from the spring of 1563 until the next outbreak of war four years later. Much of it was traditional – exhortations to peace, panegyrics of the king, ceremonies, especially the various 'entrees' staged for the king and his mother on their celebrated journey round the French provinces. Some was provocative but still not new – the problem of the minority (settled in favor of the Guises), the reception of the canons and decrees of the Council of Trent (not settled at all) and the never-ending recriminations among Calvinists and ex-Calvinists. As always there were private duels, as those between Ronsard, royal historiographer as well as poet, and his Huguenot critics, including the

---

[56] *Remonstrance envoyee au roy par la noblesse de la Religion Reformee du païs de Maine, sur les assassinats, pilleries, saccagements de maisons, seditions, violements de femmes et autres exces horribles* (n.p., 1564; LN 401); cf. royal *Verbal et information . . . de la ruine de l'Eglise . . .* etc (Lyon, 1562; BN Lb33.75), and *Doleance faicte au roy sur l'impunité des meurtres et oppressions qui se committent iournellement en ce royaulme, au prejudice de ses Edictz* (n.p., 1564; BN Lb33.148).

[57] *Lettres patentes, par laquelle est enioint prendre et enlever tous et un chacun les biens appartiens aux seditieux et rebelles*, 19 March (Paris, 1563; BN F. 46823.8).

[58] Funeral sermon for Francis of Guise by Jacques Le Hongre, 20 March (Paris, 1563; LN 351), for example, and Condé's defense and exculpation of Coligny 25 May (n.p., 1563; BN Lb33.130); *Arrest de l'innocence de monsieur l'admiral* (Paris, 1566; LN 448, 447).

[59] Geurts, *Pamfletten*, 157ff. Cf. *Rescript et declaration du Tres illustre Prince d'Orange, contenant l'occasion de la defense . . . contre l'horrible Tyrannie du Duc d'Alba et ses adherans*, 20 July 1568 (BM 9210. a. 15).

martyrologist Chandieu.[60] Ideological resentments were kept alive not only by these but also by the reprinting of Condé's partisan statements and by the beginning of historical re-examination of the origins of the war, most notably in the *Commentaries* of Pierre de la Planche of 1565. Finally, there was the argument for armed resistance. In an address to the Queen Mother in 1563 (ostensibly translated from the Italian) Jacques Spifame, councillor of Geneva (and formerly of the French king), applied the argument for justice to the problem of insurrection. 'The word of God', he wrote, 'teaches us that wars are legitimate when arms are taken up by order of the magistrate to execute public vengeance against those who, whether native or foreign, trouble the tranquility of the kingdom.'[61] Though couched in terms of legitimacy, this amounted again to a kind of crypto-revolutionary theory.

Although extremely defensive about charges of complicity made against Coligny in the killing of the Duke of Guise, propagandists did not moderate their attacks on the abominable influence of the Guise family. Long after the peace settlement a pamphleteer was still complaining, 'How monstrous and incredible it is that they have pillaged and stolen from the greatest and most honorable families of the kingdom. What cruel, inhuman butcheries are the massacres which have been committed on their behalf and at their command.'[62] Retrospectively it seemed clear that the *rapprochement* with the Lutherans, exemplified in the Saverne conference between the brothers Guise and the ultra-Lutheran leader, Duke Christoph von Württemberg, who had their suspicious meeting just before the massacre of Vassy. By such maneuvers they had not only usurped the government and dishonored the kingdom but had also promoted that Roman religion 'on which depends their whole authority'. 'Whence it follows', concluded this critic of the 'tiger', 'that whoever upholds or excuses the Cardinal in this quarrel is a sworn enemy of the king and his estate.'

One major and expanding theme was the disturbances in social order brought by foreign influence and the confusion of class distinctions. The de-classing effects of religious conversion were

---

[60] See J. Pineaux (ed.), *La Polémique protestante contre Ronsard* (Paris, 1973); also F. Charbonnier, *Pamphlets protestants contre Ronsard 1560–1577* (Paris, 1923), and *La Poésie française et les guerres de religion* (Paris, 1919), and F. Yates, *The French Academies of the Sixteenth Century* (London, 1942), 186ff.

[61] *Lettre addressee de Rome a la roine* . . . (n.p., 1563; BN Lb33.131 and LN 361), *MC*, IV, 442.

[62] *Bref discours et veritable des principales coniurations de ceux de la maison de Guyse, contre le roy et son royaume* (n.p., 1565; LN 407), Ai: 'Certes c'est une chose incroyable, et monstrueuse, des pilleries et brigandages qu'ils [les Guises] ont commis sur la plus grande partie des plus anciennes et honorables familles de ce Royaume.' Cf. *Brief discours sur les moyens, que tient le Cardinal de l'Orraine pour empescher l'establissement de la Paix, et ramener les Troubles en France* (n.p., 1568; BN Lb33.245), and *La Guerre Cardinale* (n.p., 1565; BN Lb33.160A).

proverbial, as the case of the bishop who fled France to become a miller in Switzerland illustrates (*d'evêque devenir meunier*).[63] On the other hand one gentleman complained, with a wealth of examples, about the process of 'bastardizing the nobility'.[64] Low types were regularly raised to positions of honor, he charged, and ill-advised marriages made social confusion worse. Catherine de Médicis had made a doctor's wife a duchess, her husband thus becoming a duke, while the first gentleman of the king's chamber was the son of a banker. (This was a non-too-subtle jibe at the Queen, herself descended from Florentine bankers.) What a monstrous process, he continued – 'a transubstantiation indeed to turn a gentleman into a villain and a villain into a gentleman'. The new people making their way into French society were not only low-born, complained another nobleman, but they did not even believe in God. Some pretended nobles were 'sons of tax collectors, farmers and artisans, others children of the soil who know neither their father nor their mother'. It was true that French Huguenots were forced to vacate their offices – 'The King has declared purely and simply that all offices possessed by those of the new so-called religion are vacant and untenable' – and this published *arrêt* of 1568 included a list of those who had been so expropriated.[65]

This influence extended to the highest political levels, for the royal council itself was filled with foreigners. According to another protest of 1567, 'the Italians have gained so much credit and favor in the court by their subtleties and the crafty use of their money that by contrast native Frenchmen seem to be foreigners'.[66] A translation of an anti-papal tract by Flacius Illyricus carried the attack on the 'Romanist liars' into the heart of their false tradition, and Huguenots followed this trail blazed by Lutherans.[67] One conspicuous expression of this infection was that 'papemania' derided by Rabelais. 'Papemania' was also the title of a pamphlet of 1567, which praised

---

[63] J. B. Dubédat, *Histoire du Parlement de Toulouse* (Paris, 1885), I, 333.

[64] *Lettre missive d'un gentilhomme a un sien compagnon contenant les causes du mecontentement de la Noblesse de France* (n.p., 1567; BN Lb33.191 and LN 548), and the *Response* thereto (192); cf. *Response a une lettre escrite a Compiegne* (n.p., 1567; LN 554).

[65] *Arrest de la Court de Parlement . . . sur la declaration des estats et offices vacans et impetrables, de ceux de la nouvelle Pretenduë Religion* (Paris, 1569; LN 655, cf. 658) and the Edict (Rouen, 1568; BN F. 46837. 18 and LN 585): 'le Roy a declare purement et simplement vacans et impetrables tous les estats et Offices tenuz et possedez par ceux de la nouvelle pretenduë Religion'. Cf. *Recueil des Lettres et Mandemens du Roy* (Paris, 1568; BN Ld176.29), Div, 'Roole des noms et estats de ceux qui ont esté privez de leurs Offices . . . par les Arrests', totalling 184.

[66] *Articles des plaintes et doleances du peuple* (n.p., 1567; LN 503); cf. other of Condé's pamphlets of that year (LN 509, 510) and an *Advertissement a la noblesse* (Lyon, 1568; BN Lb33.250 and LN 270) attributed to Du Tillet.

[67] *Contre la principauté de l'evesque Romain* (Lyon, 1564; LN 367), 8.

that 'great man Valla' and his exposé of the Donation of Constantine and rejected as fraudulent ecclesiastical tradition in general.[68] The principal symbols of Romanism were the Society of Jesus and especially the Council of Trent, whose published 'Canons and Decrees' (1564) constituted a storm-center of propaganda for generations. Of course, the Catholics had their own complaints about the foreign base of Huguenot power, referring not only to that 'new Jerusalem' Geneva but also to the German fatherland of 'Christian liberty' and subversive propaganda.

In fact the process of internationalization was evident on both sides. The threat to 'those of the religion' included Italy, Savoy and increasingly Spain, which had begun its own counterattack on Protestant opposition in the Netherlands. The upsurge of Dutch propaganda and counter-propaganda closely resembled and intermixed with that of France, to the extent indeed that the provenance of some pamphlets, such as the *Defense of Liberty against Tyrants*, can hardly be determined by the contents. Similar rhetorical conventions and poetic and musical expressions were employed, and similar defiance of attempts at suppression. As always, preaching was a special target, but in reply to the placards issued by the authorities against unlicensed sermons the Protestants asked, 'What if the apostles had not obeyed the command of their master?' And further, 'If a rebellion is to want to save souls . . ., then one must judge Germany, France, Scotland, Denmark, Sweden, Poland and others to have revolted.'[69] Such judgments were indeed made, and certainly the configurations of ideology in this age were European-wide.

In France the escalation of ideology is apparent in the second wave of Huguenot propaganda accompanying the second and third wars of religion (1567–70). As always the assumption was the determination of the enemy to 'exterminate the pure doctrine of the gospel', as it was put by one 'Discourse' published in Orleans (with a false imprint 'Heidelberg'), but this time the face of the enemy was closer and more menacing.[70] At the end of the royal inspection tour around France, Catherine had stopped for a meeting at Bayonne with Philip II's representative the Duke of Alba, and from the very beginning this provoked suspicions among Protestants. These suspicions were intensified two years later when Alba set out on his

---

[68] *La Papemanie de France* (n.p., 1567; Ars. 10.1).
[69] *Recueil des choses advenues en Anvers, touchant le faict de la Religion* (n.p., 1566; BM 850.b.3), Fi.
[70] *Discours au vray des conseils et moyens qu'on a tenus pour exterminer la pure doctrine de l'evangile hors ce royaume* ([Orleans], 1568; BN Lb[33].195); cf. E. Droz, *L'Imprimerie à la Rochelle* (Geneva, 1960), 1, 63. A. Joubert, *Etude sur les misères d'Anjou aux XVe et XVIe siècles* (Anjou, 1886).

mission to the Netherlands to restore order, causing panic as he marched his troops up the eastern side of France and contributing at least indirectly to the outbreak of the second war. Feelings of persecution and worse to come led Protestants to worry about this 'enterprise of Bayonne', as the author of the 'Discourse' put it, whose aim was 'to diminish and weaken those of the Religion in order to make easier the breaking and revocation of the edict' of pacification. 'The King of Spain', according to another pamphlet, 'having entered into a league with the Emperor, the Pope and other princes in order to exterminate those of the religion, summoned the King [of France] to do the same and to sign the articles of the Council of Trent, which the Cardinal of Lorraine has been so solicitous about.'[71] Here was the ideological origin, at least from Protestant perspective, of that 'Tridentine' alliance which in one form or another posed a threat for at least another generation. It also represents a locus classicus of a conspiracy theory of history.

Such were the premises of the official Huguenot propaganda which from 1567 again began issuing from the presses of Orleans and Geneva.[72] Again there was talk of 'the necessity of assembling the estates'; and reference was made not only to the meetings held a few years earlier at Fontainebleau and Orleans but also the Estates General of Tours in 1484 as described by Commines and romanticized by Huguenot critics of 'tyranny'. Still, the ultimate issue was that of armed resistance – and more important, resistance to what authority? According to a parlementary *arrêt* of November 1569, the injury was declared to be to the 'majesty' of the king, and thus lese-majesty or treason became explicitly the grounds of debate. One of the popularizers of Machiavelli in France, Jean de la Taille, also remonstrated against all the subjects 'who have taken up arms against his majesty'; and another royalist pamphlet denounced rebellion as the worst possible crime.[73] The tactics of the Huguenots

---

[71] *Bref discours contenant les causes et raisons par lesquelles ceux de la Religion reformee ont prise les armes* (in collection cited, next note), Avi: 'C'estoit que l'on attendoit que le Roy d'Epaigne d'eust passer en Itallie, comme il avoit fait courir le bruit, et qu'ayant faict ligue avec l'Empereur, le Pape et autres Princes, pour exterminer ceux de la Religion, il sommeroit le Roy de faire le semblable, et de signer les articles du Concile de Trent, dequoy le Cardinal de l'Orraine estoit diligent solliciteur.' Cf. *Lettre de deux gentilshommes* (n.p., 1567; BN Lb33.217 and LN 547).

[72] *Les Requestes, protestations, remonstrances et advertissements, faits par Monseigneur le Prince de Condé* (Orleans, 1567; BN Lb33.206), including 11 individual pamphlets, separate copies in Lb33.207–11 and LN 505–9. Cf. *De la necessité d'assembler les estats* (n.p., 1567; BN Lb33, 186, Ars. 10.2 and LN 511), and pamphlet on fifteenth-century 'Reformateurs du bien public' (n.p., 1567; LN 550); also Hauser, 184ff.

[73] La Taille, *Remonstrance pour le roy, a tous ses subiects qui ont prins les armes contre sa maiesté* (Lyon, 1567; Paris, 1569; LN 545, 675) and *Advertissement sur le pourparlé qu'on dit de paix* (n.p., 1568; LN 557).

were to reverse this argument. Their target was not royal majesty, or sovereignty, in any sense. On the contrary it was the Cardinal of Lorraine who had 'subverted the state' of France, who had conspired with Spain and other enemies of the crown. Yet the Huguenots were undeniably vulnerable themselves to charges of conspiring with foreigners. Among other German princes, the Count of Zweibrucken published to the world (and in French) his support for 'those of the reformed religion'. And so the debate went on, with agreement on nothing except that rebellion, the crime of lese-majesty, represented the fundamental issue of the age.

In its effort to maintain control over social upheavals the government continued to have recourse to legislative remedies for all manner of human activities.[74] There were edicts published to regulate questions of minority in the private law of succession and of the conditions of feudal confiscation, that is, the seizing of fiefs. As always, too, education came under surveillance, and Protestants were prohibited from establishing or teaching in any schools or colleges. Prohibitions of the printing of unapproved books were repeated, with death prescribed for a second offense. Such restrictions and the continuous attempts to forbid libels and name-calling were intended, according to the model edict of January 1562, 'to maintain our civil laws' (*pour garder nos loix politiques*)[75] and protect 'the good houses of our kingdom' according to conventional notions of 'good police'; but the criminalization of so many offenses against civil law clearly reflected an expansion of political ambition if not of power – and this in an age of resurgent neo-feudal as well as religious disorder.

Throughout these debates the Guise-Bourbon feud retained its central position, though Condé, who died in 1568, was replaced by Coligny as principal antagonist. In a remonstrance of that year Coligny rehearsed the calamities which had befallen France in the previous decade, and he pointed in particular to the cities which had joined 'the party of the Religion', as he called it, during these troubles.[76] Orleans, Valence, Auxerre and many others had joined the resistance, while Catholic cities like Amiens and Bourges had seen 'seditions' and the massacre of great numbers of those of the

---

[74] See the numerous published edicts listed in Isnard and LN.

[75] Edict, 17 Jan. 1562 (BN F. 46822.7), other copies and supplementary legislation (Isnard 1677ff. and LN 283ff., MC, III, 7.

[76] *Remonstrance au Roy* (n.p., 1568; BN Lb33.241); cf. *Responce a un certain escrit, publié par l'admiral et ses adherans, pretendans couvrir et excuser la rupture* . . . (Paris, Lyon, Poitiers, 1568; BN Lb33.244 and LN 573–5); cf. F. Deltail, 'Lettres de l'église de Saint-Lo', *BSHPF*, cxvii (1971), 84–7, and 'Accord entre Mr le Prince de Condé et ceulx de la Rochelle', 6 June 1577, in *Documents inédits pour servir à la histoire de la Réforme et de la Ligue*, ed. J. Loutchitzky (Paris, 1875), 94.

Religion. This may have seemed to be more a threat than a complaint, for Coligny himself was the one looked to by many cities as protector. Just as running attacks on the Cardinal of Lorraine had turned into a black legend, so the charisma and political menace of the Admiral was creating a dangerous public image, making him into a symbol and a scapegoat of civil disorder. In 1569 Coligny was officially condemned in an *arrêt* (the one translated into eight languages) which deprived him of his offices, declared him guilty of conspiracy and treason, and hanged him *in absentia*.[77] This act, as some later thought, prepared the ground for his assassination three years later. It did not, however, lessen his magnetic force; nor did it deter his following, especially among urban groups.

In the French wars as in those of the Netherlands the role of the cities became increasingly important. From the time of Condé's association in 1562 some cities, including Rouen, Saint Lo and Le Mans, had taken a public position in favor of the Huguenot cause; and by the third civil war such statements had became a significant part of propaganda. Most sensational were two 'declarations and protestations' made by La Rochelle in 1568 and 1569 objecting to treatment by the government as well as to actions of 'certain mutinous and seditious Italians and other degenerate and bastardized French'.[78] When one of the king's agents, upon entering the city, heard the singing of the psalms, according to the first pamphlet, 'he swore that within three days they would be singing a different tune'. This attitude was typical of the Catholics, continued the author, and 'in short one cannot imagine any cruelty, tyranny, injustice and inhumanity which has not been practiced by those of that religion'. Among the Protestant citizens there was much discussion of the principle of 'liberty of conscience' and the legitimacy of armed resistance. 'All power comes from above', the argument continued; however, 'those who battle and conspire against God are not true kings but private persons who need not be obeyed in this regard, as is the case likewise with obedience and respect to fathers

---

[77] *Arrest de la Court de Parlement contre Gaspart de Coligny, qui fut admiral de France, mis en huict langues, a sçavoir, François, Latin, Italien, Espagnol, Allemant, Flament, Anglois et Escoçois* (Paris, 1569; LN 652–3); cf. Kelley, *Hotman*, 202.

[78] *Declaration et protestation de ceux de la religion reformee de la Rochelle* ([La Rochelle], 1568; BN Lb33.226), Biii: 'L'on caressera de toutes courtoises et liberalitez un poltron et infame Italien, ou un fier sot et superstitieux Espanol, ou quelque larron banquier et thresorier, ou villain maquereau, ou impudent flatereau, ou dissimulé atheiste franc–Espanol pour tourner le dos a un prince du sang, ou quelque vertueux et vaillant chevalier, qui se sera employé toute sa vie a faire tresfidele service au Roy.' And *Second declaration . . .* (1569, with above, 227); cf. Droz, *L'Imprimerie*, 1, 61ff.; *Discours sur la rebellion de la Rochelle commis par les pretendus reformez* (Poitiers, 1569; Lb33.221); *Pourparler fait a La Rochelle* (n.p., 1571; Lb33.296).

and mothers'. The real culprit was not the young Charles IX, however; rather it was Philip II, 'the Spaniard, ancient, natural and hereditary enemy of France'. This pamphlet was shot through with xenophobic rhetoric – 'cowardly and infamous Italian', 'arrogant, stupid and superstitious Spaniard', and 'dissimulating atheist of a Franco-Spaniard'. It was against such foreign influence, not against the monarchy, that La Rochelle was struggling.

So the fiction of legality, of working within recognized political arrangements, was maintained, and no doubt this made it easier to achieve the pacification of 1570. In this famous 'Peace of Monsieur' La Rochelle and three other Huguenot cities were guaranteed, and many of the religion (Hotman among them) were allowed to return to properties, academic posts and offices. The declaration of the king in this piece of legislation, that 'the memory of everything since the troubles came to our kingdom' should be 'as if it had never happened'[79] reflected the optimism of this interlude, as did old-fashioned exhortations to peace by Louis le Roy and others. What promised to legitimize the arrangement was the projected marriage between the Huguenot Henry of Navarre and Margaret, sister of the king. The public euphoria reached its highest point in the first part of 1572 with prophecies of boundless national prosperity. Nostradamus addressed his predictions 'to the French nation', and he was seconded by Belleforest, who likewise read signs of good fortune and the 'felicity of the reign of Charles IX'.[80] They were joined by another astrologer who lauded more specifically the 'politique' union of Bourbon and Valois, scheduled for August. Hopes had not run so high since the summer of 1561, when the Colloquy of Poissy was being arranged and publicized.

Nor, in the event, had hopes ever been dashed so irreparably. In fact the peace had permitted both sides to consolidate themselves, and the Huguenots in particular to strengthen ties with the Dutch, who even used La Rochelle as a base of operations. And all the marriage plans accomplished was to bring together into Paris Coligny and other Huguenot leaders and so to set the stage for the catastrophe to follow: first the attempted, then the successful murder of the Admiral (22 and 24 August respectively), and then the mob violence which took the lives of thousands in Paris and various

[79] Including an English translation, *An Edict set forth by the French King for appeasing of Troubles in his kingdome* (London, n.d.).

[80] Nostradamus, *Propheties . . .* (Lyon, 1572; BN Lb33.304); Belleforest, *Discours sur l'heur des presages advenus de nostre temps, significantz la felicite du regne de nostre Roy Charles neufiesme tres-chrestien* (Paris, 1572; BN Lb33.303); B. Abbatia, *Prognostication touchant le mariage . . .* (Paris, 1572; LN 717).

provincial cities over the next few weeks and sent many more into exile. The massacres of St Bartholomew not only initiated another and more bitter phase of civil war but also set off an unprecedented firestorm of propaganda, perhaps the most sensational and most seminal in modern history.

THOSE OF THE CAUSE

The story of the martyrdom of Admiral Coligny and the killing of thousands of his followers, first in Paris and then in the provinces, has been told many times[81] and never so vividly as by Huguenot ideologists. Among these were both Beza and Hotman, who had been among the founders of the party line over a decade before and who now became, respectively, its philosopher and its historian. Of course both sides indulged in propaganda, pictorial and poetic as well as conventional prose forms; and the attempt to reconstruct the context and course of events has had to contend with such media interference ever since. Whatever·the facts of the matter – the motives of the actors, the numbers of the dead, the extent of the damage and the immediate consequences – the primary significance of the outburst in the long run was the impact it had on the moral and political consciousness of the members of all parties and, more indirectly, the shaping effects it had on the social and constitutional thinking of contemporary ideologists and more detached political observers.

In retrospect the Huguenots concluded that the whole thing had been planned in advance, including the false peace of St Germain itself. One of the most extreme propaganda reactions expressed this view in bitter verses:

> My father was a devil in dis-Guise
> Assuming the habit of a priest,
> A deadly monster professing all vice,
> Stirring up trouble, a terrible beast,
> Coupling with that high born whore,
> Descended from the buggers of Italy,
> Nursed by the milk of a horrible fury.[82]

Huguenots, some of whom half-expected some such catastrophe, called up recollections of earlier atrocities and two generations of

---

[81] Most recently, *The Massacre of St Bartholomew*, ed. A. Soman (The Hague, 1974), and *Actes du Colloque l'Amiral de Coligny et son temps* (Paris, 1974); H. Fazy, *La Saint-Barthélemy et Genève* (Geneva, 1879); Janine Estèbe, *Tocsin pour un massacre* (Paris, 1968); and Kelley, *Hotman*, chapters 9–10.

[82] *Reveille-Matin* (see below, p. 302, n. 2); Hauser, 249.

threats of 'extermination'; and they pointed in particular to the suspicious meeting at Bayonne in 1567 between Catherine de Médicis and the Duke of Alba. Rehearsing old resentments led directly to the discussion of the most fundamental issues, among them many of the problems debated by later historians, including the question of premeditation, the idea of a general 'conspiracy' and the determination of war guilt. For its part, the government immediately began to publish edicts charging the Parisian Huguenots, under Coligny's leadership, with having themselves planned a conspiracy to rebel against the king and others of the royal family. The condemnation of Coligny for lese-majesty made three years before was republished, and a standard form of recantation was issued for Huguenots to sign – 'I, so-and-so, native of such-and-such diocese, do abjure and anathematize all errors, whether Lutheran, Calvinist, Huguenot or any other' – and this was followed by a confession of orthodox faith.[83] Many Huguenots who could not sign this declaration went into hiding or exile, especially to Geneva. It was this exile-underground community that formed the social base of the most subversive and radical polemic of modern times.

For the next two years the propaganda war was intense, taking up where the debate had left off three years earlier but on a larger terrain and with more dangerous targets. Matters were complicated by various international issues, including official attempts to neutralize the Swiss (potential allies of the Huguenots), the increasing links with the war between Spain and the Netherlands, and especially the candidacy of Catherine's third son, Henry of Anjou, to the Polish throne, which generated its own more conventional publicity. Among the more official spokesmen for the government (aside from the legislative statements) were Pomponne de Bellièvre, ambassador to the Swiss cantons; Jean de Monluc, sent as ambassador to Poland to allay the doubts of the nobility; and Guy du Faur de Pibrac, one of the most eloquent advocates of the century.[84] Bellièvre's charges that the Huguenots had offended the royal majesty were circulated only by word of mouth, but Monluc's

---

[83] *Forme d'abjuration d'heresie, et confession de foy, que doivent par les desvoyez de la foy, pretendans estre receuz en l'Eglise*, 1 Oct. (Paris, 1572; BN Ld[176].32). 'Ie N. natif de Etc. Diocese de Etc. . . . abiure et anathematize tout erreur et heresie Lutherienne, Calviniste, Huguenotique, et toute autre heresie quelque qu'elle soit.' Relevant legislation collected in BN F. 46843, and cf. LN 729, 724.

[84] *Oratio*, 10 and 25 April 1573 (Cracow, 1573; BN Lb[34].20) and French trans., *Harangue* (Paris, 1573; BN Lb[34].21); also Monluc's *Epistola* and *Defensio* (Paris, 1574; BN Lb[34].19) and *Vera et brevis descriptio* (Cracow, 1573; BN Lb[33].313); and a Polish translation cited by François de Noailles, *Henri de Valois et Pologne en 1572* (Paris, 1867), II, 128.

oration was issued as well in pamphlet form. In general he played down the extent of the killing (only 40 in Paris, not 1200) and compared them favorably with Protestant atrocities, which he had witnessed in his own bishopric of Valence some years before. Far from being inhuman or tyrannical, the government had displayed clemency; and on the contrary it was 'les Evangeliques' who were responsible for the renewal of war. To reinforce this argument, Pibrac tried to establish in more detail the accumulation of official grievances and the background of the continuing Huguenot 'conspiracy' to murder the royal family and usurp control over the government.[85]

In support of this position two of the greatest scholars of the century, uncharacteristically, became involved in controversy. Marc-Antoine Muret charged that the 'heretiques-rebelles' had been engaged in a conspiracy, and in rhapsodic terms defended the massacres.[86] 'O memorable night which, by the ruin of a few seditious men, has delivered the king from the threat of death and the kingdom from the perpetual fear of civil war . . .! O happy day, full of glory!' (Of course, this was spoken in the presence of the pope, who himself contributed to the propaganda by a medal struck in honor of 24 August 1572.) Even more renowned as a philologist, Jacques Cujas emerged from his academic shell to support the royal position and to register his distaste at the level of Huguenot argument. Noting the flood of 'little books', Cujas added, 'and as if they are not content with their writings, they offer illustrations of the day of St Bartholomew, representing the king carrying the head of the Admiral on his lance, while others, perhaps his brother, watch a

---

[85] *Ad Stanislaum Elvidium epistola* (Paris, 1573; BN Lb33.322 and LN 770), and French translation (Lb33.323, LN 771), and in A. Cabos (ed.), *L'Apologie de la Saint-Barthélemy par Guy du Faur de Pibrac* (Paris, 1922).

[86] *Oratio* (Rome, 1573; BN Lb33.320), and French version with response by A. Buccapadulius (Paris, 1573; BN Lb33.319 and LN 767). Cf. *Discours sur les occurrences des guerres intestines de ce royaume et de la justice de Dieu contre les rebelles . . .* (Paris, 1572; LN 724), 4:

> O bien esleu de Dieu, ô Roy qui n'as iamais
> Rien plus aymé, que voir tes subiets vivre en paix,
> Embrassant lennemy de ta misericorde,
> Ennemy, meritant la faveur d'une corde.
> O huguenot ingrat, cour plein d'impieté,
> Isseu de mont Caucase, et d'un tygre alaité
> Pourtant de bien receus, quelle recognoissance?

And *ibid.*, 8:

> Iustice et Pieté, font dominee la France.
> Iustice et Pieté, y maintiennent la loy,
> Pour n'y servir qu'un Dieu, une Eglise, et un Roy.

pregnant woman being burnt and cut open'.[87] According to another critic, 'there is no gallows, cross or torture severe enough to expiate the crime of a traitor, a seditionist, a rebel, an enemy of his country and of his king'.[88]

One of the most savage critics of the Huguenots had been one of their number just a few years before. Pierre Charpentier had left the chair of law at the University of Geneva under a cloud, and in the fall of 1572 he placed his polemical talents at the disposal of Catholicism. For him the massacres were simply 'punishment' for the French who were in revolt (*François revoltez*). He attacked his former comrades at their most vulnerable point, which was their self-interest, and argued that Ramus, claimed by the rebels as one of their martyrs, had in fact been opposed to their cause. 'The persecution of the churches of France came about not through those who profess religion', he insisted, 'but through those who encourage factions and conspiracies, which go by the name of "the Cause".' '"The Cause"', he sneered; 'all this means is to carry out a successful coup.'[89]

It was precisely on this capital point – 'la CAUSE' – that Huguenot spokesmen were prepared to stake their reputations, if not their fortunes. Perhaps the earliest champion of the Huguenots was François Portus, who from his Genevan refuge defended 'the innocence of the faithful servants of God and obedient subjects of the king, massacred on 24 August 1572' against such 'defamatory letters'. The reason the word 'Cause' offends you, he told his former colleague Charpentier, is that you defend those who have no cause.[90] For him on the contrary the recent catastrophe had brought together the evangelical and constitutional demands of the Huguenots, so that 'those of the religion' has now become 'those of the Cause'. Another support of this party – 'lost and lamented cause', he called it – was the great jurist Hugues Doneau, lately exiled from Bourges to Geneva, who undertook to refute Muret and Cujas (a

---

[87] *Pro Io. Monlucio . . . adversus libellum . . . Zachariae Furnesteri* (n.p., 1575; BN Lb34.22), originally published with Monluc, *Epistola* (cited above, p. 289, n. 85), and French trans., *Defense pour monsieur de Montluc* (Paris, 1575; BN Lb34.23).

[88] Artus Desiré, *La Singerie des huguenots* (Paris, 1574; Ars. 16.6), 22; *Discours de la mort et execution de Gabriel comte de Montgomery* (Paris, 1574; LN 790), 2; and Frank S. Giese, *Artus Desiré* (Chapel Hill, 1973). Cf. *Figure des medailles* (Paris, 1572; Ars, 14.7), 'Figure et exposition des pourtraictz et dictions contenuz es medailles de la conspiration des rebelles en France, opprimee et estaincte par le Roy tres-chrestien Charles IX le 24 d'Aoust 1572.' One shows the king on his throne holding a flaming sword and sceptre; another with an olive crown and on the obverse Hercules in a lion's skin holding a torch to a hydra. The permission to cast by Seguier is dated 4 Oct.

[89] *Epistola ad Franciscum Portum Cretensem* (n.p., 1572[3]; BN Lb33.314 and LN 720), and French trans. (BN Lb33.315 and LN 721).

[90] *Ad Petri Carpentarii causidici virulentam epistolam, responsio* (n.p., 1573; BN Lb33. 316 and LN 773) and French trans. (n.p., 1574; BN Lb33.317 and LN 831).

former colleague at Bourges) as well as Charpentier.[91] Doneau tried to convict the royalist partisans out of their own mouths, especially by referring to the notorious edict published just four days after the massacres, according to which 'His Majesty declares that what has come about has been done by his express command and not for reason of religion.'[92] Presumably the intention was to deny any charge of religious persecution, but the inference drawn by many was that the king himself was assuming political guilt for the killings and for the renewal of war. Certainly this was the conclusion of Doneau, who saw consequences 'worse than the cruelest tyranny of antiquity'.

Other Huguenot pamphlets, emanating from the same partisan source, followed the same general lines, to the extent indeed that problems of individual attribution are in some cases ultimately insoluble and perhaps not greatly important: the ideology of the Cause was in effect the expression of the whole exile community prepared by a co-operative propaganda machine. A certain Wilhelm Prisback rehearsed Coligny's career and abstracted from it eight specific 'outrages' which Huguenots had suffered.[93] Pierre Fabre launched another attack on Charpentier, a mere 'chicanneur' who had falsely assumed 'the arrogant title of jurisconsult'.[94] Besides lamenting the butchery of St Bartholomew, Fabre continued the theme of reform, complaining that waiting for the pope to reform the church was like waiting for courtiers to reform their manners, drunkards the taverns and whores their bordellos. Pierre Burin, responding to Pibrac, following the image which Hotman had attached earlier to the Cardinal of Lorraine, suggested that the king himself had, to judge from royalist statements, become the 'tiger'.[95]

Underlying this vituperative journalism was a more substantial (but no less vituperative) historical literature, which reconstructed the background and events of the past generation. Perhaps most authoritative were the publications of Doneau's colleague Hotman, likewise fled from Bourges to Geneva, who composed both an authorized biography of Coligny and a narrative history called the *French Fury*, both of which circulated widely in several languages.

[91] *Zachariae Furnesteri defensio pro iusto et innocente tot millium animarum sanguine* (Lyon, 1573), and *Adversus anonymi cuiusdam pro Monlucio praescriptionum Zacaraei Furnesterii defensio* (n.p., 1575); see above, p. 290, n. 87.

[92] *Declaration du roy, de la cause et occasion de la mort de l'admiral* (Paris, 1572; LN 729); copies in BN F. 46843 (ME, II), Aii: 'Sadicte Maiesté declare que ce qui est ainsi advenu a esté par son expres commandement, et non pour cause aucune de religion . . .'

[93] *Responsio ad orationem* [by Bellièvere] (La Rochelle, 1573; BN Lb³³.321).

[94] *Traitté du quel on peut apprendre en quel cas il est permis a l'homme chrestien de porter les armes* ('Neustadt', 1575; Lb³⁴.99 and LN 854) and Latin version (Lb³⁴.98 and LN 877).

[95] *Response* (Basel, 1574; BN Lb³³.324 and LN 783), 25: 'Cesse de nous vouloir persuader que le Roy se fit Tygre.'

On the one hand Hotman portrayed Coligny as a high-minded and saintly leader who had finally achieved martyrdom; on the other he continued his invective against that bloody 'tiger' of a Cardinal, who was 'the very forger of all the former warres', going back indeed to that affair of Amboise in 1559, in which Hotman had played a part. No one contributed more than Hotman to these twin legends of political virtue and villainy, except perhaps the principals in the feud. In the St Bartholomew plot the Cardinal's partner in crime was Catherine de Médicis, and in his biography of the Admiral Hotman included an incriminating (and no doubt fabricated) letter in which she declared that 'there is no better way to restore the crown of France . . . than to kill all the Huguenots'.[96] Hotman's friend Henri Estienne, another of the pioneering scholars who turned their hand to polemic, put the finishing touches on this black legend of Catherine de Médicis in his own scathing biographical essay, which also circulated internationally and multilingually.

At the same time a deeper perspective was being opened on the ideological predicament which St Bartholomew had brought to a head. The past was ransacked by embattled scholars not only to find grounds for recrimination but also to seek deeper roots for the present troubles and perhaps even to find remedies for them. Once again Beza and Hotman were among the major figures. Beza's career from his conversion in 1548 to his accession to Calvin's ministry neatly illustrates the dynamic of the 'ideological primary group' and, on a personal level, the process of politicization discussed earlier. As Calvin was a classic case of the 'Founder', so Beza was the very archetype of the 'Second', who takes over the 'cause' in its more difficult stages and who labors to provide it with a solid social and political base. If it is true (as a sociologist has remarked) that 'The Second always had a very bad press', the reasons are not hard to grasp in this case.[97] Even more than Calvin, Beza was torn between the needs of conformity in Geneva and resistance in France. According to popular opinion, he had been involved in conspiracy at Amboise, betrayal of national unity at Poissy and seditious rabble-rousing in Paris on the eve of war. He lived through the darkest years of civil conflict and, because of St Bartholomew and the subsequent emigrations, was provoked to extend Calvin's view of resistance (barely a loophole) into a considerable theory of revolution. Those events, coupled with the later return of King Henry IV to Catholicism, confirmed Beza's exile mentality and political disillusionment.

---

[96] See Kelley, *Hotman*, 207ff. Estienne, *A mervaylous discourse upon the life, deedes, and behaviours of Katherine de Medicis* . . . ('Heidelberg', 1575).

[97] W. Stark, *A Sociology of Religion* (London, 1966), IV, 13.

Hotman also died in exile, though he did not live to see Henry's final defection from the Cause. His *Francogallia* was largely a product of the 1560s; but like the *Right of Magistrates* by his old friend (and as so often before, collaborator) Beza, this erudite defense of liberty and institutional purity caught the spirit of the 1570s. Historically, Hotman's purpose was to contrast the corrupt and 'tyrannical' legal and social heritage of Rome (imperial as well as papal, that is, civilian as well as canonist) with native Germano-Celtic – 'Francogallic' – cultural traditions. The analogy with religious reform was unmistakable. Just as evangelical reformers sought to be 'free' from papal materialism in a purified church, so Hotman sought to be free of Italianate oppression in a purified constitution. In political terms one might say that he opposed the principle of historical 'immanence' which would justify the 'Italogallic' state of the late Valois (this term Hotman himself applied to the alternative vision of his severest critic, Papire Masson), including its usurping and persecuting Parlement; and in its place Hotman substituted a kind of 'transcendent' constitution located, like the 'primitive church', in an idealized antiquity that nevertheless seemed recoverable. Here again legal and social 'reform' merged with the religious variety. Accepting a commission from that 'Solon' of France, Chancellor Michel de l'Hôpital, who himself lamented the corruption and 'chicanery' associated with civil law, Hotman had written just a few years earlier a treatise called *Anti-Tribonian* in reference to the Byzantine editor of Roman law, which proposed a basic reform of legal education and practice. In a sense the *Francogallia* represented the political basis of this social and intellectual ideal.[98]

Hotman's book, which was a locus of the major ideological themes of the next generation, permeated the debates of the civil wars. The attack by Papire Masson, who was a disciple of Hotman's old nemesis Baudouin as well as a eulogistic biographer of that 'tiger', the Cardinal of Lorraine (both of whom had died in 1573), set up what Hotman regarded as an evil Romanist counterpart of his Francogallic ideal; and the ensuing controversy, which once again raised ghosts of the old sibling rivalry with Baudouin, represented in a number of ways the culmination of partisan conflict in this incandescent age of *Kulturkampf* – of ideological warfare.[99] Endorsing Hotman's interpretation were a number of Huguenot publications, one of them a *France-Turquie*, which poured scorn on the Catholic

---

[98] *Francogallia* and *Anti-Tribonian* (Paris, 1603), on which see the thesis of A. Saint-Charmaran, 'L'Antitribonien dans l'oeuvre de François Hotman' (Paris, Ecole du droit, 1972; dactilograph). See above, p. 194, n. 40.

[99] See P. Ronzy, *Papire Masson* (Paris, 1924), and Kelley, *Hotman*, 252ff., with further references.

alternative to Hotman's vision.[100] More direct support appeared in the writings attributed to Nicolas Barnaud. His *Mirror of the French* diagnosed the disease of the body politic with particular reference to the increase in crime, usury and venality associated in the popular mind with Italian immigrants (*Italiens francisquez*), especially the *fuorusciti* patronized by Catherine.[101] It was because of such Italian influence that France possessed – so Barnaud reversed the old Gallican formula – 'neither God, nor faith nor law'. In the *Reveille-Matin* the Francogallic ideal was appealed to as the only solution to the miseries of that age.[102]

The polarity of Germanism and Italianism colored much of the propaganda of these years, and it was intensified by foreign ties on both sides. As Gallicans like Masson seemed ideologically bound to Rome, so Huguenots were unavoidably drawn to German Protestants, who were 'like brothers and [cousins-]german to the French', according to one pamphleteer, 'being linked by a common tie of religion'.[103] The standard invidious contrast between Italianate behavior and the freedom and 'frankness' of Germanic tradition was expressed by Pierre Fabre in the current etymological pun, that 'We who are French and frank do not dissimulate in Italian fashion.'[104] In the wake of the massacres libellous verses were circulated against the royal family as well as the Cardinal, and their anti-Italian character was striking. In general, Italianism, as discussed and ranted about by authors like Hotman and Estienne, ranged from Ciceronianism to sodomy; but in particular it encompassed those cardinal sins of theology and political philosophy, atheism and tyranny; and it was this aspect of the alien syndrome that Huguenots took as their principal target.

It was in this context that there began to emerge a new symbol of – and scapegoat for – Italianism. Niccolò Machiavelli, old servant of the Medici, was identified with the 'Politique' in the most pejorative sense of the word; and soon his posthumous influence was hypostasized as 'Machiavellism', a concept that has haunted European history ever since.[105] Within a few months of the massacres Portus

---

[100] *La France-Turquie, c'est a dire, conseils et moyens tenus par les ennemies de la couronne de France pour reduire le royaume en tel estat que la tyrannie turquique* (Orleans, 1576; LN 890).

[101] *Miroir des françois* (Paris, 1581), 31, *passim*; cf. L'Estoile, 58ff., 90ff., etc. There is another *Miroir françois* (n.p., n.d.; Ars. 26.2), 'representant la face de ce siecle corrumpu'.

[102] *Reveille-Matin*, 191.

[103] *Declaration des causes qui ont meu ceux de la religion a reprendre les armes pour leur conservation* (Montauban, 1574; LN 789).

[104] *Traitté* (see p. 291 above, n. 94), 64: 'Nous qui sommes François sommes francs et ne dissimulons rien a la mode Italienne.'

[105] Kelley, 'Murd'rous Machiavel in France', *Political Science Quarterly*, LXXXV (1970), 545–59.

threw this charge at that 'traitor and apostate' Charpentier, and soon it became common currency. Machiavelli was blamed not only for an immoral political style but, via Catherine de Médicis, the daughter of the man to whom the *Prince* was dedicated, for the massacres themselves, which seemed to be an adaptation of the advice given in chapter 13 of that book. In 1574 a 'remonstrance' addressed to King Henry III, successor of the unfortunate Charles IX, argued that in order to achieve peace it was necessary 'to ban Machiavelli perpetually from France as the greatest liar and imposter there has ever been'. 'Those who have introduced the precepts of Machiavelli into France', the author continued, 'have failed to realize that France is very different from his nation. For Frenchmen are naturally religious, fond of piety and never pleased to falsify their faith or to deny their honor and reputation . . .'[106] Two years later the author of this tract, Innocent Gentillet, published his famous *Anti-Machiavel*, thus inaugurating a new political genre which at the same time served as an extraordinarily vivid form of anti-Catholic propaganda. Many others, eventually Catholics as well as Protestants, took up this xenophobic and often racialist symbolism for their own polemical purposes. Later the Spanish joined with the Italians, as Huguenots saw it, in mutual ignominy – just as the Dutch joined the French in common cause.

Other expressions of resistance came, as always, from the cities, especially La Rochelle, which had such a rich tradition of civic liberties. As recently as 1539 La Rochelle had defied the authority of the king on secular, which is to say fiscal, grounds; and at that time religious motives were already coming into play.[107] Less than a month before the massacres of St Bartholomew, La Rochelle appealed to Coligny for protection; and after his death there were rumors that the city was going to renounce allegiance to the French crown and accept the sovereignty of Elizabeth of England (to which, in earlier times, the city had been subject). A justification for this was also found in the Biblical case of Libna, which figured prominently in the propaganda of the period, notably that of Hotman and Beza. It was the latter who introduced most directly the argument from civic liberties; for the point of departure for his *Right of Magistrates*, a more theoretical counterpart to his colleague Hotman's *Francogallia*, was the famous 'Magdeburg Confession', in which German Protestants had publicly defied the authority of the Emperor in 1550.

In all the publicity of these years the ideological focus remained

---

[106] *Remonstrance au Roy tres-chrestien Henry III* (Frankfurt, 1574; BN Lb³⁴.92), 92; Gentillet, *Discours contre Machiavel*, ed. A. D'Andrea and P. D. Stewart (Florence, 1974).
[107] See below, p. 320, at n. 38.

constant: it was, in the words of an anonymous Huguenot 'resolution' of 1577, that 'question posed so many times before concerning the taking of arms by inferiors'.[108] Writing after the pacification of 1576, the author of this pamphlet took a philosophical view of his task; and he began with a definition of society as 'a community of men associated by law, whether a monarchy, aristocracy or democracy, founded on certain laws, usages and customs received and approved by the common good'. In any form of government, however, law was supreme: 'justice is the soul, laws are the expression of this, and the king is only the mouthpiece [*bouche*] of the laws'. This was the true meaning of the old formula that the king's will was law, for in practice 'the king is only the simple administrator of the crown'. So it was, the author continued, that we could plead against the king in his own courts; otherwise we could only give up and say, 'Take!' The basis of society, then, was the old principle of *salus populi*, 'the good of the people is the supreme law'; and like Hotman and Beza, this author inferred from this some notion of popular sovereignty. He inferred, too, a link between popular liberty and pure religion and seemed to think that the former was a necessary condition for the latter. In Switzerland, for example, political liberty had been achieved long before Zwingli and Oecolampadius preached the gospel. In any case tyranny and evangelical religion were incompatible, and this contributed to the 'revolution's' answer to the classic question, which was that 'defense against tyranny by arms is permitted in all good conscience'. More than that, such resistance was necessary, and all those who joined in such a cause were true servants of their patria.

Of course such arguments only gave weight to the charge that, in the grudging words of this same author, 'The gospel is the seed-bed of rebellion' (*l'Evangile soit semence de rebellion*). Charpentier carried on about the 'Cause' in such terms. 'That old cause has engendered a new one', he wrote, referring to the wave of resistance that contributed to the fourth civil war.[109] 'By this they can refuse to obey the commands of the king and to take his cities away from him . . . But this new "Cause" is really the cause spoken of by rhetoricians, that is, something separated from reason.' For the Huguenots, of

---

[108] *Resolution claire et facile sur la question tant de fois faicte de la prise des armes par les inferieurs* . . . (Rheims, 1577; BN Lb³⁴.103.A), 50, 83ff.: '. . . ie demanderois volontiers pour quoy en France nous tenons inviolablement cette regle, que le Roy n'est que simple administrateur de la Couronne'. 'C'est pourquoy en toutes cours nous plaidons contre le Roy, et gaignons plus de causes que luy: car si sa puissance estoit absolue, il faudroit seulement luy dire, Prenez.'

[109] *Advertissement . . . touchant le port des armes* (Paris, 1575; BN Lb³⁴.97), and Latin version (96); for response, see p. 291 above, n. 95.

course, the term implied not only a political commitment but also a holy mission; and to understand the extreme forms which ideology had assumed in this culminating phase of civil war we should recall the ever-repeated, but now politicized, condition of martyrdom: 'What makes the martyr is not the punishment but the cause.'[110]

Having explored some of the levels of social and political consciousness, examined some of the various institutional vehicles and surveyed some of the immediate historical consequences, it is finally time to come to grips with some of the broader and longer-range aspects of the problem of ideology. The last chapter examines sixteenth-century ideology from several points of view in order to bring closer together the diverse inquiries ventured in the previous six chapters. After an attempt to assess the general character of Huguenot ideology in confrontation with its Catholic counterpart and at the height of its political organization and energy, two kinds of retrospective analyses will be undertaken, first a historical discussion of the social and institutional sources of ideology and then a structural discussion of the way these elements are combined into a coherent view of human predicaments. It seems appropriate to conclude with a discussion of the last phase of the cycle, the 'end of ideology'.

---

[110] Crespin, I, 23.

VIII · Ideology:
An autopsy of social thought

This gross Ideology of them all.

John Adams

Doctrines do not necessarily die from having been killed.

T. H. Huxley

VIII · Ideology:
An autopsy of social thought

APOLOGUE: AN ALARM SOUNDS (1573)

'A prince who refuses justice to one of his subjects is guilty before God. So much worse is a prince who refuses it to all of his subjects at once, especially those who know that death will result from this conspiracy.'[1] Thus declared a spokesman in a Huguenot dialogue published a little more than a year after the massacres of St Bartholomew. The notorious *Reveille-Matin* was the work of a man who called himself 'Eusebe Philadelphe', but who was probably Nicolas Barnaud; printed ostensibly in Edinburgh but actually in Basel, it presented the clearest, most comprehensive and perhaps most effective statement of the political position of the Huguenots yet formulated. This masterpiece of propaganda not only summed up the political and social complaints of the previous generation and exemplified the radical turn which arguments took after 1572 but also illustrated the transition from party propaganda to broader and more philosophical interpretations – the intersection, one might say, of ideology and political philosophy.

The first part of this 'alarm-bell' of 1573 appeared as a single *Dialogue*, 'in which are treated many things happening to the Lutherans and Huguenots in France, together with certain points and advice to be known and followed', which appeared less than six months after the massacres. The interlocutors are Alithie (Truth), Philalithie (Lover of Truth), the Historiographer, the Politique, the Church and a prophet, Daniel. Though executed with a certain humor and lightness of touch, the dialogue offers a fairly standard Huguenot account of the events leading up to the explosion of August 1572 and beyond. Alithie opens the conversation:

---

[1] *Le Reveille-matin des François, et de leurs voisins. Composé par Eusebe Philadelphe Cosmopolite* ('Edinburgh' [Basel], 1574), Dialogue II, 1; *Dialogue auquel sont traitees plusieurs choses advenues aux Lutheriens et Huguenots de la France . . . par Eusebe Philadelphe* (Basel, 1573) and Latin (BN Lb33.343, 342), dedicated to Elizabeth, 20 Nov. 1573. H. Bordier, *La Saint Barthélemy et la critique moderne* (Geneva, 1879), suggested that the second dialogue was by Doneau; cf. Hauser, 249–51; P. Chaix, A. Dufour and G. Moeckli, *Les Livres imprimés à Genève de 1550 à 1600* (Geneva, 1966), 82; and N. Cazaran, 'Exemples antiques dans quelques pamphlets des guerres de religion', *Association Guillaume Budé, IXe Congrès* (Paris, 1975), 570–610.

'Here comes my old friend Philalithie, it seems to me with a slow step, sad and disturbed . . . Who are these persons with you?'

'You look well, Madame . . .', Philalithie replied. 'One is the Historio-grapher and the other the French Politique.'

'I am happier to see you with the first than with the other', remarked Alithie, 'knowing as I do that he is necessary to assist the enemy and to serve posterity, while the other is more often pernicious and reprehensible, especially if he has stayed at those princely courts which you know so well. But if you remember what I have taught you, I am sure that such persons as the Politiques are these days will not turn you against me.'

The serious discussion begins when they agree that the Historio-grapher, who also claims to be a friend of Alithie, should relate the events of the age. He consents, though remarking that much of the story is perhaps better forgotten. What follows is a summary history of the spread of the gospel from the time of Luther, Bucer, Zwingli, Oecolampadius and Melanchthon, and then an account of the succeeding persecutions leading up to more organized and evenly-matched violence. The pivotal event is the uprising of Amboise, when 'Lutherans became Huguenots' and persecution became tyranny.

'Well I remember those times', interjects the Politique. The subsequent meeting of the Estates General, 'formerly the mind, eyes and ears of our better-counseled kings and bridle for the worst', was merely a cover for the machinations of the Guises. The Politique completes his digression with an anecdote about the Cardinal of Lorraine which seems to please the whole company.[2] It seems that the pope sent him, as a reward for his services to Holy Mother Church, a portrait of the Virgin done by Michelangelo. *En route* the messenger became ill, and the errand was carried on by another man from Lucca. This practical joker substituted another painting of the same size and replaced the seals. When the Cardinal opened the papal gift in the presence of the court, they were shocked to see a panoramic view of the Cardinal, the Queen Mother and the Duchess of Guise, all enjoying an orgy with their naked limbs entwined.

Alithie agrees that this well illustrates the 'force of truth' but then urges the Historiographer to get on with his story, and so he does. The principal themes of the 1560s are remarked on by other speakers, 'liberty of conscience' by Alithie and the abused 'ancient laws' by the Politique. Before coming to the bloody dénouement the Historiographer sets the scene with suggestions of premeditation and recalls in particular the principle laid down a century-and-a-half

---

[2] *Reveille-matin*, I, 13. C. S. Rowan, 'Ulrich Zasius and John Eck: "Faith need not be kept with an enemy"', *Sixteenth Century Journal*, VIII (1977), 79–95.

earlier at the Council of Constance, that it was not necessary to keep faith with heretics (a proposition – *hereticus non esse servandum fidem* – which had sent John Hus to his martyrdom). He also repeats the rumor that Henry of Navarre's mother was poisoned. After the wedding celebrations of Henry and Catherine's daughter Margaret came the great royal conspiracy; and here the Historiographer, true to his trade, introduces a damaging (though unfortunately not authentic) document to show that the royal family had been 'persuaded by the doctrines of Machiavelli'. This is a letter supposedly written by Catherine to Marshal Strozzi on the very day of the massacres: 'I am advising you that today, 24 August, the Admiral and all the Huguenots with him have been killed . . . You are ordered to make yourself master of La Rochelle and there to do the same to all the Huguenots who fall into your hands. Take care to carry this out if you fear to displease the king, Monsieur my son and myself.' And it is signed 'Catherine'. Over two weeks after that, the Historiographer continues, the king was still swearing to kill the rest of his enemies. All the listeners, now including the Church and Daniel, lament this perfidy and agree that few acts of villainy could compare with these of the Valois 'disciples of Machiavelli'.

It is Daniel who moves from these facts and arguments to a general resolution, 'That the said day of the massacre, 24 August, be forever named "the Day of Betrayal" [*la Iournee de la Trahison*] and that the king . . . be called "Charles the Traitor" and have on his arms as an anagram of this "Chasseur Deloyal"' (Faithless pursuer). The remainder of the dialogue is devoted to a Huguenot *arrêt* which contemplates, in forty articles, the restructuring of the whole French state, starting with a governing council of twenty-five and extending into all areas of civil, military and ecclesiastical life. 'Amen!', say they all; and before adjourning, all subscribe to this imaginary constitutional declaration.[3]

The conversation was resumed eight months later, when this dialogue was reissued with another one (perhaps by a different hand), and together entitled *Reveille-Matin*. This time the scene is an inn at Freiburg, and only two of the discussants are present; for some reason neither Truth nor her friend is there. The Politique appears first, chanting a psalm, and takes a moment to recognize the other. 'Good Lord, it's the Historiographer!' he cries. 'Is it possible?' 'It is indeed', says the Historiographer, embracing the Politique. The two colleagues exchange news about their travels and then return to the subject, though now in somewhat different terms. At this point

---

[3] *Reveille-matin*, I, 82, 138.

the question of how to react to a tyrant was no longer hypothetical, since Charles IX had obviously placed private above public interest, and the news had been broadcast to the world. Later in the dialogue it is established that the first conversation, the story told to Alithie, has been published by the same Catholic printer who sold the *French Fury*, a work written 'by a German soon after the massacre' (Hotman). What is more, the two friends now feel free to indulge in more general speculation about such questions as 'the power of kings, tyranny and voluntary servitude'. For the first time the Politique becomes the principal speaker, and his subject is what it is only nominally anachronistic to call revolution.

Classic question: 'If it is possible for subjects to resist the magistrate and how far this license extends.' And classic answer: 'It is indeed correct to say that after God the King comes first, but it is not absolutely true. For people have never been so stupid or ill-advised as to give anyone sovereign power . . . without keeping a good strong bridle, for fear that royalty may fall, as on a slippery road, into tyranny.'[4] So it had been with Rome and other states.

Classic lamentation, too: oppression of the estates and of their long-standing 'liberty'. In this context the Politique brings in feudal law (*le droict feudal*) to buttress his case. 'According to feudal law', he argues, 'the vassal loses his fief for the same reason that the lord loses it, that is, for felony, because the law says that the obligation between the two is mutual and reciprocal. So it is between the king and his subjects, who are as vassals to him.' In feudal society, he continues, even serfs had rights against an oppressive lord; and 'the condition of subjects should not be worse than that of serfs, for if the serf is made free when his lord abuses his power, why should it not be the same with subjects?' On such grounds, indeed, the Swiss had long since freed themselves from Austrian tyranny. And so it had been also with the free cities, especially 'our poor brothers of La Rochelle', as the Politique calls them, whose liberties were clearly listed by Froissart. But the fundamental model was always the church, especially in the Conciliar period. 'The ecclesiastical tyranny of the pope, which has corrupted all doctrine', the Politique acknowledges, 'has violated the order of the church which used to be like the three estates in political organization [*qui eust esté comme les trois estats en la police*] . . . but which now has been forbidden to assemble in a free council.'[5] As ecclesiastical resistance followed ecclesiastical tyranny, so political resistance was following political tyranny.

The upshot has been the corruption of society on every level,

[4] *Ibid.*, II, 85.　　　　　[5] *Ibid.*, II, 93.

domestic and moral as well as political and religious. Kings were indeed like fathers, but even in Roman law fathers no longer had the right to kill their children. The predicament was fundamental in emotional as well as civil terms: 'When they [the subjects–children] see him [the king–father] wielding a bloody sword, surrounded by his killers and their enemies, when they know that he himself has ordered the sacrifice, admitted the massacres and planned the treason – then how can they possibly acknowledge him in any way as a father?' No, he is a 'tyrant', a 'traitor', a 'pseudo-father'. And the Historiographer agrees with the Politique that 'the acts of the Valois require that one should not wait until after their death to declare their villainy'.

Attitudes of defiance are extended not only in psychological and philosophical terms but also in the dimension of history and tradition. The Politique singles out for praise Hotman and Pasquier, both critics of Romanism beneath their religious differences, and modern research into the history of the Albigensians. He mentions also the commission of the Council of Nîmes to seven antiquarians (*obser-vateurs de l'antiquité*) to investigate French and Gallic tradition to establish an ideal of social order and justifications for resistance.[6] The people of Dauphiné, he adds, will not lay down their arms until they see the end of tyranny and the restoration of the 'ancient laws' of France. So antiquarian efforts continued to fuel revolutionary ardor and indeed to suggest utopian ideals.

This ideological alarm-bell was a dialogue but not a debate: the real controversy was carried on from outside the confessional circle; and as an example of a reaction on the part of an orthodox Catholic critic it is appropriate that we look at a retort published the same year (1574) and represented, with more exasperation than ingenuity, as the 'true alarm-bell' – *Le Vray Reveille-Matin*. The author was Arnaud Sorbin, who billed himself as a doctor of theology and a preacher of Toulouse (notorious for its fiery sermonizers) and who somewhat indelicately prefaced his response with hymns in praise of that 'apostle of Christ', St Bartholomew. Sorbin adopted neither the dramatic form nor the attractive style of his target, but he did rival its dogmatic and often bitter tone.

Necessarily, Sorbin's approach was defensive, not to say negative. We do not love liberty less than you, he protested, nor do we want tyranny.[7] What was necessary, however, was 'Ordre', and this was

---

[6] *Ibid.*, II, 116; cf. L. Anquez, *Histoire des assemblées politiques des reformés en France* (Paris, 1889), 3.

[7] A. Sorbin, *Le Vray Reveille-Matin des Calvinistes et publicains François* (1574) (Paris, 1576; BN 8° Lb33.385), 6ff. Cf. two later works entitled *Le Reveille-matin des catholiques* (Paris, 1589; BN Lb33.184 and 186).

the central theme of Sorbin's passionate defense of orthodoxy and kingship. 'Some good Hotmanist will tell me that the Estates are above kings . . .', he wrote, but this was in complete violation of the principle of Order. He lamented the wave of crimes and atrocities but pointed out that the Catholics, too, had their martyrs. If asked whether cunning, tricks and 'finesse' were legitimate to maintain order, his answer would be, yes, against traitors and 'perturbers of the state'. And against Hotman in particular, he declared, 'we shall prove by authentic histories or received laws of France that the heretics, rebels and enemies of the state, guilty of the crime of lese-majesty, divine and human, are disturbers of public peace, destroyers of the people, incendiaries and the like . . .'. And Sorbin proposed his own set of forty articles to preserve the monarchy.

In these two competing alarms, rallying people round conflicting causes, we can see clearly not only the principal parties but the terms of the debate that would divide them for another two decades. Despite fundamental political and social transformations, and ten years later a complete turnabout between the legitimate and opposition groups, the ideological pattern was deeply fixed. Charges of sedition, atheism, betrayal, usurpation, the most malicious motives imaginable were mutually exchanged and denied. The political and religious questions were hopelessly confused for both parties; only a very radical and 'Machiavellian' divorce between the two could resolve the conflict, and this continued to be virtually unthinkable to most believing Christians. So the polemic and invective continued to pour forth at a growing rate until it reached flood stage in the 1580s. The *Reveille-Matin* was translated into various languages, reissued, banned in Geneva as well as France,[8] and of course its arguments were repeated endlessly. On the other side both the volume and the intensity of the responses likewise increased, and in the 1580s and 1590s 'alarm-bells' were still being rung to alert Frenchmen to threats of rebellion. By then, of course, this was hardly news.

[8] H. Fazy, *La Saint-Barthélemy et Genève* (Geneva, 1879), 80.

THE SHAPE OF IDEOLOGY

The sixteenth century was in many ways the seed-time of modern ideology, producing (according to Raemond) more than 200 heresies along with attendant visions of secular life.[9] This is not, of course, to make any large claims for the originality of this ideologically creative age; and indeed in conceptual terms it might be better to reverse the metaphor – to regard it, that is, rather as the harvest time of western political and social thought. For in a long perspective what is remarkable about this century is less its philosophical innovativeness than its eclecticism and conservatism. Ideologists showed their virtuosity not by divising new formulas but by adapting and re-arranging old ones. Yet for all this, the implications of political (if not social) radicalism were profound. It may be suggested, indeed, that mastery over the western political heritage made possible more fundamental departures and insights than neglect or avoidance could have done. As in other areas of the history of thought the most effective and durable changes of orientation and perspective are made possible by taking off from and transforming, rather than affecting to forget, prevailing ideas. Promoting change under the guise of preserving tradition or returning to an earlier and better state has in any case been a frequent device of ideologists, and never more so than in this period of backward-looking (whether fundamentalist or traditionalist) re-evaluations.

The Huguenot party line was many years in the making, but it was not until after 1572 that it took definite ideological shape. Before that time it had normally been hedged in qualifications and claims to political, if not religious, orthodoxy; and of course it had also been muted by the convention of taking the usurping Guises rather than the monarchy itself as the target. Such was also the attitude of the Dutch toward Philip II's 'bad ministers'.[10] St Bartholomew changed all that, at least for a time. In its wake the Huguenot 'cause' was

---

[9] Raemond, 146. Besides the standard works of G. Weill, *Les Théories sur le pouvoir royal en France pendant les guerres de religion* (Paris, 1894), V. de Caprariis, *Propaganda e pensiero politico in Francia durante le guerre di religione* (Naples, 1959) and J. M. H. Salmon, *The French Religious Wars in English Political Thought* (Oxford, 1959), useful discussions include M. Yardeni, *La Conscience nationale en France pendant les guerres de religion (1559–1598)* (Paris, 1971), Ch. Mercier, 'Les Théories politiques des Calvinistes en France au cours des guerres de religion', *BSHPF*, LXXXIII (1934), 225–60, 381–415, G. de Lagarde, *Recherches sur l'esprit politique de la Réforme* (Douai, 1926), A. Elkan, *Die Publizistik der Bartholomäusnacht* (Heidelberg, 1905), and P. Méaly, *Les Publicistes de la Réforme* (Paris, 1903). Treatments also in the standard histories of early modern political thought by Figgis, J. W. Allen, P. Mesnard and especially Q. Skinner, *The Foundations of Modern Political Thought* (Cambridge, 1978).

[10] P. A. Geurts, *De nederlandse Opstand in Pamfletten 1566–1580* (Nijmegen, 1956), 23.

clearly and even philosophically defined; and all the second thoughts and back-tracking of later years could not dull the initial impact nor impede the long-range influence of its ideological off-spring. The party line itself continued to be publicized in familiar terms. Henry of Navarre, like Condé and Coligny before him, issued position papers, and of course the feud with the Guises continued unabated until the death of Henry of Guise in 1588.[11] The deeper conclusions were drawn by private persons like Hotman and Beza, and it was through their relatively unfettered investigations and speculations that the shape of ideology was transformed from propaganda to something approaching political philosophy.

Within the space of less than a decade there appeared, in fact, a series of fundamental works which have some claims to be numbered among the classics of the western political tradition. Besides various distinguished historiographical works and the *Reveille-Matin*, there were Hotman's *Francogallia* (1573), his friend Beza's *Right of Magistrates* (1574), the anonymous *Political Discourse* (1574), La Boétie's posthumous *Voluntary Servitude* (1574), Gentillet's *Contre-Machiavel* (1576), Jean Bodin's monumental *Republic* (1576) and the *Defense of Liberty against Tyrants* (1579), usually attributed to Philippe du Plessis Mornay.[12] Although these works touch upon many other matters and carry us beyond the embattled terrain of sixteenth-century ideology, they are the product of the same dilemma, belong to the same world of discourse, and deserve to be read in part in this same context.

The most influential of these works, those of Hotman, Beza, Bodin and Mornay, were engaged in the same set of debates, but they differed in a number of important respects. Hotman's *Francogallia*, largely a product of the first decade of the civil wars, represents a scholar's search for the causes of the national predicament – historical and antiquarian in substance though legalistic in style and argument. Emotionally as well as conceptually, it was analogous to the Protestant search for a pure and undefiled religion. Although some of its more radical themes were later justified by Hotman as being historical and descriptive and not legal and prescriptive in character, most readers, friends like Barnaud as well as enemies like Belleforest, thought differently; and Hotman himself privately expressed

---

[11] *Declaration de Henry de Bourbon* . . . (La Rochelle, 1574; BN Lb34.85).

[12] Among other discussions, see R. Giesey, 'The Monarchomach triumvirs: Hotman, Beza and Mornay', *BHR*, xxxII (1970), 41–56, Salmon's introduction to *Francogallia*, J. Franklin, *Constitutionalism and Resistance in the Sixteenth Century* (New York, 1969), and J. Denert, *Beza, Brutus, Hotman: Calvinistische Monarchomachen* (Cologne, 1968); also *Jean Bodin, Verhandlungen der internationalen Bodin Tagung in München*, ed. H. Denzer (Munich, 1973), especially the contribution by Salmon.

satisfaction at striking a blow against tyranny. Beza's *Right of Magistrates* not only reinforced but often overlapped with Hotman's book, especially in terms of legal and institutional history. Taking off as it did from Calvin's view of resistance as well as the Magdeburg Confession, it had a more religious orientation and depended more on the martyrological conception of 'cause'; and in fact its fundamentalism prevented it, like Hotman's book, from being published in Geneva. The *Defense of Liberty*, which seemed to pertain to the Dutch as much as to the French scene, represents a further radicalization because it was more abstract, more Biblical (and less institutional) and because it countenanced resistance on an international basis. The *Political Discourse*, combining Biblical and legal arguments, was even more insistent on notions of popular sovereignty and tyrannicide. As for Bodin's *Republic*, though designed as a systematic vision of society, it can also be read as a counterattack on 'monarchomach' conceptions like those of Beza and Hotman.

In France the concept of sovereignty, or majesty, was the center of attention in the 1570s, and it was no accident that Bodin's classic formulation of the idea appeared at this time. On many levels of thought and action sovereignty was being challenged. Privately, Hotman suggested his own doubts in a rhetorical question: 'How can there be any majesty in such a monster [as Charles IX], and how can one accept as a king a man who has spilled the blood of 30,000 persons in eight days?'[13] Publicly, he seemed to express a similar view that was hardly less inflammatory for all its scholarly and conceptual embroidery. To many, Hotman's defense of 'mixed government' was a flagrant violation of 'majesty'; and few, friends or enemies, put much faith in his disclaimers that he was writing history not political theory. In any case his arguments were drawn into the public sphere by critics and by friendly interpreters like Prisbach and the author of the *Reveille-Matin*, whose last pages represented a sort of popularization of Francogallicanism. And Bodin's famous definition of sovereignty (*majestas* in Latin, he reminded his readers) as both 'indivisible and perpetual' can be seen as an explicit contradiction of this thesis. In this polarity we can see the issue dividing the parties formulated on the highest theoretical level.

In agreement with less celebrated Huguenots of the time, 'monarchomachs' like Beza and Hotman inclined more or less consciously toward the principle of popular sovereignty. Behind his scholarly cover Hotman seemed to advocate the idea of elective kingship and the right of people to condemn and depose kings for cause, and in

---

[13] Letter to Gualter, 10 Jan. 1573 (cited in Kelley, *Hotman*, 227); in general see R. Mousnier, *The Assassination of Henry IV*, trans. J. Spencer (London, 1973), and B. Hundeshagen, *Calvinismus und staatsbürgerliche Freiheit* (Zurich, 1946).

the second edition of the *Francogallia* (1576) he inserted several times, in capital letters, the famous Roman formula, *SALUS POPULI SUPREMA LEX ESTO*, 'The Welfare of the People should be the Supreme Law', which was virtually a code phrase for lese-majesty.[14] Beza was in general agreement with this view, while making more extensive use of Biblical illustrations before applying to legal and historical sources. He also introduced the old conciliarist argument which had survived in France as well as Germany, that the oecumenical council was above the pope, and by analogy he suggested that the secular estates were likewise above the king.[15] So did the Defender of liberty, but characteristically this author was much more dogmatic about the issue. He argued not only that 'kings are made by the people' but 'the people are above kings' and 'kings receive laws from the people'. Nor could time or prescription run contrary to popular sovereignty so conceived. These opinions rested upon an even more fundamentalist and Biblical view of society than those of Beza or Hotman.[16]

Contractualism was of course a common mode of thought and argument among lawyers; and it affected propaganda in several ways – in the form not only of the feudal contract but also of private law, which demanded good faith in any social relationship, and above all of the famous Roman regal law, the *lex regia*. Pierre Fabre introduced this formula, by which the Roman people had bestowed their 'majesty' on the prince, into his critique of Charpentier in 1575. 'When first a people created a king', he wrote, 'they wanted to choose a father who would be a wise governor of faith and of the affairs which they committed to him, and so they also ordered certain and good laws in which they restrained and limited his power; and if the king transgressed them, he was no longer a true king but a usurper and a tyrant.'[17] Hotman introduced the concept into the second (1576) edition of the *Francogallia* and indeed used the term (*leges regiae*) to refer to all the 'fundamental laws' which circumscribed the king. The Roman idea that majesty was vested originally in the people is also discussed by Beza and by the Defender of liberty. 'Has the king made the people?', asked one spokesman in Barnaud's *French Mirror*. 'By no means', answered the Politique, 'but the people have made the king.'[18]

Much more complex was the question of legal and institutional

---

[14] *Francogallia*, chapter XII (1576); *Discours politique*, ME, III, fol. 213.
[15] *Du Droit des magistrats*, ed. R. Kingdon (Geneva, 1970), 24ff.; *De Iure magistratuum*, ed. K. Sturm (Neukirchen, 1965).
[16] *Vindiciae contra tyrannos* (n.p., 1580).   [17] *Response* (n.p., 1575; BN Lb34.99), 103.
[18] *Miroir des François*, 261.

restraints on royal power, and here we return to the eristic and casuistic world of lawyers, in which were lodged precedents and arguments for almost every conceivable position. Seyssel's old notion of three 'bridles' was revived, by Hotman among others, and each played a certain role in opposition propaganda.[19] First, religion was taken as a limit to the king's will in the sense not only that he was supposed to live up to its commandments but also, a more ominous suggestion, that a subject's duty was always to God first and only then to the king. Second, justice implied that the king was bound by certain fundamental laws, such as the Salic law, the principle of the inalienability of the domain, and the need to rule with some sort of conciliar 'consent', which at least tacitly qualified his 'absolute power'. (The Parlement of Paris, on the other hand, had been discredited in the eyes of the Huguenots, and Hotman in particular attacked it as the 'kingdom of pettifoggers'.)[20] Finally, the 'police' of the kingdom required that specific laws, agreements, customs and privileges of other groups and institutions be respected. Huguenot propagandists drew heavily upon this medieval view of an organic society with a rich tradition of liberties and corporate privileges and in the process contributed to various kinds of institutional mythology – 'constitutional antiquarianism' it has been called – celebrating the antiquity and national superiority of the Estates, the legal system, the peerage, the communes and other products of French society.

The two themes most emphasized in the propaganda of the 1570s were the so-called 'inferior magistrates' and the assembly of Estates, both of which had been part of the Huguenot party program from the beginning. The first involved the highest stratum of the feudal aristocracy, though it could be rationalized in terms of civil as well as feudal law. This concept, made famous in Calvin's *Institutes*, was employed by both Beza and the Defender of liberty, though specific evidence in its support could be adduced also from Hotman's book.[21] The Estates General were celebrated extensively in all three works and indeed in many other contemporary tracts. For Hotman this meant the whole glorious tradition of the 'great Council' (*Magnum Concilium*), continuous from Merovingian if not (*pace* Tacitus) prehistorical times, and the structure of 'mixed government' it implied. Beza followed the same line of argument, using many of the same examples and precedents, and seemed to grant to the Estates an even greater share in sovereignty. So, with less interest in institutional arrangements, did the *Defense of Liberty*.

The ultimate Question, however, was the legitimacy of resistance,

[19] *Francogallia*, chapter xxv (1586); cf. chapter xvii. [20] See above, pp. 182–85.
[21] *Institutes*, IV, xx, 31–2.

or rather the conditions under which resistance was legitimate. Beza and the Defender posed it in the crassest manner – asking 'Whether tyranny can be lawfully checked by armed force', in Beza's words; or as the other put it, 'Whether it be lawful to resist a Prince which doth oppress or ruin a public State, and how far such resistance may be extended. By whom, how and by what right it is permitted.'[22]

For Beza, the Defender and the Political Discourser the answer was a qualified 'yes'. The latter displayed a radical willingness to celebrate the right of a community to 'exterminate a tyrant', adding aphoristically that 'the surest remedy for a tyrant is defiance'.[23] Beza would not recognize armed resistance by a private person, except against violence, but did acknowledge the authority of the 'inferior magistrate', such presumably as Coligny and William of Orange. In any case, argued Beza with reference to the old notion of the 'king's two bodies', a subject's allegiance was to the office not to the person of the supreme magistrate. The principal source of resistance, however, was the assembly of Estates, and indeed a major function of this body was to seek redress for tyranny. Upon it Hotman bestowed all the 'marks of sovereignty' which Bodin and orthodox apologists normally reserved for the king, and later the Defender of liberty was even more assertive about this point. He had no doubt that it was the Estates' business 'to drive out a tyrant, or other unworthy king, or to establish a good one in his place'. And of course the emphasis was always on the word 'king', for none of these three authors could accept the notion of a female ruler, all questions of tyranny aside.

The correlative version of this fundamental question was how to react to religious persecution.[24] It was in the nature of Hotman's book that he avoided the religious issue, although in the preface, composed in the heat of the excitement over the massacres, he did suggest that the corruption of true religion was the principal cause of the corruption of society and the 'Francogallic' constitution. Beza, on the other hand, did not scruple to denounce 'the unjust and sinful submissiveness with which kings have bound themselves by oath to the Roman Antichrist'. In general his answer to the question was that resistance to religious persecution could be undertaken in good conscience if 'true religion' had been guaranteed by law, which was the case in France through the edicts of pacification. And the Defender of liberty responded by a rhetorical question: 'Briefly, if God calls us on the one side to enroll us in His service, and the king

---

[22] *Droit des magistrats*, Q. 10; *Vindiciae*, iii.   [23] *ME*, iii, fols. 213, 177.
[24] *Francogallia*, preface; *Droit des magistrats*, Q. 1; *Vindiciae*, iv.

on the other, is any man so void of reason that he will not say we must leave the king, and apply ourselves to God's service?'

There is little dqubt that such attitudes were common among members of the Huguenot community, especially those in exile or in arms, although specific forms of argument may well have differed. In fact what is striking about the idea of resistance in this period is the great variety of grounds on which it was justified. Partly this was a result of the eclecticism of the age and the attitude of many ideologists that any argument in a good cause was valuable. But it reflected, too, the great range of beliefs and emotions as well as ideas and theories. The means of legitimizing may be arranged on a sort of scale ranging from the most conventional authority to the most free-floating rationalizing: Biblical and literary texts, historical example and legal rules, analogies from private and feudal law, arguments from morality and natural law, and appeals to common sense and pure reason. Far from Luther's principle of 'scripture alone', Huguenot secular ideologists more closely approximated the view taken at the Council of Trent, that demonstration could be achieved in terms of tradition and custom as well as scriptures. In this sense, too, Huguenot propaganda appeared to be 'total' and to touch on every level of experience.

Yet in terms of political thought a certain drift can be detected from an empirical and authoritarian mode of persuasion to more rational methods of proof. Common to all four authors is a tendency to draw illustrations in a comparative way from the experience and institutions of disparate societies – that is, from the field that corresponded to the old law of nations, the *jus gentium* – and then to infer, by a sort of inductive process, patterns that seemed to be universal and, arguably, in conformity with the 'natural law'. In this spirit appeal was made to the oaths of English kings and the Aragonese nobility (the famous 'si no, no' formula), to fundamental laws and to various kinds of representative assemblies.[25] So there emerged a kind of argument from 'natural law' in a modern, empirical and comparative, as well as a medieval and *a priori* sense which would reach maturity in the more sophisticated formulations of the next century. This can be seen above all in the *Defense of Liberty*, in which an almost pure theory of social contract is put forward and in which the absolutist moral tone is so dominant that, in the face of rampant nationalism, even the notion of foreign assistance for the 'cause' is given rational defense.

It is well known that the arguments of the so-called 'monarcho-machs' were adopted and applied not only by Catholics of the next

[25] *Francogallia*, chapter XII; *Droit des magistrats*, Q. 7; cf. R. Giesey, *If Not, Not* (Princeton, 1968).

generation, when Henry of Navarre's candidacy for the throne cast them into opposition, but also seventeeth-century English and eighteenth-century American revolutionaries.[26] To some extent these adaptations represent a specific transmission of arguments in a continuum of intellectual history; but it must also be admitted that resistance arguments, as they became more abstract, rationalized and grounded in philosophy and natural law rather than legal precedent or historical tradition, also became universalized and applicable to many predicaments. Notions of tyranny, natural rights, social compact and the right of revolution were elaborated in other contexts, American as well as English and European, and represent at least an indirect legacy of the sixteenth-century wars, as John Adams and many seventeenth- and eighteenth-century men of affairs believed. But these represent other cycles of ideology with their own 'beginnings' and go beyond the present inquiry.

THE ELEMENTS OF IDEOLOGY

How analyze the ideological upsurge of the international Protestant community in the 1570s? How evaluate this epiphenomenal creation that represents perhaps the most intense and coherent expression of a 'total' ideology, at least in public terms and on a world-wide scale, in early modern history? Certainly the visible propaganda involved drew strength from a great variety of social discontents as well as long-standing political division, but no less certainly religious enthusiasm constituted its vital force. This was the view taken not only by partisans of all sorts (despite earlier expressions of doubt about the sincerity of religious motivation on the part of leaders) but also by disinterested observers and professional social critics like the Venetian ambassador to France, Marc' Antonio Barbaro. The turmoil of the age was unheard of, Barbaro wrote in a report of 1564, 'and this great mutation proceeds from no other cause than from religion'.[27] He then went on to list five means by which society was being subverted: the growing inclination of the nobility toward heretical ideas, the popularity of disputations, the intrusion of churchmen into law offices, the failure to punish 'crime' in Huguenot cities, and the favor shown by the great (presumably men of political consequence like Condé and Coligny) toward heresy. These were at least

---

[26] See especially Salmon, *French Religious Wars*.

[27] Marc' Antonio Barbaro, 1564, in E. Alberi (ed.), *Relazioni degli Ambasciatori veneti al senato*, ser. 1, vol. IV (Florence, 1958), 159–63.

the most perceptible conditions for the generation of ideology in the sixteenth century.

Where Barbaro saw heresy and anti-social behavior we may, on closer scrutiny, detect a more general pattern of opposition signifying more than political inconvenience. Among French, Swiss, German and Dutch Calvinists, or Calvinist sympathizers, an integrated and militant view of the world was formed, if only temporarily, by the convergence of intellectual conviction and social necessity; and the result was a general vision of human nature that went beyond particular confessional formulations. Although this vision was nowhere expressed in anything like systematic form, partial views are apparent in the enormous range of propaganda which has been exploited here; and it may be useful to suggest here a kind of hypothetical reconstruction. What follows is an attempt to draw together some of the main elements of the Protestant ideological creation which previous chapters have approached in a more historical fashion.

Most basic is the psychological element, the taproot of discontent and of social and generational upheaval. There does not seem to be any satisfactory way to isolate and to trace the effects of ego-energy on a social level, and certainly an appeal to a generalized 'individualism' is inadequate. Yet some patterns with anti-social implications are undeniably the product of particular acts of will, especially the emergence of heroic models – the 'magisterial' reformers – which came to replace social norms. The wider repercussions of this can be seen in various kinds of unconventional behavior, including the flight from parental control and monastic institutions, the pursuit of martyrdom and more active and militant kinds of resistance. It may be presumptuous in terms of existing evidence to speculate about psychohistorical causes, but the results are indisputable. So is the general inclination to justify actions on the basis of non-conventional standards of conscience and transcendent values, which in practice often meant values of an outlawed or alien community. It is of course true that within a generation this behavior and these values tended themselves to become socialized and conventionalized, just as the magisterial reformers were followed by that less charismatic replacement that has been called 'the Second' – Bullinger following Zwingli, for example, and Beza following Calvin. But this is precisely the process which, according to the various channels we have followed, transforms ideals into ideology.

Secondly, and considerably more accessible to observation, is the evangelical element. In some ways this was the most active ingredient of ideology, just as the major vehicle of propaganda and of the legitimation of unorthodox behavior was the Bible. The theme of 'Christian liberty' sounded by Luther, Pupper van Goch, Farel and many others was not political at first, but it was unmistakably anti-authoritarian and easily accommodated to political causes, as Luther soon found in his contacts with the 'protesting' German princes. Most essentially, according to Erich Fromm's famous formulation of the 'negative freedom' of post-medieval society, the evangelical idea of liberty promised release from the tyranny of materialism and idolatry, from an ignominious 'human' conception of divinity and of course from foreign domination.[28] The implication was that the standard of judgment and action came not from human authority, tradition or institutions but from a transcendent 'word' to be derived from scriptures without any ecclesiastical 'interpretation'. Projected into the secular sphere, the notion of a free and purified faith also provided a means of criticizing and perhaps rejecting human authority. The analogy is with the metaphor of 'the king's two bodies': just as the mass was purged of idolatrous 'real presence', so secular power was separated from its human agency; and the argument was that allegiance, like faith, was due only to the transcendent aspect.[29] With regard to the monarch, in other words, respect was due to his 'majesty' but perhaps not to 'his majesty'. In various ways the 'reformed' religion furnished a model and emotional source of secular ideology. In historical terms Hotman's *Francogallia* was a secular projection of the primitive church; in political terms the *Defense of Liberty* was a secular projection of the Biblical covenant; and both represented analogues to the notion of Christian liberty.

It is also possible to recognize a corporate element, including a variety of group or institutional privileges, which involved in some sense an allegiance separate from that owed to church or state. Guilds, professions, offices and other institutions all had their specially defined and jealously guarded 'liberties' which even the government could not violate with impunity.[30] The Gallican church, the University of Paris, the lawyers' *barreau* and the Parlement, the guild of printers and even the family, as there has been reason to notice, had all of them their time-honored privileges which the crown periodically confirmed and sometimes added to or subtracted from. It will not do to follow older historians in associating too closely such accumulations of corporate privilege with modern liberal atti-

[28] Erich Fromm, *Escape from Freedom* (New York, 1941).
[29] E. H. Kantorowicz, *The King's Two Bodies* (Princeton, 1957).
[30] F. Olivier Martin, *L'Organisation corporative de la France d'ancien régime* (Paris, 1938), is a useful discussion, but there is no intellectual history of the subject.

tudes, in identifying the defiance of sixteenth-century printers and professors with modern 'freedom of the press' or the principles of *Lern-* and *Lehrenfreiheit*, or the 'liberty of speech' enjoyed by sixteenth-century *parlementaires* with more recent conceptions. Certainly there were inequities and authoritarian patterns in earlier notions of 'liberty' at odds with those of the nineteenth and twentieth centuries. Yet recognizing differences does not mean denying historical connections. Earlier social and professional groups were indeed sources of resistance to uniformitarian and oppressive political forces; and in terms at least of ideology the habits, traditions and formulations of protests for corporate 'liberties' contributed to attitudes of heterodoxy, resistance and eventually revolution.

Fourthly, there is the feudal element, which has been and would continue to be a permanent obstacle to royal authority and to national consolidation.[31] In a sense the major precedent for this was the rebellious party of 'protesting' German princes formed in 1529, given an ideological base by the Confession of Augsburg the next year, and devoted for a quarter of a century to a civil war for 'German liberties' against an intractable Emperor. 'He declared them', according to De Thou, 'traitors, rebels, seditious men, criminals guilty of lese-majesty and disturbers of public peace.'[32] While supporting such behavior outside France, the king professed to be shocked by it at home. In particular the 'treason' of the Constable Charles de Bourbon was still fresh in the minds of older people at the time when his descendants, and finally his cousin Henry of Navarre, took up arms for their 'cause', which De Thou was not alone in believing contained 'more discontent than Huguenotterie'. The notion of feudal contract, with its attendant rights and duties for both parties, was implicit in the position taken by the 'conspirators' of Amboise and explicit in that taken by Condé in his 'treaty of association'. It was evident in various complaints by spokesmen for the nobility in particular, which was forced to fight for its 'honor', which is to say its landed property, as well as for religious and political principle. Arguments from and analogies with feudal 'liberty' permeated the propaganda of the civil wars and after the massacres found a prominent place in such more systematic statements as the *Reveille-Matin* and the *Francogallia*. Even the idea of

---

[31] F. Kern, *Kingship and Law in the Middle Ages*, trans. S. Chrimes (Oxford, 1948), and P. L. Cardauns, *Die Lehre vom Widerstandsrecht* . . . (Bonn, 1903).

[32] De Thou, I, 154, on the 'libertez germaniques' and Charles V's statement about his princely opponents: 'il les declaroit traitres, Rebelles, Seditieux, Criminels de Leze-Majesté et Perturbateurs du repos public'.

popular sovereignty depended in a sense on this neo-feudal ideal, since the assumption tended to be that 'the people' could act directly through the agency of the 'inferior magistrates', which is to say the grandest of the 'grandes familles'.

It would probably be an exaggeration and historically premature to emphasize a classical element in the political and social consciousness of the civil wars. There is some evidence of republican hyperbole and the precedent of Brutus was occasionally invoked, but even with regard to the issues of tyrannicide and assassination this sort of remote antiquarianism was of secondary importance. In most respects, sixteenth-century ideology did not attempt to extricate itself from the framework and assumptions of feudal society. This was evident even in those most forceful expressions of resistance to 'sovereign' claims, such as those of Philip of Hesse in Germany, Condé and Coligny in France, and especially William of Orange in the Netherlands. Like the defense of Hesse, the 'Apology' of Orange of 1582 was based in large part on his feudal objections (as Duke of Brabant) to treatment at the hand of his suzerain Philip II of Spain.[33] The neo-feudal basis of resistance arguments is apparent also in the continuous calls for assemblies of the Estates both in France and in the Netherlands, where the Estates in 1581 finally 'abjured' the sovereignty of Philip II on the grounds that their relationship was basically contractual – unlike that between Philip and his colonies in the New World. It is of course true that Roman law furnished many arguments and precedents for all these dilemmas and to that extent represents links with classical antiquity, but in general the law involved was modernized and, so to speak, naturalized. Feudalism – if we can so render that rationalized structure of European customs called the *jus feudisticum* – continued to provide the primary ideological context.

Related to feudal ideas and even more disturbing to royalist orthodoxy was the civic element of sixteenth-century ideology. Here classical antiquity had more to offer, and in intellectual terms the independence of 'reformed' cities of the sixteenth century, or at least their pretensions thereto, represented a continuation of attitudes associated with the 'civic humanism' of Italian city-states of the previous century. Yet once again medieval patterns seemed predominant. Urban freedoms, while they might be nourished by classical republicanism, had their own indigenous roots and peculiar character. The old proverb 'City air makes free', *Studtluft macht frei*, was

---

[33] *Apologie ou defense du tresillustre prince Guillaume, par la grace de Dieu prince d'Orange . . . contre le ban et edict publié par le roi d'Espaigne . . .*, ed. A. Lacroix (Brussels, 1858).

given new life when joined to notions of Germanic and Christian 'liberty'; and of course free cities like Strasbourg and Magdeburg had given practical application to such attitudes by taking their place in the front ranks of resistance to the Emperor Charles V.[34] Similar examples can be found in the claims of Dutch cities resisting the Emperor's son, Philip II. The convergence of religious and civic liberties is apparent in the case of the city of Brabant, which supported 'those of the religion' on the basis of certain 'ancient liberties' which forbade the Duke (that is, Philip) to 'pursue' his subjects except by due process of law, to impose taxes without calling the estates and to appoint foreigners to office. According to the published manifesto, the arrangement was like the feudal contract: 'And if the Duke violates or derogates from these liberties, the citizens are absolved from their oath and can do freely what seems best to them.'[35] These manifestos issued by insurgent cities contributed directly to more formal resistance theory, most notably through Beza's *Right of Magistrates*, which purported to be a commentary on the famous 'Magdeburg Confession' of 1550, and through the *Defense of Liberty against Tyrants*, which had recourse to Dutch precedents.

Most significant were the precedents furnished by the cities of Switzerland, which were held up as ideals in particular by Dutch propagandists. The libertarian traditions of Geneva, enhanced by the interrelated process of 'reformation' and the struggle for independence from Savoy, were consolidated by two generations of conflict with that power. Nowhere is the union of religious commitment and political independence – the spiritual and material components of ideology – so clearly illustrated as in the Genevan oath of allegiance: the old civic requirements are maintained (owning property in the city, asking permission to leave or to import foreign goods, giving military service when necessary, and others), but to this was added from the 1540s the prerequisite that citizens 'live according to the reformation of the gospel'.[36] This was, of course, in the name of civic as well as Christian liberty, and not the liberty of Genevans only. 'We are convinced', Beza wrote after the first war of religion in France, 'that if the city falls, it will affect its neighbors and be a disaster even for those who know nothing of it. It would be the

---

[34] Analogous with the 'civic humanism' discussed by Hans Baron and William Bouwsma in the context of the Italian Renaissance, the urban ideology of Reformation cities has only begun to receive comparable treatment (most notably by Moeller and Ozment) in general terms; see p. 36 above, n. 35.

[35] [Theophile], *Histoire des troubles et guerres civiles du pays pas* (n.p., 1582), 12–13.

[36] In Kelley, *Hotman*, 346.

end of liberty.' Like the earlier 'myth of Venice', the 'myth of Geneva' – what a contemporary called 'la legende du Lac Leman' – was publicized by friends and foes alike. For ultramontane Catholicism Geneva seemed a fearful 'grotto' of heresy and subversion, for the disillusioned Antoine Fromment (in a sermon which sent him into exile) a second Sodom, for Protestants a 'new Jerusalem' and a 'new republic'; but for all it was a dominating symbol of Reformation ideology.[37]

For France the classic case of civic defiance was La Rochelle, a city which traced its liberties back at least to the twelfth century and indeed claimed descent from a fortification of Caesar.[38] Before 1200 the city had the privilege of establishing a 'senate', which (like the Parlement of Paris) followed the Roman precedent of 100 members. In the sixteenth century the civic liberties of La Rochelle became menacing as the people allegedly began arming themselves against the king's 'majesty' in 1534. La Rochelle's 'rebellion' against the *gabelle* was apparently settled in 1542, but already the religious question was looming. 'I have been warned', wrote Francis I two years later, 'that in La Rochelle and environs there are several persons, greatly tainted with these accursed and damned Lutheran errors, who have joined themselves together in flocks and who go about the country causing endless scandal, sowing among the people their unfortunate and damned doctrine, a thing which displeases me.'[39] But royal displeasure did not prevent the advance of heresy, especially as it gathered support among the nobility. In 1558 it was reported that a band of comedians ridiculed Roman rites in the presence of the visiting King and Queen of Navarre. Four years later the massacre of Vassy provoked 'a mania for pulling down idols', and this soon escalated into armed conflict. During the 1560s La Rochelle began to demand respect for its 'ancient liberties'

---

[37] Raemond, 13; and cf. A. Dufour, 'Le Mythe de Genève au temps de Calvin', *Schweizerisches Zeitschrift für Geschichte*, IX (1959), 489–518. Cf. *Remonstrance faicte a Monseigneur le Duc de Savoy, par ung gentilhomme François* (Lyon, 1589; Ars. 31. 10), representing Geneva as a 'Ville remplie de larrons, assassins, et de toutes les miseres que l'un sçauroit trouver au monde. Ville que les bannis, les apostatz, les pilleurs, et les homicides, ont eslüe pour choisir leurs demeurs . . ., refuge des heretiques bannis d'Italie, d'Espagne, de Flandres, de France, de Paris, et de Lyon, Ville ou les blasphemes contre Dieu et l'Eglise sont ouiz. Ou les livres des heretiques ont esté imprimés, bref, Ville qui est l'origine, et la source de tous les maulx advenus depuis cinquante ans en toute la Chrestienté.' Cf. H. Meylan, *Silhouettes du XVIe siècle* (n.p., n.d.), 51.

[38] Arcère, *Histoire de la ville de la Rochelle* (La Rochelle, 1756), I, 430, and cf. G. Procacci, *Classi sociali e monarchia assoluta nella Francia della prima meta del secolo XVI* (Turin, 1955).

[39] *Voyage du Roy François I en sa ville de la Rochelle en l'an 1542*, repr. AC, III; cf. L. Delmas, *The Huguenots of La Rochelle*, trans. G. Catlin (New York, 1880), 11.

but also for the more modern 'liberty of conscience'. By 1572 the city was virtually an independent republic, creating a 'myth' to rival that of Geneva and contributing directly to the civic element of the propaganda of the 1570s.

In the ideological movements of the sixteenth century the national element was undeniably visible, but its function was in some ways ambivalent and deceptive, even divisive for some adherents of the evangelical–political 'cause'.[40] This was especially the case in the Empire, in which Luther raised the flag of nationalism in his address of 1521 against the ecclesiastical establishment and inadvertently against the Emperor. In the Netherlands nationalism was based largely on anti-Spanish sentiment and a sort of popular front of feudal, civic and evangelical interests which in many ways was powerless to overcome deeply rooted particularist tendencies. In France the situation was also complicated. The rhetoric and arguments of both Gallicans and Huguenots could be intensely nationalistic, and yet both parties had increasingly entangling alliances with foreign powers – Italian and Spanish on the one hand and German, Swiss, Dutch and, to a lesser extent, English on the other. The paradoxical conclusion seems to be that nationalism was a powerful ideological force, but its effect even within particular states was more divisive than unifying, at least in the short run. Indeed it is a measure of the strength of sixteenth-century ideological movements that they could resist as well as make use of national sentiment.

In general, ideological movements of the sixteenth century were extraordinarily concrete in provenance and in formulation: they reflected immediate human dilemmas and interests, that is, and they appealed to particular precedents and traditions. Yet attempts were made to go beyond the authority of history, law and even scriptures and to elevate protests and programs to a philosophic level. In this connection natural law and rational theology reappear as devices of legitimation, reason and universal values replacing human custom and convention. As monarchy seemed to be founded on reason, so might ideas of social contract and popular sovereignty. Ultimately, whatever the claims of positive law, 'God chooses and the people establish a king' (*Eligit Deus et constituit Regem populus*), and parties could choose either or both parts of this proposition to justify a course of action.[41] This was the case also with active resistance, for it was a formula in agreement with reason as well as

---

[40] Yardeni, *La Conscience nationale*.

[41] Cf. Claude Gousté, *Tractatus de potestate regia in ecclesia* (1561), in Melchior Goldast (ed.), *Monarchia S. Romani Imperii* (Hanover, 1611), 656.

civil law that force may be used to repel force (*vim vi repellere licet*).[42] In the works of Bodin and the monarchomachs in particular, all the elements discussed here, and more, are combined into synthetic views of the human condition as it essentially is or ought to be in social and political terms. It may be going too far to argue, with the historian of the Politique party, that Hotman's *Francogallia* led directly to Rousseau's *Social Contract*, but in terms of the history of ideology the family resemblance seems unmistakable.[43] In sublimated form, in other words, sixteenth-century views of resistance and revolution have been passed on to a series of posterities, each with its own set of dilemmas – ours as well as Rousseau's and John Adams's among them.

THE LEVELS OF IDEOLOGY

The manifold intellectual legacy of western civilization provided the materials for ideological expression; particular institutional and social structures gave it form and direction; but it was specific human predicaments that gave it immediacy and intensity. These predicaments, created by the religious, social and political divisions of Reformation Europe, forced even uncommitted persons to confront the most basic questions of obedience and defiance, of loyalty and betrayal, of dissembling or fleeing, even of life and death. Such questions cut through every level of experience, familial, religious, educational, professional, communal and national; and to obtain a full appreciation of the historical process, it would be a mistake to give priority to any single level. Seizing upon a particular dimension of human experience, economic, political or religious, in the name of explanation is simply too restrictive for certain kinds of historical investigation, especially one that attends to the contours and changes in consciousness and the cultural and institutional patterns of society. Such an enterprise, drawing perhaps more on cultural anthropology than on social science, may surrender some capacity for answering pointed questions (especially the child's question, 'Why?'); but in fact while such pointed questions may penetrate the surface of history, they may also violate it in certain ways, especially in the search for general structures. The primary questions here are not cause and blame, then, but rather means and patterns – how, in what forms and in what contexts. Again the form of analysis follows not causal sequence but rather the model of human experience, that is, levels of thought and behavior.

As an illustration consider the problem of 'authority', a theme that

[42] *Digest*, 43, 16, 27.   [43] Francis De Crue, *Le Parti des politiques* (Paris, 1892), 82.

does indeed touch every level of experience and that is central to early modern history in many ways. The richness of connotation, the resonances which it creates, can be appreciated by reviewing the variety of forms taken by the term and concept of 'authority' in the foregoing chapters. On the most basic social level is the authority of parents, especially of the father. Temporally and emotionally this has priority in human experience; for if one did not grasp the principle of authority on this level, if one could not learn to obey parents and especially Father, how could one be expected to show obedience or reverence to teacher, to master, to magistrate, perhaps even to God?[44] This is not to suggest that attitudes formed within the family were in any meaningful way 'causes' of the later collective behavior of adults; large-scale social upheaval cannot be explained by a generation of recalcitrant children, though some social critics have tried to make such a connection. Yet in the sixteenth century some link can be seen in prominent cases, such as those of Beza and Hotman, and the correlation is surely significant.

So is that with pedagogical authority, insofar as the schoolmaster and professor became surrogate parents with powers of reward and punishment. To begin with at least, academic authority was personal. But a major difference emerged as 'authority' was broadened to include academic tradition in the form of particular and usually old 'authors'.[45] Here it was that a separation could occur between *auctoritas* and particular human or bookish manifestations. In universities 'moderns' were chronically breaking with 'ancients' by shifting allegiances to different intellectual authorities, often as represented by rival faculties. So humanists, for example, from their base in the arts faculty broke with scholasticism, whose strength was located in philosophy, theology, and law. In some cases defiance approached iconoclasm; and so Lorenzo Valla refused to accept any domination, even from Cicero, turning instead to the 'authority of antiquity' in general, which in effect meant his own judgment, his own scholarly conscience. He was followed in this liberal (some would say 'libertine') attitude by Erasmus and others, perhaps most notably by Peter Ramus, although his claim to reform philosophy on the basis of reason alone was perhaps iconoclastic more in appearance than in reality, especially as his views became organized and petrified into another authoritarian system.

A more decisive break with authority, denigrated as 'human tradition', was made by the magisterial reformers. Luther's burning of the books of canon law was an unmistakable declaration of his

---

[44] See chapter II.   [45] See chapter IV; cf. Kelley, *Foundations*, chapter I.

fundamental, and fundamentalist, anti-authoritarian position, one tenet shared by all reformers. In practical human terms the idea of the 'authority' of God's scriptural word was not necessarily binding, not authoritarian in any inconvenient way, as Luther's own liberal view of 'interpretation' illustrates. The significant thing was that Biblical standards permitted the criticism and potentially the rejection of any merely human authority. So in fact did the idea of absolute subjection to the divine will, the 'terrible sovereignty of God' (*horribilis maiestas Dei*), as Calvin called it.[46] Absolute monarchy and popular sovereignty, divine right of kings and divine right of resistance, were all justifiable in scriptural terms, and so was almost any other conceivable position. On this level, conscience was not only guide but in effect law, and perhaps king.

Probably the most crucial and intimidating symbol of established authority in the sixteenth century was the Catholic mass; certainly it was one of the first and most controversial targets of evangelical reformers. The idea of 'real presence', analogous to the holy attributes of pope and priesthood, embodied on the most fundamental emotional (as well as theological) level the assumption of ecclesiastical legitimacy and continuing divine sanctions of the established church and by association established governments as well.[47] The illicit cohabitation of human and divine in the eucharist seemed to reformers the ultimate corruption; but it was paralleled by similar confusions in society and institutional arrangements, which, though human in origin and maintenance, had pretensions to transcendent and sacred character. Analogous to the rejection of the mass was the rejection of the tradition and 'authority' on which it was based and finally the rejection of the political institutions which guaranteed it. Such at least was the rationale and the potential of sixteenth-century evangelical 'protest', and it seems to me that the most radical expressions of ideology bear this out. That this may have been a violation of the conscious intent of Luther, Calvin, and other responsible leaders does not alter the case.

Although 'authority' almost by definition was not to be defied, in fact the problem of authority in various senses was the object of interminable debate and disagreement. Indeed it was the chief and recognized target of certain licensed experts, namely, the professional 'scientists' of that age, especially university-trained theologians, philosophers, lawyers and physicians, all of whom had the most sensitive and responsible positions with regard to the values, goals and structures of European culture and society. Many aspects of intellectual history can be understood largely as a process of ques-

[46] *Institutes*, III, xx, 17.   [47] See p. 19.

tioning, criticizing and sometimes rejecting authorities in philosophy, natural science and other fields, including the new field of 'political science'; and in many cases this process was seen as a threat to the stability of church and society in general. Faculties of philosophy and medicine in particular harbored naturalistic critics whose views could not be accommodated to prevailing theological orthodoxy. And doctors of theology, the 'queen of sciences' itself, were capable of the most subversive challenges to authority.

Most interesting and relevant to this discussion is the position of the faculties of law, the theorists and practitioners of jurisprudence.[48] It is clear in the first place that they refused the claims to intellectual precedence of any other science or profession. Their doctrinal imperialism included even theology, so that civil lawyers almost instinctively placed ecclesiastical under secular authority. Second and more ominously, lawyers were committed to a fundamental process of 'interpretation' which could be more crucial than authority itself; and in general they were trained to take a utilitarian, casuistic and literally 'duplicitous' view of legal tradition. Not only the pedagogical conventions of disputation and the scholastic method of arguing *in utramque partem* but also the need to serve a particular 'cause' made them institutionally and constitutionally critical-minded; and of course they brought these disruptive talents into the arena of politics when summoned into its service. The common and interconfessional view that 'a lawyer's a bad Christian' had more than a theological significance; it referred also to the belief, expressed voluminously in satirical literature, that men of law were partisans by profession and liars by nature – purveyors of 'false consciousness', we might say.

All these issues and attitudes should be taken into account when we confront the most explosive of all questions, that of public authority, the power and legitimacy of controlling political institutions.[49] In the sixteenth century this meant especially kingship and empire (*regnum* and *imperium*), which combined attributes of paternity, community and divinity as well as office in their authority. The western political tradition is filled with conflicting theories about the classic (and scholastic) *quaestio* of the limits and conditions of political authority, although lawyers, ancient as well as medieval and modern, seldom cared to venture opinions unless specifically solicited. Exceptions to this included conflicts of interest between powers, whether church and state, rival states or cities, and the complex problems of relations between lord and vassal in feudal law; but these were not central to the problem of authority as such. In

---

[48] See chapter v.   [49] See chapter vi.

general it was in the context of particular crises that authority was subjected to questioning, and never so massively and so publicly as in the sixteenth century. The result was a spectacular convergence of ideas not only from other dimensions of human experience, domestic as well as professional and religious, but also from disparate parts of the European intellectual heritage, classical as well as medieval, lay as well as ecclesiastical, moral as well as political. This complex of ideas, reaching out toward a broad view of private and public life, uncompromising in its assumptions and activist in its implications, has all the marks of a mature and perhaps 'total' ideology.

Like 'authority' the concept of liberty was multi-valent and many-levelled, and as a term 'liberty' spanned the poles of sixteenth-century controversy, signifying to Protestants the most precious of divine gifts and to their enemies a false license that brought schism and social chaos. On the level of individual psychology, 'liberty' posed an excruciating paradox. On the one hand it suggested the insidious notion of free will, which had been the point of divergence between Erasmus and Luther; on the other hand it called up to Protestant consciousness that 'Christian liberty' which declared humanity potentially free of material commitments and corruption, an idea endorsed by Erasmus as well as Luther and Calvin. In the context of early modern society 'liberty' signified particular privilege and 'immunity' from various higher authorities, lay and ecclesiastical, but even in this sense it was clearly acquiring positive force, connoting an admirable human ideal. Although granted from a higher level of the social hierarchy, 'liberties' became distinguishing features – defining attributes – both of particular institutions and of the individuals associated with them. As universities and members of academic communities celebrated and fought for a larger measure of 'academic freedom', so the legal profession and the Parlement of Paris defended its 'freedom of speech' and rights of registration and remonstrance to the crown. Each group, seeking to enhance its own authority, contributed to a broader conception of 'liberty'.

On the political level individual liberty was hardly acknowledged in any explicit way, and yet there was a basis for such a conception in jurisprudence. In customary law, privileges tended to be attached to the land, to particular provinces; but civil law gave first priority to personality. Definition and application of the law presupposed determination of the 'human condition' (*De Statu hominum* was one of the first rubrics of civil law), and in this determination degree of 'liberty' was the prime subject of discussion.[50] In this context

---

[50] *Digest*, 1, 5.

medieval and modern jurists commonly moved from consideration of juridical to philosophical 'liberty', celebrating the 'dignity and excellence of man' on this ground and by implication the virtues of a system of law and a society that accommodated such liberty. In the religious and especially the political propaganda of the later sixteenth century there were at least overtones of this legal conception of liberty, although it remains true that the principal sources of 'political' liberty in a modern sense are associated with the claims and pretensions of princes, great lords and cities. Feudal and civic 'liberties', it is clear, represent the original grounds for the cultivation of political liberty; but of course even in these restricted senses broader implications could be drawn – and were in fact drawn, perhaps most notably in the *Defense of Liberty against Tyrants*.

In any case the concept of liberty, expanded and in many ways politicized in the course of the sixteenth century, tended to reinforce ideas of resistance, active as well as passive. Possessing a largely negative signification, 'resistance' was not a concept that could easily be legitimized in traditional terms; for it seemed always to be associated with exceptional circumstances. Nevertheless, there seemed to be grounds for defiance of authority on every social level. Disobedience to parents could be justified on religious grounds; to religious authority by recourse to higher, which is to say divine, principle; to academic authority on grounds, arguably, of reason. Resistance to political authority drew upon all these modes of justification, and attempts to synthesize them contributed significantly to the coherence of ideological constructions, the point at which all these levels are joined.

As construed here, the ideological process is not dependent upon a particular content. Apart from its substance, its pattern, on a social as well as an individual level, can be seen as corresponding in a general way to life experience; and the major phases in the Reformation can be defined in the following rough fashion. Identification: the activation of conscience toward a commitment, whether or not through a discrete 'conversion'. Socialization: the process of committing, of joining a community that had at least a tacit basis, and of acknowledging this membership. Intellectualization: the rationalizing of this commitment in terms of particular branches of knowledge and educational institutions. Legitimation: the justification of this commitment in terms of a defensible tradition, or at least of society and the public as a whole, characteristically accomplished by the legal profession and other secular intellectuals. Publication: the propagation of this commitment through various media, most conspicuously printing. And finally organization: the implementation and enforcement of an ideological program in a form that in some ways prefigured the modern political party, which also became the basis for military resistance.

This analysis may seem excessively abstract, and it is undeniable that particular expressions of ideology are generated in specific social contexts in response to particular human predicaments. But even historically it is possible to distinguish levels of ideology in the sense of escalating stages. The first stage .was, as always, religious and stemmed from long-standing demands for liberty of conscience and of worship under government sponsorship, or at least protection. When religious demands joined with secular protest in the late 1550s, the first propaganda was represented mostly by *ad hominem* attacks on the Guise family, especially the Cardinal of Lorraine. Both in France and in the Netherlands, where Cardinal Granvelle and Alba served as primary targets of polemic, the monarchy itself came under fire only after the most desperate stages of war, following the massacres of 1572. As we have seen, it was especially the counsel of lawyers that elevated such protest to the constitutional level and that led eventually to justifications of armed resistance. The final stage is defined by attempts to raise these arguments still higher to the level of political theory, posing in a general form the most searching questions about the nature of obedience, sovereignty, constitutional tradition, social structure and ultimate sources of legitimacy. At this point, however, we leave our subject and come to the final stage of the process we have been reconstructing – that is, to the 'end of ideology'.

THE END OF IDEOLOGY

By the end of the 1570s the most fundamental expressions of Huguenot ideology had been published and had made their impact, but in quantitative terms the high tide of propaganda was yet to come. So were some of the worst horrors of civil war and private criminality. For political controversy the noise-level at least continued to rise until that 'annus mirabilis' of pamphlet production, 1588, which also saw the failure of the Spanish Armada, the day of the barricades in Paris and the assassination of the younger Duke of Guise (followed the next year by that of Henry III, last of the Valois). In 1580 Henry of Navarre published his own 'declaration', following the pattern established by Coligny and Condé before him.[51] Four

---

[51] *Declaration et Protestation du Roy de Navarre, sur les iustes occasions qui l'ont meu de prendre armes, pour la defense et tuition des Eglises reformees en France* (n.p., 1580; Lb34.187). No attempt will be made here to confront directly the massive propaganda of these later years, discussed most recently by F. J. Baumgartner, *Radical Reactionaries: The Political Thought of the French Catholic League* (Geneva, 1975).

years later, however, with the death of the Duke of Anjou and the obvious fact that Henry III would die without issue, Navarre became the presumptive heir; and the Huguenot party line took a legitimist and conservative turn. Hôtman, for example, deleted references to the principle of elective monarchy in the third edition of his *Francogallia*. On the other hand the anti-Romanist line became even more intense, especially in 1585, when the papal bull of excommunication against Navarre and Condé once more sharpened exchanges.

From this time on, it was the Catholic party that was forced into an opposition posture in France; but while the predicament had changed and the party roles were reversed, the patterns of ideological conflict remained much the same. Now the Catholic 'princes, lords and cities' issued declarations against those trying 'by all means to subvert the Catholic Religion and State' and demonstrated in their turn 'the causes which have constrained Catholics to take up arms, and to charge King Henry III with "tyranny".'[52] Ideologically, however, their weapons had already been forged for them. 'The Huguenots', according to a pamphlet of 1589, 'have shown the way to the Catholics . . .'[53] As for the arguments for resistance, the author added, 'It is certain that if they have any color and plausibility for the assumption of arms and war against the king, they are so much the stronger in support of the Catholics, who have taken up arms to destroy the heretics.' And so Catholic propagandists did not hesitate to appeal to the principle of elective kingship popularized by Beza, Hotman and Barnaud, and some even to the idea of tyrannicide.[54]

So the polarization, which one Huguenot spokesman compared to the conflict of Guelfs and Ghibellines in fourteenth-century Italy, continued unabated. Du Laurier denounced the screaming priests who addressed their crowds as if they had Calvin and Beza by the hair.[55] Indeed the sermonizing of the *ligueur* priests rivalled that of the evangelical reformers in the earlier part of the century. According to a 'manifesto of France' of 1589, some of them declared the entire French nobility to be heretical and enemies of the people.[56]

---

[52] *Apologie catholique contre les libelles, declarations, avis et consultations faites, ecrites et publiees par les ligues perturbateurs du repos du royaume de France* (n.p., 1585; BN Lb34.240); *Responce faicte a la ligue . . .* (n.p., 1585; LN 1123).

[53] *Coppie de trois epistres catholiques* (Orleans, 1589; BN Lb34.700).

[54] *Discours sur les calomnies imposees aux Princes et seigneurs Catholiques, par les Politiques de nostre temps* (n.p., 1588; BN Lb34.434), using Hotman's elective arguments against Navarre.

[55] *De l'Estat present de ce royaume quant a la religion, justice et police* (Paris, 1583; BN Lb34.213).

[56] *Le Manifest de la France* (n.p., 1589; LN 1559–60).

The fanaticism of parties was mutually reinforcing. On the Catholic side, extremists like Louis Dorléans kept alive the charge of conspiracy. The Huguenot 'league', he argued, had been formed as early as 1563 (the time of the assassination of the first Duke of Guise); and he attacked in particular the 'assassin' Beza, who had carried Calvinism over into the political realm.[57] Naturally, he also defended the necessary bloodshed of St Bartholomew. On the other hand Pierre de Belloy, writing in 1587 on behalf of Navarre, denounced 'the crimes of lese-majesty committed daily by the league' established in opposition to 'the dignity of the king'.[58] In that same year the more radical author of the *Antiguisart* also assailed the 'rebel league' of Catholics and went on to justify the assassination of Francis of Guise almost a quarter-century earlier – and this just a year before the Duke's son Henry was to meet a similar fate – on the grounds that this dynasty had been responsible for opening the 'Pandora's box' of civil war.[59] As they had been blamed for their 'foreign' Lorraine origins and Italian (not to speak of Scottish) ambitions, now they were charged with another sort of international intrigue. As one of Louis Dorleans' critics wrote, 'I do not recognize as French those who have their hearts in Spain.'[60]

One opinion shared by both parties helped keep the ideological fires burning, and this was the old assumption that religious indifference was even worse than error. Not long after St Bartholomew one royalist lawyer declared that 'the scorner of religion is the true subverter of the republic', and of course partisans could not agree more.[61] So Dorléans was horrified by 'those indifferent folk who have held that everyone can be saved in their own faith'.[62] Even worse was the attempt to hide or to disguise the difference – to 'dissemble' or 'dissimulate' – as did certain 'tacit Huguenots'. Du Laurier was especially incensed at those perverse and unnatural 'hermaphrodites' (the same charge that had been thrown at Baudouin in his irenic efforts a generation before) who dissembled their opinions in order to preserve their properties and offices, pretend-

---

[57] *Premier et Second Advertissements des Catholiques Anglois aux François* (Paris, 1590; BN Lb³⁴.312); cf. B. Richter, 'French Renaissance pamphlets in the Newberry Library, I. The debate between Philippe du Plessis-Mornay and Louis Dorleans', *Studi francesi*, XI (1960), 220–40.

[58] *De l'autorité de roi et crimes de lese majesté qui se committent par ligues, designations de successeur, et libelles ecrites contre la personne et dignité du prince* (n.p., 1587; BN Lb³⁴.329); cf. *Responce* (Paris, 1589; BN Lb³⁴.330).

[59] *Antiguisart* (Rheims, 1587; BN Lb³⁴.333), 29.

[60] *Briefve responce d'un Catholique françois* (Bordeaux, 1586; BN Lb³⁴.309 and LN 1125–6), 7.

[61] Jean de la Madeleyne, *Discours de l'estat et office d'un bon Roy* . . . (Paris, 1575).

[62] *Apologie ou defense des Catholiques* (n.p., 1586; BN Lb³⁴.308), 6.

ing to accept both religions.[63] This was 'to reason à la Machiavel', and the name of this old Florentine dissimulator – 'doctor of tyranny', in the words of one 'good Catholic' – pervaded the polemic of the last wars of religion.[64]

Once again, then, the issue came to center on the familiar term and concept of the political man, 'le Politique', which increasingly was associated with libertinism and atheism as well as 'Machiavellism'. 'The name "politique" was once a name of honor', wrote one orthodox pamphleteer in 1588, 'of a just governor and prudent magistrate who knew how to rule a city through civil reason and create concord out of the divergent interests of different citizens . . . Today this fine name, associated with a thousand vices, is a name of horror and destructive of order, a name of filth and contempt because of those who have abused it.'[65] And he added, 'The honor of a "politique" is that of a fox, his eye always on the prince's face and agreeing with him in everything, even against God.' What so many people believed about the lawyer, in short, could be charged against the Politique: he was, from the standpoint of any faith, a 'bad Christian'. Another author presented an exhaustive 'catalogue of errors' characteristic of the politique mentality – among them the proposition that 'he gives first priority to the civil and political affairs of the state'; that 'these political affairs are placed in particular above religion'; that 'nature is the only guide to and mirror of the conservation of man'; and that 'in order to maintain a civil state in peace it is necessary to preserve all religions that have arisen'. And the conclusion: 'Here is the purpose of all Huguenots and Politiques associated with that of the Libertines, Epicureans and Atheists.' It was altogether worthy of 'that atheist Machiavelli, evangelist of today's Politiques'.[66] One author even suggested that it was 'machiavellian' to be unwilling to carry on war against religious aggression.

At the same time, however, there were signs of a changing mood.

---

[63] Du Laurier, *De l'Estat present*, 63.

[64] *Advis aux Catholiques françois* (Paris, 1589; LN 1393), 13, and *Conseil d'ung gentilhomme françois et bon catholique* (n.p., 1585; BN Lb34.244).

[65] *La Description des Politiques de nostre temps* (Paris, 1588; LN 1238), 3: 'Ce nom de Politique estoit un nom d'honneur, c'estoit le iuste nom d'un iuste gouverneur, d'un prudent Magistrat qui par raison civille sçavoit bien policer les membres d'une ville, et qui sage et accord par accordant discords de citoyens divers tiroit de bons accords . . . Auiourd'huy ce beau nom souillé de mille vices, n'est plus qu'un nom d'horreur qui destruit les polices . . . L'humeur du Politique c'est un humeur Renarde, son oeil incessament sur les Prince regard, et leur agree en tout, et fuisse contre Dieu . . .' Cf. *Histoire de la ligue*, ed. C. Valois (Paris, 1914), 135.

[66] *La Foy et religion des politiques de ce temps* (Paris, 1588; LN 1258). Cf. *Epistre aux delicats et flatteurs machiavelistes* (n.p., 1575; BN Lb34.100), 3.

Even before the massacres of St Bartholomew, disillusionment was settling over some persons who had lost their taste for combat. Even the belligerent *Political Discourses* identified as one cause of the civil war the presence of men who simply had no other métier than that of war. Jacques Cujas, though he had defended the government's position, had contempt for the way in which scholarship had been inundated by controversy. 'I have never read or heard of a century', he wrote, 'more fertile in spirits devoted to calumny than ours.'[67] The *guisard* advocate Du Tillet, in a message intended for his posterity, lamented the evils brought by partisanship, and even his bitter and excitable opponent Hotman changed his belligerent stance during the dark days of siege in Sancerre and sought 'consolation' and inner peace in Augustinian contemplation. The militant spirit they deplored carried over into every sphere of life; and some reflective types, Montaigne most notable among them, began to think that the most serious problem was not in theological disagreement but in human nature itself. As one versifier observed,

> The elephant's big, the lion strong,
> The tiger fierce, but all in vain:
> By hand of Man – or hands of men –
> The beasts are, all of them, often slain.[68]

It was to counteract such instinctive urges to violence disguised as religious fervor that some 'Politiques' presented a counsel of moderation. 'They are called "politiques"', wrote one of the most prominent of their number, Pierre Belloy, 'who do not want to dip their hands in the blood of Christians.'[69] This, too, could be a matter of conscience.

Among Huguenots attitudes of realism emerged with the destructive effects of war. The strictures addressed by Du Laurier to Henry of Navarre appeared in the context of a general Seysselian assessment 'of the present state of the kingdom with respect to religion, justice and police', and his conclusion was pessimistic. Each of Seyssel's three 'bridles' needed reforming in the most thorough-

---

[67] *Defense pour monsieur de Monluc* (Paris, 1575).

[68] J. Spifame, *Discours sur le conge impetre par monsieur le cardinal de Lorraine, de faire porter armes defensives a ses gens* . . . (n.p., 1565; LN 444), 60:

> L'Elefant est grand, et le Lyon fort,
> Le Tigre furieux: toutesfois sont
> Par main de l'homme souvent mis a mort,
> Ce qu'un ne peut faire plusieurs le font.

[69] *Replique faicte a la responce que ceux de la ligue ont publiee contre l'Examen* . . . (n.p., 1587; BN Lb34.328).

going fashion.[70] Less than a decade after the *Reveille-Matin*, Barnaud had launched into his extensive projects to estimate the social and economic costs of the wars, and his results were staggering. Still arguing the 'Francogallican' case and still speaking through the persona of 'le Politique', Barnaud acknowledged in his *French Mirror* that, to reverse the old Gallican formula, there was in France 'neither God, nor faith nor law'.[71] There was at least a suggestion that more attention should be given to 'political' matters before the 'grand monarchy of France' fell into total disrepair, and along with it religion, justice and police.

So we return to the old pre-war themes of religious toleration and 'conciliation', or rather to the complex devices of legal recognition, coexistence and legislative settlement. Before the massacres of St Bartholomew one 'exhortation to peace' suggested the conditions of such a settlement. 'We have two forms of religion in France', this pamphlet acknowledged. 'It remains only to prescribe certain rules for each . . . [to ensure] that one does not have too great advantage over the other and that we should enjoy equal liberty and favor in our religions.'[72] The internationalization of controversy in the last quarter of the century complicated this solution, but there did not seem to be alternatives. A pamphlet of 1586 reported the arguments of ambassadors from Germany pleading for 'pity' toward the French evangelicals and for some such political resolution of religious differences.[73] As a family needed a stable structure, a 'bonne police' to regulate the relationships between husband and wife, so a society required a reasonable and mutually accommodating arrangement for its ideological groupings. Bipartisan political agreements might seem as paradoxical and 'duplicitous' as religious hermaphrodeity, but in the wake of St Bartholomew the compromising Politiques did emerge as an identifiable 'party' and acquired a power base with the candidacy of Henry of Navarre to the French throne. Despite its national claims, however, this 'political party' had, except for opposition to Romanism, only the most attenuated ideology.

There is no question here of reviewing the complex ideological patterns of the last quarter of the sixteenth century. In quantitative terms the outpouring of propaganda reached new heights, and so did the international character of the polemics. The new intelligent-

---

70 See above p. 88, n. 26, and p. 329, n. 55.
71 *Miroir des françois*, 69. Cf. *Le Miroir françois representant la face de ce siecle corrumpu* (n.p., 1588[?]; Ars. 26.2).
72 *Exhortation a la paix* (n.p., 1568; LN 571); cf. *Discours sur la comparison et ellection des deux partis qui sont par le iourd'huy en ce Royaume* (Montauban, 1586; BN Lb34.320).
73 *Discours des ambassadeurs d'Allemagne qui sont venus vers le Roy pour moyenner la paix en la France* (Paris, 1586; BN Lb34.297).

sia made possible by printing was creating all kinds of specialisms, one of them the propaganda trade itself. Extremism and verbal abuse became professionalized as well as habitual, especially when reinforced by violence and a variety of social turmoils which had little in common with the confessional conflicts of an earlier generation except for the emotional momentum derived from them. Ideological patterns persisted despite the confusion of political and religious interests, for instance in the competing legislations of all 'three Henries' as well as Mayenne and 'Charles X', all of whom issued 'declarations du roy' to carry on the old tradition of ordinances. Tyrannicide, beyond *ad hoc* political assassination, emerged as an explicit issue, as did ideas of popular sovereignty. There were even published appeals on behalf of orphans and the poor, victims of civil conflict without a power base or a 'cause'.[74] But in rhetorical, behavioral and institutional terms the publicity of these years represents variations on established themes and an extension of the same ideological process. What is striking from the perspective chosen here is the growing futility of centrifugal partisanship and the hollow repetitiousness of most propaganda, and what seems significant is the growing tendency to end party strife and to achieve a national settlement and solidarity on political grounds.

Not only in retrospect but also in the view of many a Gallican as well as Huguenot and 'politique', the settlement depended upon the person and position of Henry IV; and the arguments centered, however voluminously, on two core issues. The first was the problem of his legitimacy (in religious as well as genealogical terms), and here the notorious 'Salic law' became the center of attention.[75] Both national tradition and political realism seemed to insure that the question would be resolved in favor of Navarre rather than the Spanish-supported Cardinal of Bourbon, who assumed the title of Charles X. The second issue was the problem of Henry's 'abjuration', that is, his return to the Catholic faith which was unquestionably dominant in French society and institutions. This step of course had *politique* overtones of the most pejorative sort, especially in view of Henry's previous vacillations. To earnest Protestants and Catholics alike a third conversion seemed to be 'Machiavellism' of the most

---

[74] Fr. Le Breton, *Remonstrance aux trois Estatz de la France, et a tous les peuples chrestien pour la deliverance du Pauvre et des Orphelins* (Paris, 1586; BN rés. Lb34.321).

[75] [Belloy], *Moyens d'abus entreprises et nullitez du rescrit et bulle du Pape Sixte Ve, en date du mois de septembre 1585* (n.p., 1586), and Hotman, *Brutum Fulmen* (n.p., 1586), on which see Kelley, *Hotman*, 304.

reprehensible sort and an unconscionable violation of 'conscience'.[76] In national terms, however, there seemed no other way out of the dilemma.

So Henry IV returned to 'the religion of Machiavelli', as Beza put it. After his reception (specifically at the hands of his own Gallican clergy) back into Catholicism, his coronation in Chartres and his return to Paris, the king began the work of restoration; and once again published propaganda was the most visible vehicle for the reaffirmation of monarchy and national unity. A series of acts and edicts set forth the program of restoration for every part of French society.[77] The reduction of rebellious cities, the restoration of the Parlement and the University of Paris, the reinstatement of corporate liberties and particular offices and other legislative actions began the long effort to re-establish order. Religious pacification took several years more but followed the guidelines of earlier edicts. By such 'political' means the structure of French monarchy and society – religion, justice and police – was stabilized, and the excesses of controversy were curbed. Discontents and tensions remained; but in political terms this Bourbon restoration represented, at least for that age, 'the end of ideology'.

Yet this was but the political expression of a mood that had been increasingly apparent in the late sixteenth century – apparent at least if we do not restrict ourselves to the drums and trumpets and mounting waves of pamphlets. Nowhere is that mood more evident than in the work of that disillusioned magistrate, Michel de Montaigne, who secluded himself even before the massacres of St Bartholomew and began to reflect not only on the state of his own consciousness but also on levels of social life below the noises of religious and political controversy. Though he celebrated the ego, he denounced egoism and that 'natural and original disease' of intellectual presumption. He deplored disputation and other inflations and abuses of the arts of discourse.[78] 'Grammar is that which creates most disturbance in the world', he declared, and the notorious litigiousness of his age was simply an extension of this. 'Our suits', he continued, 'only spring from disputations as to the interpretation of laws.' What suffered most, of course, was faith. 'When has this been seen better than in France in our day?', he remarked about the

---

[76] E.g., *Advertissement au Roy . . .* (n.p., 1589; BN Lb35.89) and J. Boucher, *Sermons de la simulee conversion et nullité de la pretendue absolution de Henry de Bourbon* (Paris, 1594; BN Lb35.480). Cf. *Refutation des calomnies et impostures des Huguenots Politiques et Atheistes de ce temps* (n.p., n.d.; BN Lb34.586), *La Vie et condition des politiques et atheistes de ce temps* (Paris, 1589; BN Lb34.624), etc., etc.

[77] See Isnard, nos. 4129, 4170ff. For a modern parallel to these disillusioning times see A. de Moreuil, *Resistance et collaboration sous Henri IV* (Paris, 1960).

[78] 'Apologie pour Raimond Sebonde', *Essais*, I, 12.

variations in religion. 'Those who have taken it to the right, those who have taken it to the left, those who call it black, those who call it white, use it so similarly for their violent and ambitious enterprises . . .' Montaigne dismissed contemporary religious enthusiasms as nothing more than insolent egoism. 'See the horrible impudence with which we bandy reasons about and how irreligiously we have both rejected them and taken them again, according as fortune has changed our places in these public storms.'

Unmistakably, Montaigne is referring here to what has been called the 'politicization' of religious movements; but beyond that he also laments the virtuosity with which parties employ religion. The justice of particular causes has been merely alleged, he charged, 'as in the mouth of an advocate, not as in the heart and affection of the party'. This duplicity was most evident in the reversal of party positions that occurred during the mid 1580s, and the revolutionary hypocrisy of this shift Montaigne found most distasteful. 'This proposition, so solemn, whether it is lawful for a subject to rebel and to take arms against his prince in defense of religion', he quoted: 'remember in whose mouth, this year past, the affirmative of this was the buttress of one party, the negative was the buttress of what other party; and hear . . . whether the weapons make less din for this cause than for that.' Here indeed was the 'end of ideology'.

Epilogue:
Ideology and utopia

How, having made these various soundings into sixteenth-century experience, shall we map out the historical process in general? How shall we assess the sixteenth-century phenomena of reformation, rebellion, reaction and civil war? John Adams viewed that scene from a distance of two centuries; and another two hundred years stand between us and those alien times of decaying chivalry, moral callousness, technological innocence and religious fanaticism. Yet in some ways the harrowing experiences of our century may allow us to appreciate post-Reformation turmoil better than did the enlightened second president. Whether we can (as he implicitly did) classify the French civil wars as 'revolutionary' is debatable, but in the context of 'ideology' such a suggestion seems historically defensible. Obviously sixteenth-century upheavals occurred in a society that was 'pre-industrial' and 'underdeveloped' (as some historians, in their retrospective wisdom, like to observe), a society in which class distinctions in a modern sense were lacking, and mass media existed in a very rudimentary form. Any prescription for 'revolution' that insists on such ingredients, therefore, is bound to come to the conclusion that Huguenot and Catholic political behavior in the wake of the Reformation fails to live up to the modern standard in terms either of consciousness or of social depth.[1]

The problem is not merely terminological. Clearly the phenomena examined here do not constitute the same *kind* of revolution as those of 1917, 1848 or 1789: the relevant question is whether they belong to the same class of events, to the same continuum of history. Contemporaries certainly regarded the turmoil of the later sixteenth century – 'seditious', 'subversive' and 'rebellious', they variously called their enemies – to be profoundly destructive of society and institutions as well as threatening to the state. They saw their rivals working for social as well as for political transformation – for a 'changement de leur estat', in the language of contemporary pamphlets, as well as 'subversion de l'Estat'. It cannot be said that Huguenot resistance was the product of class division in a modern sense, but then the

---

[1] See P. Zagorin, 'Theories of revolution in contemporary historiography', *Political Science Quarterly*, LXXXVIII (1973), 23–52.

high crest of most revolutionary movements has resulted from the temporary coalition of class interest, especially between cities and landed aristocracy. The French civil wars, as Adams realized, offered a classic illustration of this in the alliance between the dissenting 'malcontent' nobility, led in the first instance by Condé, and the chronically 'rebellious' cities, which attached themselves to his party and especially to his successor Coligny. Ideologues, whether religious enthusiasts or unscrupulous 'politiques', labored to maintain this unstable popular front, often deluding themselves in the process about the coherence and viability of their program; and so likewise did their comrades in the Netherlands.

Revolutionary or not, sixteenth-century dissent is bound up with one question of fundamental historical (as well as sociological and political) interest: 'why men rebel'.[2] In this connection the notion of 'relative deprivation' seems most pertinent, since the historical process of the sixteenth century, especially from the affair of the placards to the massacres of St Bartholomew, seemed to fulfill in a striking manner the most extreme conditions of 'RD': namely, a rise of expectations encouraged by evangelism (socially potent despite its 'transcendent' appeal) and a decline in the capability of achieving these expectations because of official repression (as well as a lack, indeed a rejection, of realism). This discrepancy was intensified by two other factors identified by Gurr: the phenomenon of 'conversion', used in a sociological as well as a religious sense, referring to the abandonment of old norms and beliefs and their replacement by new ones, which were often unrealizable; and the rise and eventual confrontation of 'dissident coercion' and 'regime coercion', preparing the ground for that organized sort of violence which has been called 'internal war'.[3] The rise of a 'new ideology', in short, combined with increasing (and more and more commonly justified) violence, establish the necessary preconditions for rebellion – whether or not the social configurations and goals permit the label 'revolution'.

The question posed here, however, has been less why men rebel than why men think they must rebel (and how they legitimize this); and to answer this we must consider the particular predicament of sixteenth-century France – the social forms, levels and qualities of dissent. Random anxieties and discontents are brought into focus by particular ideological forces which have the capacity to unite disparate groups. Men and women from all levels of experience and

[2] Ted Robert Gurr, *Why Men Rebel* (Princeton, 1970).
[3] H. Eckstein, 'On the etiology of internal wars', *History and Theory*, IV (1965), 133–63.

expectations, ranging from venturesome adolescence to cautious old age, from poverty-bound resentment to affluent ambition, must join their private loves and hates with public antagonisms and enterprises and direct their energies, at least for a time, to a single goal or set of ideals. When this rare condition exists, when private interests are overridden, the process of history can be profoundly affected in terms of social patterns and institutions as well as individual anguish and outcry. Needless to say, the final outcome may bear little resemblance to the designs of any of the contending parties. This ironic (or tragic) aspect of history is vividly represented in a dialogue published in 1622, which represents Luther and Calvin returning to earth to survey their handiwork. Although their ideals had not changed, they were of course shocked and chagrined to see the predictions of their opponents in a sense fulfilled – that liberty of conscience had brought schism, and schism civil war.[4]

It has not been the purpose of this book to identify discrete 'causes' for the tumultuous conflicts of the later sixteenth century, and indeed such an ambition would hardly be consistent with its methods and multi-layered design. Nevertheless, it may be useful to consider this question, almost classically (it seems to me) *mal posée*, in general terms. One recent theoretical discussion has suggested a wide variety of (overlapping and perhaps contradictory) causal factors, or rather 'preconditions of internal war'; and the generous list of suggestions in this essay provokes certain reflections about the historical process in the Reformation period. Of the 'political factors', for example, one would surely be welcomed by the Catholic party, namely, 'excessive toleration of alienated groups', and another, 'responses to oppressive government', would doubtless be popular with the Huguenots; but a modern perspective might incline rather to what Eckstein classifies as 'divisions among the governing classes'. Among the 'social factors' of apparent relevance we may notice those which emphasize 'circulation of elites', or the restrictions thereon, since the control of offices, patronage and professional opportunities were fundamental issues both in France and the Netherlands. In many respects, however, social and economic factors seem considerably less weighty for this period of economic 'underdevelopment' and social corporatism than for a society dependent on modern industry and technology.

The implication, at least for the sixteenth century, is that 'intellectual factors' played a much larger role; and in fact all four of the

---

[4] *Le Dialogue de Calvin et Luther revenus du nouveau monde sur les affaires de l'Europe* (n.p., 1622; Bibliothèque du Protestantisme Française).

particular 'preconditions' suggested by Eckstein would seem to be significant for the troubles and transformations of Reformation Europe. The 'failure of a regime to perform adequately the functions of socialization', although it expresses well enough the legislative agenda of the French monarchy and the Empire, is perhaps too anachronistic; but it does provide a relevant commentary on the deficiencies of sixteenth-century 'police'. More to the point are the conditions defined as 'coexistence in a society of conflicting social "myths"' (corresponding ultimately to respective Catholic and evangelical views of tradition and novelty, transcendence and immanence, liberty and authority) and, consequently, the 'existence in a society of unrealizable values or corrosive social philosophies'. Finally and perhaps most obviously, there is the 'alienation (desertion, transference of allegiance) of the intellectuals'. All these factors (and others which could be inferred) point to the intensification of social and political consciousness associated with the 'beginning of ideology'.

Problems of large-scale social transformation aside, it seems clear that in the sixteenth century social and political as well as religious consensus was disintegrating in a fundamental way. Arthur Koestler's remark that 'man's deadliest weapon is language' has never been so vividly illustrated as in the polemic of this period.[5] Even taking into account the excesses of evangelical and orthodox invective, preoccupation with and ubiquitous charges of 'libertinism' and 'atheism' suggest a basic breakdown of communications. Calvin defined a 'libertine' simply as one without scriptures; but the broader implication was that such a person, Rabelais for instance, lacked conventional and communal values in general. On the other hand Calvin's own call for a 'liberty' beyond law seemed to his opponents to promote a similar anarchy. Both attitudes seemed to be based on a conception of conscience that gave little thought either to social convention or to political consequence. It is not surprising that this age of ideological pandemonium, of subversion not only of values but even of language, produced extreme statements both of resistance and of authority. This age of iconoclasm, assassination and tyrannicide also produced, in Bodin's *Republic*, the ultimate statement (at least before Hobbes) of political absolutism, and remedy for the collapse of a social consensus undermined by ideological differences.

Once established, these ideological extremes could not be forgotten, though they might be repressed temporarily: ideology be-

---

[5] *Janus* (New York, 1978), 15.

comes, in sublimated ways, a permanent part of the intellectual heritage. And even when the substance is laid aside or becomes outmoded, the form of ideology may be preserved. Conscience, or at least the appeal thereto, continues to be a prominent factor in western public thought and action; and the conversion experience has extended far beyond its original religious field of cultivation. In various ways religious modes have been injected into secular social and political movements, with attendant analogues of kinship, brotherhood and sisterhood. Even more conspicuously the academy has continued to be a carrier and generator of ideologies and causes with or without roots in society at large. The legal profession has lost its central role, but only because the business of legitimation and political propaganda has generated its own professional specialities. Printing too has in some ways been overshadowed by higher-powered media, but it continues to be a model and mainstay of publicity and persuasion. The institution of the political party, finally, has evolved far beyond its quasi-feudal, quasi-military or quasi-congregational form; but again it has preserved at least a family resemblance and certain rhetorical and social if not specifically institutional ties with its remote ideological ancestor of the sixteenth century.

About the preservation or continuity of ideals less can be said with any assurance. Confessional forms are of course still with us, Tridentine Catholicism as well as fundamentalist Protestant sects descended at least nominally from Reformation times; but central as they may be to the human condition privately, in public terms they can be only marginal to ideological conflict in most of western society. Industrialism, the emergence of classes, 'integral' national-ism, technological progress, the experience of total war, exposure to homogenizing media and all the other forces of 'modernization' make it virtually impossible for old-time religion to function as an organizing principle for ideology in either individual or group terms – even indeed to form the basis of an effective political party. Yet it must not be forgotten that in the sixteenth century 'religion' encompassed much more than matters of Providence and the private conscience: in all confessional forms it implied a total view of life, secular as well as sacred, material as well as spiritual, social and political as well as moral and ecclesiastical. Religious allegiance entailed fundamental assumptions about every level of society, from family to school, social calling and government; and so it contained, and concealed, attitudes and potential behavior most basic to the beginning – or the end – of ideology.

It may be suggested further that the religious core of social attitudes, with their internalizing and spiritualizing tendencies, actually encouraged the transformation of secular interests into more universal values.[6] What may be regarded as the idealizing aspect of sixteenth-century ideology can be seen on various institutional levels. Evidence of this can be seen in the family, to the extent that it promoted (or provoked) values that transcended, if only temporarily, blood ties, property and the succession thereto, and political allegiance. Universalizing tendencies are also reflected in the academy, to the extent that it raised reason above authority and supported values that were not merely corporate, ecclesiastical or political; in the legal profession, to the extent that it lived up to its claims to be the curator of 'true philosophy' and the promoter of equity as well as the letter of the law; and in printing, to the extent that it served public enlightenment and that advancement of learning to which earlier humanists had devoted their rhetoric, if not always their energies. As for the political party, it could hardly by definition be universalizing; and yet for a time it could stand for larger and even non-partisan goals, to the extent that it opposed abuses and inequalities. All of these tendencies were given momentum and direction by religious ideals.

The heyday of these ideals, of course, came in the early period of trials, oppression and attempts to identify the problem of evil in human terms; and indeed the best way to understand emergent Protestant ideology is in its negative impulse. As the idea of Christian liberty was itself largely negative (freedom from not freedom to, in Erich Fromm's words – from the law, from materialism and from authority),[7] so Protestant social and political consciousness may best be understood in term of its targets; and these in turn may be most appropriately summarized by recalling the proto-sociological categories of Seyssel: religion, justice and police. What evangelical reformers were opposing were, first, the Gallican (as well as the Roman) view of religion as a material construction and as a 'human tradition'; secondly and analogously, the legist (explicitly *parlementaire*, implicitly royalist) view of justice as the accumulation of ordinances and official acts; and above all the bureaucratic proliferation of juridical and fiscal offices which, despite its venal character, formed the basis of 'la police'. What they proposed in the re-forming of these categories was, first, a purified, de-ritualized and de-politicized faith; secondly, a legal order likewise purged of foreign and 'tyrannical' rules and open to local autonomy; and finally

---

[6] A. Greeley, *Unsecular Man* (New York, 1922).
[7] *Escape from Freedom* (New York, 1941), 24.

a popularly-based social organism free of litigiousness, persecution (fiscal as well as religious) and tyranny. It is true that they proposed these reforms under the guise of conservatism, of a return to an earlier purer state; but even this appeal to tradition, such as Hotman's 'Francogallican' program, represented a sort of universalizing impulse. The point is that the quality of 'antiquity', so highly prized in the sixteenth century, signified not only seniority but also a temporal approximation to a set of universal – tried and true if not always rational – values, invidiously contrasted with the later, mutable and 'foreign' innovations of corrupt outsiders.

It was hardly to be expected that such ideals could have a permanently enhancing effect on European society. In fact the 'politicization' of Protestantism and subsequent emergence of parties soon provided the originally 'transcendent' Protestant faith with its own kind of immanence, its own evolving 'human traditions'. The 'pure faith', the 'true church' of the Huguenots itself developed a complex and corruptible institutional base, and it assumed an increasingly threatening form through the agency of the same legislative tradition which had originally attempted to 'exterminate' it. The 'primitive constitution' and pristine legal and social tradition reconstructed by Hotman were not only ideals but also instruments of partisan propaganda, and very flexible ones at that. And as for 'popular government', this was in social terms even more of a covering fiction for particular and very 'political' interest groups. As ideological conflict turned into civil war, transcendent invocations of 'conscience' and the 'liberty' thereof, of 'piety' and its marriage to 'learning', of 'true philosophy' and 'equity' all became party slogans and subterfuges – the basis for that 'gross ideology' which John Adams considered to be 'taught in the school of folly',[8] and which indeed deserved a place on the agenda of Erasmus's *Encomium Moriae*, if only as a recurrent feature of the human condition.

The rational formulation of ideological differences did not create but it did vastly intensify social and political division in French and European society as a whole. There is a behavioral continuum, it seems to me, between the verbal excesses of the early reformers – their vilification not only of pope and priest but also of Mary and the mass, not only of the corrupters of religion, that is, but also of its central symbols – and their civil violence. The movement from reform to revolution followed a trajectory traced by rhetoric and its gestural counterpart, iconoclasm, from propaganda to civil and finally military resistance. It is clear that violence was initiated and so

---

[8] See above, p. 2, at n. 3.

in effect condoned by political and ecclesiastical authorities, but it is equally clear that violence was a conventional (and in some ways justifiable) means of reacting, especially collectively. Sporadic violence, which found expression in iconoclasm and rioting, was transformed by politics and civil war into more purposeful destruction, including terrorism, assassination and massacre. In a gruesome way extremism helped further to define and to clarify ideological positions. It contributed also, let us note, to disillusionment and that return to 'politics as usual' that marked, for that age, 'the end of ideology'.

Disillusionment may be an unavoidable part of the human condition, the end of the ideological cycle; but it does not constitute the final lesson of history. The 'end of ideology', as Daniel Bell put it, referring to the formula of Mannheim, does not mean the end of utopia.[9] The realization of particular transcendent principles may always be doomed to failure in the process of history but, for all that, consciousness does not cease its formations and reformations. There is always a past which we may, for our ideological needs, try to reconstruct in order to make sense of and perhaps to justify our achievements and mistakes. There is always a future which we may, for our utopian hopes, envisage as· fulfilling our traditions and efforts. There are always values and ideals toward which we aim these efforts, or at least by which we judge our failures. And perhaps, whether or not it can be given human expression, there is always what Reinhold Niebuhr called 'the God whom we meet as "The Other" at the final limit of our consciousness . . .'.[10] These forms of transcendence will always be, if we care to think about it, on the edge of history; and it is a shallow view of the historical process that ignores this potential, a potential underlying not only religion but, in one way or another, each new 'beginning of ideology'.

[9] In Chaim I. Waxman (ed.), *The End of Ideology Debate* (New York, 1968).
[10] *The Nature and Destiny of Man* (New York, 1941–3), 130.

Index of names